PA-RISC 2.0

Architecture

Hewlett-Packard Professional Books

Blinn	Portable Shell Programming: An Extensive Collection of Bourne Shell Examples
Costa	Planning and Designing High Speed Networks Using 100VG-AnyLAN, Second Edition
Fristrup	USENET: Netnews for Everyone
Fristrup	The Essential Web Surfer Survival Guide
Grady	Practical Software Metrics for Project Management and Process Improvement
Grosvenor, Ichiro, O'Brien	Mainframe Downsizing to Upsize Your Business: IT-Preneuring
Gunn	A Guide to NetWare® for UNIX®
Helsel	Graphical Programming: A Tutorial for HP VEE
Kane	PA-RISC 2.0 Architecture
Lewis	The Art & Science of Smalltalk
Malan, Letsinger, Coleman	Object-Oriented Development at Work: Fusion In the Real World
Madell, Parsons, Abegg	Developing and Localizing International Software
McMinds/Whitty	Writing Your Own OSF/Motif Widgets
Phaal	LAN Traffic Management
Poniatowski	The HP-UX System Administrator's "How To" Book
Poniatowski	HP-UX 10.x System Administration "How To" Book
Thomas	Cable Television Proof-of-Performance: A Practical Guide to Cable TV Compliance Measurements Using a Spectrum Analyzer.
Witte	Electronic Test Instruments

PA-RISC 2.0 Architecture

Gerry Kane

For book and bookstore information

http://www.prenhall.com

Prentice Hall PTR
Upper Saddle River, New Jersey 07458

Acknowledgements

Special thanks to Martin Whittaker who was the impetus behind this book and provided leadership and direction at every turn and to Dale Morris and Jim Hull who contributed key sections. Many other folks at Hewlett-Packard provided critical information: among them Ruby Lee, and Jerry Huck.

Personal thanks go to the usual suspects: Sean, Kyle, Ambrose, Marcella

Editorial/production supervision: *Joanne Anzalone*
Manufacturing manager: *Alexis R. Heydt*
Acquisitions editor: *Karen Gettman*
Editorial assistant: *Barbara Alfieri*
Cover design: *Design Source*
Cover design director: *Jerry Votta*
Book Design: *Suzanne Hayes*
Patricia Pekary, Manager Hewlett-Packard Press

Published by Prentice Hall PTR
Prentice-Hall, Inc.
A Simon & Schuster Company
Upper Saddle River, New Jersey 07458

The publisher offers discounts on this book when ordered in bulk quantities.
For more information, contact:
Corporate Sales Department
Prentice Hall PTR
1 Lake Street
Upper Saddle River, NJ 07458

Phone: 800-382-3419, Fax: 201-236-7141
E-mail: corpsales@prenhall.com

ISBN 0-13-182734-0

Prentice-Hall International (UK) Limited, *London*
Prentice-Hall of Australia Pty. Limited, *Sydney*
Prentice-Hall Canada Inc., *Toronto*
Prentice-Hall Hispanoamericana, S.A., *Mexico*
Prentice-Hall of India Private Limited, *New Delhi*
Prentice-Hall of Japan, Inc., *Tokyo*
Simon & Schuster Asia Pte. Ltd., *Singapore*
Editora Prentice-Hall do Brasil, Ltda., *Rio de Janeiro*

Foreword

"Everything should be made as simple as possible, but not simpler."

A. Einstein

When the first PA-RISC systems were shipped in 1986, the architecture was clearly recognized as a break with the past, with regular, hardware-inspired instructions rather than variable, interpretive forms. But its simple instructions were somewhat richer than other RISC designs, providing basic support for operations on strings and other data types prevalent in commercial applications. This semantic richness, unusual in the RISC designs of the time, was a direct result of the breadth of markets for HP computers and the decision to optimize PA-RISC for the full range of technical and commercial applications.

In the intervening years, PA-RISC has become the basis of a large family of computer systems, currently spanning a capacity range of over two orders of magnitude. As the product family has grown, the range of applications has also expanded geometrically. PA-RISC workstations now host applications which were once the province of supercomputers. Database servers now supply realtime streams of compressed video and audio. And PA-RISC has evolved to meet the demands for leadership performance in these emerging application domains.

The purpose of a processor architecture is to define a stable interface which can efficiently couple multiple generations of software investment to successive generations of hardware technology. Stability and efficiency are the goals, and the range of software and hardware technologies expected during the architecture's life determine the scope for which the goals must be achieved.

The desired stability does not rule out change, but it does require that any evolution of the architecture contain the prior definition as a subset. This is the principle of "forward compatibility" which ensures that all prior software will continue to work on all later machines—a straightforward idea whose value to users is obvious. Over the last decade, PA-RISC has evolved in response both to significant changes in the nature of customer applications and to rapid advances in technology, particularly chip fabrication technology and compiler technology.

Efficiency also has evident value to users, but there is no simple recipe for achieving it. Optimizing architectural efficiency is a complex search in a multidimensional space, involving disciplines ranging from device physics and circuit design at the lower levels of abstraction, to compiler optimizations and application structure at the upper levels.

Because of the inherent complexity of the problem, the design of processor architecture is an iterative, heuristic process which depends upon methodical comparison of alternatives ("hill climbing") and upon creative flashes of insight ("peak jumping"), guided by engineering judgement and good taste.

To design an efficient processor architecture, then, one needs excellent tools and measurements for accurate comparisons when "hill climbing," and the most creative and experienced designers for superior "peak jumping." At HP, this need is met within a cross-functional team of about twenty designers, each with depth in one or more technologies, all guided by a broad vision of the system as a whole.

Since the inception of PA-RISC, nearly fifty people have contributed directly to its definition as members of the architecture team. With the generous support of colleagues and managers in their respective organizations, they have made careful measurements of application workloads, designed ingenious tools and methods to analyze data, created novel semantics and encodings, deliberated intently to hone the best cost-performance design, and crafted clear, unambiguous descriptions. It was my great privilege and pleasure to lead this team of talented designers, and it is their achievement which is documented in this book.

— *Michael Mahon*
Principal Architect
Hewlett-Packard
August, 1995

Contents

Figures

Tables

Preface

Hewlett-Packard's PA-RISC architecture was first introduced in 1986. Although there have been interim improvements in the intervening years, the PA-RISC 2.0 architecture described in this book is the most significant step in the evolution of the PA-RISC architecture. While the primary motivation for PA-RISC 2.0 was to add support for 64-bit integers, 64-bit virtual address space offsets, and greater than 4 GB of physical memory, many other more subtle enhancements have been added to increase the performance and functionality of the architecture.

Compatibility with PA-RISC 1

From an unprivileged software perspective, PA-RISC 2.0 is forward compatible with the earlier PA-RISC 1.0 and PA-RISC 1.1 architectures – all unprivileged software written to the PA-RISC 1.0 or PA-RISC 1.1 specifications will run unchanged on processors conforming to the PA-RISC 2.0 specification.

However, unprivileged software written to the PA-RISC 2.0 specification will not run on processors conforming to the PA-RISC 1.0 or PA-RISC 1.1 specifications.

PA-RISC 2.0 Enhancements

PA-RISC 2.0 contains 64-bit extensions, instructions to accelerate processing of multimedia data, features to reduce cache miss and branch penalties, and a number of other changes to facilitate high performance implementations. The 64-bit extensions have the highest profile and the greatest impact on the programming model for both applications and system programs. The paragraphs that follow provide thumbnail sketches of some of the more significant features of PA-RISC 2.0.

64-bit Extensions

PA-RISC has always supported a style of 64-bit addressing known as "segmented" addressing. In this style, many of the benefits of 64-bit addressing were obtained without requiring the integer datapath to be larger than 32 bits. While this approach was cost-effective, it did not easily provide the simplest programming model for single data objects (mapped files or arrays) larger than 4 billion bytes (4GB). Support of such objects calls for larger-than-32-bit "flat" addressing, that is, pointers longer than 32 bits which can be the subject of larger-than-32-bit indexing operations. Since nature prefers powers of two, the next step for an integer data path width greater than 32 bits is 64 bits. PA-RISC 2.0 provides full 64-bit support with 64-bit registers and data paths. Most operations use 64-bit data operands and the architecture provides a flat 64-bit virtual address space.

Multimedia Extensions

Since multimedia capabilities are rapidly becoming universal in desktop and notebook machines, and since general purpose processors are becoming faster than specialized digital signal processors, it was seen as critical that PA-RISC 2.0 support these multimedia data manipulation operations as a standard feature, thus eliminating the need for external hardware.

PA-RISC 2.0 contains a number of features which extend the arithmetic and logical capabilities of PA-RISC to support parallel operations on multiple 16-bit subunits of a 64-bit word. These operations are especially useful for manipulating video data, color pixels, and audio samples, particularly for data compression and decompression.

Cache Prefetching

Because processor clock rates are increasing faster than main memory speeds, modern pipelined processors become more and more dependent upon caches to reduce the average latency of memory accesses. However, caches are effective only to the extent that they are able to anticipate the data and instructions that are required by the processor. Unanticipated surprises result in a cache miss and a consequent processor stall while waiting for the required data or instruction to be obtained from the much slower main memory.

The key to reducing such effects is to allow optimizing compilers to communicate what they know (or suspect) about a program's future behavior far enough in advance to eliminate or reduce the "surprise" penalties. PA-RISC 2.0 integrates a mechanism that supports encoding of cache prefetching opportunities in the instruction stream to permit significant reduction of these penalties.

Branch Prediction

A "surprise" also occurs when a conditional branch is mispredicted. In this case, even if the branch target is already in the cache, the falsely predicted instructions already in the pipeline must be discarded. In a typical high-speed superscalar processor, this might result in a lost opportunity to execute more than a dozen instructions. This is known as the mispredicted branch penalty.

PA-RISC 2.0 contains several features that help compilers signal future data and likely instruction needs to the hardware. An implementation may use this information to anticipate data needs or to predict branches more successfully, thus avoiding the penalties associated with surprises.

Some of these signals are in the nature of "hints" which are encoded in "don't care" bits of existing instructions. These hints are examples of retroactive additions to PA-RISC 1.1, since all existing code will run on newer machines, and newly annotated code will run correctly (but without advantage) on all existing machines. The benefit of making such retroactive changes is that compilers are thereby permitted to implement the anticipatory hints at will, without "synchronizing" to any particular hardware release.

Memory Ordering

When cache misses cannot be avoided, it is important to reduce the resultant latencies. The PA-RISC 1 architecture specified that all loads and stores are observed to be performed "in order," a characteristic known as "strong ordering."

Future processors are expected to support multiple outstanding cache misses while simultaneously performing loads and stores to lines already in the cache. In most cases this effective reordering of loads and stores causes no inconsistency, and permits faster execution. The latter model is known as "weak ordering," and it is intended to become the default model in future machines. Of course, strongly ordered variants of loads and stores must be defined to handle contexts in which ordering must be preserved – mainly related to synchronization among processors or with I/O activities.

Coherent I/O

As the popularity and pervasiveness of multiprocessor systems increase, the traditional PA-RISC model of I/O transfers to and from memory without cache coherence checks has become less advantageous. Multiprocessor systems require that processors support cache coherence protocols. By adding similar support to the I/O subsystem, the need to flush caches before and/or after each I/O transfer can be eliminated. As disk and network bandwidths increase, there is increasing motivation to move to such a cache coherent I/O model. The incremental impact on the processor is small, and is supported in PA-RISC 2.0.

How This Book is Organized

The audience for this book might be divided into the following broad categories (listed in decreasing order of probable size – though, one hastens to add, not in any presumed order of importance):

- application programmers
- operating system programmers
- compiler programmers
- hardware/system designers.

The book has been organized to make information easily accessible to each of these audience categories based on the assumption that each category requires an additional level of detail. For example, application programmers are primarily concerned with such things as data types, addressing capabilities, and the instruction set. Operating system programmers need all of that information and also must concern themselves with such things as page table structures and cache operations, topics that application programmers do not usually need to worry about. Accordingly, chapters are generally structured so that the information that is of interest to the broadest audience is presented at the beginning, and details that have a more limited audience come later. Similarly, the book contains a rather large number of appendices: they are used to provide specialized information which, if included in the main body of the book, might add unneeded complexity to topics that are otherwise of broad interest.

Conventions Used in This Book

Several typographical and notation conventions are used throughout this book to simplify, emphasize, and standardize presentation of information.

Fonts

In this book, fonts are used as follows:

Italic	is used for instruction fields and arguments. For example: "The completer, *compte*, encoded in the *u* and *m* fields of the instruction,...".
	Italic is also used for references to other parts of this and other books or manuals. For example: "As described in *Chapter 4, Flow Control and* ...".
Bold	is used for emphasis and the first time a word is defined. For example:

"Implementations provide seven registers called **shadow registers** ...".

UPPER CASE   is used for instruction names, instruction mnemonics, short (three characters or less) register and register field names, and acronyms. For example: "The PL field in the IIAOQ register ...".

Underbar (_)   characters join words in register, variable, and function names. For example: "The boolean variable cond_satisfied in the Operation section ...".

Numbers

The standard notation in this book for addresses and data is hexadecimal (base 16). Memory addresses and fields within instructions are written in hexadecimal. Where numbers could be confused with decimal notation, hexadecimal numbers are preceded with 0x. For example, 0x2C is equivalent to decimal 44.

Instruction Notations

Instruction operation is described in a C-like algorithmic language. This language is the same as the C programming language with a few exceptions. These are:

- The characters "{}" are used to denote bit fields.

- The assignment operator used is "←" instead of "=".

- The functions "cat" (concatenation), and "xor" (logical exclusive OR) take a variable number of arguments, for which there is no provision in C.

- The switch statement usage is improper because we do not use constant expressions for all the cases.

- The keyword "parallel" may appear before loop control statements such as "for" and "while" and indicates that the loop iterations are independent and may execute in parallel.

Bit Ranges

A range of bits within a larger unit, is denoted by "unit{range}", where unit is the notation for memory, a register, a temporary, or a constant; range is a single integer to denote one bit, or two integers separated by ".." to denote a range of bits.

For example, "GR[1]{0}" denotes the leftmost bit of general register 1, "CR[24]{59..63}" denotes the rightmost five bits of control register 24, and "5{0..6}" denotes a 7-bit field containing the number 5. If $m > n$, then {m..n} denotes the null range.

Registers

In general, a register name consists of two or three uppercase letters. The name of a member of a register array consists of a register name followed by an index in square brackets. For example, "GR[1]" denotes general register 1.

The named registers and register arrays are:

Register	Range	Description
GR[t]	t = 0..31	General registers
SHR[t]	t = 0..6	Shadow registers
SR[t]	t = 0..7	Space registers
CR[t]	t = 0, 8..31	Control registers
CPR[uid][t]	t = 0..31	Coprocessor "uid" registers
FPR[t]	t = 0..31	Floating-point coprocessor registers

The Processor Status Word and the Interruption Processor Status Word, denoted by "PSW" and "IPSW", are treated as a series of 1-bit and multiple-bit fields. A field of either is denoted by the register name followed by a field name in square brackets, and bit ranges within such fields are denoted by the usual notation. For example, PSW[C/B] denotes the 16-bit carry/borrow field of the PSW and PSW[C/B]{0} denotes bit 0 of that field.

Temporaries

A temporary name comprises three or more lowercase letters and denotes a quantity which requires naming, either for clarity, or because of limitations imposed by the sequential nature of the operational notation. It may or may not represent an actual processing resource in the hardware. The length of the quantity denoted by a temporary is implicitly determined and is equal to that of the quantity first assigned to it in an operational description.

Operators

The operators used and their meanings are as follows:

←	assignment	|	bitwise or
+	addition	==	equal to
−	subtraction	<	less than
*	multiplication	>	greater than
~	bitwise complement	!=	not equal to
&&	logical and	<=	less than or equal to
&	bitwise and	>=	greater than or equal to
||	logical or		

All operators are binary, except that "~" is unary and "−" is both binary and unary, depending on the context.

Control Structures and Functions

The control structures used in the instruction notation are relatively standard and are described in Appendix E, "Instruction Notation Control Structures".

1   Overview

In the mid 1980s, there was much heated discussion on the subject of the RISC (Reduced Instruction Set Computer) versus CISC (Complex Instruction Set Computer) approach to computer architecture and design. Those arguments have mostly been put to rest and the viability of RISC is universally acknowledged. Now, the argument is usually RISC versus RISC and often, "who is RISC-iest?"

During these more recent arguments, the first three letters of RISC - "Reduced Instruction Set"- are sometimes given undo emphasis when evaluating architectures. This rather simplistic method of evaluating an architecture (how many different instructions does a machine support) does a general disservice to the concept of RISC and can especially distort the value of mature RISC architectures such as PA-RISC. Although it has not yet caught on as a buzzword in the way that RISC has, it can certainly be argued that the term "Precision Architecture" - as in PA-RISC - is actually a much better description of what the design technique known as RISC is all about. This overview chapter will briefly describe the traditional RISC characteristics that are shared by PA-RISC and then provide some detail on the differences between the precision PA-RISC approach and other RISC architectures.

Traditional RISC Characteristics of PA-RISC

There are number of specific characteristics that have come to be associated with most RISC architectures. PA-RISC supports the following traditional RISC features:

- Direct hardware implementation of instruction set — The instruction set can be hardwired to speed instruction execution. No microcode is needed for single cycle execution. Conventional machines require several cycles to perform even simple instructions.

- Fixed instruction size — All instructions are one word (32-bits) in length. This simplifies the instruction fetch mechanism since the location of instruction boundaries is not a function of the instruction type.

- Small number of addressing modes — The instruction set uses only short displacement, long displacement, and indexed modes to access memory.

- Reduced memory access — Only load and store instructions access memory. There are no computational instructions that access memory; load/store instructions operate between memory and a register. This simplifies control hardware and minimizes the machine cycle time.

- Ease of pipelining — The instructions are designed to be easily divisible into parts. This and the fixed size of the instructions allow the instructions to be easily pipelined.

- Optimizing compilers — The PA-RISC instruction set is designed to be an excellent target for optimizing compilers and is optimized for simple, frequently used instructions that execute in one CPU cycle. Implementation of more complex functions is assigned to system software or to assist processors such as the floating-point coprocessor.

- A floating-point coprocessor for IEEE floating-point operations.

PA-RISC - The Genius is in the Details

There is no single aspect of PA-RISC that can be pointed to as making it radically different from other RISC architectures. However, there are a myriad of details that combine to enable implementation of PA-RISC machines that are significantly more efficient than competing RISC machines. The essence of the "precision" approach is that the architecture should be designed precisely to support the operations of applications that will run on a given machine in the most efficient possible manner. Additionally, in order to keep pace with evolving demands, that architecture must also be simple to implement and manufacture. Although it could be argued that these same "essential" statements could be made about other architectures, there are three general categories of features that define the key differences between PA-RISC and other RISC architectures:

- Pathlength reduction features
- Integrated CPU features
- Extensibility and longevity features

The sections that follow will provide details for each of these feature categories.

A Critical Calculus: Instruction Pathlength

All RISC architectures strive to enhance performance by including only those features that allow simple, pipelined implementations with very short cycle times and an instruction execution rate of one per CPU cycle. However, since RISC machines provide a simpler and less varied set of instructions than CISC machines, they are often criticized for instruction pathlength expansion: since fewer and simpler instructions are supported, more of these instructions must be executed to accomplish the same task as compared to a CISC machine. This effect mitigates some of the performance advantages of RISC machines and can also increase memory requirements and, therefore, system costs.

Most RISC architectures, including PA-RISC, combat this valid criticism by using optimizing compilers. PA-RISC goes further, however, by providing efficient instruction-level parallelism: frequent operations are combined into single instructions and sub-word data are operated on in parallel. These techniques enable PA-RISC to reduce instruction pathlength without impacting either the cycle time or the cycles-per-instruction goals of RISC architectures.

Reducing the number of instructions required to perform a given function benefits applications in two ways. First, less code space is required which reduces memory requirements and therefore can reduce the hardware cost of complete systems. Second, reducing the number of instructions in programs provides higher performance or lets the system run at a lower frequency, thus permitting the use of cheaper components.

PA-RISC achieves reductions in instruction pathlength in four different areas:

- Memory accessing instructions
- Functional operation instructions
- Instruction sequencing techniques
- Simple hardware requirements

The sections that follow provide more details on these mechanisms.

Memory Accessing Features for Pathlength Reduction

Like most RISC architectures, PA-RISC is a load-store architecture. Therefore, making these memory access operations efficient is critical in reducing the instruction pathlength since these operations are performed so frequently. The following table highlights some of the features provided to optimize the load-store operations.

Feature	Discussion
Indexed Loads	The most common addressing mode for loads adds the contents of a base and index register to obtain the effective address. Most RISC machines require two instructions for this operation. PA-RISC implements indexed loads with a single instruction.
Scaled-Indexed Loads	A single PA-RISC instruction provides index scaling into a data structure to easily accommodate loading of bytes, halfwords, words, or doublewords - operations typically requiring three instructions in other RISC machines.
Address Updates	Operations that repetitively access every nth item in an array or other data structure are quite common and in most RISC machines require two instructions - one to load the data and a second to update the base address register. PA-RISC performs this operation with a single load or store instruction.
32-bit Static Displacements	A 2-instruction sequence in PA-RISC permits specification of a full 32-bit static displacement from a base address. This sequence typically requires 3 instructions in other RISC machines.

Functional Operation Features for Pathlength Reduction

Some critical or frequently performed functional operations that often require more than one instruction are combined in PA-RISC, often by judicious use of existing hardware. The following table briefly describes some of the functional operations where pathlength reduction features are implemented.

Feature	Discussion
Shift and Add	Integer multiplication by a constant can be accomplished using a sequence of a shift left instruction and an add instruction. PA-RISC combines these two operations into a single shift-left-and-add instruction for the most common cases - shift by 1, 2, or 3 bit positions. Other RISC machines typically require two instructions for the shift-and-add operation. Some RISC machines (including PA-RISC) provide an integer multiply instruction, but this instruction typically has a longer latency than shift-and-add.

Feature	Discussion
Bit-Field Instructions	Bit-field operations can be unwieldy and require multiple instructions in most RISC machines. PA-RISC provides a powerful set of bit-field instructions such as the Extract and Deposit instructions which combine a shift operation with a mask or merge operation. Additionally, a double shift instruction which simplifies dealing with operands that cross word boundaries is provided and conditional branches based on a single bit are also supported.
Floating-Point Multiply and Fused Add	Within the large class of applications that make significant use of floating-point arithmetic, the most frequent floating-point operations are multiply and add (or subtract) which require two separate instructions in most machines. PA-RISC combines these operations into a single multiply-add or multiply-subtract instruction.
Parallel Subword Operations	Although applications frequently operate on a mix of 4-bit decimal numbers, 8-bit characters, and 16-bit international characters, most RISC machines do not use their data path efficiently for these subword operations. PA-RISC, however, samples carry out bits at 4-bit boundaries of the data path. This allows parallel operation on subword data and can result in requiring significantly fewer instructions to operate on characters and BCD numbers.
Multimedia Audio and Video	Processing multimedia data requires arithmetic operations and flexible manipulation of subword data. PA-RISC provides a compact set of instructions with minimal architectural impact to support processing of multimedia data in single instruction operations.

Conditional Instruction Sequencing Features for Pathlength Reduction

Control flow instructions are very common in most programs, and complicate the desired smooth flow of instructions through the pipeline. PA-RISC provides a number of features that mitigate the impact of control flow instructions and result in requiring execution of fewer instructions. The following table summarizes the pathlength reduction features provided for conditional instruction sequencing.

Feature	Discussion
Combined Operation and Conditional Branch	A significant percentage of dynamic instruction paths consist of conditional branch instructions - many with short branch distances. Most RISC machines require two instructions for this operation: a functional operation which sets a condition code and a conditional branch based on that code. PA-RISC provides eight conditional branch instructions covering the most frequent cases which combine the functional operation and the conditional branch in a single instruction.

Feature	Discussion
Branches with Conditional Nullification	Many RISC machines require that the delay slot of a conditional branch instruction be filled with a NOP instruction - needlessly increasing path-length. In PA-RISC, each conditional branch instruction contains a "nullify" bit that selects whether the next instruction (in the delay slot) is always executed or conditionally executed. This approach ensures that delay slots can always be filled with useful operations.
Operation with Conditional Nullification	PA-RISC arithmetic, logical, and bit-manipulation instructions also include the mechanism for conditionally nullifying the next instruction. The condition is evaluated in the same cycle as the data operation and, if true, causes the following instruction to be skipped. This technique allows generation of "in-line" conditional execution without the pipeline penalties normally associated with conditional branching, thus allowing optimal operation of the instruction pipelining and prefetch mechanisms.
Operation and Conditional Trap	High-level languages often require a range-checking capability to ensure that addresses are within set boundaries. PA-RISC provides trapping variants of Add, Subtract, and Shift-and-Add instructions which cause a software trap to occur on overflow or a condition being met. These instructions allow simple, compact implementation of such operations as range-checking.

Simple Hardware Required to Enable Pathlength Reduction Features

Many of the pathlength reduction features described in the preceding paragraphs could be implemented in other RISC machines - by adding significant amounts of silicon and complexity. A key to the efficiency of PA-RISC is that these features are enabled with minimal additional hardware complexity. The following table briefly describes the simple hardware used to implement some of the pathlength reduction features. In each case, the additional hardware requirements are minimal compared to the improved performance that is obtained. Figure 1-1 illustrates the PA-RISC datapath.

Feature	Discussion
Scaled Indexing & Shift-and-Add	Typical RISC processors require an adder unit to perform basic address calculations such as base+displacement for loads and stores. Both of these enhanced features are accommodated in PA-RISC by simply widening the multiplexor in front of one port to the ALU that performs a shift of one, two, or three bits.
Parallel Subword Operations	These single-instruction-multiple-data type of instructions are supported by just sampling the ALU carry-out bits at intervals of 4 bits. Since many 32-bit ALUs are designed by replicating 4-bit ALU slices, this has no impact on the speed or complexity of the ALU.
Combined Operation and Conditional Branch	Typical RISC processors include a separate branch adder, in addition to the ALU, to quickly calculate target addresses for better pipeline architecture. PA-RISC makes additional use of this already available branch adder to calculate program-counter relative branch addresses during the same cycle as the functional operation is being performed.

Feature	Discussion
Bit-Field Operations	In typical RISC machines, a multiplexor is provided at the output of the shifter used for sign extension for right shifts. Support for bit-field operations is obtained simply by slightly widening the multiplexor already provided to perform a masking operation for extracts and deposits.
Floating-Point Multiply and Add	Since floating-point units typically have separate multiplier and adder functional units, adding a dual-operation multiply-and-add instructions requires only two extra ports on the floating-point register.
Address Updates on Loads	Since loads have a longer latency than ALU operations, typical RISC designs use a dedicated general register write port to avoid the complications of arbitrating with ALU operations for the port. This typically leaves the normal write port unused on loads. PA-RISC exploits this situation and makes use of this unused write port for address updates.

Figure 1-1. PA-RISC Datapath

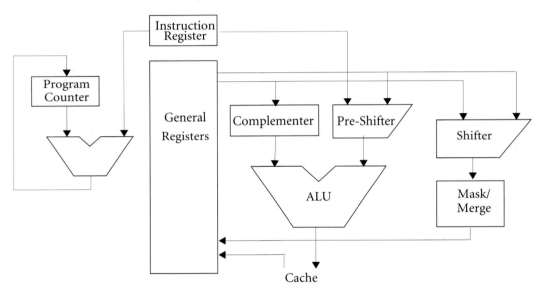

Multimedia Support: The Precision Process Illustrated

PA-RISC's implementation of multimedia support provides an excellent illustration of how the precision architecture approach works. The process begins with the recognition of a significant need – that is, a need that is deemed to be long-lasting and broad-based. Multimedia support meets these criteria since it is becoming obvious that scalable multimedia interfaces will replace current graphical interfaces, and multimedia communications and databases are already beginning to replace text-based systems. Soon, most systems will be expected to handle the ubiquitous transmission, storage and processing of different information media such as audio, video, images, graphics and text.

When this significant need was identified, the PA-RISC team began a thorough investigation of what would be required to provide efficient multimedia support. Although separate specialized hardware units had been previously used to support such operations as video compression, it seemed that the time was right to make efficient support of multimedia a standard feature in the microprocessor rather than an optional hardware feature tacked on with additional cost. Further, the fact that multimedia standards and algorithms are continually changing argued for flexible hardware primitives that could be used by software.

Next, it was determined that the most computation-intensive algorithms are based on such video decompression standards as MPEG and JPEG. These standards needed halfword (16-bit) arithmetic to provide sufficient dynamic range for internal pixel computations but further investigation suggested that they did not usually require byte arithmetic. This latter fact was used to minimize hardware changes since the implementation would be simpler if not all possible subword sizes needed to be accommodated.

The final stage of the process was to determine what instructions were needed to provide the most efficient support and how to implement these instructions with minimum impact on existing hardware resources. Of the multimedia algorithms studied, the most common operations on pixels were ADD, SUBTRACT, AVERAGE, and MULTIPLY of two numbers. The first three operations could be readily implemented using the existing ALU datapath to operate on two pairs of halfwords in parallel using a single instruction in a single cycle. Thus, the HADD, HSUB, and HAVG instructions were easily provided.

Halfword multiplication could not be implemented in a single cycle and would have required new datapaths separate from the ALU datapath. The solution was to provide partial support using halfword multiplication by constants with parallel Halfword-Shift-and-Add instructions (HSHLADD and HSHRADD.) These instructions could be implemented using existing hardware that was already being used for scaled indexing, word and doubleword shift-and-add, and parallel subword operations (as described in the previous section) and, when used as primitives to do constant multiplication, resulted in efficient support for the key compression algorithms.

The architecture team then went one step further. Their investigations made it clear that to fully utilize halfword parallel arithmetic instructions in a 64-bit architecture, it is desirable to be able to rearrange halfwords in registers without incurring the overhead of memory load and store instructions. Since processing of multimedia data often requires rearrangement of packed pixel data structures, the team determined that they could provide support for these operations at very little cost in complexity. Accordingly, the PERMH, MIXH, MIXW instructions were implemented to support rearrangement of words and halfwords in registers with no memory load/store overhead. This support was provided with minimal hardware changes since the existing shift-merge-unit datapath already handled a general 4-to-1 MUX for each result halfword with some restrictions.

The end result of this process was significant performance gains for critical multimedia algorithms with only small changes being required to the existing datapaths.

Integrated CPU

In addition to the instruction set features which reduce the execution time and pathlength of programs, PA-RISC integrates the following features into the CPU which reduce the hardware and development costs of a system:

- Security and protection

- Uniquely powerful interrupt system

- Debugging aids

Security and Protection Features

Controlling access to data in a multi-user environment is an essential requirement in most systems. PA-RISC provides a comprehensive set of protection and security features to simplify these critical requirements.

Feature	Discussion
Four Privilege Levels	Most architectures have two privilege levels - user and supervisor. PA-RISC defines four distinct privilege levels to enable implementation of multiple hierarchical rings of security in very secure environments. This would allow, for example, an operating system microkernel to run at privilege level 0, the surrounding system services at levels 1 and 2, and user processes at level 3.
Access Rights on a Per-Page Basis	Access rights determine the privileges needed to read, write or execute a memory page. In PA-RISC, these rights are embedded for each virtual page in the page directory and TLB entry which contain the Access Rights and Access ID for that page. The Access ID, which is enabled by a bit in the Processor Status Word, is compared against four Protection IDs associated with the current process to determine if access should be allowed.
Gateway Instruction	This instruction performs a branch and promotes the privilege level of the current process to that specified in the access ID for the destination page. This provides an efficient mechanism to perform operating system calls without the need for a software interrupt, process switch, or passing through the most privileged level.

Interrupt System Features

The PA-RISC interrupt system is simpler yet more flexible than those provided in most other RISC machines. It provides fast, single-cycle context switching and precise interruptions even with delayed branching. The following table describes several interrupt system features that particularly distinguish PA-RISC.

Feature	Discussion
Software Control of Interrupt Groups	Most architectures set interrupt priorities in special purpose hardware. In PA-RISC, software can independently disable one or more interrupt groups, delaying their processing to a more convenient time. Software can also select the order, and hence the priority, in which it services unmasked interrupts.
Logging of Low-priority Interrupts	Most architectures interlock low-priority devices while higher priority interrupts are being handled thus requiring low-priority devices to continue requesting interrupts until they are recognized. PA-RISC logs low-priority interrupts even while higher priority interrupts are being handled.

Debugging Features

A significant portion of any software development project is the debugging process. PA-RISC includes a unique set of features to aid in system-level debugging.

Feature	Discussion
Program Tracing Assistance	The Processor Status Word (PSW) contains three bits that can be set to cause a trap on any taken branch, on transfers to a higher privilege level, or a transfer to a lower privilege. This permits program flow to be traced and allows for auditing of the interface between programs and more privileged code in system calls.
Specialized Breakpoint Support	The Recovery Counter is a special mechanism that can be programmed to produce a trap after a specified number of instructions have been executed. This is useful for breaking at a particular point in execution, as opposed to when a particular instruction address is reached.
Breakpoint Support	The BREAK instruction can be used for straightforward breakpoint capability. The instruction also contains a parameter field, which is ignored by the hardware, and lets it be used as a fast Supervisor Call instruction.
Trapping on Page Accesses	Each page in the virtual address space can be tagged to enable traps when any references are made to the page or only when the page is modified.
Special Diagnostic Instructions	The DIAGNOSE instruction provides access to processor state not normally directly accessible to software. The instruction has a parameter field to encode implementation-dependent operations relating to initialization, reconfiguration, or diagnostics.

Extensibility and Longevity

An architecture that can not be extended has a limited life and is a technological dead end. It is also critical that extensibility be an inherent part of the architecture - attempts to tack it on as an afterthought inevitably result in inefficient jury rigs. PA-RISC has, from the outset, incorporated several architectural features to ensure that this architecture will have a long life and enable future growth and extensions. These features include an assist architecture that supports incorporation of the special function unit and coprocessor interfaces, and the large, scalable virtual physical address space. These features are briefly described in the following table.

Feature	Discussion
Assist Architecture	PA-RISC includes instructions to invoke special, optional, hardware functions provided by two types of processor assists: Special Function Units (SFUs) and Coprocessors. SFUs are tightly coupled to the main processor and use its general registers as the operands and targets of operations. Coprocessors are less tightly coupled to the main processor and use either memory (via the cache) or their own registers for the operands and targets of operations. PA-RISC supports up to eight each of SFUs and coprocessors. Two coprocessors, the Floating-point and Performance Monitor coprocessors, are already defined.
Address Space	Virtual address space requirements have been increasing unpaced as memory demands of software systems accelerate. PA-RISC accommodates scalable virtual memory systems ranging from 64 to 96 bits of virtual address space. The smaller virtual address spaces permit lower cost processors. The same address space image is presented to a program independent of the virtual address space supported by a particular system. Physical address spaces ranging from 32 to 64 bits are accommodated and the same image and the same image is presented to software independent of the physical space supported by a particular system.

System Organization

The PA-RISC processor is only one element of a complete system. A system also includes memory arrays, I/O adapters, and interconnecting busses. The processor module is organized to provide a high-performance computation machine. The Central Processing Unit (CPU) includes a general register set, virtual address registers and machine state registers. A cache is optional, but it is such a cost-effective component that nearly all processors incorporate this hardware. To support virtual memory addressing, a hardware translation lookaside buffer (TLB) is included on processors to provide virtual to absolute address translations.

Any processor may include Special Function Units (SFUs) and coprocessors. These dedicated hardware units substantially increase performance when executing selected hardware algorithms. Collectively, SFUs and coprocessors are called **assist processors**. For example, floating-point functions are provided by a coprocessor, while a signal processing algorithm could be enhanced with a specialized SFU.

Figure 1-2 shows a typical processor module with a cache, a TLB, one coprocessor and one SFU.

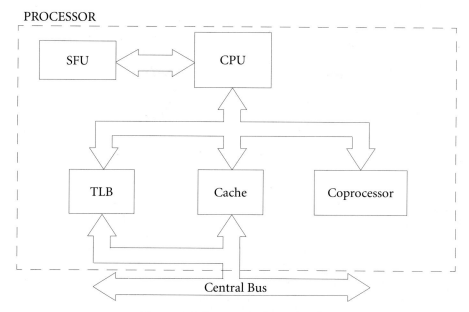

PROCESSOR

Figure 1-2. Processor Organization

Register-intensive computation is central to the architecture. Calculations are performed only between high-speed CPU registers or between registers and immediate constants. Register-intensive operation simplifies data and control paths thereby improving processor performance.

Load and store instructions are the only instructions that reference main memory. To minimize the number of memory references, optimizing compilers allocate the most frequently used variables to general-purpose registers.

Storage System

The PA-RISC storage system is an explicit hierarchy that is visible to software. The architecture provides for buffering of information to and from main memory in high-speed storage units (visible caches).

The memory hierarchy achieves nearly the speed of the highest (fastest and smallest) memory level with the capacity of the lowest (largest and slowest) memory level. The levels of this memory hierarchy from highest to lowest are the general registers, caches (if implemented), main memory and direct access storage devices such as disks. Figure 1-3 illustrates the hierarchical speed/size relationship between the various elements of a typical memory system.

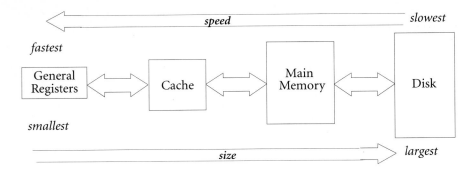

Figure 1-3. Memory Hierarchy

A cache system, when implemented, is an integral part of the processor. Caches hold frequently accessed data and instructions in order to minimize access time to main memory. A system may have a separate instruction cache (I-cache) and data cache (D-cache), or may have a single, combined cache that holds both instructions and data.

System support of virtual addressing is provided by a hardware feature called the Translation Lookaside Buffer (TLB) which performs translations from virtual addresses to absolute addresses. The TLB contains translations for recently accessed virtual pages. Each TLB entry also contains information used to determine valid access to that memory page and the type of access permitted. While the TLB determines the proper translation of the virtual address, access information is checked and access is either granted or denied. TLBs may be split on a processor, one for instructions (ITLB) and one for data (DTLB).

Virtual Addressing

A generalized virtual memory system is an integral part of the architecture on all PA-RISC systems. The virtual memory system supports virtual addresses between 64 and 96 bits wide. Program-supplied addresses are treated as logical addresses and translated to absolute addresses by the TLB when memory is referenced. Address translations are made at the page level. Direct access to physical memory locations is also supported in the instruction set.

The global virtual memory is organized as a set of linear spaces with each space being between 4 Gbytes and 16 Exabytes long. Each space is specified with a space identifier and divided into variable sized pages with each page being between 4 Kbytes and 64 Mbytes in size.

Input/Output Organization

The PA-RISC I/O architecture is **memory-mapped**, which means that complete control of all attached modules is exercised by the execution of memory read and write commands. Processors invoke these operations by executing load and store instructions to either virtual or absolute addresses.

This approach permits I/O drivers to be written in high-level languages. Since the usual page-level protection mechanism is applied during virtual-to-absolute address translation, user programs can be granted direct control over particular I/O modules without compromising system integrity.

Direct I/O is the simplest and least costly type of system I/O interface because it has little or no local state and is controlled entirely by software. Since direct I/O responds only to load and store instructions and never generates memory addresses, it may be mapped into virtual space and controlled directly by user programs.

Direct Memory Access (DMA) I/O adapters contain sufficient state to control the transfer of data to or from a contiguous range of absolute addresses and to perform data chaining. This state is initialized prior to the start of a transfer by a privileged driver which is responsible for the mapping and validation of virtual addresses. During the transfer, the virtual page(s) involved must be locked in physical memory and protected from conflicting accesses through software.

Assist Processors

Assist processors are hardware units that can be added to the basic PA-RISC system to enhance its performance or functionality. Two categories of assist processors are defined and are distinguished by the level at which they interface with the memory hierarchy.

The first type of assist processor is the **special function unit** (SFU) which interfaces to the memory hierarchy at the general register level. This acts as an alternate ALU or as an alternate path through the execution unit of the main processor. It may have its own internal state.

The second type of assist processor is the **coprocessor**, which shares the main processor caches. Coprocessors are typically used to enhance performance of special operations such as high-performance floating-point calculations. Coprocessors generally have their own internal state and hardware evaluation mechanism. The floating-point coprocessor is defined in Chapter 8, "Floating-point Coprocessor", and the performance monitor coprocessor is defined in Chapter 11, "Performance Monitor Coprocessor".

Multiprocessor Systems

Multiprocessor support for various types of multiprocessor systems is built into the architecture. Multiprocessors can be configured to provide incremental performance improvement via distribution of the system workload over multiple CPUs, or can be configured redundantly to provide fault-tolerance in the system. In systems sharing a single virtual address space, the architecture defines a model of a single consistent cache and TLB. Software is still responsible for maintaining coherence for modifying instructions, and for virtual address mapping. Systems may choose to only share physical memory and form more loosely-coupled configurations. All multiprocessor systems synchronize using a semaphore lock in shared main memory.

Instruction Set Overview

PA-RISC provides a compact, yet full-functioned instruction set. The following table summarizes the capabilities provided by the various categories of instructions.

Category	Discussion
Memory Reference Instructions	Transfer data between the general registers and main memory or the I/O system. Load and store instructions are the only instructions that reference memory. Operands required for a given operation are first brought into a CPU register from memory with a load instruction. The result of the operation is explicitly saved to memory with a store instruction. There are two primary addressing modes for memory accesses: base relative and indexed. Memory references can be specified by either virtual or absolute addressing. System I/O is memory-mapped: that is, I/O modules are mapped into physical pages which are not part of the main memory, but which are addressed in the same way. This provides the same flexibility, security, and protection mechanisms for I/O operations as are provided for main memory.
Arithmetic and Logical Instructions	Provide a simple but powerful set of functions. Besides the usual arithmetic and logical operations, there are shift-and-add instructions to accelerate integer multiplication, extract and deposit instructions for bit manipulations, and several instructions to provide support for packed and unpacked decimal arithmetic.
Special Arithmetical and Logical Instructions	These include saturating arithmetic, averaging, shifting, and permuting, which operate on packed 16-bit integers four at a time. These instructions are particularly valuable in multimedia applications such as video decompression.
Multiple-precision Arithmetic	Carry-sensitive instructions support multi-precision arithmetic. More complex arithmetic functions (including packed, unpacked and zoned decimal operations) are supported by language compilers through execution of a sequence of simple instructions.
Program Control Flow Instructions	Branch instructions and instructions that conditionally skip the following instruction affect the control flow of a program. The condition resulting from an operation can immediately determine whether or not a branch should be taken. Unconditional branch and procedure call instructions are provided to alter control flow. The need for some branch sequences is eliminated as most computational instructions can specify skipping of the next instruction. This permits such common functions as range checking to be performed in a simple, non-branching instruction sequence.

Category	Discussion
Multimedia Instructions	Provide efficient support for the most frequent multimedia operations since these operations are assuming greater importance in many applications. The multimedia instructions in PA-RISC perform multiple parallel computations, with each of the results being tested and forced to the appropriate value if necessary, in a single cycle. The result is a sizeable reduction in pathlength and fewer disruptive breaks in control flow in multimedia algorithms.
Floating-point Instructions	Support the defined IEEE standard operations of addition, subtraction, multiplication, division, square root, conversions, and round-to-integer.
System Control Instructions	•Provide the support needed to implement an operating system including: returning from interruptions, executing instruction breaks and probing access rights. They also control the Processor Status Word, special registers, caches, and translation lookaside buffers.

2   Processing Resources

The PA-RISC instruction set is only one aspect of the processor architecture; the following components are also specified:

- Processing Resources — what registers and register sets are available to the user and to system software

- Data Types — how data is organized and what data types are available to the user

- Memory and I/O Addressing — how system memory and the input/output facilities are organized and accessed.

This chapter describes the processing resources and data types in a PA-RISC system. The memory and I/O addressing aspects are described in Chapter 3, "Addressing and Access Control".

The software-accessible registers (that is, the processing resources) are the storage elements within a processor that are manipulated by the instructions. These resources participate in instruction control flow, computations, interruption processing, protection mechanisms, and virtual memory management. The software-accessible registers can be divided into two groups: non-privileged registers and privileged registers. Privileged registers are those that generally can be accessed using instructions that can be executed only when at the most privileged level. Figure 2-1 illustrates the registers provided in the PA-RISC architecture.

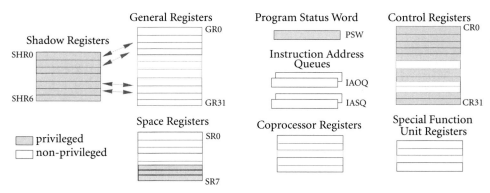

Figure 2-1. Software Accessible Registers

Non-Privileged Software-Accessible Registers

These registers can be accessed by any program at any time, regardless of the current privilege level and include those typically needed by application software (as opposed to system software.)

- General Registers (GR 0..GR 31)
- Space Registers (SR 0..SR 7 - SR5-SR7 are privileged.)
- Instruction Address Queues
- Coprocessor Registers
- Special Function Unit Registers
- subset of Control Registers (Timer, SAR, CR26,27))

General Registers

Thirty-two 64-bit **general registers** provide the central resource for all computation (Figure 2-2). They are numbered GR 0 through GR 31, and are available to all programs at all privilege levels.

GR 0, GR 1, GR2, and GR 31 have special functions.

- GR 0, when referenced as a source operand, delivers zeros. When GR 0 is used as a destination, the result is discarded.
- GR 1 is the implicit target of the ADD IMMEDIATE LEFT instruction.
- GR 2 is the instruction address offset link register for the long displacement form of the normal call instruction (BRANCH AND LINK).
- GR 31 is the instruction address offset link register for the base-relative interspace procedure call instruction [BRANCH EXTERNAL instruction with the (optional) L (for link) completer].

GR 1, GR2, and GR 31 can also be used as general registers; however, software conventions may at times restrict their use.

	0	63
GR 0	Permanent zero	
GR 1	Target for ADDIL or General use	
GR 2	Target for long displacement form of B,L or General use	
GR 3	General use	
	• • •	
GR 30	General use	
GR 31	Link register for BLE or General use	

Figure 2-2. General Registers

Space Registers

A PA-RISC system provides eight **space registers**, numbered SR 0 through SR 7, which contain space IDs for virtual addressing. Instructions specify space registers either directly in the instruction or indirectly through general register contents.

Instruction addresses, computed by branch instructions, may use any of the space registers. SR 0 is the instruction address space link register for the base-relative interspace procedure call instruction [BRANCH EXTERNAL instruction with the (optional) L (for link) completer]. Data operands can specify SR 1 through SR 3 explicitly, and SR 4 through SR 7 indirectly, via general registers.

SR 1 through SR 7 have no special functions; however, their use will normally be constrained by software conventions. For example, the following convention supports non-overlapping process groups. SR 1 through SR 3 provide general-use virtual pointers. SR 4 tracks the instruction address (IA) space and provides access to literal data contained in the current code segment. SR 5 points to a space containing process private data, SR 6 to a space containing data shared by a group of processes, and SR 7 to a space containing the operating system's public code, literals, and data. Figure 2-3 illustrates this convention.

SRs 5 through 7 can be modified only by code executing at the most privileged level.

SR 0	Link code space ID
SR 1	General use
SR 2	General use
SR 3	General use
SR 4	Tracks IA space
SR 5	Process private data
SR 6	Shared data
SR 7	Operating system's public code, literals, and data

Figure 2-3. Example Space Register Usage Convention

Space registers, as well as IASQ, IIASQ, and ISR which are described later, may be any size between 32 bits and 64 bits to support a virtual address size between 64 and 96 bits.

Instruction Address Queues

The Instruction Address Queues hold the address of the currently executing instruction and the address of the instruction that will be executed after the current instruction, termed the **following** instruction. Note that the following instruction is not necessarily the next instruction in the linear code space. These two queues are each two elements deep. The Instruction Address Offset Queue (IAOQ) elements are each 64 bits wide. The high-order 62 bits contain the word offset of the instruction while the 2 low-order bits maintain the **privilege level** of the corresponding instruction. There are four privilege levels: 0, 1, 2, and 3 with 0 being the most privileged level.

The Instruction Address Space Queue (IASQ) contains the space ID of the current and following instructions. The IASQ may be from 32 to 64 bits in size. The space ID of the current instruction, when executing without instruction address translation enabled, is not specified and may contain any value.

The front elements of the two queues (IASQ_Front and IAOQ_Front) form the virtual address of the current instruction while the back elements of the two queues (IASQ_Back and IAOQ_Back) contain the address of the following instruction. Figure 2-4 shows this structure. Two addresses are maintained to support the delayed branching capability (See "Concept of Delayed Branching" on page 4-1).

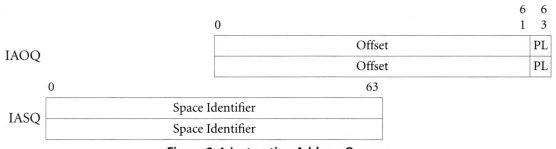

Figure 2-4. Instruction Address Queues

Control Registers (non-privileged)

Although most of the Control Registers can be accessed only by privileged instructions, the Shift Amount Register (SAR), Interval Timer, and temporary registers CR26,27 are accessible at any time and are described in the paragraphs that follow.

Shift Amount Register

The Shift Amount Register or SAR (CR 11), is a 6-bit register used by the variable shift, extract, deposit, and branch on bit instructions. It specifies the number of bits a quantity is to be shifted. The remaining 58 bits are ignored bits.

Interval Timer

The Interval Timer (CR 16) consists of two internal registers. One of the internal registers is a 64-bit counter which continually counts up by 1 at a rate which is implementation-dependent and between twice the "peak instruction rate" and half the "peak instruction rate". Reading the Interval Timer returns the value of this internal 64-bit register. The other internal register contains a 32-bit comparison value and is set by writing to the Interval Timer. When the least significant 32 bits of the counter register and the comparison register contain identical values, a bit in the External Interrupt Request Register is set to 1. This causes an external interrupt, if not masked. The W bit (Wide enable) in the Processor Status Word (PSW - see Table 2-1) determines which bit of the EIRR is set. If the W bit is 0, the timer comparison causes bit 32 to be set to 1. If the W bit is 1, the timer comparison causes bit 0 of the EIER to be set to 1.

The Interval Timer can only be written by code executing at the most privileged level. If the PSW S-bit is 1, the Interval Timer can only be read by code executing at the most privileged level; otherwise, it can be read by code executing at any privilege level.

In a multiprocessor system, each processor must have its own Interval Timer. Each Interval Timer need not be synchronized with the other Interval Timers in the system, nor do they need to be clocked at the same frequency.

If, as part of a power-saving mode, the processor clock is reduced below the "peak instruction rate", the Interval Timer continues to count at its peak rate. If the processor clock is stopped, the Interval Timer may also stop.

Temporary Registers

Two of the eight 64-bit temporary registers (CRs 26 and 27) are readable by code executing at any privilege level and writable only by code executing at the most privileged level.

Coprocessor Registers

Each coprocessor may have its own register set. The coprocessor mechanism is described in "Assist Instructions" on page 6-19. The floating-point coprocessor registers are described in Chapter 8, "Floating-point Coprocessor". The performance monitor coprocessor registers are described in Chapter 11, "Performance Monitor Coprocessor".

SFU Registers

Each special function unit may have its own register set. The SFU mechanism is described in "Assist Instructions" on page 6-19.

Branch Target Stack

The Branch Target Stack (or BTS) is an optional processing resource which is used to accelerate indirect branches, such as subroutine returns. The BTS is managed by software, and in processors which implement it, can provide the branch target address in place of the general register specified in the branch instruction.

Conceptually, the BTS is a stack of 63-bit registers. The number of registers is implementation dependent, and can be 0. Each register holds an instruction address plus a valid bit. Although the BTS is not directly readable, it can be thought of as being laid out as in Figure 2-5.

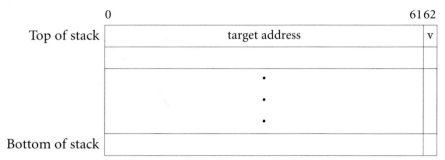

Figure 2-5. Branch Target Stack

Certain instructions push an address onto the top of the stack, forcing all other entries down one register, with the old value of the last register (bottom of stack) being discarded. When a value is pushed onto the stack, the valid bit is set to 1 for that entry.

Other operations pop an address from the top of the stack. If the valid bit associated with the address is 1, the address may be used as a branch target, to decrease the latency of the branch. If the entry is invalid, it is ignored, and the branch target is calculated the normal way (using the specified general register). When the stack is popped, each entry moves up one register, and the register at the bottom of the stack is marked invalid.

The Branch Nomination Register (or BNR) is a register which holds one instruction address. It also has a valid bit associated with it. The BNR allows software to make use of the BTS in a called function, even though the caller function does not attempt to use the stack (perhaps because it is older code).

Figure 2-6. Branch Nomination Register

Implementation of the BTS is optional. Hardware may invalidate entries in the stack at any time, so software may not rely on entries remaining valid.

For more details, see the related instruction pages.

Privileged Software-Accessible Registers

These registers can be accessed only when the processor is in the most privileged mode and are intended for use by system software.

- Processor Status Word (PSW)
- Shadow Registers (SHR 0..SHR 6)
- Control Registers (CR 0..CR 31)

Processor Status Word (PSW)

Processor state is encoded in a 64-bit register called the Processor Status Word (PSW). When an interruption occurs, the current value of the PSW is saved in the Interruption Processor Status Word (IPSW) and usually all defined PSW bits are set to 0. The format of the PSW is shown in Figure 2-7.

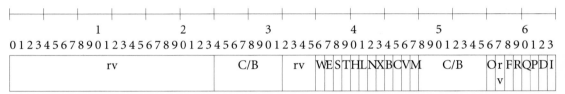

Figure 2-7. Processor Status Word

The PSW is set to the contents of the IPSW by the RETURN FROM INTERRUPTION instruction. The interruption handler may restore the original PSW, modify selected bits, or may change the PSW to an entirely new value.

The E, O, W, F, R, Q, P, D, and I bits of the PSW are known as the **system mask**. Each of these bits, with the exception of the Q-bit, may be set to 1, set to 0, written, and read by the system control instructions that manipulate the system mask. The Q-bit is specially defined. It can be set to 0 by system control instructions that manipulate the system mask, but setting it to 1 when the current value is 0 is an undefined operation. The only instruction that can set the Q-bit to 1 is the RETURN FROM INTERRUPTION instruction.

Some of the PSW bits are termed **mask/unmask** bits whereas others are termed **disable/enable** bits. Interruptions that are masked remain pending whereas those that are disabled are ignored.

The PSW fields are described in Table 2-1.

Table 2-1. Processor Status Word

Field	Description
rv	**Reserved** bits.
W	**Wide 64-bit address formation enable.** When 1, full 64-bit-offset addressing is enabled. When 0, addresses are truncated to 32-bit offsets, for compatibility with existing PA-RISC 1.0 and 1.1 applications.
E	**Little endian memory access enable.** When 0, all memory references are big endian. When 1, all memory references are little endian. Implementation of this bit is optional. If it is not implemented, all memory references are big endian and this bit is a reserved bit.
S	**Secure Interval Timer.** When 1, the Interval Timer is readable only by code executing at the most privileged level. When 0, the Interval Timer is readable by code executing at any privilege level.
T	**Taken branch trap enable.** When 1, any taken branch is terminated with a taken branch trap.
H	**Higher-privilege transfer trap enable.** When 1, a higher-privilege transfer trap occurs whenever the following instruction is of a higher privilege.
L	**Lower-privilege transfer trap enable.** When 1, a lower-privilege transfer trap occurs whenever the following instruction is of a lower privilege.
N	**Nullify.** The current instruction is nullified when this bit is 1. This bit is set to 1 by an instruction that nullifies the following instruction.
X	**Data memory break disable.** The X-bit is set to 0 after the execution of each instruction, except for the RETURN FROM INTERRUPTION instruction which may set it to 1. When 1, data memory break traps are disabled. This bit allows a simple mechanism to trap on a data store and then proceed past the trapping instruction.
B	**Taken branch.** The B-bit is set to 1 by any taken branch instruction and set to 0 otherwise. This is used to ensure that the BRANCH instruction with the ,GATE completer (the privilege increasing instruction) cannot be used to compromise system security.
C	**Code (instruction) address translation enable.** When 1, instruction addresses are translated and access rights checked.
V	**Divide step correction.** The DIVIDE STEP (integer division primitive) instruction records intermediate status in this bit to provide a non-restoring divide primitive.
M	**High-priority machine check mask.** When 1, high-priority machine checks (HPMCs) are masked. Normally 0, this bit is set to 1 after an HPMC and set to 0 after all other interruptions.

Table 2-1. Processor Status Word (Continued)

C/B	**Carry/borrow bits.** The following instructions update the PSW carry/borrow bits from the corresponding carry/borrow outputs of the 4-bit digits of the ALU:
	
	    ADD* ADDI DS
	    SHLADD* SUB SUBI
	
	The instructions marked with an asterisk set the carry/borrow bits only if the ,L (logical) completer is not specified.
	
	After an add which sets them, each bit is set to 1 if a carry occurred out of its corresponding digit, and set to 0 otherwise. After a subtract which sets them, each bit is set to 0 if a borrow occurred into its corresponding digit, and set to 1 otherwise. Bits {24..31} hold the digit carries from the upper half of the ALU, and bits {48..55} hold the digit carries from the lower half.

O	**Ordered references.** When 1, virtual memory references to pages with the corresponding TLB O-bit 1, and all absolute memory references, are ordered. When 0, memory references (except those explicitly marked as ordered or strongly ordered) may be weakly ordered. Note that references to I/O address space, references to pages with the TLB U-bit 1, semaphore instructions, and TLB purge instructions are always strongly ordered.
F	**Performance monitor interrupt unmask.** When 1, the performance monitor interrupt is unmasked and can cause an interruption. When 0, the interruption is held pending. Implementation of this bit is required only if the performance monitor is implemented and the performance monitor has the ability to interrupt. If it is not implemented, this bit is a reserved bit.
R	**Recovery Counter enable.** When 1, recovery counter traps occur if bit 0 of the recovery counter is a 1. This bit also enables decrementing of the Recovery Counter.
Q	**Interruption state collection enable.** When 1, interruption state is collected. Used in processing the interruption and returning to the interrupted code, this state is recorded in the Interruption Instruction Address Queue (IIAQ), the Interruption Instruction Register (IIR), the Interruption Space Register (ISR), and the Interruption Offset Register (IOR).
P	**Protection identifier validation enable.** When this bit and the C-bit are both equal to 1, instruction references check for valid protection identifiers (PIDs). When this bit and the D-bit are both equal to 1, data references check for valid PIDs. When this bit is 1, probe instructions check for valid PIDs.
D	**Data address translation enable.** When 1, data addresses are translated and access rights checked.
I	External **interrupt**, power failure interrupt, and low-priority machine check interruption **unmask.** When 1, these interruptions are unmasked and can cause an interruption. When 0, the interruptions are held pending.

Shadow Registers

There are seven registers **shadow registers**. Upon interruption, if the PSW Q-bit was 1, the contents of

GRs 1, 8, 9, 16, 17, 24, and 25 are copied into shadow registers SHR 0, 1, 2, 3, 4, 5, and 6, respectively. If an interruption is taken with the PSW Q-bit equal to 0, the shadow registers are unchanged. The contents of these general registers are restored from their shadow registers when a RETURN FROM INTERRUPTION instruction with the (optional) R (for restore) completer is executed.

Control Registers

There are twenty-five defined **control registers**, numbered CR 0, and CR 8 through CR 31, which contain system state information.

The control registers are shown in Figure 2-8 and described in the following sections. (The control registers that can be accessed in the non-privileged state are described earlier in the section "Control Registers (non-privileged)" on page 2-5.) Moving the contents of a control register to a general register copies the register contents right aligned into the general register. Moving the contents of a general register to a control register copies the entire general register into the control register.

Control registers 1 through 7 are reserved registers.

	0		31 32		63
CR 0	nonexistent		Recovery Counter		
	reserved				
CR 8	Protection ID 1	WD	Protection ID 2		WD
CR 9	Protection ID 3	WD	Protection ID 4		WD
CR 10	reserved			SCR	CCR
CR 11	ignored				SAR
CR 12	Protection ID 5	WD	Protection ID 6		WD
CR 13	Protection ID 7	WD	Protection ID 8		WD
CR 14	Interruption Vector Address			reserved	
CR 15	External Interrupt Enable Mask				
CR 16	Interval Timer				
CR 17	Interruption Instruction Address Space Queue				
CR 18	Interruption Instruction Address Offset Queue				
CR 19	reserved		Interruption Instruction Register		
CR 20	Interruption Space Register				
CR 21	Interruption Offset Register				
CR 22	Interruption Processor Status Word				
CR 23	External Interrupt Request Register				
CR 24	Temporary Register				
	•				
	•				
	•				
CR 31	Temporary Register				

Figure 2-8. Control Registers

Recovery Counter

The Recovery Counter (CR 0) is a 32-bit counter that can be used to provide software recovery of hardware faults in fault-tolerant systems, and can also be used for debugging purposes. CR 0 counts down by 1 during the execution of each non-nullified instruction for which the PSW R-bit is 1. The Recovery Counter is restored if the instruction terminates with a group 1, 2, or 3 interruption (see Chapter 4, "Control Flow"). When the leftmost bit of the Recovery Counter is 1, a recovery counter trap occurs. The trap and the decrement operation can be disabled by setting the PSW R-bit to 0. The value of the Recovery Counter may be read reliably only when the PSW R-bit is 0. (Reading the Recovery Counter when the PSW R-bit is 1 returns an undefined result.) The Recovery Counter may be written reliably only when the PSW R-bit is 0. (Writing the Recovery Counter when the PSW R-bit is 1 is an undefined operation.) If the PSW R-bit is set to 0 by either the RESET SYSTEM MASK or the MOVE TO SYSTEM MASK instruction, the Recovery Counter may not be read or written reliably prior to the execution of the eighth instruction after the RESET SYSTEM MASK or the MOVE TO SYSTEM MASK instruction. An interruption, or a RETURN FROM INTERRUPTION instruction which sets the PSW R-bit to 0, does not have this restriction.

Protection Identifiers

The protection identifiers (CRs 8, 9, 12, 13) designate up to eight groups of pages which are accessible to the currently executing process. When translation is enabled, the eight protection identifiers (PIDs) are compared with a page access identifier in the TLB entry to validate an access. (See "Access Control" on page 3-11.) The rightmost bit of each of the eight PIDs is the write disable (WD) bit. When the WD-bit is 1, that PID cannot be used to grant write access. This allows each process sharing memory to have different access rights to the memory without the overhead of changing the access identifier and access rights in the TLB. When the PSW P-bit is 0, the PIDs, including the WD-bits, are ignored.

Each of the 8 PID registers can be from 16 to 32 bits wide (including the WD bit), with the remaining bits being reserved bits. The length of the PIDs is implementation dependent.

Coprocessor Configuration Register (CCR)

The Coprocessor Configuration Register or CCR (bits 56..63 of CR 10) is an 8-bit register which records the presence and usability of coprocessors. The bit positions are numbered 0 through 7, and correspond to a coprocessor with the same unit identifier. Bits 0 and 1 correspond to the floating-point coprocessor, and bit 2 corresponds to the performance monitor coprocessor. Bit 7 is the rightmost bit of the CCR. It receives bit 63 from a general register when a general register is written to CR 10. The upper 48 bits of CR 10, and bits within the CCR corresponding to coprocessors which are not present, are reserved bits.

The behavior of the floating-point coprocessor with respect to the state of CCR bits 0 and 1 and the behavior of the performance monitor coprocessor with respect to the state of CCR bit 2, are specified in "Coprocessor Instructions" on page 6-22. For other coprocessors, setting a bit in the CCR to 1 enables the use of the corresponding coprocessor, if present and operational. If a CCR bit is 0, the corresponding coprocessor, if present, is logically decoupled. This decoupling must ensure that the state of a coprocessor does not change as long as its corresponding CCR bit is 0. When a CCR bit is set to 0 and an attempt is made to execute an instruction which references the corresponding coprocessor, it causes an assist emulation trap. It is an undefined operation to set to 1 any CCR bit corresponding to a coprocessor which is not present.

SFU Configuration Register (SCR)

The SFU Configuration Register or SCR (bits 48..55 of CR 10), is an 8-bit register which records the presence and usability of special function units. The bit positions are numbered 0 through 7, and correspond to an SFU with the same unit identifier. Bit 7 is the rightmost bit of the SCR. It receives bit 55 from a general register when a general register is written to CR 10. The upper 48 bits of CR 10, and bits within the SCR corresponding to SFUs which are not present, are reserved bits.

For all SFUs, setting a bit in the SCR to 1 enables the use of the corresponding SFU, if present and operational. If an SCR bit is 0, the corresponding SFU, if present, is logically decoupled. This decoupling must ensure that the state of an SFU does not change as long as its corresponding SCR bit is 0. When an SCR bit is set to 0 and an attempt is made to execute an instruction which references the corresponding SFU, it causes an assist emulation trap. The operation of an SFU when its corresponding SCR bit is 0 is explained in more detail in "Special Function Unit (SFU) Instructions" on page 6-20. It is an undefined operation to set to 1 any SCR bit corresponding to an SFU which is not present.

Interruption Vector Address (IVA)

The Interruption Vector Address or IVA (CR 14) contains the absolute address of the base of an array of service procedures assigned to the interruption classes. The lower 11 bits of the IVA are reserved Therefore, the address written to it must be a multiple of 2048. For implementations with fewer than 64 bits of physical address, the upper bits of the IVA corresponding to unimplemented physical address bits are reserved. The array of interruption service procedures is indexed by the interruption numbers given in Chapter 4, "Control Flow".

External Interrupt Enable Mask (EIEM)

The External Interrupt Enable Mask or EIEM (CR 15), is a 64-bit register containing a bit for each of the 64 external interrupts. Each 0 bit in the EIEM masks external interrupts corresponding to that bit position.

Interruption Instruction Address Queues

The Interruption Instruction Address Space Queue or IIASQ (CR 17) and the Interruption Instruction Address Offset Queue or IIAOQ (CR 18) are collectively termed the interruption instruction address or IIA queues. They are used to save the Instruction Address and privilege level information for use in processing interruptions. The registers are arranged as two two-element deep queues. The queues generally contain the addresses (including the privilege level field in the rightmost two bits of the offset part) of the two instructions in the IA queues at the time of the interruption. The IIASQ may be from 32 to 64 bits wide.

The IIA queues are continually updated whenever the PSW Q-bit is 1 and are frozen by an interruption (PSW Q-bit becomes 0). After such an interruption, the IIA queues contain copies of the information from the IA queues. The IIAOQ contains the address offsets of the interruption point in the same format as the IAOQ. The IIASQ has a different format from that of the IASQ. The IIASQ contains the upper portion of the GVA (global virtual address) of the interruption point, if code address translation was enabled. (Note that if the PSW W-bit was 0, the upper portion of the GVA is simply the space ID.)

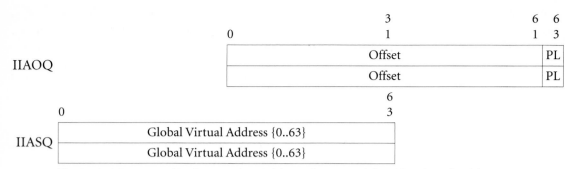

Figure 2-9. Interruption Instruction Address Queues with Wide Virtual Addresses

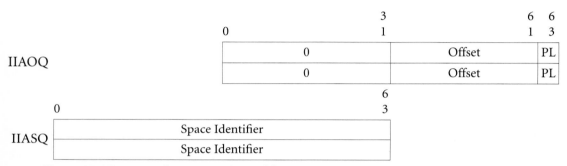

Figure 2-10. Interruption Instruction Address Queues with Narrow Virtual Addresses

If code address translation was disabled at the time of the interruption, then the IIAOQ contains the absolute offsets of the interruption point, and the IIASQ contains zeros. (Note that if the PSW W-bit was 0, the absolute offsets in the IIAOQ may be truncated to only those bits of the physical address space that are implemented, and the upper bits forced to zeros.)

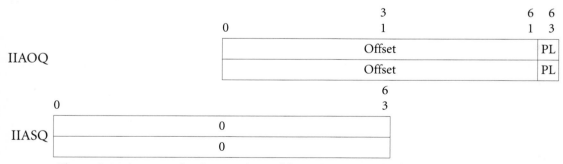

Figure 2-11. Interruption Instruction Address Queues with Absolute Addresses

On a return from interruption, the values in the IIA queues are used to reform the IA queues for the return point. The values in the IIAOQ are copied to the IAOQ. The new values for the IASQ are formed as follows (see also Figure 2-12): the lower 30 bits of the IASQ are formed by taking the bitwise AND of the lower 30 bits of the values in the IIASQ with the complement of bits {2..31} of the values in the

IIAOQ. Bits {32..33} of the IIASQ are copied to the same bits in the IASQ. The upper 32 bits of the IIASQ (or as many as are implemented) are copied to the corresponding bits of the IASQ. This reforms the original space identifiers.

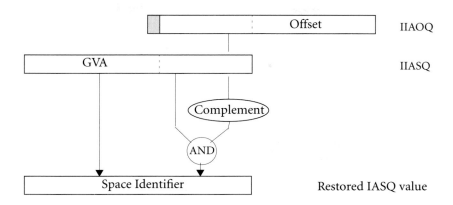

Figure 2-12.   Reforming Space Identifiers

Reading the IIAOQ (CR 18) while the PSW Q-bit is 0 retrieves the offset and privilege level portions of the front element in the IIAOQ. Writing into IIAOQ while the PSW Q-bit is 0 advances the IIAOQ and then sets the offset and privilege level portions of the back element of the IIAOQ. Reading the IIASQ (CR 17) while the PSW Q-bit is 0 retrieves the GVA portion of the front element of the IIASQ. Writing into IIASQ while the PSW Q-bit is 0 advances the IIASQ and then writes into the back element of the IIASQ. The effect of reading or writing either queue register while the PSW Q-bit is 1 is an undefined operation.

The state contained in the IIA queues is undefined when a RETURN FROM INTERRUPTION instruction sets the PSW Q-bit to 0, or when system control instructions are used to set the PSW Q-bit to 0. If an interruption is taken with the PSW Q-bit equal to 0, the IIA queues are unchanged.

Interruption Parameter Registers (IPRs)

The Interruption Parameter Registers (IPRs) are used to pass an instruction and a virtual address to an interruption handler. Three registers comprise the IPRs: the Interruption Instruction Register or IIR (CR 19), Interruption Space Register or ISR (CR 20), and Interruption Offset Register or IOR (CR 21). They are used to pass an instruction and a virtual address to an interruption handler. The values in these registers for each interruption class are specified in Chapter 4, "Control Flow". These values are set (or frozen) at the time of the interruption whenever the PSW Q-bit is 1. The ISR may be from 32 to 64 bits wide.

The value loaded into the IOR is the lower 32 bits of the virtual address offset without truncating the rightmost bits or setting them to 0, plus the 2 bits of the base register which was used to form the address. If the PSW W-bit was 1, the upper 2 bits of the IOR (called the b field) are equal to bits {0..1} from the base register. If the PSW W-bit was 0, the b field is equal to bits {32..33} from the base register. The other bits of the IOR are forced to 0.

The value loaded into the ISR is the upper portion of the GVA, if data translation was enabled. (Note that if the PSW W-bit was 0, the upper portion of the GVA is simply the space ID.)

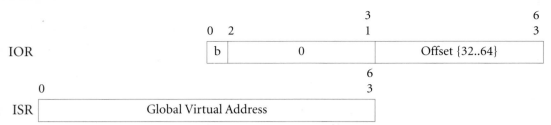

Figure 2-13. Interruption Space and Offset Registers with Virtual Address

If data translation was disabled at the time of the interruption, the IOR contains the lower 32 bits of the absolute offset. The upper 2 bits of the IOR are undefined, and may be set to any value. The other bits in the IOR are forced to 0. The ISR contains the upper portion of the absolute offset, zero-extended. If the PSW W-bit was 0 as well, the ISR contains 0.

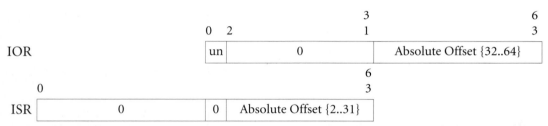

Figure 2-14. Interruption Space and Offset Registers with Absolute Address

The interruption parameter registers can be read or written reliably only when the PSW Q-bit is 0. (Reading an interruption parameter register when the PSW Q-bit is 1 returns an undefined result.) The state contained in the IPRs is undefined when a RETURN FROM INTERRUPTION instruction sets the PSW Q-bit to 0, or when system control instructions are used to set the PSW Q-bit to 0. If an interruption is taken with the PSW Q-bit equal to 0, the IPRs are unchanged.

Interruption Processor Status Word (IPSW)

The Interruption Processor Status Word or IPSW (CR 22) receives the value of the PSW when an interruption occurs. The format of the IPSW is identical to that of the PSW. The IPSW always reflects the state of the machine at the point of interruption, regardless of the state of the PSW Q-bit. As in the PSW, the unnamed bits are reserved bits.

The IPSW can be read or written reliably only when the PSW Q-bit is 0. (Reading the IPSW when the PSW Q-bit is 1 returns an undefined result.) The state contained in the IPSW is undefined when a RETURN FROM INTERRUPTION instruction sets the PSW Q-bit to 0, or when system control instructions are used to set the PSW Q-bit to 0.

External Interrupt Request Register (EIRR)

The External Interrupt Request register or EIRR (CR 23) is a 64-bit register containing a bit for each external interrupt. When 1, a bit designates that an interruption is pending for the corresponding external interrupt. Both the PSW I-bit (external interrupt, power failure interrupt, and low-priority machine check unmask) and the corresponding bit position in the External Interrupt Enable Mask (CR 15) must be 1 for an interruption to occur.

A MOVE TO CONTROL REGISTER instruction with CR 23 as its target bitwise ANDs the complement of the contents of the source register with the previous contents of CR 23, and places this result in CR 23. Thus the processor can only set the EIR register bits to 0.

A processor's EIR register is also memory mapped into the physical address space as the IIO_EIR register to enable other processors and I/O modules to interrupt the processor. When a module writes to it, the bit specified by the value written is set to 1. The W bit (Wide enable) in the Processor Status Word (PSW - see Table 2-1) determines whether the EIRR operates as a 32-bit register or a 64-bit register. When the W bit is 0, the EIRR operates effectively as a 32-bit register. Values written to the IO_EIR are interpreted as 5-bit numbers, which cause one of the bits in the range {32..63} to be set to 1. When the W bit is 1, the EIRR operates as a 64-bit register. Values written to the IO_EIR are interpreted as 6-bit numbers, which cause one of the bits in the range {0..63} to be set to 1.

Temporary Registers

Six of the eight 64-bit temporary registers (CRs 24, 25, 28..31) are accessible only by code executing at the most privileged level. They provide space to save the contents of the general registers for interruption handlers in the operating system kernel.

The other two temporary registers (CRs 26 and 27) are readable by code executing at any privilege level and writable only by code executing at the most privileged level.

Unused Registers and Bits

Currently, there are several registers and bit-fields within registers that do not have any function assigned to them. All such processing resources are classified into four categories:

1. Reserved bits — Currently unused bits, but reserved for possible future use. A READ operation is legal, and the value read back is all zeros. A WRITE operation is legal but the value written must be all zeros. Writing ones is an undefined operation. (For example, writing ones may cause these bits to no longer read as zeros.)

2. Nonexistent bits — Architecturally these bits do not exist. A READ operation is legal and may return zeros or what was last written. A WRITE operation is also legal but does not have any effect on system functionality.

3. Undefined bits — Architecturally these bits are undefined. A READ operation is legal and the value read is undefined. A WRITE operation is also legal but does not have any effect on system functionality.

4. Ignored bits — Architecturally these bits are ignored. A READ operation is legal and the value read is all zeroes. A WRITE operation is also legal but does not have any effect on system functionality.

5. Reserved registers — A register that is numbered but currently unused. Both READ and WRITE operations are undefined operations.

Data Types

The fundamental data types that are recognized are bits, bytes, integers, floating-point numbers, and decimal numbers. Their formats are described briefly in this section. Each item of data is addressed by its lowest-numbered byte.

Bits

Memory is not addressed to the resolution of bits; however, efficient support is provided to manipulate and test individual bits in the general registers.

Bytes

Bytes are signed or unsigned 8-bit quantities:

Signed Byte

Unsigned Byte

Bytes are packed four to a word and may represent a two's complement signed value in the range -128 through +127, an unsigned value in the range 0 through 255, an arbitrary collection of eight bits, or an ASCII character.

Integers

Integers may be 16, 32, or 64 bits wide, signed or unsigned:

Signed Halfword

s	value
1	15

Unsigned Halfword

value
16

Signed Word

s	value
1	31

Unsigned Word

value
32

Signed Doubleword

s	value
1	63

Unsigned Doubleword

value
64

Signed integers are in two's complement form. Halfword integers can be stored in memory only at even byte addresses, word integers only at addresses evenly divisible by four, and doubleword integers only at addresses evenly divisible by eight.

Floating-Point Numbers

The binary floating-point number representation conforms to the ANSI/IEEE 754-1985 standards. Single-word (32-bit), double-word (64-bit), and quadruple-word (128-bit) binary formats are supported.

Single-precision floating-point numbers must be aligned on word boundaries. Double-precision and quad-precision numbers must be aligned on doubleword boundaries. See Chapter 8, "Floating-point Coprocessor", for detailed information on the floating-point formats.

Packed Decimal Numbers

Packed decimal data is always aligned on a word boundary. It consists of 7, 15, 23, or 31 BCD digits, each four bits wide and having a value in the range of 0x0 to 0x9, followed by a 4-bit sign as shown in the following figure:

MSD		• • •	LSD	sign
4	4		4	4

The standard sign for a positive number is 0xC, but any value except 0xD will be interpreted as positive. 0xD indicates a minus sign for a negative number. 0xB is not supported as an alternative minus sign.

Byte Ordering (Big Endian/Little Endian)

The optional E-bit in the PSW controls whether loads and stores use big endian or little endian byte ordering. When the E-bit is 0, all larger-than-byte loads and stores are big endian — the lower-addressed bytes in memory correspond to the higher-order bytes in the register. When the E-bit is 1, all larger-than-byte loads and stores are little endian — the lower-addressed bytes in memory correspond to the lower-order bytes in the register. Load byte and store byte instructions are not affected by the E-bit. The E-bit also affects instruction fetch.

Processors which implement the PSW E-bit must also provide an implementation-dependent, software writable default endian bit. The default endian bit controls whether the PSW E-bit is set to 0 or 1 on interruptions and also controls whether data in the page table is interpreted in big endian or little endian format by the hardware TLB miss handler, if implemented (See "Hardware TLB Miss Handling" on page F-3).

Figure 2-15 shows various loads in big endian format. Figure 2-16 shows various loads in little endian format. Stores are not shown but behave similarly.

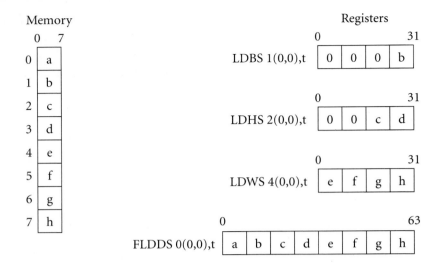

Figure 2-15. Big Endian Loads

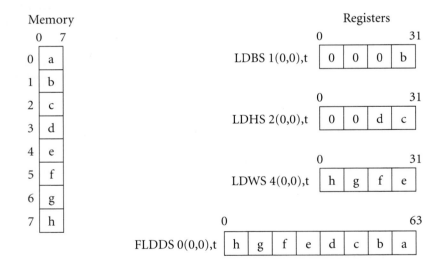

Figure 2-16. Little Endian Loads

The E-bit also affects instruction fetch. When the E-bit is 0, instruction fetch is big endian — the lower-addressed bytes in memory correspond to the higher-order bytes in the instruction. When the E-bit is 1, instruction fetch is little endian — the lower-addressed bytes in memory correspond to the lower-order bytes in the instruction.

Architecturally, the instruction byte swapping can occur either when a cache line is moved into the instruction cache (I cacheor as instructions are fetched from the I-cache into the pipeline.

Processors must support running code with either endian form from the same cache line. This relieves software of the responsibility of keeping track of what might have been brought in under different forms.

Engineering Note

For processors which swap instructions on I-cache move-in, one way to meet this requirement is to implement endian tag bits and force a miss if the tag does not match the current value of PSW[E].

Processors which swap instructions as they are fetched from the I-cache do not need to do anything extra to meet this requirement.

Since the PSW E-bit is an instruction fetch resource (see "Instruction Pipelining" on page 4-9), SET SYSTEM MASK, RESET SYSTEM MASK or MOVE TO SYSTEM MASK instructions which change the PSW E-bit must be followed by seven palindromic NOP instructions — that is, instructions which are NOPs when interpreted in either big or little endian order

---

Programming Note

One example of a palindromic NOP instruction is LDI 26,0 (opcode 0x34000034)

---

3   Addressing and Access Control

Data storage is organized as a storage hierarchy based on speed of access: user-accessible registers are at the highest level followed by the memory system which consists of high-speed buffers that hold recently referenced instructions and/or data, and main memory. The high-speed buffers, called **instruction** and/ or **data caches**, reduce the effective access time to main memory.

The I/O system is memory-mapped with I/O modules mapped into physical pages that, although not part of the main memory, are addressed in the same way. With virtual pages mapped into physical pages and I/O registers represented by words in a page, communication between a processor and an I/O module can be performed with load and store instructions to virtual addresses. The privilege level and access rights of such a page provide versatile protection. Non-privileged code may therefore be given direct access to some I/O modules without compromising system security.

PA-RISC processors use byte addressing to fetch instructions and data from main memory or the I/O registers. The byte addresses may be either virtual addresses or absolute addresses. Virtual addresses are translated to absolute addresses and undergo protection and access rights checking. Memory accesses using virtual addresses are called **virtual accesses**. When absolute addresses are used directly, no protection or access rights checks are performed. Memory accesses using absolute addresses are called **absolute accesses**.

The instructions that reference memory are load (memory-to-register), store (register-to-memory), and semaphore instructions. Additionally, several system control and cache-related instructions generate addresses that use the address translation, protection, and access rights checking mechanisms. Computation instructions do not reference memory, but perform data transformations by using values obtained from general registers and returning results to these registers.

Physical and Absolute Addressing

Objects in the main memory and I/O system reside in a 64-bit **physical address space** and can be accessed using byte addresses which may be either virtual addresses or absolute addresses. The physical address space and absolute accesses are described in the paragraphs that follow. Virtual accesses are described later in this chapter.

Physical Address Space

The Physical Address Space is 64 bits in size as shown in Figure 3-1 and has three components:

- **Memory Address Space** - Addresses 0 through 0xEFFFFFFF FFFFFFFF can reference 15 Exabytes of memory. This space represents 15/16ths of the Physical Address Space.

- **PDC Address Space** - Addresses 0xF0000000 00000000 through 0xF0FFFFFF FFFFFFFF reference Processor Dependent Code (PDC) and it associated resources. This space represents 1/256th of the Physical Address Space.

- **I/O Address Space** - Addresses 0xF1000000 00000000 through 0xFFFFFFFF FFFFFFFF can reference nearly 1 Exabyte of I/O registers. The I/O and PDC Address Spaces together represent 1/16th of the Physical Address Space.

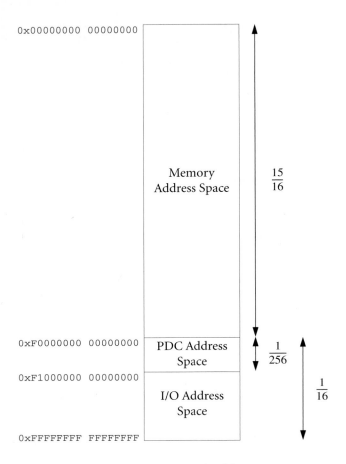

Figure 3-1. 64-bit Physical Address Space

Although software views the Physical Address Space as being 64 bits in size, implementations are only required to support physical address spaces between 32 and 64 bits in size. If less then 64 bits of physical address space are supported, the following rules must be observed:

- The Memory, PDC, and I/O Address Spaces must each occupy the same fraction of the implemented physical address space as they do in the 64-bit physical address space, as shown in Figure 3-2.

- In an n-bit physical address space implementation, implementations must ignore the most significant 64-n bits of a 64-bit physical address for references to the Memory and I/O Address Spaces. For references to the PDC Address Space, implementations may transform a 64-bit physical address into an n-bit physical address in a processor-specific fashion provided the eight most significant bits of both addresses are identical.

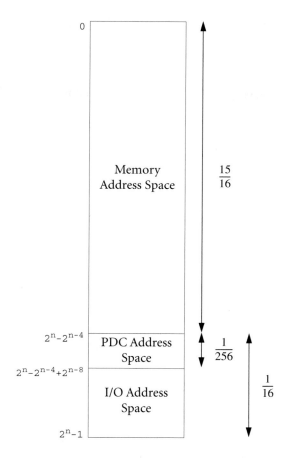

Figure 3-2. n-bit Physical Address Space Implementation

Absolute Accesses

Accesses made with LOAD WORD ABSOLUTE and STORE WORD ABSOLUTE instructions, or when virtual address translation is disabled (the PSW D-bit is 0 for data accesses or the PSW C-bit is 0 for instruction accesses) are called **absolute accesses**.

Absolute Accesses when PSW W-bit is 1

When the PSW W-bit is 1 (see "Processor Status Word (PSW)" on page 2-7 for the definition of the PSW W-bit), an absolute address is a 62-bit unsigned integer whose value is the address of the lowest-addressed byte of the operand it designates (see Figure 3-3).

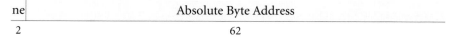

ne	Absolute Byte Address
2	62

Figure 3-3. 62-bit Absolute Pointer

Refer to "Absolute Accesses when PSW W-bit is 1" on page H-10 for details on address formation for these accesses.

Absolute Accesses when PSW W-bit is 0

When the PSW W-bit is 0, an absolute address is a 32-bit unsigned integer whose value is the address of the lowest-addressed byte of the operand it designates (see Figure 3-4)

non-existent	Absolute Byte Address
32	32

Figure 3-4.   32-bit Absolute Pointer

Refer to "Absolute Accesses when PSW W-bit is 0" on page H-11 for details on address formation for these accesses.

Memory Addressable Units and Alignment

Memory is always referenced with byte addresses, starting with address 0 and extending through the largest defined non-I/O address (0xEFFFFFFF FFFFFFFF). Addressable units are bytes, halfwords (2 bytes), words (4 bytes), and doublewords (8 bytes). A comparison of the addressable units is shown in Figure 3-5 with the relative byte numbers indicated inside the blocks.

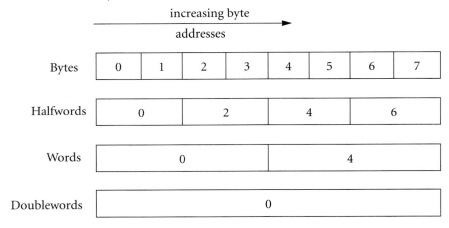

Figure 3-5.   Physical Memory Addressing and Storage Units

All addressable units must be stored on their naturally aligned boundaries. A byte may appear at any address, halfwords must begin at even addresses, words must begin at addresses that are multiples of 4, and doublewords must begin at addresses that are multiples of 8. If an unaligned virtual address is used, an interruption occurs.

Bits within larger units are always numbered from 0 starting with the most significant bit.

I/O address space is referenced in doublewords, words, halfwords, and bytes. I/O registers are accessed using the normal load and store instructions.

Virtual Addressing

Virtual memory is organized into linear spaces. These spaces can range in size from 2^{32} bytes each to 2^{64} bytes each. The object within the space is specified by a 32-bit to 64-bit offset. The space identifier is combined with the offset to form a complete **global virtual address (GVA.)** The offset and space portions are aligned as shown, and bits 34..63 of the space are ORed together with bits 2..31 of the offset to form the GVA. The lower 32 bits of the GVA come directly from the offset, and the upper 34 bits come directly from the space.

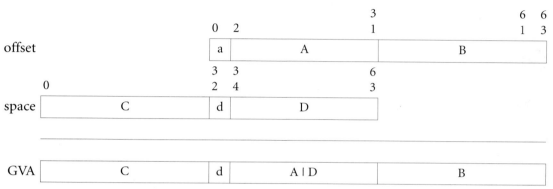

Figure 3-6.   Global Virtual Address Formation

A bit in the Processor Status Word (PSW[W]) provides compatibility with older programs. When PSW[W] is 0, offsets are truncated to 32 bits (the upper 32 bits of the offset are forced to 0). The GVA is then formed in the same way, by ORing the offset with the space. Since the offset is truncated, though, this is simply equivalent to concatenating the space with the lower 32 bits of the offset.

Implementations also provide an implementation-dependent, software-writable default width bit. The default width bit controls whether the PSW W-bit is set to 0 or 1 on interruptions, and also whether the EIRR is treated as a 32-bit or a 64-bit register. (See "Processor Status Word (PSW)" on page 2-7.)

Translation from virtual to absolute addresses is accomplished by translation lookaside buffers (TLBs), which are described in Chapter 3, "Addressing and Access Control". Fields in the TLB entry for a particular page permit control of access to the page for reading, writing or execution. Such access may be restricted to a single process, or a set of processes, or may be permitted to all processes.

To a user application, the virtual address space appears to be flatly addressable and 64 bits in size. User applications are concerned only with the 64-bit address offset. Full support for 32-bit applications with 32-bit pointers is also provided.

To Operating System software, the address space can be thought of as consisting of a set of address spaces, each with its own space identifier, and where each address space can be between 32 and 62 bits in size, depending on the needs of the individual application. For example, an implementation with 32-bit space identifiers would allow for 4 billion 32-bit spaces, or 1 million 44-bit spaces, or 4 62-bit spaces, or any combinations of these. Space identifiers can range up to 64 bits in size, allowing for a 96-bit virtual address. The virtual address model in PA-RISC provides a powerful means for efficiently managing a large address space.

For memory management purposes, the address space is logically subdivided into **pages**, each of which can range in size from 4 Kbytes to 64 Mbytes in length. The byte offset into the page is specified by the least significant 12 to 26 bits of the virtual address, depending on the page size. Figure 3-7 illustrates the structure of spaces, pages, and offsets.

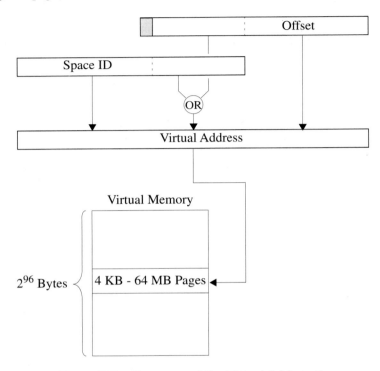

Figure 3-7. Structure of the Virtual Address Space

Pointers and Address Specification

For virtual accesses, addresses can be specified two different ways. With **explicit pointers**, an instruction computes an address offset and explicitly specifies a space identifier. This provides efficient access to the entire global virtual address space. With **implicit pointers**, an instruction computes an address offset, and this offset calculation implicitly specifies a space ID. This provides the appearance of a single 64-bit (or 32-bit) flat address space. The offset and space ID are combined to form the full virtual address.

Eight Space Registers hold space identifiers used in forming virtual addresses. Additionally, the Instruction Address Space Queue holds the space ID for the current instruction address, and two control registers are used to hold space ID information after interruptions.

Data Addresses

Data addresses are computed for regular memory reference instructions (load, store, and semaphore instructions) and for system instructions used in managing the address space (access probe, and data cache and data TLB control instructions). A 64-bit offset is calculated by adding a 64-bit base register plus a 64-bit index register or a sign-extended immediate displacement. One of the Space Registers is selected, either implicitly, by the top two bits of the base register, or explicitly, by a field in the instruction. The space ID is then logically ORed with the offset of form the virtual address.

The space identifier is selected from Space Registers 1 through 7 as follows, based on the presence and value of the 2-bit *s* field in the memory reference instruction.

- If the instruction does not have an *s* field, or if the value of the *s* field is zero, space ID selection is implicit. The top two bits of the base register are used to select one of Space Registers 4 through 7. This permits the addressing of four distinct spaces selected by program data, and is called implicit pointer addressing, since a regular 64-bit value specifies the offset and space ID for a full virtual address.

- If the instruction does have an *s* field, and the value of the *s* field is non-zero, the s-field explicitly selects one of Space Registers 1, 2 or 3. Figure 3-8 illustrates space identifier selection.

Instruction Addresses

Instruction addresses for instruction fetch are computed from the IA queues and as a result of branch target calculations. Instruction addresses are also computed for system instructions used in managing the address space (instruction cache and instruction TLB control instructions).

The current instruction address (IA) consists of a space identifier and a 64-bit byte offset. The byte offset is a word-aligned address and contains, in its least significant two bit positions, the current privilege level. This privilege level controls both instruction and data references. The current instruction address is maintained in the front elements of the Instruction Address Queues (IA queues).

In forming instruction addresses, the space ID can either remain unchanged from the last address (as with in-line instruction fetching and with intraspace branches), or the space ID can be selected from one of the Space Registers. The selection of the Space Register is either implicit (one of Space Registers 4 through 7 selected by the top two bits of the base register), explicit with a 2-bit *s* field, like data addressing (one of SRs 1, 2 or 3 selected by the instruction), or explicit with a 3-bit *s* field (one of SRs 0 through 7 selected by the instruction). See Figure 3-8.

As with data addresses, the space ID is logically ORed with the offset to form the virtual address.

Executing or branching beyond the end of the current space is undefined.

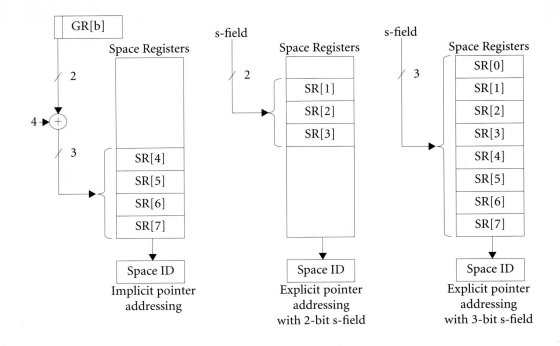

Figure 3-8. Space Identifier Selection

32-bit Addresses

Programs which use 32-bit data and 32-bit pointers are fully supported. A bit in the Processor Status Word (PSW W-bit) is used to control address formation. For 32-bit programs, address offset calculations are done just as for 64-bit programs, but then the offset is truncated to a 32-bit value. Space identifier selection for implicit pointers is done with the upper two bits of the lower 32-bits, just as in PA-RISC 1.1.

For 32-bit PA-RISC 1.1 programs that directly manipulate space identifiers to gain access to an address space larger than 32 bits, Space Registers appear to be 32 bits in size, and the virtual address is formed just as in PA-RISC 1.1. (The space identifier is concatenated with the lower 32-bits of the address offset to form the virtual address. This happens automatically as a result of the offset being truncated to a 32-bit value.)

In brief, the addressing model of PA-RISC 2.0 is fully compatible with 32-bit programs written for PA-RISC 1.1.

Absolute Addresses

For absolute accesses, the space identifiers are unused, and the absolute address is calculated from the offset alone. If the most significant 4 bits of the offset are 1, the address accesses the I/O address space and the absolute address is simply equal to the offset. (See "Absolute Accesses" on page 3-3.) If not all of the most significant 4 bits of the offset are 1, the address accesses the memory address space, and the absolute address is formed by taking the offset and forcing the most significant 2 bits to 0.

This way of forming absolute address for memory allows software more flexibility in address space layout. Note that this has no impact on machine implementing fewer than 62 bits of physical address.

Address Resolution and the TLB

Virtual addresses are translated to absolute addresses using a hardware structure called the **Translation Lookaside Buffer** (TLB). A TLB accepts a Virtual Page Number and returns the corresponding Physical Page Number. The TLB is organized as two parts. The instruction TLB (ITLB) is only used for instruction references, while the data TLB (DTLB) is only used for data references. A system may implement a **combined** TLB which is used for both instruction and data references.

A TLB is typically not large enough to hold all the current translations. Translations for all pages in memory are stored in a memory structure called the **Page Table**. Multiple page sizes are supported, from 4 Kbytes to 64 Mbytes. This allows large contiguous regions to be mapped with a single TLB entry. This increases the virtual address range of the TLB, thereby minimizing the virtual address translation overhead.

Given a virtual address, the selected TLB is searched for an entry matching the Virtual Page Number. If the entry exists, the 38 to 52-bit Physical Page Number (contained in the TLB entry) is concatenated with the original 12 to 26-bit page offset (depending on the page size in the matching entry) to form a 64-bit absolute address. If no such entry exists, the TLB is updated by either software TLB miss handling or hardware TLB miss handling.

In systems with software TLB miss handling, a TLB miss fault interruption routine performs the translation, explicitly inserts the translation and protection fields into the appropriate TLB, and restarts the interrupted instruction. To insure the completion of instructions, the TLBs must be organized to simultaneously hold all necessary translations.

In implementations that provide hardware for TLB miss handling, the hardware attempts to find the virtual to physical page translation in the Page Table. If the hardware is successful, it inserts the translation and protection fields into the appropriate instruction or data TLB. No interruption occurs in this case. If hardware is not successful, due to a search of the Page Table that was not exhaustive or due to the appropriate translation not existing in the Page Table, an interruption occurs so that the software can complete the process.

The translation lookaside buffer performs other functions in addition to the basic address translation. The other functions include access control, program debugging support and operating system support for virtual memory. Figure 3-9 summarizes the information maintained for each TLB entry.

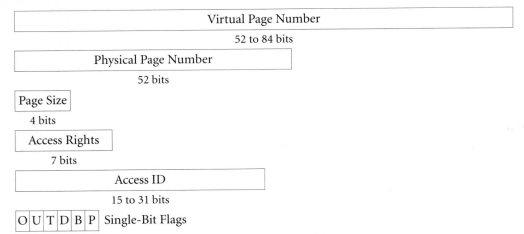

Figure 3-9.   TLB Fields

The following describes the function of each of the 1-bit fields.

O   **Ordered.** When 0, data memory references using this translation (except those explicitly marked as ordered or strongly ordered) may be weakly ordered. When 1 and the PSW[O] bit is 1, data memory references using this translation are ordered. See "Ordering of References" on page G-1.

U   **Uncacheable.** When 0, data references to a page from memory address space may be moved into the cache. When 1, data references to a page from I/O address space or memory address space must not be moved into the cache. The U-bit must be set to 1 for pages which map to the I/O address space, and is commonly set to 1 for pages in the memory address space where I/O module written data and processor written data must co-exist within the same cache line. Referencing a page which maps to the I/O address space and for which the U-bit is 0 is an undefined operation. Implementation of the U-bit is optional. See "Data Cache Move-In" on page F-8 for additional details.

T   **Page Reference Trap.** When 1, data references using this translation cause a page reference trap. The T-bit is most commonly used for program debugging.

D   **Dirty.** When 0, store and semaphore instructions cause a TLB dirty bit trap. When 1, no trap occurs. The D-bit may be used by the operating system to determine which pages have been modified.

B   **Break.** When 1, instructions that could modify data using this translation (store and semaphore instructions, and the PURGE DATA CACHE instruction) cause a data memory break trap, if enabled. The B-bit is most commonly used for program debugging.

P   **Prediction** method for branching. When 0, branch prediction is performed based on static prediction hints encoded in the instructions. When 1, branch prediction is performed based on dynamic prediction hardware, on implementations so equipped. This bit functions solely as a performance hint. Implementation of the P-bit is optional.

Since the ITLB is not used for data operands, the O, U, T, D, and B bits are only implemented in the DTLB or a combined TLB. Similarly, since the P-bit controls branch prediction, it is only implemented in the ITLB or combined TLB.

The TLB is managed by a mixture of hardware and software mechanisms. Translations are brought into the TLB by either hardware or software when a TLB miss occurs. In systems which provide hardware for TLB miss handling, the Page Table holds the information needed for the TLB. For systems with software TLB miss handling, and for explicit insertion of a translation by systems with hardware TLB miss handling, TLB management instructions provide the TLB with this information. The INSERT INSTRUCTION TLB TRANSLATION instruction places the complete translation and access control information into the ITLB. A similar instruction (INSERT DATA TLB TRANSLATION) places the complete translation and access control information and also initializes the system software and debugging support bit fields in the DTLB.

TLB miss traps do not occur on nullified instructions.

Page Size

The TLBs support a range of page sizes, in multiples of four, from 4 Kbytes to 64 Mbytes. Each page is aligned to an address which is an integer multiple of its size. The page size is inserted into the TLB with each translation, and is encoded as shown in Table 3-1. TLB purge instructions can also specify a page size, allowing a large contiguous address range to be purged in a single instruction.

Table 3-1.   Page Sizes

Encoding	Page size
0	4 KB
1	16 KB
2	64 KB
3	256 KB
4	1 MB
5	4 MB
6	16 MB
7	64 MB
8-15	Reserved

Access Control

User processes can be provided with a secure and protected environment via a part of the architecture's address translation mechanism. Processor resources, including the PSW, Control Registers, and TLB entries, contain information used to determine the allowed use of a page. Access control is available only when address translation is enabled, and is done on a per-page basis.

An access is validated if the check of the access rights and the protection identifiers both succeed. If the access is validated, the instruction reference or data reference is completed. If the access is not validated, the instruction is terminated with a protection trap. Instruction access violations are reported with instruction memory protection traps. Data read and write access violations are reported with data memory access rights or data memory protection ID traps. Probe instructions are special; they save the result of the access validation in a General Register and do not cause a protection trap. An access rights check is based on the type of access and the current privilege level. The protection identifier check compares the Protection ID Registers with a page-based access identifier in the TLB. State bits within the PSW determine when these checks are enabled.

Process Attributes

The type of access, privilege level, the current values in the Protection ID Registers, and the state of the PSW completely describes the access to the TLB. These resources are managed for each process by the operating system and collectively termed the **process attributes**. The following defines each of the process attributes.

Privilege Level (PL)

> Every instruction is fetched and executed at one of four privilege levels (numbered 0, 1, 2, 3) with 0 being the most privileged. The privilege level is kept in the least significant two bits of the current instruction's address (the front element of IAOQ). For all accesses, except the probe instructions, the privilege check uses the privilege level of the current instruction. The probe instructions explicitly specify the privilege level to be used in the access rights check.

Access type

> The access type is either read, write, or execute. Load, semaphore, and read probe instructions make **read accesses** to their operands. Store, semaphore and write probe instructions and cache purge operations make **write accesses** to their operands. Note that semaphore instructions make both read and write accesses to their operands. An **execute access** occurs when an instruction is fetched for execution.

Protection IDs

> The four Control Registers CR 8, CR 9, CR 12, and CR 13 contain the protection identifiers associated with the current process (Figure 3-10). These registers are used to allow several different protection groups to be accessed. The least significant bit of each protection ID is the write-disable (WD) bit. When 0, write accesses that match that protection ID are allowed. The remaining 15 to 31 bits hold the protection ID. Figure 3-10 depicts the maximum width of the protection identifier.

Figure 3-10.   Protection ID

PSW access attributes

> The PSW protection validation (P-bit), code address translation (C-bit), and data address translation (D-bit) bits further qualify the process attributes. When address translation is enabled and the P-bit is 1, the protection ID check is performed. When 0, the protection ID check is always considered successful. An execute access uses the C-bit to determine if address translation and access rights check are enabled. When 1,

address translation is performed and execute access rights checks are made. When 0, no address translation is performed and the access is always allowed. Read and write accesses use the D-bit in an equivalent manner. For probe instructions, address translation is performed, and access rights checks are made independent of the state of the PSW D-bit.

Access ID and Access Rights

For each entry in the TLB, the **access ID** and the **access rights** fields determine if an access is allowed. The access ID is a 15- to 31-bit field in the TLB that is used with the protection IDs in the protection ID check. The length of the access ID is implementation dependent but must match the length of the protection ID (excluding the WD bit).

The access rights field (Figure 3-11) is a 7-bit field that encodes the allowed access types and the needed privilege levels. In some cases a minimum privilege is specified, while other access types may be specified with an upper and a lower bound. The three sub-fields **type**, **PL1** (privilege level 1), and **PL2** (privilege level 2) combine to form the access rights field. The type sub-field defines the type of access that can be made to this page. Any of read-only, read/write, read/execute, read/write/execute, or execute-only is allowed. The PL1 sub-field qualifies read and execute accesses. The PL2 sub-field qualifies write and execute accesses.

Type	PL1	PL2
3	2	2

Figure 3-11.   Access Rights Field

The access rights check compares the current privilege level with the appropriate sub-field of the TLB access rights field and checks if the type of access is allowed. For a read access, the current privilege level must be at least as privileged as PL1 and the type field must allow read access. The read probe instructions explicitly specify the privilege level.

For a write access, the current privilege level must be at least as privileged as PL2 and the type field must allow write access. The write probe instructions explicitly specify the privilege level.

For an execute access, the current privilege level must be at least as privileged as PL1 and no more privileged than PL2. PL1 and PL2 are a lower and an upper bound, respectively, for execute access. The type field must also allow execute access.

For the PURGE DATA CACHE instruction, if implemented as a purge operation, the access rights check has a special case. The access rights check is done normally, except that if the access rights matches this binary pattern: "111 0X 1X" (where each X stands for either a 1 or a 0), then access is allowed. This facilitates cache management. See "Cache Flushing" on page F-10. If PURGE DATA CACHE is implemented as a flush operation, then no access rights check is performed.

The type field is also used by the BRANCH instruction with the ,GATE (for gateway) completer to specify the new privilege level. When the type value is 4 or greater and the encoded new privilege level is of greater privilege, then promotion occurs at the target of the branch.

Table 3-2 defines the type encodings and the necessary conditions of the PL1 and PL2 fields with the current privilege level (PL). This table uses the actual binary encoding when doing the privilege level comparison.

The protection identifier check compares the eight Protection ID Registers with the TLB entry's access ID. This check is validated if one or more of the protection IDs compare equal with the access ID. In case of a write access, the write disable bit of at least one of the matching protection IDs must be zero for the check to be validated. An access ID of zero is special and specifies a public page. A public page always satisfies a protection ID check for any type of access and only an access rights check is performed. If no match occurs and a public page is not being referenced, then the access is not allowed.

The PSW P-bit determines whether the protection ID check is performed. When 0, no protection check occurs and only the access rights check is performed. Figure 3-12 on page 3-15 illustrates the access rights and protection ID checks and the processor resources that participate.

Table 3-2. Access Rights Interpretation

Type value (in binary)	Allowed access types and B,GATE promotion	Privilege check
000	Read-only: data page	read: $PL \leq PL1$ write: Not allowed execute: Not allowed
001	Read/Write: dynamic data page	read: $PL \leq PL1$ write: $PL \leq PL2$ execute: Not allowed
010	Read/Execute: normal code page	read: $PL \leq PL1$ write: Not allowed execute: $PL2 \leq PL \leq PL1$
011	Read/Write/Execute: dynamic code page	read: $PL \leq PL1$ write: $PL \leq PL2$ execute: $PL2 \leq PL \leq PL1$
100	Execute: promote to privilege level 0*	read: Not allowed write: Not allowed execute: $PL2 \leq PL \leq PL1$
101	Execute: promote to privilege level 1*	read: Not allowed write: Not allowed execute: $PL2 \leq PL \leq PL1$
110	Execute: promote to privilege level 2*	read: Not allowed write: Not allowed execute: $PL2 \leq PL \leq PL1$
111	Execute: remain at privilege level 3*	read: Not allowed write: Not allowed execute: $PL2 \leq PL \leq PL1$

*Change of privilege level only occurs if the indicated new value is of higher privilege than the current privilege level; otherwise the target of the BRANCH instruction with the ,GATE completer executes at the same privilege as the BRANCH itself.

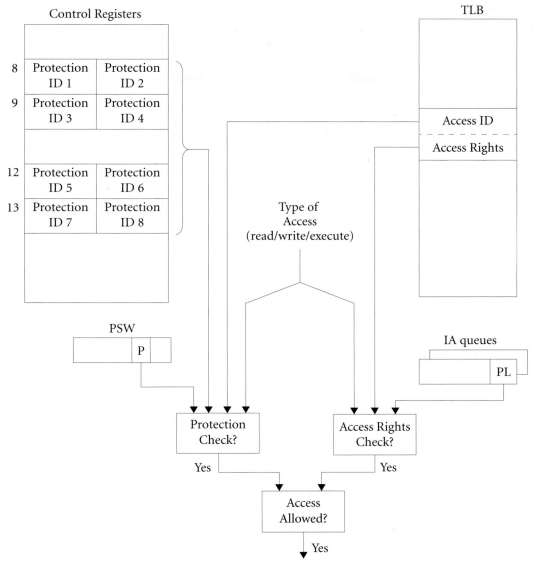

Figure 3-12. Access Control Checks

Page Table Structure

Address translations are stored in memory in a structure called the Page Table. The exact form of these tables is a software convention, but many aspects of the page tables are common and are described in this section.

The most common use of the Page Table is to translate a virtual address to a physical address after a TLB miss. The virtual address space is quite large, and a traditional approach of a multi-level forward mapped table, where each level is directly indexed by a portion of the virtual address, requires too many memory accesses and hence is an inefficient way to provide virtual to physical translations.

A better approach is to index the Page Table using the result of a hash function applied to the virtual address. The purpose of the hash function is to translate virtual addresses to a smaller, more uniform name space. The particular function used is implementation dependent. Collisions created by multiple addresses hashing to the same entry can be resolved using a sequentially searched linked list or some other structure.

The number of entries in the Page Table is typically a power of two. One possible format of a table entry is shown in Figure 3-13.

V	Tag (Virtual Page Number) (63)					
0 0 T D B Acc R (7) U O P 0 (3) s(3) R	s (10)			Access ID (31)		s
s 0 (5)	Physical Page Number (52)				0	Siz(4)
Next Page Table Entry (64)						

Figure 3-13. Page Table Entry

The fields are:

V   is the valid bit. If V = 1, this entry represents a valid translation.

Tag   is a unique key used to identify the virtual address that this entry translates.

R   is the reference bit. If R = 1, the page has been accessed (read, write, or execute) by a processor since the bit was last cleared to 0.

Physical Page Number

            is the physical page number corresponding to the virtual address, provided this entry is valid and the virtual address matches the tag.

Size   is the page size, encoded as in Table 3-1 on page 3-11.

Next Page Table Entry

            is an index/pointer to perhaps another structure containing overflow page table entries.

0   is a reserved bit field.

s   is a bit field reserved for operating system use.

The **O, U, T, D, B, P, Access Rights**, and **Access ID** fields correspond to those for TLB entries (see "Address Resolution and the TLB" on page 3-9).

Caches

Caches are high-speed intermediate storage buffers which contain recently accessed instructions and data. The caches are visible to software due to the fact that:

• The architecture supports virtually-indexed caches

- Hardware does not maintain coherence between the instruction cache and the data cache

- In some systems, hardware does not maintain coherence between I/O and processor caches.

For these reasons, the caches are managed by software in certain circumstances.

System software can control which portions of memory may be brought into cache. Additionally, software can explicitly remove items from the cache. As a result, software can control which portions of memory may be present in the cache. In some situations, such as self-modifying code, the use of non-equivalent address aliasing, and coordination with non-coherent I/O, software uses this control of the caches to effect coherence.

Items in the cache may be removed by hardware at any time. Software may therefore not rely on particular items remaining in the cache.

A consistent software view of cache operation requires that implementations never write a clean cache line back to memory. (A cache line can be 16, 32, or 64 bytes in length.) **Clean** means "not stored into" as opposed to "not changed". **Dirty** means "stored into". A cache line which was stored into in such a way that it was unchanged is considered to be dirty.

To insure memory system coherence, and to minimize cache flushing, instructions and data in memory may be brought into the caches only under certain circumstances. This operation of bringing information from memory into a cache is referred to as **move-in**. In general, when address translation is enabled, any data or instructions for which there is a valid translation in the TLB may be moved in. When translation is disabled, generally only data or instructions referenced by executed instructions may be moved in. Software may use reference bits and other mechanisms controlled by interruptions to determine when lines are potentially in the instruction cache, data cache, or both. See "Cache Move-in Restrictions" on page F-7.

The U (uncacheable) bit in the data TLB entry also affects caching. A page from the memory address space which has its U-bit set to 0 is called a **cacheable** page. Pages from the I/O address space and pages which have their U-bit set to 1 are called **uncacheable** pages. It is possible for data cache lines from an uncacheable page to exist in a data cache. This case may be caused by changing a cacheable page to uncacheable after references to this page were moved into the data cache. Changing the state of the U-bit for a page has no effect on the data cache lines from that page which already exist in the cache.

4   Control Flow

The PA-RISC architecture defines a model in which the flow of control passes to the next sequential instruction in memory unless directed otherwise by branch instructions, nullification of instructions, or interruptions. The architecture requires that a CPU program appear to execute instructions in the order in which they occur in memory although in reality the order may be changed internally. The instruction execution model described in this chapter provides a logical view of the steps involved in instruction execution. The sections on nullification, branching, and interruptions show how flow control can be altered during the course of program execution.

Branching

Branches alter the control flow during program execution. The architecture provides both unconditional and conditional branch instructions. Unconditional branch instructions always branch to the specified target. Conditional branch instructions first perform some operation (for example, move, compare, add, or bit test) and then branch if the outcome of the specified condition is met.

Concept of Delayed Branching

All branch instructions exhibit the delayed branch behavior; that is, the major effect of the branch instruction, the actual transfer of control, occurs one instruction after the execution of the branch. As a result, the instruction following the branch (located in the **delay slot** of the branch instruction) is executed before control passes to the branch destination. Figure 4-1 illustrates the concept of delayed branching.

Execution of the delay slot instruction, however, may be skipped ("nullified") by setting the "nullify" bit in the branch instruction to 1.

PROGRAM SEGMENT		
Location	Instruction	Comment
100	STW r3, 0(r6)	; non-branch instruction
104	BLR r8, r0	; branch to location 200
108	ADD r7,r2, r3	; instruction in delay slot
10C	OR r6,r5, r9	; next instruction in linear code sequence
.	.	
.	.	
.	.	
200	LDW 0(r3), r4	; target of branch instruction

EXECUTION SEQUENCE		
Location	Instruction	Comment
100	STW r3, 0(r6)	;
104	BLR r8, r0	;
108	ADD r7,r2, r3	; delay slot instruction is executed before
200	LDW 0(r3), r4	; execution of target instruction

Figure 4-1.   Delayed Branching Illustrated

Conditional and Unconditional Branches

There are two kinds of branches: **unconditional** branches are not dependent on the outcome of any test operation while **conditional** branches provide a mechanism to branch based on the outcome of a specified test. When the test is successful, the conditional branch is said to be **taken**, and, when the test is unsuccessful, the conditional branch is said to be **not-taken**. Unconditional branches are always **taken**.

Branching and Spaces

Certain branch instructions can only branch to a location within the same space, while others can branch to another space. Branches within the same space are referred to as **intraspace** or **local** branches. Branches to another space are referred to as **interspace** or **external** branches.

Target Address Computation

The target of a branch instruction, just like any instruction address, consists of a space ID and an offset.

The space ID of the target of an intraspace branch is not changed by the branch instruction. A space ID calculation is performed for interspace branches. The offset portion of the address is computed in one of several ways based on the particular branch instruction. When a displacement is added to the current instruction address offset, the branch is called **IA-relative**. When a general register is used as a base offset, it is called **base-relative**. Also, if the displacement is a fixed value that is known at compilation, it is known as **static** displacement. If the value is computed during the course of program execution, and is read from a general register, it is known as **dynamic** displacement.

For interspace branches, the space ID of the target address is always specified in a space register, and is copied into the IASQ when the branch is performed. The space register used can either be explicitly specified in the instruction or implicitly specified by the upper 2 bits of the base register. For explicit interspace branches, the offset of the target is computed by adding a 17-bit signed word displacement to the base register specified in a general register. The two rightmost bits in the base register denote the new privilege level and are ignored during the offset computation. Also, the 17-bit signed word displacement is shifted left by two before adding to the base register. For implicit interspace branches, the offset of the target is directly specified by the base register with no displacement. The two rightmost bits in the base register denote the new privilege level and are not part of the offset. Interspace branches are always base-relative.

In the case of intraspace branches, the space ID is not changed by the branch. The offset of the target, however, can be computed in one of three ways. For IA-relative branches with static displacement, a 12-bit, 17-bit, or 22-bit signed word displacement is shifted left by two and added to the current instruction address offset plus eight. For IA-relative branches with dynamic displacement, the value specified in the index register is shifted left by three and added to current instruction address offset plus eight. For base-relative branches with dynamic displacement, the value specified in the index register is shifted left by three and added to the value in the specified base register.

It should be noted that for IA-relative branches, the target is computed from the current instruction by adding a displacement or an index value. Since the instruction in the delay slot must be executed if it is not nullified, an additional value of eight is added in the offset computation to arrive at the target correctly. This is done to ensure that a branch with a displacement of zero will branch to the instruction following the delayed instruction. Also, this helps users build case tables immediately following the delay slot instruction.

Linkage

Linkage is provided in certain branch instructions to allow a return path for procedure calls. The return point is four bytes after the following instruction. Since the execution of all branches is followed by the execution of the instruction in the delay slot (or null if nullified), it should be noted that the return point is always specified as four bytes after the following instruction and **not** eight bytes after the BRANCH instruction. When the following instruction is not spatially sequential, then four bytes after the following instruction is not the same as eight bytes after the BRANCH instruction.

The linkage mechanism is available for both intraspace and interspace branches. For intraspace branches, the offset of the return point is saved in the specified target register GR t. For explicit interspace branches, the offset of the return point is always saved in GR 31, and the space ID of the return point is saved in SR 0. For implicit interspace branches, the offset of the return point is always saved in GR 2.

Conditional Branching and Nullification

When nullification is specified by a conditional branch instruction, the effect of nullification depends on the direction of the branch. This maximizes useful work done during loops and "if-then" constructs.

For a backward conditional branch, the following instruction is nullified only when the backward conditional branch is **not** taken. For forward conditional branches, the following instruction is nullified only when the forward conditional branch **is** taken. For unconditional branches, if nullification is specified, the following instruction is nullified **independent** of the direction of branch.

Branching and Address Queues

The concept of delayed branching makes it necessary to maintain the instruction address (IA) in a pair of two element queues. The **front** elements point to the currently executing instruction and the **back** elements point to the following instruction that will be executed. The term **next** refers to the Space Identifier and the offset of the next instruction address, which will enter the back elements of the queues when the queues are updated. The queues are said to be updated when the **back** elements become the **front** and **next** become the **back** elements.

For taken branches, the IA queues get updated with the address of the branch target. Both the word offset and the privilege level are updated. IAOQ_Next receives the value of the branch target offset. For not-taken branches, IAOQ_Next gets IAOQ_Back + 4. The privilege level is obtained from the back element of the queue. For interspace branches, IASQ_Next gets the value of the branch target Space ID. Otherwise, IASQ_Next receives the content of IASQ_Back. Figure 4-2 shows how the IA queues are updated, using a pseudo-code representation.

Instruction Address Offset Queue (IAOQ)

IAOQ_Front ← IAOQ_Back;
IAOQ_Back ← IAOQ_Next;
if (taken branch)
      IAOQ_Next ← Branch target offset;
else
      IAOQ_Next ← IAOQ_Back + 4;

Instruction Address Space Queue (IASQ)

IASQ_Front ← IASQ_Back;
IASQ_Back ← IASQ_Next;
if (interspace branch)
      IASQ_Next ← Branch target Space ID;
else
      IASQ_Next ← IASQ_Back;

Figure 4-2.   Updating Instruction Address Queues

Consider the situation shown in Figure 4-3; a taken branch instruction, I2, is executed in the delay slot of a preceding taken branch, I1. When this occurs, the first branch I1 schedules its target instruction, I3, to execute after I2, and the second branch, I2, schedules its target instruction, I4, to execute after I3. The net effect is the out-of-line execution of I3, followed by the execution of I4. Also, if I3 were to be a taken branch, its target, I5, would execute after I4, and I4 would also have been executed out of its spatial context.

Note that if nullification is specified in the instruction currently executing, the nullification affects the instruction to be executed next, regardless of whether that instruction immediately follows the currently executing instruction in the linear code sequence. For example, if the instruction, I2, specified nullification of the next instruction, then I3 would have no effect except that the PSW X-bit, N-bit, and B-bit would be set to 0.

Privilege Level Changes

Branch instructions may change the privilege level depending on the type of branch performed. Since privilege levels are determined by the two rightmost bits in the offset part of the instruction address, privilege level changes are a function of the offset computation.

Unconditional branches can be IA-relative or base-relative. IA-relative branches compute the target address relative to their own IA value, and since the two rightmost bits are unchanged, the privilege level of the branch instruction and the target are the same. base-relative branches (intraspace or interspace) may lower the privilege level if the two rightmost bits in the base register are of a lower privilege level. The GATE completer of the BRANCH instruction performs an IA-relative branch, however, it behaves differently for privilege computation. It can promote the privilege level to that specified by the two rightmost bits of the **type** field, located in the TLB entry for the page from which the BRANCH-with-GATE instruction is fetched.

Conditional branch instructions always perform IA-relative branches and the privilege level of the target instruction and the branch instruction is the same.

The change of privilege level always takes effect at the target instruction.

Programming Note

Since a branch instruction may be executed in the delay slot of another branch instruction, an interesting case arises because of the way the privilege level changes are defined to take effect.

Consider the case where a taken IA-relative branch is placed in the delay slot of a base-relative branch that lowers the privilege level of its target instruction. First, the base-relative branch will execute and schedule change of privilege level for its target. Then, in the delay slot, the IA-relative branch will execute and it will schedule its target to execute at the same privilege level as its own. Then, the target of the base-relative branch will execute at the new (demoted) privileged level. The next instruction, however, which is the target of the IA-relative branch, will have the same privilege level as that of the IA-relative branch, and thus will cause the privilege level to be restored to the original (higher) value as shown in the following:

PROGRAM SEGMENT		
Location	Instruction	Comment
100	STW r7, 0(r8)	; non-branch instruction
104	BV r0(r7)	; branch vectored to 200 and change priv -> 2
108	BLR r4, r0	; IA-relative branch to location 400
10C	ADD r2,r6, r9	; next instruction in linear code sequence
.	.	
.	.	
.	.	
200	LDW 0(r3), r11	; target of branch vectored instruction
.	.	
.	.	
.	.	

PROGRAM SEGMENT			
400	LDW	0(r15), r4	; target of IA-relative branch instruction
404	STW	r4, 0(r18)	

EXECUTION SEQUENCE		
Location	Instruction	Comment
100	STW r7, 0(r8)	; priv = 0
104	BV r0(r7)	; priv = 0
108	BLR r4, r0	; priv = 0
200	LDW 0(r3), r11	; priv = 2 decreased by branch vectored instr
400	LDW 0(r15), r4	; priv = 0 changed back by IA-relative branch
404	STW r4, 0(r18)	; priv = 0

Traps Associated with Branches

Branch instructions may cause various traps based on the value of PSW bits. If the PSW T-bit is 1, and a branch is taken, a taken branch trap occurs. This trap may be used for the purposes of debugging. If the PSW H-bit is 1, and a branch instruction raises the privilege level, a higher-privilege transfer trap occurs. If the PSW L-bit is 1, and a branch instruction lowers the privilege level, a lower-privilege transfer trap occurs.

Restrictions in Branching

It is illegal for a BRANCH with GATE instruction to execute in the delay slot of a taken branch instruction. The PSW B-bit ensures that this sequence is not permitted. Whenever a branch is taken, the PSW B-bit is set to 1 and, if the next instruction is a BRANCH with GATE, an illegal instruction trap occurs.

PROGRAM SEGMENT				
Location	Instruction		Comment	
100	STW	r7, 0(r8)	; non-branch instruction	
104	BV	r0(r7)	; branch vectored to location 200	I1
108	BLR	r4, r0	; IA-relative branch to location 400	I2
10C	ADD	r2,r6, r9	; next instruction in linear code sequence	
.	.			
.	.			
.	.			
200	LDW	0(r3), r11	; target of branch vectored instruction	I3
204	ADD	r11,r12, r14	;	
.	.			

.	.			
.	.			
.	.			
400	LDW	0(r15), r4	; target of IA-relative branch instruction	I4
404	STW	r4, 0(r18)	;	I5

EXECUTION SEQUENCE			
Location	Instruction	Comment	
100	STW r7, 0(r8)	;	
104	BV r0(r7)	; schedules execution at 200 after delay instr	I1
108	BLR r4, r0	; schedules execution at 400 after delay instr	I2
200	LDW 0(r3), r11	; target of first branch executes out of context	I3
400	LDW 0(r15), r4	; target of second branch (is a non-branch)	I4
404	STW r4, 0(r18)	; next instruction is in linear code sequence	I5

Figure 4-3.   Branch in the Delay slot of a Branch

Nullification

A nullified instruction is an instruction that is skipped over. It has no effect on the machine state (except that the IA queues advance and the X-bit, N-bit, and B-bit in the PSW are set to 0). The recovery counter **is not** decremented for a nullified instruction. Nullified instructions do not take group 3 interruptions (although they may take group 1, 2, or 4 interruptions).

All branch instructions and most computational instructions can nullify the execution of the following instruction. For branch instructions, nullification can be specified explicitly. In the case of computational instructions, nullification is performed conditionally based on the outcome of a test.

Instruction Execution

Instruction flow involves calculating the address of the current instruction and then fetching, decoding, and executing that instruction. This process involves performing the sequence of events listed below regardless of the instruction type. (Although these events are listed in sequence, many of them may occur in parallel. It is only necessary that they appear to be logically sequential.) In the description that follows, the values of the PSW bits are the values that exist before the instruction is executed. Changes to the PSW bits only affect instructions after the current instruction. This flow of instruction execution is shown in Figure 4-4.

1. If the PSW M-bit is 0, then high priority machine checks (HPMCs) may occur.

2. The processor checks for group 2 interruptions:

   a. A power failure interrupt that is not masked by the PSW I-bit.

   b. A recovery counter trap. This trap is enabled when the PSW R-bit) is 1 and the most-significant bit of the recovery counter is 1.

   c. An external interrupt or low-priority machine check, both of which are unmasked by the PSW I-bit.

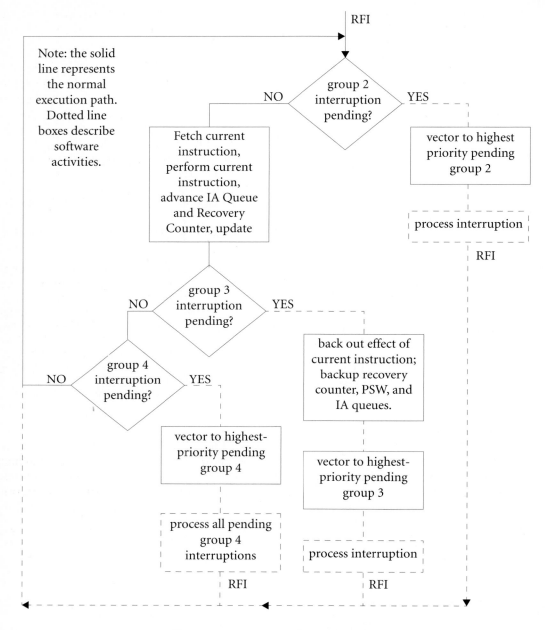

RFI

Note: the solid line represents the normal execution path. Dotted line boxes describe software activities.

group 2 interruption pending?

NO

YES

vector to highest priority pending group 2

Fetch current instruction, perform current instruction, advance IA Queue and Recovery Counter, update

process interruption

RFI

group 3 interruption pending?

NO

YES

group 4 interruption pending?

NO

YES

back out effect of current instruction; backup recovery counter, PSW, and IA queues.

vector to highest-priority pending group 4

vector to highest-priority pending group 3

process all pending group 4 interruptions

process interruption

RFI

RFI

RFI

Figure 4-4.   Interruption Processing

d. A performance monitor interrupt that is not masked by the PSW F-bit.

3. Depending on the state of the PSW N-bit, one of two events occur:

a. If the current instruction is **nullified** (the PSW N-bit is 1), group 3 interruptions must not be taken. The instruction address queue is advanced and the back of the queue is written with the new front element + 4. The privilege level is the same as the new front element. The PSW X-bit, N-bit, and B-bit are set to 0.

b. If the current instruction is **not nullified** (the PSW N-bit is 0), then the instruction is fetched using the front elements of the instruction address (IA) queues. If a group 3 interruption occurs during execution, the processor rolls back the effect of the current instruction by restoring the beginning state and takes the interruption. If the PSW C-bit is 1, virtual address translation of the instruction address is performed. The PSW P-bit enables protection checking. On a split TLB system, the instruction TLB is used for instruction address translation. The fetching of the current instruction may result in an instruction TLB miss fault/ instruction page fault or an instruction memory protection trap.

The Recovery Counter is decremented if the PSW R-bit is 1. The current instruction is executed and the PSW X-bit is set to 0. If the next instruction is to be nullified, the PSW N-bit is set to 1, and the instruction address queues are updated. The nature of that update depends on whether the current instruction is a taken branch:

- For a taken branch: the instruction address queues are advanced, the back of the queue is loaded with the target address including the privilege level which is computed by the branch instruction, and the PSW B-bit is set to 1.

- For a branch that is not taken: the instruction address queues are advanced, the back of the instruction address offset queue is written with the new front element + 4, the privilege level of the back element is set the same as the new front element, and the PSW B-bit is set to 0.

- If the current instruction is a RETURN FROM INTERRUPTION instruction, the IA queues and the PSW are updated with the new values and the following instruction is executed based on these new values.

4. Group 4 traps are handled after execution is complete. If the new privilege level is lower than that of the just completed instruction and the PSW L-bit was 1, a lower-privilege transfer trap is taken. If the new privilege level is higher than that of the just completed instruction and the PSW H-bit was 1, a higher-privilege transfer trap is taken. The term "new privilege" level refers to the privilege level at which the following instruction executes.

If neither transfer trap is taken, the instruction just completed is a taken branch, and the PSW T-bit was 1, then a taken branch trap occurs.

Instruction Pipelining

The architecture permits implementations to prefetch up to seven instructions from the cache (including branch prediction) beyond the instruction currently executing. Instructions may modify resources which affect instruction fetch on the machine they are executing on. Instruction fetch resources include protection identifier registers, the PSW, and TLB entries. When such an event takes place, it affects instructions that are fetched 8 instructions later (at the latest), or after the next RETURN FROM INTERRUPTION instruction, whichever occurs first.

Instructions may also modify resources on other processors in a multiprocessor system, which affect the instruction fetch of the target processors. When such an event takes place (the modification of the resource is acknowledged), it affects instructions that are fetched, on the target processors, after they have finished executing 8 instructions (at the latest) except as noted below.

When a processor executes an instruction which purges an instruction TLB entry in other processors, the target processors must acknowledge completing the purge. The target processors may not complete a move-in, which was initiated using the purged translation, after acknowledging the removal. Acknowledgment of a data TLB purge request from another processor must not be made until after the purge has logically been performed.

Modification of code, while discouraged, may be performed using the following protocol:

1. Modify the code in the data cache.

2. Flush the modified code from the data cache.

3. Issue a SYNCHRONIZE CACHES instruction to ensure the flush is completed and subsequent move-in will observe the memory version.

4. Flush the location of the modified code from the instruction cache.

5. Issue a SYNCHRONIZE CACHES instruction to ensure the flush is completed.

6. Delay at least an additional seven instructions or execute a RETURN FROM INTERRUPTION instruction.

In a multiprocessor system, software must ensure that no other processor is executing code that is in the process of being modified.

5   Interruptions

Interruptions are anomalies that occur during instruction processing, causing transfer of the flow control to an interruption handling routine. In the process, the hardware automatically saves certain processor state. Upon completion of interruption processing, a RETURN FROM INTERRUPTION instruction is executed, which restores the saved processor state, and the execution proceeds with the interrupted instruction.

From the viewpoint of response to interruptions, the processor behaves as if it were not pipelined. That is, it behaves as if a single instruction is fetched and executed, and any interruption conditions raised by that instruction are handled at that time. If there are none, the next instruction is fetched, and so on.

Interrupt Classes

Faults, traps, interrupts, and **checks** are the different classes of interruptions that may happen during instruction processing. Definitions of the four classes of interruptions are as follows:

Fault   The current instruction requests a legitimate action which cannot be carried out due to a system problem, such as the absence of a page from main memory. After the system problem has been corrected, the faulting instruction will execute normally. Faults are synchronous with respect to the instruction stream.

Trap   Traps include two sorts of possibilities: either the function requested by the current instruction cannot or should not be carried out, or system intervention is desired by the user before or after the instruction is executed. Examples of the first type include arithmetic operations that result in signed overflow and instructions executed with insufficient privilege for their intended function. Such instructions are normally not re-executed. Examples of the second type include the debugging support traps. Traps are synchronous with respect to the instruction stream.

Interrupt   An external entity (for example, an I/O device or the power supply) requires attention. Interrupts are asynchronous with respect to the instruction stream.

Check   The processor has detected an internal malfunction. Checks can be either synchronous or asynchronous with respect to the instruction stream.

All four classes of interruptions are handled in the same way. The interruptions are categorized into four groups based on their priorities:

Group 1:	1	High-priority machine check
Group 2:	2	Power failure interrupt
	3	Recovery counter trap
	4	External interrupt
	5	Low-priority machine check
	29	Performance monitor interrupt

Group 3:	6	Instruction TLB miss fault/Instruction page fault
	7	Instruction memory protection trap
	8	Illegal instruction trap
	9	Break instruction trap
	10	Privileged operation trap
	11	Privileged register trap
	12	Overflow trap
	13	Conditional trap
	14	Assist exception trap
	15	Data TLB miss fault/Data page fault
	16	Non-access instruction TLB miss fault
	17	Non-access data TLB miss fault/Non-access data page fault
	26	Data memory access rights trap
	27	Data memory protection ID trap
	28	Unaligned data reference trap
	18	Data memory protection trap/Unaligned data reference trap
	19	Data memory break trap
	20	TLB dirty bit trap
	21	Page reference trap
	22	Assist emulation trap
Group 4:	23	Higher-privilege transfer trap
	24	Lower-privilege transfer trap
	25	Taken branch trap

The interruption numbers in the above list are the individual vector numbers that determine which interruption handler is invoked for each interruption. The group numbers determine when the particular interruption will be processed during the course of instruction execution. The order the interruptions are listed within each group (**not** the interruption numbers) determines the priority of simultaneous interruptions (from highest to lowest).

Interruption Handling

Interruption handling is implemented as a fast context switch (which is much simpler than a complete process swap). When an interruption occurs, the hardware takes the following actions:

1. The PSW in effect at the time of the interruption is saved in the IPSW. For group 2 and 3 interruptions, the saved PSW is the value at the beginning of execution. For group 4 interruptions, the saved PSW is the value after the execution of the instruction.

2. The defined bits in the PSW are set as follows:

W	Set to the value of the default width bit.
E	Set to the value of the default endian bit.

M   Set to 1 if the interruption is a high-priority machine check; otherwise, set to 0.

all other bits   Set to 0 (interrupts are masked, absolute accesses are enabled, etc.).

3. IA information in the IIA queues is frozen (as a result of setting the PSW Q-bit to 0 in step 2 above).

   In order to enable restarting of instructions in the presence of delayed branching, at least two addresses must be saved, pointing to the next two instructions to be executed after returning from the interruption. The hardware, therefore, maintains IIA Space and IIA Offset queues, which have two elements and contain the addresses and privilege levels of these instructions. The IIA queues are kept up-to-date whenever the Q-bit in the PSW is 1. When an interruption is taken, the addresses of the pending instructions are preserved in the queues. The elements of the queues may be obtained by reading the IIASQ and IIAOQ registers (CRs 17 and 18, respectively).

4. The current privilege level is set to the highest privilege level (zero).

5. Information about the interrupting instruction is saved in the Interruption Parameter Registers (IPRs) if the PSW Q-bit was 1 at the time of the interruption. If the PSW Q-bit was 0, the IPRs are unchanged. If the details of an instruction associated with the interruption are potentially useful in processing it, the instruction is loaded into the Interruption Instruction Register (IIR or CR 19). If there is an address associated with the interruption, it is loaded into the Interruption Space and Interruption Offset registers (ISR or CR 20, and IOR or CR 21). See "Interruption Parameter Registers (IPRs)" on page 2-15 for a description of the format of these registers.

6. General registers 1, 8, 9, 16, 17, 24, and 25 are copied to the shadow registers if the PSW Q-bit was 1 at the time of the interruption. If the PSW Q-bit was 0, the shadow registers are unchanged.

7. Execution begins at the address given by:

$$\text{Interruption Vector Address} + (32 * \text{interruption\_number})$$

   Interruption_number is the unique integer value assigned to that particular interruption. Vectoring is accomplished by performing an indexed branch into the Interruption Vector Table indexed by this integer. The Interruption Vector Table contains the first eight instructions of each of the interruption handling routines. The value in the Interruption Vector Address register (CR 14) must be aligned on a 2 Kbyte boundary.

Programming Note

It is the responsibility of interruption handlers to unmask external interrupts (by setting the PSW I-bit to 1) as soon as possible, so as to minimize the worst-case latency of external interrupts.

Instruction Recoverability

When execution of instructions is interrupted, the minimal processor state that is required to be saved and restored is that necessary to correctly continue execution of the instruction stream after processing of the interruption. Processor state is defined to include any register contents, PSW bits, or other information that may affect the operation performed by an instruction. For example, if an interruption is taken immediately before an ADD instruction, its source registers must be restored, but its target register need not be (unless it is also one of the source registers).

Masking and Nesting of Interruptions

Disabling an interruption prevents it from occurring. The interruption does not wait until re-enabled. It is not kept pending. **Masking** an interruption does not prevent the recognition of a pending interruption condition, but delays the occurrence of the interruption until it is "unmasked".

The IA state is collected in the IIA queues only while the PSW Q-bit is 1; it is usually not possible to resume execution after an interruption which is taken while the PSW Q-bit is 0.

The machine state is saved in registers rather than memory when an interruption occurs, and interruption handlers must leave interruptions disabled until they have saved the machine state in memory. Once the machine state is saved, nested interrupts can be allowed.

Since it is desirable to catch hardware faults as soon as possible, interruption handlers should generally not mask high-priority machine checks. If a machine check occurs before the machine state has been saved, the interrupted process may need to be aborted. The occurrence of traps and faults within interruption handlers can be avoided by careful writing of the handlers.

Interruption Priorities

High-priority machine checks (which belong to Group 1) may occur and be processed at any time. They may be synchronous or asynchronous with instruction processing, may be associated with more than one instruction, and their precise meaning and processing is implementation dependent.

All interruptions other than high-priority machine checks are taken between instructions. Multiple simultaneous interruptions may occur because a number of instructions are capable of raising several synchronous interruptions simultaneously, and because certain interruptions are asynchronous with respect to the instruction stream.

Group 2 interruptions occur asynchronously with respect to the instruction stream.

Group 3 interruptions are synchronous with respect to the instruction stream and are signalled before completion of the instruction that produces them.

Group 4 interruptions are synchronous with respect to the instruction stream and are signalled either after completion of the instruction that causes them, or when a change in privilege level is about to happen.

Relative priorities are not assigned to the 64 external interrupts by the hardware. When multiple external interrupts occur simultaneously, software may select their order of service, based on the contents of EIR.

Return from Interruption

The RETURN FROM INTERRUPTION instruction restores the PSW and the instruction address queues. If the old PSW stored in IPSW (CR 22) has interruptions enabled (or unmasked), interruptions are re-enabled before execution of the first of the continuation instructions. The PSW Q-bit may reliably be set to 1 only by a RETURN FROM INTERRUPTION instruction. An attempt to set the PSW Q-bit to 1 with a SET SYSTEM MASK or MOVE TO SYSTEM MASK instruction is an undefined operation.

Adding the ",R" (restore) completer to the RETURN FROM INTERRUPTION instruction does everything that a normal RETURN FROM INTERRUPTION instruction does, and in addition causes the values in the shadow registers to be copied to GRs 1, 8, 9, 16, 17, 24, and 25. Execution of a RETURN FROM INTERRUPTION with the ",R" completer leaves the contents of the shadow registers undefined.

Executing a RETURN FROM INTERRUPTION instruction with the PSW Q-bit 0 and the IPSW Q-bit 0 leaves the IPRs unchanged.

Programming Note

Only those interruptions which are themselves uninterruptible (they leave the PSW Q-bit 0) may return from the interruption using the RFI,R instruction. Interruption handling code which is interruptible (they set the PSW Q-bit to 1) must return from the interruption using the RFI instruction.

Fast interruption handling is achieved using shadow registers, since GRs 1, 8, 9, 16, 17, 24, and 25 are copied to the shadow registers on interruptions. In this example, it is assumed that at most seven general registers need to be used in the interruption handling routine.

Using RFI	Using RFI,R
interrupt	interrupt
save GRs	<no save>
[process interrupt]	[process interrupt]
restore GRs	<no restore>
RFI	RFI,R

Interruption Descriptions

The sections that follow provide descriptions of each of the interrupts defined in the PA-RISC architecture.

Group 1 Interruptions

High-priority Machine Check (1)

Cause: A hardware error has been detected that must be handled before processing can continue

Parameters: Implementation dependent

IIA Queue: Front – Implementation dependent
Back   – Implementation dependent

Notes: The actions taken when a hardware error is detected depend on the seriousness of the error. Damage extensive enough to prevent proper execution of instructions will halt the machine and generate an external indication of the occurrence of the check. Damage which allows a subset of the instructions to execute (e.g., inoperative TLB) generates a high-priority machine check interruption. This is maskable by setting the PSW M-bit to 1, so that machine checks within the machine check handler can be prevented. The causes of high-priority machine checks are implementation dependent, as is the means of controlling their reporting.

Group 2 Interruptions

Power Failure Interrupt (2)

Cause: The machine is about to lose power

Parameters: none

IIA Queue: Front – Address of the instruction to be executed at the time of the interruption
                  Back   – Address of the following instruction

Notes: This interruption is masked and kept pending when the PSW I-bit is 0.

Recovery Counter Trap (3)

Cause: Bit 0 of the recovery counter is 1 and the PSW R-bit is 1

Parameters: none

IIA Queue: Front – Address of the instruction to be executed at the time of the interruption
                  Back   – Address of the following instruction

Notes: The recovery counter can be used to log interruptions during normal operation and to simulate interruptions during recovery from a fault.

External Interrupt (4)

Cause: A module writes to the processor's IO_EIR register, or the interval timer compares equal to its associated comparison register

Parameters: none

IIA Queue: Front – Address of the instruction to be executed at the time of the interruption
                  Back   – Address of the following instruction

Notes: Each external interrupt level has associated with it one bit in the External Interrupt Enable Mask Register (CR 15) and one bit in the External Interrupt Request Register (CR 23). When a module writes into the EIR register, the bit position corresponding to the value written is set to 1. If the default width bit is 1, the bit to set directly corresponds to the value; if 0, the bit to set is the value + 32. For example if the value 5 is written, then bit 5 of the EIR register is set to 1 if the default width bit is 1, and bit 37 of the EIR is set if the default width bit is 0. If the corresponding bit in CR 15 is 1 and the PSW I-bit is 1, an external interrupt is taken; otherwise, the interrupt is masked, and is kept pending.

Interrupt handling software sets bits in the EIR to 0 by executing a MOVE TO CONTROL REGISTER instruction with the appropriate mask.

If multiple sources can set the same interrupt, it is the responsibility of software to correctly respond to all of the interrupting sources.

Low-priority Machine Check (5)

Cause: A hardware error has been detected which is recoverable and does not require immediate handling

Parameters: Implementation dependent

IIA Queue: Front – Address of the instruction to be executed at the time of the interruption
Back – Address of the following instruction

Notes: Errors which have been detected and recovered from by hardware to the point that operation can continue in a degraded fashion are reported via the low-priority machine check interruption. This interruption is masked and kept pending when the PSW I-bit is 0. The causes of low-priority machine checks are implementation dependent, as is the means of controlling their reporting.

Performance Monitor Interrupt (29)

Cause: An implementation-dependent event related to the performance monitor coprocessor requires software intervention

Parameters: Implementation dependent

IIA Queue: Front – Address of the instruction to be executed at the time of the interruption
Back – Address of the following instruction

Notes: This interruption is masked and kept pending when the PSW F-bit is 0.

Group 3 Interruptions

Instruction Tlb Miss Fault/instruction Page Fault (6)

Cause: The instruction TLB entry needed by instruction fetch is absent, and if instruction TLB misses are handled by hardware, the hardware miss handler could not find the translation in the Page Table

Parameters: none

IIA Queue: Front – Address of the instruction causing the fault
Back – Address of the following instruction

Notes: Only if an instruction is to be executed can an instruction TLB miss fault occur.

Instruction Memory Protection Trap (7)

Cause: Instruction address translation is enabled and the access rights check fails for an instruction fetch or instruction address translation is enabled, the PSW P-bit is 1, and the protection identifier checks fails for an instruction fetch

Parameters: none

IIA Queue: Front — Address of the instruction causing the trap
                     Back — Address of the following instruction

Notes: This interruption does not occur for absolute accesses.

Illegal Instruction Trap (8)

Cause: An attempt is being made to execute an illegal instruction or to execute a BRANCH with GATE instruction with the PSW B-bit equal to 1

Parameters: IIR – The illegal instruction causing the trap

IIA Queue: Front — Address of the instruction causing the trap
                     Back — Address of the following instruction

Notes: Illegal instructions are the unassigned major opcodes. Unassigned sub-opcodes are undefined operations (undefined sub-opcodes may cause the illegal instruction trap). On some implementations, DIAGNOSE may be an illegal instruction.

Break Instruction Trap (9)

Cause: An attempt is made to execute a BREAK instruction

Parameters: IIR – The BREAK instruction causing the trap

IIA Queue: Front — Address of the instruction causing the trap
                     Back — Address of the following instruction

Privileged Operation Trap (10)

Cause: An attempt is being made to execute a privileged instruction without being at the most privileged level (priv= 0)

Parameters: IIR – The privileged instruction causing the trap

IIA Queue: Front — Address of the instruction causing the trap
                     Back — Address of the following instruction

Notes: The list of privileged instructions is: DIAG, IDTLBT, IITLBT, LCI, LDDA, LDWA, LPA, MTSM, PDTLB, PDTLBE, PITLB, PITLBE, RFI, RSM, SSM, STDA, STWA.

Privileged Register Trap (11)

Cause: An attempt is being made to write to a privileged space register or access a privileged control register without being at the most privileged level (priv= 0)

Parameters: IIR – The instruction causing the trap

IIA Queue: Front — Address of the instruction causing the trap
                     Back — Address of the following instruction

Notes: This interruption may be caused by the MOVE TO SPACE REGISTER, MOVE TO CONTROL REGISTER, or MOVE FROM CONTROL REGISTER instructions.

Overflow Trap (12)

Cause: A signed overflow is detected in an instruction which traps on overflow

Parameters: IIR – The instruction causing the trap

IIA Queue: Front – Address of the instruction causing the trap
Back   – Address of the following instruction

Conditional Trap (13)

Cause: The condition succeeds in an instruction which traps on condition

Parameters: IIR – The instruction causing the trap

IIA Queue: Front – Address of the instruction causing the trap
Back   – Address of the following instruction

Assist Exception Trap (14)

Cause: A coprocessor or special function unit has detected an exceptional condition or operation. An exceptional operation may include unimplemented operations or operands.

Parameters: IIR – For immediate traps, the SFU or coprocessor instruction that was executing when an exception is reported with a trap. It may or may not be related to the condition causing the exception. For delayed traps, any instruction corresponding to the SFU or coprocessor. See "Interruptions and Exceptions" on page 10-4.

IIA Queue: Front – Address of the instruction causing the trap
Back   – Address of the following instruction

Data Tlb Miss Fault/data Page Fault (15)

Cause: The data TLB entry needed by operand access of a load, store, or semaphore instruction is absent, and if data TLB misses are handled by hardware, the hardware miss handler could not find the translation in the Page Table

Parameters: ISR – space identifier of data address
IOR – offset of data address
IIR – The instruction causing the fault

IIA Queue: Front – Address of the instruction causing the fault
Back   – Address of the following instruction

Notes: This interruption does not occur for absolute accesses.

Non-access Instruction Tlb Miss Fault (16)

Cause: The instruction TLB entry needed for the target of a FLUSH INSTRUCTION CACHE instruction is absent, and if TLB misses are handled by hardware, the hardware miss handler could not find the translation in the Page Table

Parameters: ISR – space identifier of virtual address to be flushed
IOR – offset of virtual address to be flushed

IIR – The instruction causing the fault

IIA Queue: Front – Address of the instruction causing the fault
Back – Address of the following instruction

Notes: This interruption source is distinguished from other TLB misses because a page fault should not result in reading the faulting page from disk. This interruption does not occur for absolute accesses.

Non-access Data Tlb Miss Fault/non-access Data Page Fault (17)

Cause: The data TLB entry needed by a LOAD PHYSICAL ADDRESS, PROBE ACCESS, PROBE ACCESS IMMEDIATE, FLUSH INSTRUCTION CACHE, PURGE DATA CACHE, or a FLUSH DATA CACHE instruction is not present, and if TLB misses are handled by hardware, the hardware miss handler could not find the translation in the Page Table

Parameters: ISR – space identifier of virtual address
IOR – offset of virtual address
IIR – The instruction causing the fault

IIA Queue: Front – Address of the instruction causing the fault
Back – Address of the following instruction

Notes: These interruption sources are distinguished from other TLB misses because a page fault should not result in reading the faulting page from disk. This interruption does not occur for absolute accesses.

Data Memory Access Rights Trap (26)

Cause: Data address translation is enabled, and an access rights check fails on an operand reference for a load, store, or semaphore instruction, or a cache purge operation

Parameters: ISR – space identifier of the virtual address
IOR – offset of the virtual address
IIR – The instruction causing the trap

IIA Queue: Front – Address of the instruction causing the trap
Back – Address of the following instruction

Notes: This interruption does not occur for absolute accesses.

Data Memory Protection Id Trap (27)

Cause: Data address translation is enabled, the PSW P-bit is 1, and a protection identifier check fails on an operand reference for a load, store, or semaphore instruction, or a cache purge operation

Parameters: ISR – space identifier of the virtual address
IOR – offset of the virtual address
IIR – The instruction causing the trap

IIA Queue: Front – Address of the instruction causing the trap
Back – Address of the following instruction

Notes: This interruption does not occur for absolute accesses.

Unaligned Data Reference Trap (28)

Cause: Data address translation is enabled, and a load or store instruction is attempted to an unaligned address

Parameters: ISR – space identifier of the virtual address
IOR – offset of the virtual address
IIR – The instruction causing the trap

IIA Queue: Front – Address of the instruction causing the trap
Back   – Address of the following instruction

Notes: Unaligned data reference traps are not detected for absolute accesses or semaphore instructions – they are undefined operations. Only unaligned virtual memory loads and stores (including coprocessor loads and stores) are defined to terminate with the unaligned data reference trap.

Data Memory Protection Trap/unaligned Data Reference Trap (18)

Cause: Data address translation is enabled, and an access rights check or a protection identifier check fails on an operand reference for a load, store, or semaphore instruction, or a cache purge operation; a load or store instruction is attempted to an unaligned address with virtual address translation enabled (unaligned absolute references and semaphore instructions are undefined operations)

Parameters: ISR – space identifier of the virtual address
IOR – offset of the virtual address
IIR – The instruction causing the trap

IIA Queue: Front – Address of the instruction causing the trap
Back   – Address of the following instruction

Notes: This interruption does not occur for absolute accesses. Only unaligned virtual memory loads and stores (including coprocessor loads and stores) are defined to terminate with the data memory protection trap. Execution of a semaphore instruction with unaligned (16 byte boundaries) addresses is an undefined operation.

This trap is retained for compatibility with the earlier revisions of the architecture. In PA-RISC 1.1 (Second Edition) and later revisions, processors must use traps 26, 27, and 28 which provide equivalent functionality.

Data Memory Break Trap (19)

Cause: Store and semaphore instructions or cache purge operations to a page with the B-bit 1 in the data TLB entry

Parameters: ISR – space identifier of the virtual address
IOR – offset of the virtual address
IIR – The instruction causing the trap

IIA Queue: Front − Address of the instruction causing the trap
                   Back − Address of the following instruction

Notes: This trap is disabled if the PSW X-bit is 1. This interruption does not occur for absolute accesses.

Tlb Dirty Bit Trap (20)

Cause: Store and semaphore instructions to a page with the D-bit 0 in the data TLB entry

Parameters: ISR − space identifier of the data address
                   IOR − offset of the data address
                   IIR − The instruction causing the trap

IIA Queue: Front − Address of the instruction causing the trap
                   Back − Address of the following instruction

Notes: Software is invoked to update the dirty bit in the data TLB entry and the Page Table. This interruption does not occur for absolute accesses.

Page Reference Trap (21)

Cause: Load, store, and semaphore instructions to a page with the T-bit 1 in its data TLB entry

Parameters: ISR − space identifier of the virtual address
                   IOR − offset of the virtual address
                   IIR − The instruction causing the trap

IIA Queue: Front − Address of the instruction causing the trap
                   Back − Address of the following instruction

Notes: This interruption does not occur for absolute accesses.

Assist Emulation Trap (22)

Cause: An attempt is being made to execute an SFU instruction for an SFU whose corresponding bit in the SFU Configuration Register (SCR) is 0 or to execute a coprocessor instruction for a coprocessor whose corresponding bit in the Coprocessor Configuration Register (CCR) is 0

Parameters: ISR − space identifier of the data address
                   IOR − offset of the data address
                   IIR − The instruction causing the trap

IIA Queue: Front − Address of the instruction causing the trap
                   Back − Address of the following instruction

Notes: ISR and IOR contain valid data only if the instruction is a coprocessor load or store.

Group 4 Interruptions

Higher-privilege Transfer Trap (23)

Cause: An instruction is about to be executed at a higher privilege level than the instruction just completed and the PSW H-bit is 1

Parameters: none

IIA Queue: Front – Address of the instruction with the higher privilege level
Back   – Address of the following instruction

Lower-privilege Transfer Trap (24)

Cause: An instruction is about to be executed at a lower privilege level than the instruction just completed and the PSW L-bit is 1

Parameters: none

IIA Queue: Front – Address of the instruction with the lower privilege level
Back   – Address of the following instruction

Taken Branch Trap (25)

Cause: A taken branch was executed, and the PSW T-bit is 1

Parameters: none

IIA Queue: Front – Address of the instruction to be executed after the branch
Back   – Address of the branch target

Notes: This interruption occurs after the execution of the branch instruction, and the address of the branch instruction itself is not available. The address at the front of the IIA queue is the address of the instruction to be executed next. If the branch has nullification specified, this is the address of the nullified instruction (the PSW N-bit is 1 in this case).

6   Instruction Set Overview

This chapter provides an overview of the PA-RISC instruction set. The instructions can be divided into the following functional groups:

- Computation instructions.

- Multimedia instructions.

- Memory Reference instructions.

- Long Immediate instructions.

- Branch instructions.

- System Control instructions.

- Assist instructions.

The instruction set consists of defined, undefined, illegal, and null instructions. This chapter discusses the concepts of undefined and null instructions and includes descriptions of the conditions, their completers, and the notation used in the instruction descriptions. Each instruction is described in detail in Chapter 7, "Instruction Descriptions". Each description includes the full name of the instruction, the assembly language mnemonic and syntax format, machine instruction format, purpose, a narrative description, an operational description, exceptions, and notes concerning usage. In some cases, programming notes are included for additional guidance to programmers.

Instructions are always 32 bits in width. A 6-bit major opcode is always the first field. Source registers, if specified, are often the next two 5-bit fields and are always in the same place. Target registers, if specified, are not fixed in any particular 5-bit field. Depending on the major opcode, the remainder of the instruction word is divided into fields that specify immediate values, space registers, additional opcode extensions, conditions, and nullification.

Computation Instructions

Computation instructions are comprised of the arithmetic, logical, shift, extract, and deposit instructions which operate on the general registers. The two 5-bit fields following the 6-bit opcode field can specify the following combinations:

1. Two source registers.

2. A source register and a target register.

3. A source register and a 5-bit immediate.

4. A target register and a 5-bit immediate.

Table 6-1 summarizes the computation instructions that are provided.

Table 6-1. Computation Instruction Summary

3-Register Arithmetic & Logical Instructions	
ADD, SHLADD, SUB, OR, XOR, AND, ANDCM, UADDCM, UXOR, DS, CMPCLR, DCOR	Perform arithmetic and logical operations with two operands in registers and store the result in a third register.
Immediate Arithmetic Instructions	
ADDI, SUBI, CMPICLR	Perform arithmetic operations between a sign-extended immediate and the contents of a register. The result is placed in a register.
Shift Pair, Extract & Deposit Instructions	
SHRPD, SHRPW,	The shift pair operations allow for a concatenation of two registers followed by a shift of 0 to 63 bit positions.
EXTRD, EXTRW,	Extract instructions take a field from a source register and insert it right-justified into the target register.
DEPD, DEPDI, DEPW, DEPWI	Deposits either set the target to zero or leave it unchanged (merge operation). The deposit instructions then take a right-justified field from a source and deposit it into any portion of the target.

The three-register arithmetic and logical instructions take two source arguments from two general registers. These source registers are specified by the two 5-bit fields following the opcode specifier. The rightmost 5-bit field specifies the target register.

Some of the computation instructions have a signed immediate argument which is either five bits or eleven bits in length. The 5-bit immediate is encoded in the second 5-bit field following the opcode field and the target specifier in the first 5-bit field following the opcode field. The 11-bit immediate is encoded in the rightmost 11-bit field, and the target specifier in the second 5-bit field following the opcode specifier.

Many computation instructions may nullify the instruction following, given the correct conditions. The instruction condition completers are used to determine if the instruction following is nullified, based on the contents of the source operands and the operation performed.

Three-Register Arithmetic and Logical Instructions

These instructions perform arithmetic and logical operations between two operands in registers and store the result into a register. Each arithmetic/logical instruction also specifies the conditional occurrence of either a skip or a trap, based on its opcode and the condition field. Not all options are available on every instruction. Only those operations and options considered useful are defined.

Immediate Arithmetic Instructions

The immediate arithmetic instructions operate between a sign-extended 11-bit immediate and the contents of a register. The result is placed in a register. Immediate operations may optionally trap on overflow. In addition, immediate adds may trap on a specific condition.

The 11-bit immediate field has the sign bit in the rightmost position, but the other 10 bits are in the usual order. The 1-bit opcode extension field determines whether overflow causes a trap.

Shift Pair, Extract, and Deposit Instructions

The shift pair operations allow for a concatenation of two registers followed by a shift of 0 to 63 bit positions. The rightmost 64 bits are placed in a general register. Depending on the choice of the source registers, this operation allows the user to perform right or left shifts, rotates, bit field extractions when the bit field crosses word boundaries, unaligned byte moves, and so on.

Extract instructions take a field from a source register and insert it right-justified into the target register. This field is either zero extended or sign extended. This way, the extract instructions support both logical and arithmetic shift operations.

The deposit instructions either set the target to zero or leave it unchanged (merge operation) and then take a right-justified field from a source and deposit it into any portion of the target. The source can be either a register or a 5-bit signed immediate value. The 5-bit immediate field has the sign bit in the rightmost position, but the other 4 bits are in the usual order. Deposit instructions support left shift operations and simple multiplication by powers of two.

Multimedia Instructions

PA-RISC provides efficient support for the most frequent multimedia operations because these operations are assuming greater importance in many applications. Instructions in this category perform **multiple parallel operations** in a single cycle.

In multimedia workloads, a large portion of the arithmetic can be thought of as **saturation arithmetic**. This means that if the result of a calculation would be too large in magnitude to be represented in a given format, the calculation delivers the largest representable number (as opposed to wrapping to the other end of the representable range, as with modular arithmetic). Commonly, this must be implemented by testing each result (twice, for signed results), and performing conditional branches or skips to force the result to a maximum value. The multimedia instructions in PA-RISC perform multiple parallel computations, with each of the results being tested and forced to the appropriate value if necessary, in a single cycle. The result is a sizeable reduction in pathlength and fewer disruptive breaks in control flow in multimedia algorithms.

Re-arrangement instructions provide efficient support for packed pixel data structures in memory, allow algorithms to make full use of the parallel computation instructions, and enable the use of the full load/store bandwidth of the processor in accessing pixel data.

The multimedia instructions are comprised of halfword arithmetic, halfword shift, and rearrangement instructions. The instructions operate on 16-bit signed or unsigned numbers. The signed representations are two's complement numbers in the range 2^{15}–1 to 2^{15}. Table 6-2 summarizes the multimedia instructions provided.

Table 6-2. Multimedia Instruction Summary

Parallel Halfword Arithmetic Instructions	
HADD, HSUB, HAVG	Parallel halfword add, subtract, and average instructions operate on two 64-bit registers, each containing four 16-bit operands.
Parallel Halfword Shift Instructions	
HSHLADD, HSHRADD, HSHL, HSHR	Parallel halfword shift instructions allow multiple halfword shifts with the shift amount encoded in the instruction. Bits are blocked from being shifted across halfword boundaries. The parallel halfword shift-and-add instructions support halfword multiplication and division by constants.
Rearrangement Instructions	
PERMH, MIXH, MIXW	These instructions allow full utilization of halfword parallel instructions by supporting rearrangement of words and halfwords in registers with no memory load/store overhead.

Parallel Halfword Arithmetic Instructions

In multimedia applications, the most common operations on pixels are addition, subtraction, averaging and multiplication (especially multiplication by constants).

The HALFWORD ADD, HALFWORD SUBTRACT and HALFWORD AVERAGE instructions operate on two 64-bit general registers, each containing four 16-bit operands, and produce four 16-bit results, delivered to a general register. Saturation can be optionally performed. For the HALFWORD AVERAGE instruction, unbiased rounding is performed, to reduce the accumulation of rounding errors.

Halfword multiplication and division by constants is supported through parallel halfword shift-and-add instructions. The HALFWORD SHIFT LEFT AND ADD and HALFWORD SHIFT RIGHT AND ADD instructions perform four parallel halfword shift and add operations. These instructions are used as primitive operations in performing halfword integer multiplication and division by a constant.

Saturation

The halfword addition, subtraction, and shift-and-add instructions can be performed with normal modular arithmetic or with **signed saturation** or **unsigned saturation**. Saturation arithmetic occurs frequently in multimedia algorithms. When an intermediate result of an operation cannot be represented in the target register, saturation is said to occur and the result is forced to a maximum or minimum value. Thus, when a result is out of range (too large or too small to be represented in the target register) the saturation result is automatically delivered and no extra instructions are required to test for these boundary conditions. Saturation is performed independently on each of the 16-bit results.

Optional saturation is specified via instruction completers. In the instruction descriptions, the term *cmplt* is used to denote the completer field which encodes the *sat* field. If no completer is specified, the operands are added or subtracted with modular arithmetic. If signed saturation is specified, both operands are treated as signed numbers and are added or subtracted producing a signed result with signed saturation. If unsigned saturation is specified, the first operand is treated as an unsigned number and the second as a signed number. These are added or subtracted producing an unsigned result with unsigned saturation.

The results for **maximum saturation** and **minimum saturation** are defined for halfword arithmetic instructions in the following tables. **Signed saturation** results are defined in Table 6-3 and **unsigned saturation** results are defined in Table 6-4.

Table 6-3. Signed Saturation Results

Instructions	Maximum Saturation	Minimum Saturation
HADD, HSUB, HSHRADD	Intermediate result of an operation is greater than $2^{15}-1$. The result is forced to $2^{15}-1$.	Intermediate result of an operation is less than -2^{15}. The result is forced to -2^{15}.
HSHLADD	Intermediate result of an operation is greater than $2^{15}-1$. The result is forced to $2^{15}-1$. In addition, the result is also forced to $2^{15}-1$ if the leftmost bit of the first operand is 0, and one or more of the bits shifted out differs from the leftmost bit following the shift.	Intermediate result of an operation is less than -2^{15}. The result is forced to -2^{15}. In addition, the result is also forced to -2^{15} if the leftmost bit of the first operand is 1, and one or more of the bits shifted out differs from the leftmost bit following the shift.

Table 6-4. Unsigned Saturation Results

Instructions	Maximum Saturation	Minimum Saturation
HADD, HSUB	Intermediate result of an operation is greater than $2^{16}-1$. The result is forced to $2^{16}-1$.	Intermediate result of an operation is less than 0. The result is forced to 0.

Parallel Halfword Shift Instructions

The halfword shift instructions allow multiple parallel halfword shifts. The shift amount is encoded in the instruction and shifting can be done by any amount, from 0 to 15 bits. These instructions generally use the main shifter, except that they block any bits from being shifted across halfword boundaries. The HALFWORD SHIFT LEFT instruction allows multiplication by 2^n in a single instruction. The HALFWORD SHIFT RIGHT instruction allows division by 2^n and the shift can be either signed or unsigned. The completer, *cmplt*, determines which type of shift to perform. The completer is encoded in the *se* field of the instruction.

Rearrangement Instructions

The PERMUTE HALFWORDS, MIX HALFWORDS, and MIX WORDS instructions allow full utilization of the halfword parallel arithmetic instructions by supporting the rearrangement of words and halfwords in registers without incurring the overhead of memory load and store instructions. These instructions allow arbitrary permutations and combinations of words and halfwords in a register.

The PERMUTE HALFWORDS instruction can generate any arbitrary combination or permutation of the four halfwords from its source operand.

In the MIX HALFWORDS instruction, two halfwords from the first operand are merged with two halfwords from the second operand to produce the result. The completer, *cmplt*, determines which halfwords are selected. The completer is encoded in the *ea* field of the instruction.

In the MIX WORDS instruction, a word from the first operand is merged with a word from the second operand to produce the result. The completer, *cmplt*, determines which words are selected. The completer is encoded in the *ea* field of the instruction.

Memory Reference Instructions

Memory reference instructions load values into and store values from the general registers. Table 6-5 summarizes the memory reference instructions.

Table 6-5. Memory Reference Instruction Summary

Load/Store	
LDB/STB, LDH/STH, LDW/STW, LDD/STD	Load/Store a byte, halfword, word, or doubleword using a memory address formed using short or long displacement or indexed.
Load/Store Absolute	
LDWA/STWA, LDDA/STDA	Load/Store a word or doubleword using an absolute memory address formed using short or long displacement or indexed.
Load and Clear	
LDCW, LDCD	Read (load) and lock a word or doubleword semaphore in main memory.
Store Bytes/DoubleWord Bytes	
STBY, STDBY	Implement fast byte moves (stores) to unaligned word or doubleword destination.

Memory reference instructions work directly between the registers and main memory. They also can operate between the registers and the data cache on implementations so equipped. A load instruction loads a general register with data from the data cache. A store instruction stores a data value from a general register into the data cache. Normally this distinction is transparent to the programmer, but provisions are made for cache and TLB operations requiring cognizance of the data cache (see "System Control Instructions" on page 6-17).

The address formation mechanisms supported include: short displacement, long displacement, and indexed. It is possible to modify the base value in a general register by the displacement or index. The rightmost bits of computed addresses are not ignored. Unaligned load and store instructions with data address translation enabled to halfwords, words, or doublewords cause an unaligned data reference trap. Semaphore operations and absolute accesses to unaligned data are undefined operations.

Program synchronization can be done using the LOAD AND CLEAR instructions, which perform indivisible semaphore operations. These instructions are required to use 16-byte aligned addresses.

When using semaphores to synchronize with I/O, care must be taken in placing other information in the same cache line as the semaphore. Data which is writable, can only be placed in the same cache line as a semaphore if access to write the data is controlled by the semaphore.

Depending on the state of the PSW D-bit (data address translation bit), most load and store instructions perform virtual accesses (when the PSW D-bit is 1) or physical accesses (when the PSW D-bit is 0, or when executing LOAD ABSOLUTE, STORE ABSOLUTE instructions).

The state of the PSW E-bit determines whether the data which is loaded or stored is big endian (when the PSW E-bit is 0) or little endian (when the PSW E-bit is 1).

Memory is accessed using the following procedures:

```
mem_load(space,offset,low,high,hint)
{
    if (PSW[D] == 0)
        return(phys_mem_load(offset,low,high,hint));
    else
        return(virt_mem_load(space,offset,low,high,hint));
}

mem_store(space,offset,low,high,hint,data)
{
    if (PSW[D] == 0)
        phys_mem_store(offset,low,high,hint,data);
    else
        virt_mem_store(space,offset,low,high,hint,data);
}
```

There are some restrictions on which instructions can be used for referencing the I/O address space and uncacheable memory. See "Operations Defined for I/O Address Space" on page F-12. For a description of memory reference atomicity, see "Atomicity of Storage Accesses" on page G-1.

LOAD OFFSET, LOAD IMMEDIATE LEFT, LOAD PHYSICAL ADDRESS, LOAD COHERENCE INDEX, and LOAD SPACE IDENTIFIER are not memory reference instructions.

Programming Note

Execution may be faster if software avoids dependence on register interlocks. Instruction scheduling to avoid the need for interlocking is recommended. A register interlock will occur if an instruction attempts to use a register which is the target of a previous load instruction that has not yet completed. This does not restrict the length of the delay a load instruction may incur in a particular system to a single execution cycle; in fact, the delay may be much longer for a cache miss, a TLB miss, or a page fault.

Debugging is facilitated by the data memory break trap. This trap occurs whenever a store, a semaphore, or a purge data cache operation is performed to a page with the B-bit 1 in its TLB entry and the PSW X-bit is 0.

Address Formation

Addresses are formed by the combination of a Space ID and an address Offset. Address Offsets may be formed as the sum of a base register and any one of the following: a long displacement, a short displacement (which leaves more instruction bits for other functions), or an index register. Figure 6-1 on page 6-9 illustrates typical examples of the various methods of forming addresses for the memory reference instructions. For detailed illustrations of address calculations for each of the available addressing methods refer to "Memory Reference Instruction Address Formation" on page H-1.

Not all address formation methods are available with every memory reference instruction. Table 6-6 summarizes the address formation methods and the instructions where each is available.

Table 6-6. Address Formation Options for Memory Reference Instructions

Instructions	Indexed	Short Displacement	Long Displacement	Base Register Modification
LDD, LDW, LDH, LDB	X	X	X	X
STD, STW, STH, STB		X	X	X
LDDA, LDWA, LDCD, LDCW	X	X		X
STDA, STWA, STBY, STDBY		X		X

Base Register Modification

All of the address formation methods provide the option of modifying the contents of the Base Register either before or after the address calculation is performed. The address can be formed by using the contents of Base Register before it is modified (sometimes known as post-increment) or by using the contents of the Base Register after it has been modified by the displacement or index (sometimes known as pre-increment.)

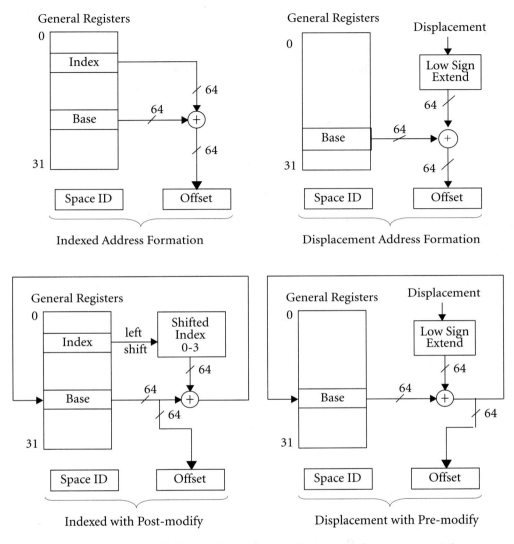

Figure 6-1. Example Address Formation for Memory Reference Instructions

Cache Control

Some memory reference instruction formats contain a 2-bit cache control field, *cc*, which provides a hint to the processor on how to resolve cache coherence. The processor may disregard the hint without compromising system integrity, but performance may be enhanced by following the hint.

There are three different categories of cache control hints: load instruction cache control hints, store instruction cache control hints, and semaphore instruction cache control hints. The cache control hints are specified by the *cc* completer to the instruction and encoded in the *cc* field of the instruction.

The cache control hints for load instructions are shown in Table 6-7. Implementation of the hints by a processor is optional, but the processor must treat unimplemented and Reserved hints as if no hint had been specified.

The Spatial Locality cache control hint is a recommendation to the processor to fetch the addressed cache line from memory but to not displace any existing cache data because there is good spatial locality but poor temporal locality.

Table 6-7. Load Instruction Cache Control Hints

Completer	Description	cc
<none>	No hint	00
	Reserved	01
SL	Spatial Locality	10
	Reserved	11

The cache control hints for store instructions are shown in Table 6-8. Implementation of the hints by a processor is optional, but the processor must treat unimplemented and Reserved hints as if no hint had been specified.

Table 6-8. Store Instruction Cache Control Hints

Completer	Description	cc
<none>	No hint	00
BC	Block Copy	01
SL	Spatial Locality	10
	Reserved	11

The Block Copy cache control hint is a recommendation to the processor not to fetch the addressed cache line if it is not found in the cache. Instead, the processor may create a cache line for the specified address and perform the store instruction on the created line. If the cache line is not fetched then the processor must zero the rest of the created cache line if the privilege level is 1, 2, or 3. The processor may optionally zero the rest of created the cache line if the privilege level is 0. If the store instruction with the Block Copy hint does not store into at least the first byte of the cache line, the processor must perform the store as if the cache control hint had not been specified.

The Block Copy cache control hint is a way for software to indicate that it intends to store a full cache line worth of data. Note that this hint should only be used if the rest of the memory in the addressed cache line is no longer needed.

The cache control hints for the LOAD AND CLEAR semaphore instructions are shown in Table 6-9. The implementation of the hints by the processor is optional. If no hints are implemented, the processor must treat all hints as if no hint had been specified. If the Coherent Operation hint is implemented, the processor must treat Reserved hints as if the Coherent Operation hint had been specified.

Table 6-9. Load And Clear Word Instruction Cache Control Hints

Completer	Description	cc
<none>	No hint	00
CO	Coherent Operation	01
	Reserved	10
	Reserved	11

The Coherent Operation cache control hint is a recommendation to the processor that, if the addressed data is already in the cache, it can operate on the addressed data in the cache rather than having to update memory.

All software users of a semaphore must access the semaphore using the same cache control hint. Sharing a semaphore using different cache control hints is undefined.

Data Prefetch Instructions

Data prefetch instructions are used to initiate a prefetch of the addressed data into the data cache before it is required by later memory reference instructions, thus hiding some or all of the cache-miss latency.

Data prefetch instructions are encoded as normal load instructions with a target register of GR0. All of the normal load addressing modes (long displacement, short displacement, and indexed), base register modification, and cache hints are available. The prefetch address is never unaligned — the low-order address bits are ignored and the cache line containing the address is fetched.

All interruptions normally associated with memory reference instructions (Data TLB miss fault/data page fault, Data memory access rights trap, Data memory protection ID trap, Page reference trap) are suppressed for data prefetch instructions. If one of these exceptions would occur, the prefetch is simply ignored, but any base register modification specified by the instruction still occurs.

There are four data prefetch instructions, corresponding to targeting GR0 for each of the four load instruction data sizes, as shown in Table 6-10. The two reserved encodings do not perform any prefetch, but otherwise operate as described in this section (e.g., interruptions are suppressed, base modification still occurs).

Table 6-10. Data Prefetch Instructions

Instruction	Description
LDD	Prefetch cache line for read
LDW	Prefetch cache line for write
LDH	Reserved
LDB	Reserved

Prefetch for read indicates that the cache line is likely to be used in a subsequent load operation while prefetch for write indicates that a subsequent store will use the cache line. These are distinguished in order to allow the line to be brought into the cache in the correct state.

A prefetch for write is allowed to bring the cache line into the cache in the modified state, in which case the instruction must check access rights as if it was a store and check for the Data memory break and TLB dirty bit traps and suppress the prefetch if any of these checks fails.

A LOAD AND CLEAR instruction with a target register of GR0 may be implemented as a normal LOAD AND CLEAR, which clears the data in memory and discards the original contents, or may be aliased to the equivalent-size load instruction (LDCD to LDD, LDCW to LDW), in which case it behaves exactly like that prefetch instruction and does not clear the data in memory.

Store Bytes Instructions

STORE BYTES and STORE DOUBLEWORD BYTES provide the means for doing unaligned byte moves efficiently. These instructions use a short 5-bit displacement to store bytes to unaligned destinations. The short displacement field is in two's complement notation with the sign bit as its rightmost bit.

The space identifier is computed like any other data memory reference (see Figure H-1 on page H-2). The calculation of the offset portion of the effective address for different completers is shown in Figure H-5. Space and offset are combined like any other data memory reference (see Figure H-3 on page H-3).

The actual offset and modified address involves some alignment and other considerations. Refer to the instruction description pages for an exact definition.

Long Immediate Instructions

The long immediate instructions do not reference memory. They compute values either from a shifted long immediate (21 bits long), from a shifted long immediate and a source register, or from a base register plus a 16-bit displacement. This computed value is then stored in another general register. These instructions are typically used to compute the addresses of data items. The LOAD OFFSET instruction can also be used to simply load a 16-bit immediate into a register.

Table 6-11. Immediate Instruction Summary

Immediate Instructions	
LDO, LDIL, ADDIL,	The three immediate instructions load a computed value into a register or add an immediate value into a register.

Figure 6-2 on page 6-13 illustrates the operation of the immediate instructions.

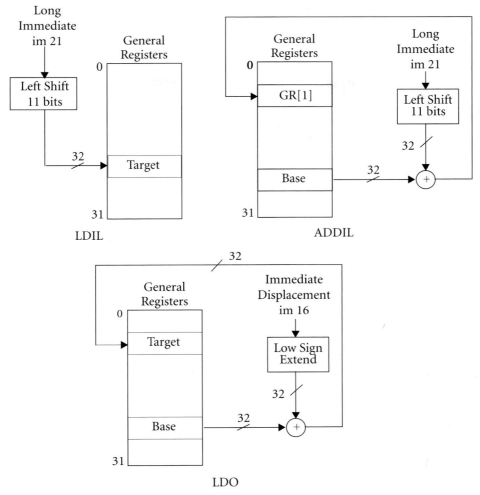

Figure 6-2. Immediate Instructions

Branch Instructions

Branch instructions are classified into three major categories: unconditional local branches, unconditional external branches, and conditional local branches. Within these categories there is sub-classification based on how the target address is computed, whether or not a return address is saved, and whether or not privilege changes can occur. Not all of the options are available for each category. The following sections describe the types of branches. The operation of each branch instruction is detailed in the instruction description in Chapter 7, "Instruction Descriptions". Table 6-12 summarizes the categories of branch instructions.

Table 6-12. Branch Instruction Summary

Unconditional Local Branches	
B, BLR, BV	Branch, branch and link, or branch vectored unconditionally within the current space using IA- or base-relative addressing.
Unconditional External Branches	
BE, BVE	Branch or branch vectored unconditionally to another space using base-relative addressing.
Conditional Local Branches	
ADDB, ADDIB, BB, CMPB, CMPIB, MOVB, MOVIB	Branch within the current space if the specified condition is satisfied using IA-relative addressing. Categories include: move and branch, compare and branch, add and branch, and branch on bit.

Unconditional Local Branches

The unconditional local branch instructions are used for intraspace control transfers, procedure calls, and procedure returns. Three types of relative addressing are provided:

1. IA-relative branches with static displacement use the IAOQ_Front plus either a 17-bit or 22-bit signed word displacement. This allows a branch target range of up to plus or minus 8 Mbytes within a space.

2. IA-relative branches with dynamic displacement use the IAOQ_Front plus a shifted index register.

3. Base-relative branches with dynamic displacement use the value in a base register plus a shifted index register.

The BRANCH instruction satisfies most of the requirements for unconditional branching. The branch target is IA relative with a 17-bit static displacement.

A BRANCH instruction with the optional ,L (for link) completer is used for procedure calls. The branch target is IA relative with a 22-bit displacement if GR 2 is specified as the link register, and with a 17-bit displacement if any other general register is specified. In addition, this variant of the instruction places the offset of the return point (or link) in the specified GR. The return point is the location four bytes beyond the address of the instruction which executes after the BRANCH.

A BRANCH instruction with the optional ,GATE (for gateway) completer is used for intraspace branching with a process privilege level promotion. The branch target is IA relative with a 17-bit static displacement.

The BRANCH AND LINK REGISTER instruction is used for intraspace procedure calls in which the branch target is outside the range for a BRANCH instruction with the ,L completer, or when a dynamic target displacement is needed. The branch target address is base relative with a dynamic displacement. Link handling is performed the same way as for a BRANCH instruction with the ,L completer.

The BRANCH VECTORED instruction is used for intraspace branching through a table and for procedure returns. The branch target address is base relative with a dynamic displacement. The process privilege level may be demoted.

Unconditional External Branches

The unconditional external branch instructions are used for interspace control transfers, procedure calls, and procedure returns. All unconditional external branch instructions use base-relative addressing and may demote the process privilege level based on the rightmost bits of the base register.

Two types of base-relative addressing are provided:

- Base-relative branches with static displacements use a base register plus a 17-bit signed word displacement. This allows a branch target range of up to plus or minus 256 Kbytes across space boundaries. The target space comes from a Space Register which is specified explicitly.

- Base-relative branches with no displacement or index value. The target space comes from an SR which is specified implicitly by the base register.

The BRANCH EXTERNAL instruction is used for interspace branching and procedure returns.

A BRANCH EXTERNAL instruction with the optional ,L completer is used for interspace procedure calls. It places the offset of the return point in GR 31 and copies the space ID into SR 0. The return point is the location four bytes beyond the address of the instruction which executes after the branch.

The BRANCH VECTORED EXTERNAL instruction is used for interspace branching through a table and for procedure returns. The target space is specified implicitly by the base register.

A BRANCH VECTORED EXTERNAL instruction with the optional ,L completer is used for interspace procedure calls. It places the offset of the return point in GR 2. The return point is the location four bytes beyond the address of the instruction which executes after the branch.

Conditional Local Branches

The conditional local branch instructions are used to perform an operation and then branch if the condition specified is satisfied. All conditional local branch instructions use IA-relative addressing with static displacements. The target address is the current IAOQ_Front plus a 12-bit signed word displacement. This allows a branch target range of up to plus or minus 8 Kbytes within a space.

There are four categories of conditional local branch instructions: move and branch, compare and branch, add and branch, and branch on bit. The branch may be taken if the condition specified is true or false. There are two forms of each instruction, the two-register form and the register plus 5-bit immediate form. The 5-bit immediate operand provides data values in the range from -16 to +15.

Branch Target Stack

The Branch Target Stack (or BTS) is an optional processing resource which is used to accelerate indirect branches, such as subroutine returns. The BTS is managed by software, and in processors which implement it, can provide the branch target address in place of the general register specified in the branch instruction.

Operations which push an address onto the stack:

- B,L,PUSH - Used for normal function calls.
- BVE,L,PUSH - Used for intra-space calls, such as calls to library functions.

- PUSHBTS - Used to push a value from a GR onto the stack, in preparation for a dynamic branch.
- PUSHNOM - Pushes the value in BNR onto the stack; used in the called function if the caller did not push the return address on the stack.

Operations which pop an address from the stack:

- BVE,POP - An address is popped from the stack, and if valid, it is used as the target address. Otherwise, the BVE branches to an address given by a GR.
- POPBTS - Pops a specified number of entries from the stack and discards them; used for stack unwinding.
- CLEARBTS - Pops all entries from the stack, discarding them all and leaving the stack invalid; this is used in situations where the sequence of calls and returns is reset, such as with LONGJMP in Unix systems.

All branch-and-link instructions nominate their link value. That is, the link value which is written to a GR is also copied into BNR.

So, for call/return acceleration, one of these two scenarios is used:

- The caller uses a B,L,PUSH or BVE,L,PUSH to call. The callee uses a BVE,POP to return. (This is the normal scenario.)
- The caller does not explicitly push a value onto the stack (it does not specify a ,PUSH completer on the branch used to call). The callee does a PUSHNOM to push the link onto the stack. The callee uses a BVE,POP to return.

For dynamic branches (such as may be generated by C-language switch statements), this scenario is used:

- A PUSHBTS is done as soon as the target address has been calculated. Then, at the point the branch is done, a BVE,POP is done.

Branch Characteristics

Figure 6-3 categorizes the characteristics of the branch instructions.

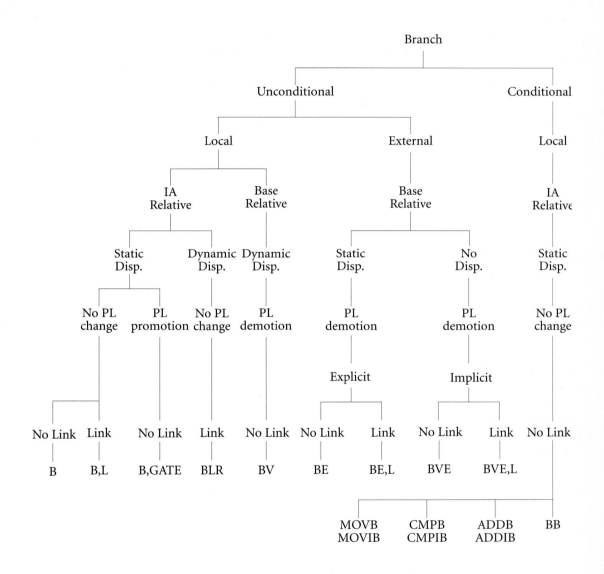

Figure 6-3. Classification of Branch Instructions

System Control Instructions

The system control instructions provide special register moves, system mask control, return from interruption, probe access rights, memory management operations, and implementation-dependent functions. Table 6-13 summarizes the System Control instructions that are provided.

Table 6-13. System Control Instruction Summary

Special Register Move Instructions	
LDSID, MTSP, MFSP, MTCTL, MFCTL, MTSARCM, MFIA,	These instructions move values to and from the space registers, control registers, the shift amount, and instruction address register.
System Mask Control Instructions	
SSM, RSM, MTSM	These instructions set, reset, and move values to the system mask portion of the PSW.
Return From Interrupt & Break Instructions	
RFI, BREAK	Restore state and restart interrupted instruction stream or cause a break for debugging purposes.
Memory Management Instructions	
SYNC, SYNCDMA, PROBE, PROBEI, LPA, LCI, PDTLB, PITLB, PDTLBE, PITLBE, IDTLBT, IITLBT, PDC, FDC, FIC, FDCE, FICE	These instructions synchronize memory operations, probe addresses to determine access rights, load a physical address or a coherence index, purge or insert TLB entries or translations, and purge or flush data or instruction caches or cache entries.
Implementation-Dependent Instruction	
DIAG	Provide implementation-dependent operations for diagnostic purposes.

The memory management instructions generate instruction and data addresses. Address formation is similar to that of the indexed load instructions. The only difference is that the index register is never shifted before adding to the base register. .

Memory management instructions select a space identifier either implicitly or explicitly as shown in Figure 3-8 on page 3-8. The calculation of the offset portion of the address is shown in Figure 6-4.

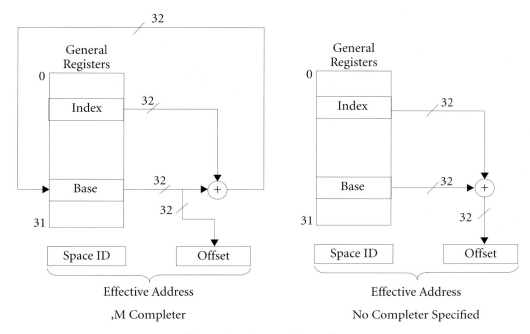

Figure 6-4. System Operations

Assist Instructions

The PA-RISC design generally conforms to the concept of a simple instruction set implemented in cost-effective hardware. Certain algorithms can benefit from substantial performance gains by dedicating specialized hardware to execute specialized instructions. Since few algorithms rely solely upon the specialized hardware alone, it is usually advantageous to combine the central processor with additional assist processors closely coupled to it.

In addition to the instructions executed by a central processor, the instruction set contains instructions to invoke the special, optional, hardware functions provided by the two types of assist processors: Special Function Units (SFUs) and coprocessors. Table 6-14 summarizes the assist instructions that are provided for SFUs and coprocessors.

Table 6-14. Assist Instruction Summary

Special Function Instructions	
SPOP0, SPOP1, SPOP2, SPOP3	These instructions invoke SFU operations, copy SFU register or result to a general register, and perform a parameterized SFU operation.
Coprocessor Instructions	
COPR, CLDD, CLDW, CSTD, CSTW	These instructions invoke a coprocessor operation and load or store words or doublewords to or from a coprocessor register.

Special function units are closely coupled to the central processor and provide extensions to the instruction set. They use the general registers as operands and targets of operations.

Coprocessors provide functions that use either memory locations or coprocessor registers as operands and targets of operations. Coprocessors are less closely coupled to the central processor, and so are more easily provided as configuration options for an implementation than special function units. Coprocessors may also directly pass doubleword quantities to and from the coprocessor and memory. This is suited to the manipulation of quantities that are too large to be directly handled in general registers.

The special function unit and coprocessor instructions are intended to encapsulate all of the optional hardware features used for non-system-level code. An emulation facility is provided that permits PA-RISC family members to execute code using the standard instruction set when optional hardware is not present. The emulation facility is provided by the assist emulation trap, which passes information in control registers, substantially reducing the instruction path length for emulation.

The assist exception trap permits partial implementations of standard "hardware" functions in a combination of hardware and software. This handles functions that are difficult or not cost-effective to implement fully in hardware.

Compatibility Among Implementations

The standard PA-RISC instruction set contains all defined instructions, including those for all defined assist processors. Particular implementations may choose to implement these instructions in hardware, software, or some combination of the two, using assist emulation traps and/or assist exception traps to complete the implementation. Thus, these instructions can be used by compilers and assemblers without sacrificing object-code portability. Software emulation of the extended functions is also used to permit execution of the object code in a degraded mode for high-availability systems.

Special Function Unit (SFU) Instructions

The SFU mechanism is intended for certain architecturally defined instruction extensions, such as hardware fixed-point binary multiply/divide or encryption hardware, as well as for implementation-specific extensions, such as emulation assist processors or direct I/O controller connections.

SFUs are connected to the general register interface and are invoked by special operation instructions. These instructions cause the execution unit to perform any of several operations (determined by the opcode extension), which may use the contents of registers, or may write back a result. Some instructions conditionally nullify the following instruction.

Some special function operations overlap their execution with succeeding instructions. These operations require that the special function unit's state be saved and restored when a context switch is made. An interlock occurs if a special function result is requested before the operation has completed, or the special function unit is busy.

An SFU is not required to hold its state in addressable registers. Instead, SFU operations are used to save and restore the state, as well as to pass it operands and receive results from it.

Defined special function units will conform to the requirements of the defined SFU instructions, so that they may be implemented either as built-in or interfaced special function units. The assist emulation trap permits software implementation of any defined special operation instruction.

The processor must also provide the current privilege level to special function units. Privilege levels could be broadcast each time they change or could be transmitted with each SFU operation. Use of the privilege level by the SFU is specific to each of the units. The operation paragraph of each SFU instruction description specifies the necessary information that must be available to the SFU in the *sfu_operation* function.

There is one SFU instruction, the IDENTIFY SFU (SPOP1) instruction, that is defined for all SFUs. It must be implemented.

SFU Configuration Register

The SCR (SFU Configuration Register) is an 8-bit control register (within CR 10 bits 16..23) that is used to indicate the presence and usability of a hardware implementation of an SFU. For all bits in the SCR, SCR{i} corresponds to an undefined SFU with a unit identifier that is the same as the bit position, that is the SFU with uid i.

When SCR{i} is 1, the SFU with uid i is implied to be present and usable. SFU instructions are passed to the SFU and the defined operation occurs. Exceptions resulting from the operation cause the instruction to be terminated with an assist exception trap. Assist emulation traps are not allowed to occur for the SFU with uid i when SCR{i} is 1. It is an undefined operation to set to 1 the SCR bit corresponding to a nonexistent SFU.

When SCR{i} is 0, it is not implied that the SFU with uid i is absent from the system, but rather that the SFU, if present, is not currently being used. When the SCR bit is 0, the SFU instruction is terminated with an assist emulation trap. Assist exception traps are not allowed to occur for the SFU with uid i when SCR{i} is 0.

Setting the SCR{i} bit to 0 must logically decouple the SFU with uid i. This must ensure that the state of the SFU with uid i is frozen just prior to the transition of SCR{i} from 1 to 0 and that the state does not change as long as SCR{i} is 0. When SCR{i} is 0, the SFU with uid i must not respond to any SFU operations for the SFU with uid i. The frozen state of an SFU, for example, could also be a state in which the SFU is left "armed" to trap any subsequent operations. For example, if the SFU with uid i is in an "armed-to-trap" state and SCR{i} is 0, any operation involving that SFU must not cause an assist exception trap.

The precedence of the interruptions that are applicable to operations for the SFU with uid i depends on the state of SCR{i}. The assist exception trap and assist emulation trap are always taken in the priority order as described in "Interruption Priorities" on page 5-4.

NOTE

Logical decoupling may be accomplished in a variety of ways. Processors may use abort signals or other schemes to notify SFUs that the current instruction is to be ignored.

When the SCR bit is 0, logical decoupling suppresses any exception traps from an SFU and causes the emulation trap to occur (if it is the highest priority).

Coprocessor Instructions

The coprocessor mechanism is intended for special-purpose data manipulations, for example to handle data larger than will fit in a general register. The interconnection method allows for instruction set extensions with minimal effect on the instruction execution rate, while maintaining short data communication paths between the coprocessors and the rest of the system. Coprocessor instructions can be executed by the coprocessor hardware or emulated by software. Combinations of instructions implemented in hardware and emulated by software are possible even when the coprocessor hardware is present in a system.

When caches are implemented, coprocessors are connected to the CPU-cache interface. For systems that do not have a cache, coprocessors are connected to the CPU-memory bus interface. Coprocessors manipulate data in their own register sets, but use the data cache or memory bus and central processor's address generation logic. Under control of the CPU, coprocessor load instructions pass data from the data cache or memory bus to a coprocessor, and coprocessor store instructions pass data from a coprocessor to the data cache or memory bus. Coprocessor operations use only the coprocessor's registers. Some coprocessor operations may nullify the following instruction.

Coprocessor operation, load, and store instructions may overlap their execution with succeeding instructions. An interlock occurs if a coprocessor operation is requested before the coprocessor is able to perform it, and for loads and stores involving busy coprocessor registers.

The coprocessor load and store instructions contain a 5-bit field which normally specifies a coprocessor register, but may also be interpreted by coprocessors as a sub-operation field. Coprocessors keep their state in their registers, so that storing the coprocessor registers and reloading them is sufficient to save and restore the state of a coprocessor.

Some coprocessors are capable of supporting doubleword load and store operations. These operations are implemented on all systems that support such coprocessors, even though they may require additional cycles for some machines. Coprocessor load and store operations must be atomic.

The operation section of each coprocessor instruction description specifies the necessary information that must be available to the coprocessor in the *coprocessor_op* and *send_to_copr* functions. There is one coprocessor instruction, the IDENTIFY COPROCESSOR (COPR,uid,0) instruction, that is defined for coprocessors with unit identifiers 4 through 7. Coprocessors with unit identifiers 0 and 3 have a mechanism to identify themselves that is individually defined.

NOTE

An unaligned data reference trap is taken if the appropriate number of rightmost bits of the effective virtual address are not zeros for the COPROCESSOR LOAD WORD, COPROCESSOR LOAD DOUBLEWORD, COPROCESSOR STORE WORD, and COPROCESSOR STORE DOUBLEWORD instructions. Absolute accesses to unaligned data are undefined operations.

Coprocessor Configuration Register

The CCR (Coprocessor Configuration Register) is an 8-bit control register (within CR 10 bits 24..31) that is used to indicate the presence and usability of a hardware implementation of a coprocessor. Bits 0 and 1 in the CCR correspond to the floating-point coprocessor and bit 2 in the CCR corresponds to the performance monitor coprocessor. For all other bits in the CCR, CCR{i} corresponds to an undefined coprocessor with a unit identifier that is the same as the bit position, that is the coprocessor with uid i.

Execution of any floating-point instruction with CCR{0} and CCR{1} not set to the same value is an undefined operation. Execution of a coprocessor operation instruction (major opcode 0x0C) with CCR{0}, CCR{1}, and the uid field in the instruction all set to 1 is an undefined operation.

When CCR{i} is 1, the coprocessor with uid i is implied to be present and usable. Coprocessor instructions are passed to the coprocessor and the defined operation occurs. Exceptions resulting from the operation cause the instruction to be terminated with an assist exception trap. Assist emulation traps are not allowed to occur for the coprocessor with uid i when CCR{i} is 1. It is an undefined operation to set to 1 the CCR bit corresponding to a nonexistent coprocessor.

When CCR{i} is 0, it is not implied that the coprocessor with uid i is absent from the system, but rather that the coprocessor, if present, is not currently being used. When the CCR bit is 0, the coprocessor instruction is terminated with an assist emulation trap. Assist exception traps are not allowed to occur for the coprocessor with uid i when CCR{i} is 0.

Setting the CCR{i} bit to 0 must logically decouple the coprocessor with uid i. This must ensure that the state of the coprocessor with uid i is frozen just prior to the transition of CCR{i} from 1 to 0 and that the state does not change as long as CCR{i} is 0. When CCR{i} is 0, the coprocessor with uid i must not respond to any coprocessor operations for the coprocessor with uid i. The frozen state of a coprocessor, for example, could also be a state in which the coprocessor is left "armed" to trap any subsequent operations. For example, if the coprocessor with uid i is in an "armed-to-trap" state and CCR{i} is 0, any operation involving that coprocessor must not cause an assist exception trap.

The precedence of the interruptions that are applicable to operations for the coprocessor with uid i depends on the state of CCR{i}. The assist exception trap and assist emulation trap are always taken in the priority order as described in "Interruption Priorities" on page 5-4.

NOTE

Logical decoupling may be accomplished in a variety of ways. Processors may use abort signals or other schemes to notify coprocessors that the current instruction is to be ignored.

When the CCR bit is 0, logical decoupling suppresses any exception traps from a coprocessor and causes the emulation trap to occur (if it is the highest priority).

Conditions and Control Flow

Many instructions utilize conditions derived from the values of the operators and the operation performed. The architecture defines several sets of conditions that affect control flow:

- Arithmetic/Logical Conditions.
- Unit Conditions.
- Shift/Extract/Deposit Conditions.
- Branch On Bit Conditions.

Every instruction that tests conditions uses one of these sets. Each set contains a maximum of sixteen separate conditions and their negations. Most instructions that use conditions may also select the negation of a condition.

The condition completer field, *cond*, in the assembly language form of the instructions specifies a condition or the negation of a condition. This field expands in the machine language form to fill the condition field, *c*, (normally 3 bits wide), the 1-bit negation field, *f*, and the 1-bit doubleword field, *d*, as required. For some instructions, the negation or doubleword attributes of the condition are controlled by the opcode.

The result of an operation and the specified condition can affect control flow in the following ways:

- Branching – the result determines whether or not the branch is taken.

- Nullifying – the result determines whether or not the next instruction is nullified.

- Trapping – the result determines whether a conditional trap is taken or execution proceeds normally.

Additional Notes on the Instruction Set

This section defines how the architecture and instruction notation handles such details as undefined, illegal, null, and unimplemented instructions.

Undefined and Illegal Instructions

Not all of the 64 possible major opcodes of the instruction set are defined as valid instructions. (See Appendix C, "Operation Codes", for a list of the valid instruction opcodes.) An undefined major opcode is considered an **illegal instruction**. Execution of an illegal instruction causes an illegal instruction trap.

Within each major opcode, there may be undefined opcode extensions and modifiers (these are **undefined instructions**). Interpretation of these opcodes is left to the implementor, but system integrity is not compromised. An undefined instruction, or sequence of undefined instructions, executed at a given privilege level has no effect on system state other than what would have been produced by a sequence of defined instructions running at the same privilege level. This limits the possible side-effects that could result from undefined instructions.

Undefined operations are equivalently specified. These result from normally defined instructions but with operands or specifiers that are explicitly disallowed.

Executing an optional special operation or coprocessor instruction may cause an assist exception trap or an action that depends on the definition of the specific special function unit or coprocessor.

Reserved Instruction Fields

In the Format section of the instruction description pages in Chapter 7, instruction fields marked *rv* are Reserved instruction fields. These fields are reserved for future architectural definition. To avoid incompatibility with future revisions of the architecture, software must provide zeros in all Reserved fields. When decoding instructions, processors must ignore Reserved instruction fields.

Reserved Values of an Instruction Field

Certain values of some instruction fields are Reserved for future architectural definition. To avoid incompatibility with future revisions of the architecture, software must not use the Reserved values. When decoding instructions, processors must treat the Reserved values as described for the specific field.

Null Instructions

Null instructions occur when unimplemented features of the architecture are accessed. The effect of a null instruction is identical to a nullified instruction except that the Recovery Counter is decremented. There is no effect on the machine state except that the IA queues are advanced and the PSW B-bit, N-bit, X-bit, Y-bit, and Z-bit are set to 0.

7   Instruction Descriptions

This chapter provides a description of each of the instructions (except floating-point instructions which are described in Chapter 9, "Floating-Point Instruction Set") supported by the PA-RISC architecture. The instructions are listed in alphabetical order, according to the instruction's mnemonic.

Figure 7-1 illustrates the information presented in each of the instruction descriptions. The information presented in this figure is for illustrative purposes only and does not represent a valid instruction.

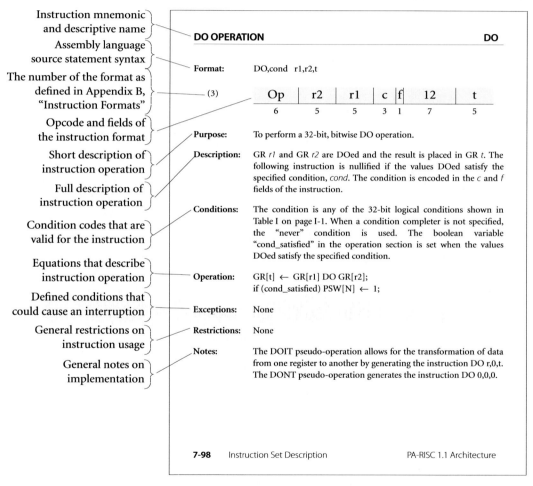

Figure 7-1. Instruction Description Example

Format: ADD,cmplt,carry,cond   r1,r2,t

(8)

02	r2	r1	c	f	e1	1	e2	0	d	t
6	5	5	3	1	2	1	1	2	1	5

Purpose: To do 64-bit integer addition and conditionally nullify the following instruction.

Description: GR $r1$ and GR $r2$ are added. If no trap occurs, the result is placed in GR t. The variable "carry_borrows" in the operation section captures the 4-bit carries resulting from the add operation. The completer, *cmplt*, encoded in the *e1* field, specifies whether the carry/borrow bits in the PSW are updated and whether a trap is taken on signed overflow. The completer, *carry*, encoded in the *e2* field, specifies whether the addition is done with carry in.

The following instruction is nullified if the values added satisfy the specified condition, *cond*. The condition is encoded in the *c*, *d*, and *f* fields of the instruction. The boolean variable "overflow" in the operation section is set if the operation results in a 32-bit signed overflow ($d=0$) or a 64-bit signed overflow ($d=1$.) For addition with carry in, the *d* field encodes whether the word carry (PSW C/B{8}, $d=0$), or the doubleword carry (PSW C/B{0}, $d=1$) is used.

The *e1* field encodes whether the carry/borrow bits in the PSW are updated and whether a trap is taken on overflow ($e1=1$: carries updated, no trap, $e1=2$: carries not updated, no trap, $e1=3$: carries updated, trap on overflow.) The *e2* field encodes whether addition with carry in is performed ($e2=0$: no carry in, $e2=1$: addition performed with carry in.) The combination $e1=2$, $e2=1$ is not defined. The following table shows the allowed combinations:

Completer	Description	e1	e2
<none>	Add	1	0
C or DC	Add with carry/doubleword carry	1	1
L	Add logical	2	0
TSV	Add and trap on signed overflow	3	0
C,TSV or DC,TSV	Add with carry/doubleword carry and trap on signed overflow	3	1

Conditions: The condition is any of the 32-bit add conditions shown in Table D-6 on page D-5 or any of the 64-bit add conditions shown in Table D-7 on page D-6. When a condition completer is not specified, the "never" condition is used. The boolean variable "cond_satisfied" in the operation section is set when the values added satisfy the specified condition.

Operation: switch (carry) {
           case C: res ← GR[r1] + GR[r2] + PSW[C/B]{8};
                          break;
           case DC: res ← GR[r1] + GR[r2] + PSW[C/B]{0};
                          break;
           default: res ← GR[r1] + GR[r2];
                          break;
        }
        if (cmplt == TSV && overflow)
            overflow_trap;
        else {
            GR[t] ← res;
            if (cmplt != 'L')
                PSW[C/B] ← carry_borrows;
            if (cond_satisfied) PSW[N] ← 1;
        }

Exceptions: Overflow trap

Notes: When the ,C completer is specified, only 32-bit conditions are available. When the ,DC completer is specified, only 64-bit conditions are available.

Format: ADDB,cond,n   r1,r2,target

(17)	28/2A	r2	r1	c	w1	n	w
	6	5	5	3	11	1	1

Purpose: To add two values and perform an IA-relative branch conditionally based on the values added.

Description: GR *r1* and GR *r2* are added and the result is placed in GR *r2*. If the values added satisfy the specified condition, *cond*, the word displacement is assembled from the *w* and *w1* fields, sign extended, and added to the current instruction offset plus 8 to form the target offset. The branch target, *target*, in the assembly language format is encoded in the *w* and *w1* fields.

If nullification is not specified, the following instruction is not nullified. If nullification is specified, the instruction following a taken forward branch or a failing backward branch is nullified. The ,N completer, encoded in the *n* field of the instruction, specifies nullification.

Conditions: The condition, *cond*, is any of the 32-bit add conditions shown in Table D-6 on page D-5 or any of the 64-bit add and branch conditions shown in Table D-8 on page D-6 and is encoded in the *c* and *opcode* fields of the instruction. When the PSW W-bit is 0, only the 32-bit conditions are available. Opcode 28 is used for the 32-bit non-negated add conditions (those with f = 0 in Table D-6) and opcode 2A is used for the 32-bit negated add conditions (those with f = 1 in Table D-6.) When the PSW W-bit is 1, a subset of the 32-bit and 64-bit conditions are available. Opcode 28 is used for the non-negated conditions (those with f = 0 in Table D-8) and opcode 2A is used for the negated conditions (those with f = 1 in Table D-8.) When a condition completer is not specified, the "never" condition is used. The boolean variable "cond_satisfied" in the operation section is set to 1 when the values added satisfy the specified condition and set to 0 otherwise.

Operation: GR[r2] ← GR[r1] + GR[r2];
disp ← lshift(sign_ext(assemble_12(w1,w),12),2);
if (cond_satisfied)
    IAOQ_Next ← IAOQ_Front + disp + 8;
if (n)
    if (disp < 0)
        PSW[N] ← !cond_satisfied;
    else
        PSW[N] ← cond_satisfied;

Exceptions: Taken branch trap

Add to Immediate

Format: ADDI,cmplt,trapc,cond   i,r,t

(9)

2C/2D	r	t	c	f	e1	im11
6	5	5	3	1	1	11

Purpose: To add an immediate value to a register and conditionally nullify the following instruction.

Description: The sign-extended immediate value *i* is added to GR *r*. If no trap occurs, the result is placed in GR *t* and the carry/borrow bits in the PSW are updated. The immediate value is encoded into the *im11* field. The variable "carry_borrows" in the operation section captures the 4-bit carries resulting from the add operation.

The completer, *cmplt*, encoded in the *e1* field, specifies whether a trap is taken on a 32-bit signed overflow (*e1*=0: no trap, *e1*=1: trap on 32-bit signed overflow.) The completer, *trapc*, encoded in the opcode, specifies whether a trap is taken if the values added satisfy the condition specified (no trap for opcode 2D, trap on condition for opcode 2C.) The table below shows the *cmplt* and *trapc* combinations.

Completer	Description	Opcode	e1
\<none\>	Add to immediate	2D	0
TSV	Add to immediate and trap on signed overflow	2D	1
TC	Add to immediate and trap on condition	2C	0
TSV, TC	Add to immediate and trap on signed overflow or condition	2C	1

For opcode 2D, the following instruction is nullified if the values added satisfy the specified condition, *cond*. The condition is encoded in the *c* and *f* fields of the instruction. The boolean variable "overflow" in the operation section is set if the operation results in a 32-bit signed overflow.

Conditions: The condition is any of the 32-bit add conditions shown in Table D-6 on page D-5. When a condition completer is not specified, the "never" condition is used. The boolean variable "cond_satisfied" in the operation section is set when the values added satisfy the specified condition.

Operation: res ← low_sign_ext(im11,11) + GR[r];
if (cmplt == TSV && overflow)
      overflow_trap;
else if (trapc == TC && cond_satisfied)
      conditional_trap;
else {
      GR[t] ← res;
      PSW[C/B] ← carry_borrows;
      if (cond_satisfied) PSW[N] ← 1;
}

Exceptions: Overflow trap   Conditional trap

Format: ADDIB,cond,n   i,r,target

(17)

29/2B	r	im5	c	w1	n	w
6	5	5	3	11	1	1

Purpose: To add two values and perform an IA-relative branch conditionally based on the values added.

Description: The sign-extended immediate value *im5* is added to GR *r* and the result is placed in GR *r*. If the values added satisfy the specified condition, *cond*, the word displacement is assembled from the *w* and *w1* fields, sign extended, and added to the current instruction offset plus 8 to form the target offset. The branch target, *target*, in the assembly language format is encoded in the *w* and *w1* fields.

If nullification is not specified, the following instruction is not nullified. If nullification is specified, the instruction following a taken forward branch or a failing backward branch is nullified. The ,N completer, encoded in the *n* field of the instruction, specifies nullification.

Conditions: The condition, *cond*, is any of the 32-bit add conditions shown in Table D-6 on page D-5 or any of the 64-bit add and branch conditions shown in Table D-8 on page D-6 and is encoded in the *c* and *opcode* fields of the instruction. When the PSW W-bit is 0, only the 32-bit conditions are available. Opcode 29 is used for the 32-bit non-negated add conditions (those with f = 0 in Table D-6) and opcode 2B is used for the 32-bit negated add conditions (those with f = 1 in Table D-6.) When the PSW W-bit is 1, a subset of the 32-bit and 64-bit conditions are available. Opcode 29 is used for the non-negated conditions (those with f = 0 in Table D-8) and opcode 2B is used for the negated conditions (those with f = 1 in Table D-8.) When a condition completer is not specified, the "never" condition is used. The boolean variable "cond_satisfied" in the operation section is set to 1 when the values added satisfy the specified condition and set to 0 otherwise.

Operation: GR[r] ← low_sign_ext(im5,5) + GR[r];
                 disp ← lshift(sign_ext(assemble_12(w1,w),12),2);
                 if (cond_satisfied)
                      IAOQ_Next ← IAOQ_Front + disp + 8;
                 if (n)
                      if (disp < 0)
                           PSW[N] ← !cond_satisfied;
                      else
                           PSW[N] ← cond_satisfied;

Exceptions: Taken branch trap

Format: ADDIL   i,r,r1

(7)

0A	r	im21
6	5	21

Purpose: To add the upper portion of a 32-bit immediate value to a general register.

Description: The 21-bit immediate value, *i*, is assembled, shifted left 11 bits, sign extended, added to GR *r* and placed in GR1. Overflow, if it occurs, is ignored.

Operation: GR[1] ← sign_ext(lshift(assemble_21(im21),11),32) + GR[r];

Exceptions: None

Programming Note

ADD IMMEDIATE LEFT can be used to perform a load or store with a 32-bit displacement. For example, to load a word from memory into general register *t* with a 32-bit displacement, the following sequence of assembly language code could be used:

```
ADDIL   l%literal,GRb
LDW     r%literal(0,GR1),GRt
```

Format: AND,cond   r1,r2,t

(8)

02	r2	r1	c	f	0	1	0	0	d	t
6	5	5	3	1	2	1	1	2	1	5

Purpose: To do a 64-bit, bitwise AND.

Description: GR *r1* and GR *r2* are ANDed and the result is placed in GR *t*. The following instruction is nullified if the values ANDed satisfy the specified condition, *cond*. The condition is encoded in the *c*, *d*, and *f* fields of the instruction.

Conditions: The condition is any of the 32-bit logical conditions shown in Table D-9 on page D-7 or any of the 64-bit logical conditions shown in Table D-10 on page D-7. When a condition completer is not specified, the "never" condition is used. The boolean variable "cond_satisfied" in the operation section is set when the values ANDed satisfy the specified condition.

Operation: GR[t] ← GR[r1] & GR[r2];
if (cond_satisfied) PSW[N] ← 1;

Exceptions: None

Format: ANDCM,cond   r1,r2,t

(8)	02	r2	r1	c	f	0	0	0	0	d	t
	6	5	5	3	1	2	1	1	2	1	5

Purpose: To do a 64-bit bitwise AND with complement.

Description: GR *r1* is ANDed with the one's complement of GR *r2* and the result is placed in GR *t*. The following instruction is nullified if the values ANDed satisfy the specified condition, *cond*. The condition is encoded in the *c*, *d*, and *f* fields of the instruction.

Conditions: The condition is any of the 32-bit logical conditions shown in Table D-9 on page D-7 or any of the 64-bit logical conditions shown in Table D-10 on page D-7. When a condition completer is not specified, the "never" condition is used. The boolean variable "cond_satisfied" in the operation section is set when the values ANDed satisfy the specified condition.

Operation: GR[t] ← GR[r1] & ~GR[r2];
if (cond_satisfied) PSW[N] ← 1;

Exceptions: None

Format:

B,cmplt,stack,n   target,t

(20)

3A	t/w3	w1	0/1/4/5	w2	n	w
6	5	5	3	11	1	1

Purpose: To do IA-relative branches with optional privilege level change and procedure calls with a static displacement.

Description: The word displacement is assembled from the w, w1, w2, and (when the ,L completer is specified with GR 2 as the link register) w3 fields in the instruction. The displacement is sign extended, and the result plus 8 is added to the offset of the current instruction to form the target offset.

The completer, *stack*, specifies whether the offset of the return point is pushed onto the branch target stack. If the ,L completer is specified and the ,PUSH completer is specified, either the offset of the return point or an "invalid" value is pushed onto the branch target stack. On machines that do not implement the branch target stack, the instruction executes the same as if the ,PUSH completer had not been specified.

The completer, *cmplt*, specifies whether a return link is saved, or whether a privilege-increasing GATEWAY function is performed. If the ,L completer is specified, the offset of the return point is placed in GR *t*. The return point is 4 bytes beyond the following instruction.

If the ,GATE completer is specified and the PSW C-bit is 1, the privilege level is changed to that given by the two rightmost bits of the type field in the TLB entry for the page (when the type field is greater than 3) from which the BRANCH instruction is fetched if that results in a higher privilege. If privilege is not increased, then the current privilege is used at the target. In all cases, the privilege level of the BRANCH instruction is deposited into bits 62..63 of GR *t*. The privilege change occurs at the target of the BRANCH. If the PSW C-bit is 0, the privilege level is changed to 0. An illegal instruction trap is taken if a BRANCH instruction is attempted with the ,GATE completer and the PSW B-bit is 1.

If the ,GATE completer is specified, sub-opcode 1 is used. If the ,L completer is specified and the target register is GR 2, sub-opcode 5 is used. If the ,L completer is specified, the target register is GR 2, and the ,PUSH completer is specified, sub-opcode 4 is used. Otherwise, sub-opcode 0 is used.

The variable "page_type" is set to the value of the access rights field, bits {0..2}, from the translation used to fetch the instruction. See "Access Rights Interpretation" on page 3-14.

The following instruction is nullified if the ,N completer is specified. The completer is encoded in the *n* field of the instruction. The branch target, *target*, in the assembly language format is encoded in the w, w1, w2, and (when GR 2 is the link register) w3 fields.

Operation: if (cmplt == 'GATE' && PSW[B])
        illegal_instruction_trap;
    else {
        if (cmplt == 'L' && t == GR2) {
            disp $\leftarrow$ lshift(sign_ext(assemble_22(w3,w1,w2,w),22),2)
            if(stack == 'PUSH')
                push_onto_BTS((IAOQ_Back + 4){0..61});
        }
        else
            disp $\leftarrow$ lshift(sign_ext(assemble_17(w1,w2,w),17),2);
        if (cmplt == 'GATE') {
            GR[t] $\leftarrow$ cat(GR[t]{0..61},IAOQ_Front{62..63});
            if (PSW[C]) {
                if (page_type <= 3)
                    priv $\leftarrow$ IAOQ_Front{62..63};
                else
                    priv $\leftarrow$ min(IAOQ_Front{62..63}, page_type{1..2});
            } else
                priv $\leftarrow$ 0;
        else
            priv $\leftarrow$ IAOQ_Front{62..63};
        IAOQ_Next{0..61} $\leftarrow$ (IAOQ_Front + disp + 8){0..61};
        IAOQ_Next{62..63} $\leftarrow$ priv;
        if (cmplt == 'L') {
            GR[t] $\leftarrow$ IAOQ_Back + 4;
            BNR $\leftarrow$ (IAOQ_Back + 4){0..61};
        }
        if (n) PSW[N] $\leftarrow$ 1;
    }

Exceptions: Illegal instruction trap
Taken branch trap

Notes: When the ,GATE completer is specified, the privilege information must be captured when the TLB is read for instruction fetch and that information kept for the determination of the new execution privilege.

To perform an unconditional branch without saving a link, the B,n target pseudo-operation generates a a B,L,n target,%R0 instruction with GR0 as the link register.

The CALL,n target pseudo-operation generates a B,L,n target,%R2 instruction to perform a procedure call with GR2 specified as the link register.

Restrictions: The ,PUSH completer can be used only if the ,L completer is specified and the target register is GR2.

Programming Note

It is possible for a BRANCH to promote the privilege level so that the process cannot continue executing on that page (because it violates PL2 of the TLB access rights field.) In that case, software should ensure that the BRANCH nullifies execution of the following instruction and its target should be on a page whose range of execute levels includes the new privilege level. Otherwise, an instruction memory protection trap may result.

Format: BB,cond,n   r,pos,target

(18)

30/31	p	r	c	1	d	w1	n	w
6	5	5	1	1	1	11	1	1

Purpose: To perform an IA-relative branch conditionally based on the value of a bit in a register.

Description: If the bit in GR *r* specified by *pos* satisfies the condition, *cond*, the word displacement is assembled from the *w* and *w1* fields of the instruction, sign extended, and added to the current instruction offset plus 8 to form the target offset. The branch target, *target*, in the assembly language format is encoded in the *w* and *w1* fields.

The bit position, *pos*, can either be a constant (fixed bit position, opcode 31), or can be SAR, the Shift Amount Register (CR 11) (variable bit position, opcode 30.)

With a fixed bit position, the *p* field encodes the lower 5 bits of *pos*, and the *d* field encodes either 0 or the complement of the upper bit. If a word condition is specified (either < or >=), *pos* may take on the values 0..31, and the bit tested is one of the bits in the lower word of GR *r*. For word conditions, the *d* field is 0. If a doubleword condition is specified (either *< or *>=), *pos* may take on the values 0..63, and the complement of the upper bit of *pos* is encoded in the *d* field. Any bit in the doubleword in GR *r* may be tested.

With a variable bit position, the *p* field is 0. If a word condition is specified (either < or >=), the leftmost bit of the SAR is ignored, and 32 is added to the value in the lower 5 bits. Thus, the bit tested is one of the bits in the lower word of GR *r*. If a doubleword condition is specified (either *< or *>=), the full value of the SAR is used. Any bit in the doubleword in GR *r* may be tested. For word conditions, the *d* field is 0; for doubleword conditions, the *d* field is 1.

If nullification is not specified, the following instruction is not nullified. If nullification is specified, the instruction following a taken forward branch or a failing backward branch is nullified. The ,N completer, encoded in the *n* field of the instruction, specifies nullification.

Conditions: The condition, *cond*, is any of the branch on bit conditions from Table D-15 on page D-9. The boolean variable "cond_satisfied" in the operation section is set to 1 when the bit tested satisfies the specified condition and set to 0 otherwise.

Operation: if (variable_bit_position)
        if (cond == < || cond == >=)   /* word conditions */
            shamt ← CR[11]{1..5} + 32;
        else   /* doubleword conditions */
            shamt ← CR[11];
    else
        shamt ← cat(~cp,p);
    lshift(GR[r],shamt);
    disp ← lshift(sign_ext(assemble_12(w1,w),12),2);
    if (cond_satisfied)
        IAOQ_Next ← IAOQ_Front + disp + 8;
    if (n)
        if (disp < 0)
            PSW[N] ← !cond_satisfied;
        else
            PSW[N] ← cond_satisfied;

Exceptions: Taken branch trap

Format: BE,n   wd(sr,b)
              BE,L,n   wd(sr,b),sr0,r31

(19)	38/39	b	w1	s	w2	n	w
	6	5	5	3	11	1	1

Purpose: To do procedure calls, branches and returns to another space.

Description: The word displacement, *wd*, is assembled from the *w*, *w1*, and *w2* fields in the instruction. The displacement is sign extended and added to GR *b* to form the target offset. SR *sr* (which is assembled from the *s* field of the instruction) becomes the target space.

If the ,L completer is specified, the offset of the return point is placed in GR 31 and the space of the return point is placed in SR 0. The return point is 4 bytes beyond the following instruction. If the ,L completer is specified, opcode 39 is used; otherwise opcode 38 is used.

If the two rightmost bits of GR *b* designate a lower privileged level than the current instruction, the privilege level of the target is set to that specified by the rightmost bits of GR *b*. The decrease in privilege level takes effect at the branch target.

When a BRANCH EXTERNAL is executed with the PSW C-bit 0 (code address translation is disabled) the effect on IASQ (and SR 0 if the ,L completer is specified) is not defined.

The following instruction is nullified if the ,N completer is specified. The completer is encoded in the *n* field of the instruction.

Operation: disp $\leftarrow$ lshift(sign_ext(assemble_17(w1,w2,w),17),2);
              IAOQ_Next{0..61} $\leftarrow$ (GR[b] + disp){0..61};
              if (IAOQ_Front{62..63} < GR[b]{62..63})
                   IAOQ_Next{62..63} $\leftarrow$ GR[b]{62..63};
              else
                   IAOQ_Next{62..63} $\leftarrow$ IAOQ_Front{62..63};
              IASQ_Next $\leftarrow$ SR[assemble_3(s)];
              if (cmplt == L) {
                   GR[31] $\leftarrow$ IAOQ_Back + 4;
                   SR[0] $\leftarrow$ IASQ_Back;
              }
              if (n) PSW[N] $\leftarrow$ 1;

Exceptions: Taken branch trap

Programming Note

If a taken local branch is executed following a BRANCH EXTERNAL instruction, the target's address is computed based on the value of the IASQ set by the BRANCH EXTERNAL instruction. This results in a transfer of control to possibly a meaningless location in the new space.

Format: BLR,n   x,t

(21)

3A	t	x	2	0	n	0
6	5	5	3	11	1	1

Purpose: To do IA-relative branches with a dynamic displacement and store a return link.

Description: The index from GR x is shifted left 3 bits and the result plus 8 is added to the offset of the current instruction to form the target offset. The offset of the return point is placed in GR t. The return point is 4 bytes beyond the following instruction.

The following instruction is nullified if the ,N completer is specified. The completer is encoded in the n field of the instruction.

Operation: IAOQ_Next ← IAOQ_Front + lshift(GR[x],3) + 8;
GR[t] ← IAOQ_Back + 4;
if (n) PSW[N] ← 1;

Exceptions: Taken branch trap

Programming Note

BRANCH AND LINK REGISTER with GR 0 as the link register does a IA-relative branch without saving a link. Jump tables based on the index value can be constructed using this instruction. When the jump table begins at the instruction which is located at the BLR plus 8 bytes, an index value of 0 can be used to branch to the first entry of the table.

Format: BREAK   im5,im13

(27)

00	im13	00	im5
6	13	8	5

Purpose: To cause a break instruction trap for debugging purposes.

Description: A break instruction trap occurs when this instruction is executed.

Operation: break_instruction_trap;

Exceptions: None

Notes: *im5* and *im13* can be used as parameters to the "BREAK" processing code.

Format: BV,n   x(b)

(21)

3A	b	x	6	0	n	0
6	5	5	3	11	1	1

Purpose: To do base-relative branches with a dynamic displacement in the same space.

Description: The index from GR x is shifted left 3 bits and the result is added to GR b to form the target offset.

The following instruction is nullified if the ,N completer is specified. The completer is encoded in the n field of the instruction.

If the two rightmost bits of GR b designate a lower privilege level than the current privilege level, the privilege level of the target is set to that specified by the rightmost bits of GR b. The decrease in privilege level takes effect at the branch target.

Operation: IAOQ_Next{0..61} ← (GR[b] + lshift(GR[x],3)){0..61};
if (IAOQ_Front{62..63} < GR[b]{62..63})
     IAOQ_Next{62..63} ← GR[b]{62..63};
else
     IAOQ_Next{62..63} ← IAOQ_Front{62..63};
if (n) PSW[N] ← 1;

Exceptions: Taken branch trap

Format: BVE,stack,n   (b)
BVE,L,stack,n   (b),r2

(22)

3A	b	0	6/7	1	rv	n	p
6	5	5	3	1	10	1	1

Purpose: To do base-relative branches and procedure calls to another space.

Description: Either GR *b* or the branch target stack provides the offset of the target instruction.

The completer, *stack*, specifies whether a branch target stack operation is performed. If no completer is specified, GR *b* provides the target offset and the branch target stack is not changed.

If the ,POP completer is specified and if the branch target stack is non-empty and the top entry is valid, the target offset can be provided by either GR *b* or the top entry of the branch target stack. If the ,POP completer is specified, the top entry of the branch target stack is popped. If the ,POP completer is specified and the top entry of the branch target stack is valid and does not equal the value in GR *b*, the results are undefined. On machines that do not implement the branch target stack, GR *b* provides the target offset.

If the ,L completer is specified and the ,PUSH completer is specified, either the offset of the return point or an "invalid" value is pushed onto the branch target stack. On machines that do not implement the branch target stack, the instruction executes the same as if the ,PUSH completer had not been specified.

If a *stack* completer is specified, the *p* field is 1. Otherwise the *p* field is 0.

If the ,L completer is specified, the offset of the return point is placed in GR 2. The return point is 4 bytes beyond the following instruction. The completer is encoded in the sub-opcode field of the instruction (6: no link, 7: link.) The space of the target instruction is specified implicitly by the base register. The upper two bits of GR *b* are added to 4 to select a space register which gives the target space.

The following instruction is nullified if the ,N completer is specified. The completer is encoded in the *n* field of the instruction.

If the two rightmost bits of GR *b* designate a lower privilege level than the current privilege level, then the privilege level of the target is set to that specified by the rightmost bits of GR *b*. The decrease in privilege level takes effect at the branch target.

When a BRANCH VECTORED EXTERNAL is executed with the PSW C-bit 0 (code address translation is disabled) the effects on IASQ are not defined.

Operation: if (stack == 'POP') {
$\qquad$ tmp ← pop_from_BTS();
$\qquad$ valid ← tmp{62};
$\qquad$ if (valid)
$\qquad\qquad$ IAOQ_Next{0..61} ← tmp{0..61};
$\qquad$ else
$\qquad\qquad$ IAOQ_Next{0..61} ← GR[b]{0..61};
$\qquad$ }
$\quad$ if (IAOQ_Front{62..63} < GR[b]{62..63})
$\qquad$ IAOQ_Next{62..63} ← GR[b]{62..63};
$\quad$ else
$\qquad$ IAOQ_Next{62..63} ← IAOQ_Front{62..63};
$\quad$ if (cmplt == L) {
$\qquad$ GR[2] ← IAOQ_Back + 4;
$\qquad$ BNR ← (IAOQ_Back + 4){0..61};
$\qquad$ if (stack == 'PUSH')
$\qquad\qquad$ push_onto_BTS((IAOQ_Back + 4){0..61});
$\quad$ }
$\quad$ IASQ_Next ← space_select(0, GR[b],LONG_DISP);
$\quad$ if (n) PSW[N] ← 1;

Exceptions: Taken branch trap.

Notes: The CALL,n (b) pseudo-operation generates a BVE,L,n (b),%R2 instruction to perform an indirect procedure call with GR2 specified as the link register.

The RET,n pseudo-operation generates a BVE,n (%R2) instruction to perform a procedure return.

Format: CLDD,uid,cmplt,cc   d(s,b),t

(41)

0B	b	im5	s	a	1	cc	0	uid	m	t
6	5	5	2	1	1	2	1	3	1	5

(39)

0B	b	x	s	u	0	cc	0	uid	m	t
6	5	5	2	1	1	2	1	3	1	5

Purpose: To load a doubleword into a coprocessor register.

Description: The aligned doubleword at the effective address is loaded into register t of the coprocessor identified by uid. The offset is formed as the sum of a base register, b, and either an index register, x (Format 39), or a displacement d (Format 41.) The displacement is encoded into the immediate field. Optional base modification can also be performed.

The completer, *cmplt*, determines whether the offset is the base register, or the base register plus the index register or displacement. The completer also specifies base register modification, optional index prescaling, and ordering constraints (see Table H-3 on page H-8, and Table H-1 on page H-4 for the assembly language completer mnemonics.) The completer, *cc*, specifies the cache control hint (see Table 6-7 on page 6-10.)

For short displacements, a one in the m field specifies base modification, and the a field encodes whether pre-modification (a=1), or post-modification (a=0) is performed. For indexed loads, a one in the m field specifies base modification, and a one in the u field specifies index prescaling.

Operation: if (indexed_load)   /* indexed (Format 39)*/
         switch (cmplt) {
            case S:
            case SM: dx ← lshift(GR[x],3);
                        break;
            case M:
            default: dx ← GR[x];
                        break;
         }
       } else   /* short displacement */
         dx ← low_sign_ext(im5,5);   /* (Format 41) */
       space ← space_select(s,GR[b],format);
       switch (cmplt) {
            case MB: offset ← GR[b] + dx;
                        GR[b] ← GR[b] + dx;
                        break;
            case MA:
            case M:
            case SM: offset ← GR[b];
                        GR[b] ← GR[b] + dx;
                        break;
            default: offset ← GR[b] + dx;
                        break;
       }
       send_to_copr(uid,t);
       CPR[uid][t] ← mem_load(space,offset,0,63,cc);
       if (cmplt == O)
         enforce_ordered_load;

Exceptions: Assist exception trap   Unaligned data reference trap
           Data TLB miss fault/data page fault   Page reference trap
           Data memory access rights trap   Data memory protection ID trap
           Assist emulation trap

Restrictions: If the completer O is specified, the displacement must be 0.

Format: CLDW,uid,cmplt,cc   x|d(s,b),t

(41)

09	b	im5	s	a	1	cc	0	uid	m	t
6	5	5	2	1	1	2	1	3	1	5

(39)

09	b	x	s	u	0	cc	0	uid	m	t
6	5	5	2	1	1	2	1	3	1	5

Purpose: To load a word into a coprocessor register.

Description: The aligned word at the effective address is loaded into register t of the coprocessor identified by *uid*. The offset is formed as the sum of a base register, b, and either an index register, x (Format 39), or a displacement d (Format 41.) The displacement is encoded into the immediate field. Optional base modification can also be performed.

The completer, *cmplt*, determines whether the offset is the base register, or the base register plus the index register or displacement. The completer also specifies base register modification, optional index prescaling, and ordering constraints (see Table H-3 on page H-8, and Table H-1 on page H-4 for the assembly language completer mnemonics.) The completer, *cc*, specifies the cache control hint (see Table 6-7 on page 6-10.)

For short displacements, a one in the m field specifies base modification, and the a field encodes whether pre-modification ($a=1$), or post-modification ($a=0$) is performed. For indexed loads, a one in the m field specifies base modification, and a one in the u field specifies index prescaling.

Operation: if (indexed_load)   /* indexed (Format 39)*/
                        switch (cmplt) {
                            case S:
                            case SM: dx ← lshift(GR[x],2);
                                          break;
                            case M:
                            default: dx ← GR[x];
                                          break;
                        }
                    } else   /* short displacement */
                        dx ← low_sign_ext(im5,5);   /* (Format 41) */
                    space ← space_select(s,GR[b],format);
                    switch (cmplt) {
                        case MB: offset ← GR[b] + dx;
                                      GR[b] ← GR[b] + dx;
                                      break;
                        case MA:
                        case M:
                        case SM: offset ← GR[b];
                                      GR[b] ← GR[b] + dx;
                                      break;
                        default: offset ← GR[b] + dx;
                                      break;
                    }
                    send_to_copr(uid,t);
                    CPR[uid][t] ← mem_load(space,offset,0,31,cc);
                    if (cmplt == O)
                        enforce_ordered_load;

Exceptions: Assist exception trap   Unaligned data reference trap
                  Data TLB miss fault/data page fault   Page reference trap
                  Data memory access rights trap   Assist emulation trap
                  Data memory protection ID trap

Restrictions: If the completer O is specified, the displacement must be 0.

Clear Branch Target Stack

CLRBTS

Format: CLRBTS

(23)

3A	0	0	2	0	0	1	0	1
6	5	5	3	1	9	1	1	1

Purpose: To clear the branch target stack.

Description: The branch target stack is cleared, either by making it empty or by invalidating all entries.

If this instruction is nullified, the results are undefined.

This instruction is executed as a NOP on machines that do not implement the branch target stack.

Operation: clear_BTS();

Exceptions: none

Format: CMPB,cond,n   r1,r2,target

(17)

20/22/27/2F	r2	r1	c	w1	n	w
6	5	5	3	11	1	1

Purpose: To compare two values and perform an IA-relative branch conditionally based on the values compared.

Description: GR *r1* is compared with GR *r2*. If the values compared satisfy the specified condition, *cond*, the word displacement is assembled from the *w* and *w1* fields, sign extended, and added to the current instruction offset plus 8 to form the target offset. The branch target, *target*, in the assembly language format is encoded in the *w* and *w1* fields.

If nullification is not specified, the following instruction is not nullified. If nullification is specified, the instruction following a taken forward branch or a failing backward branch is nullified. The ,N completer, encoded in the *n* field of the instruction, specifies nullification.

Conditions: The condition, *cond*, can be any of the 32-bit compare or subtract conditions shown in Table D-3 on page D-4 or any of the 64-bit compare or subtract conditions shown in Table D-4 on page D-4 and is encoded in the *c* and *opcode* fields of the instruction. Opcode 20 is used for the 32-bit non-negated conditions (those with f = 0 in Table D-3), opcode 22 for the 32-bit negated conditions (those with f = 1 in Table D-3), opcode 27 for the 64-bit non-negated conditions (those with f = 0 in Table D-4), and opcode 2F for the 64-bit negated conditions (those with f = 1in Table D-4.) When a condition completer is not specified, the "never" condition is used. The boolean variable "cond_satisfied" in the operation section is set to 1 when the values compared satisfy the specified condition and set to 0 otherwise.

Operation: GR[r1] + ~GR[r2] + 1;
disp ← lshift(sign_ext(assemble_12(w1,w),12),2);
if (cond_satisfied)
     IAOQ_Next ← IAOQ_Front + disp + 8;
if (n)
     if (disp < 0)
          PSW[N] ← !cond_satisfied;
     else
          PSW[N] ← cond_satisfied;

Exceptions: Taken branch trap

Format: CMPCLR,cond   r1,r2,t

(8)

02	r2	r1	c	f	2	0	0	2	d	t
6	5	5	3	1	2	1	1	2	1	5

Purpose: To compare two registers, set a register to 0, and conditionally nullify the following instruction, based on the result of the comparison.

Description: GR *r1* and GR *r2* are compared and GR *t* is set to zero. The following instruction is nullified if the values compared satisfy the specified condition, *cond*. The condition is encoded in the *c*, *d*, and *f* fields of the instruction.

Conditions: The condition is any of the 32-bit compare or subtract conditions shown in Table D-3 on page D-4 or any of the 64-bit compare or subtract conditions shown in Table D-4 on page D-4. When a condition completer is not specified, the "never" condition is used. The boolean variable "cond_satisfied" in the operation section is set when the values compared satisfy the specified condition.

Operation: GR[r1] + ~GR[r2] + 1;
GR[t] ← 0;
if (cond_satisfied) PSW[N] ← 1;

Exceptions: None

Programming Note

COMPARE AND CLEAR can be used to produce the logical value of the result of a comparison (assuming false is represented by 0 and true by 1) in a register. The following example will set *ra* to 1 if *rb* and *rc* are equal, and to 0 if they are not equal:

    CMPCLR,<>   rb,rc,ra
    LDO   1(0),ra

Format: CMPIB,cond,n   i,r,target

(17)	21/23/3B	r	im5	c	w1	n	w
	6	5	5	3	11	1	1

Purpose: To compare two values and perform an IA-relative branch conditionally based on the values compared.

Description: The sign-extended immediate value *im5* is compared with GR *r*. If the values compared satisfy the specified condition, *cond*, the word displacement is assembled from the *w* and *w1* fields, sign extended, and added to the current instruction offset plus 8 to form the target offset. The branch target, *target*, in the assembly language format is encoded in the *w* and *w1* fields.

If nullification is not specified, the following instruction is not nullified. If nullification is specified, the instruction following a taken forward branch or a failing backward branch is nullified. The ,N completer, encoded in the *n* field of the instruction, specifies nullification.

Conditions: The condition, *cond*, can be any of the 32-bit compare or subtract conditions shown in Table D-3 on page D-4 or any of the 64-bit compare immediate and branch conditions shown in Table D-5 on page D-5 and is encoded in the *c* and *opcode* fields of the instruction. Opcode 21 is used for the 32-bit non-negated conditions (those with f = 0 in Table D-3), opcode 23 is used for the 32-bit negated conditions (those with f = 1 in Table D-3), and opcode 3B is used for the 64-bit conditions (those in Table D-5.) When a condition completer is not specified, the "never" condition is used. The boolean variable "cond_satisfied" in the operation section is set to 1 when the values compared satisfy the specified condition and set to 0 otherwise.

Operation: low_sign_ext(im5,5) + ~GR[r] + 1;
disp ← lshift(sign_ext(assemble_12(w1,w),12),2);
if (cond_satisfied)
        IAOQ_Next ← IAOQ_Front + disp + 8;
if (n)
        if (disp < 0)
                PSW[N] ← !cond_satisfied;
        else
                PSW[N] ← cond_satisfied;

Exceptions: Taken branch trap

Format: CMPICLR,cond   i,r,t

(9)

24	r	t	c	f	d	im11
6	5	5	3	1	1	11

Purpose: To compare an immediate value with the contents of a register, set a register to 0, and conditionally nullify the following instruction.

Description: The sign-extended immediate and GR r are compared and GR t is set to zero. The immediate value is encoded into the *im11* field. The following instruction is nullified if the values compared satisfy the specified condition, *cond*. The condition is encoded in the c, d, and f fields of the instruction.

Conditions: The condition is any of the 32-bit compare or subtract conditions shown in Table D-3 on page D-4 or any of the 64-bit compare or subtract conditions shown in Table D-4 on page D-4. When a condition completer is not specified, the "never" condition is used. The boolean variable "cond_satisfied" in the operation section is set when the values compared satisfy the specified condition.

Operation: low_sign_ext(im11,11) + ~GR[r] + 1;
                  GR[t] ← 0;
                  if (cond_satisfied) PSW[N] ← 1;

Exceptions: None

Format: COPR,uid,sop,n

(38)

0C	sop1	uid	n	sop2
6	17	3	1	5

Purpose: To invoke a coprocessor unit operation.

Description: The coprocessor operation code *sop* (assembled from the *sop1* and *sop2* fields) is sent to the coprocessor identified by *uid* and the indicated operation is performed. If nullification is specified and the coprocessor condition is satisfied, the following instruction is nullified.

Operation: sop ← cat(sop1,sop2);
coprocessor_op(uid,sop,n,IAOQ_Front{30..31});
if (n && coprocessor_condition(uid,sop,n))
        PSW[N] ← 1;

Exceptions: Assist emulation trap   Assist exception trap

Notes: The COPROCESSOR OPERATION instruction is used to implement the IDENTIFY COPROCESSOR pseudo-operation. This operation places an identification number from the coprocessor *uid* into coprocessor register 0. This value is implementation dependent and is useful for configuration, diagnostic, and error recovery.

Each implementation must choose an identification number that identifies the version of the coprocessor. The values all zeros and all ones are reserved. An assist exception trap is not allowed and this instruction must be implemented by all coprocessors with unit identifiers 4 through 7. Unit identifiers 0 and 2 have a uid-specific sequence to obtain the identification number.

The format of the identification number for the floating-point coprocessor is described in "Floating-Point Status Register" on page 8-8.

The IDENTIFY COPROCESSOR pseudo-operation is coded as follows: COPR,uid,0

Coprocessor Store Doubleword   CSTD

Format: CSTD,uid,cmplt,cc   r,xld(s,b)

(42)

0B	b	im5	s	a	1	cc	1	uid	m	r
6	5	5	2	1	1	2	1	3	1	5

(40)

0B	b	x	s	u	0	cc	1	uid	m	r
6	5	5	2	1	1	2	1	3	1	5

Purpose: To store a doubleword from a coprocessor register.

Description: Register r of the coprocessor identified by uid is stored in the aligned doubleword at the effective address. The offset is formed as the sum of a base register, b, and either an index register, x (Format 40), or a displacement d (Format 42.) The displacement is encoded into the immediate field. Optional base modification can also be performed.

The completer, $cmplt$, determines whether the offset is the base register, or the base register plus the index register or displacement. The completer also specifies base register modification, optional index prescaling, and ordering constraints (see Table H-3 on page H-8, and Table H-1 on page H-4 for the assembly language completer mnemonics.) The completer, cc, specifies the cache control hint (see Table 6-8 on page 6-10.)

For short displacements, a one in the m field specifies base modification, and the a field encodes whether pre-modification ($a=1$), or post-modification ($a=0$) is performed. For indexed stores, a one in the m field specifies base modification, and a one in the u field specifies index prescaling.

Operation: if (indexed_store)   /* indexed (Format 40)*/
        switch (cmplt) {
            case S:
            case SM: dx ← lshift(GR[x],3);
                            break;

            case M:
            default: dx ← GR[x];
                            break;
        }
    } else   /* short displacement */
        dx ← low_sign_ext(im5,5);   /* (Format 42) */
    space ← space_select(s,GR[b],format);
    if (cmplt == O)
        enforce_ordered_store;
    switch (cmplt) {
        case MB: offset ← GR[b] + dx;
                    GR[b] ← GR[b] + dx;
                    break;

        case MA:
        case M:
        case SM: offset ← GR[b];
                    GR[b] ← GR[b] + dx;
                    break;
        default: offset ← GR[b] + dx;
                    break;
    }
    send_to_copr(uid,r);
    mem_store(space,offset,0,63,cc,CPR[uid][r]);

Exceptions: Assist exception trap   TLB dirty bit trap
                  Data TLB miss fault/data page fault Page reference trap
                  Data memory access rights trap   Unaligned data reference trap
                  Data memory protection ID trap   Assist emulation trap

Restrictions: If the completer O is specified, the displacement must be 0.

Format: CSTW,uid,cmplt,cc   r,x|d(s,b)

(42)

09	b	im5	s	a	1	cc	1	uid	m	r
6	5	5	2	1	1	2	1	3	1	5

(40)

09	b	x	s	u	0	cc	1	uid	m	r
6	5	5	2	1	1	2	1	3	1	5

Purpose: To store a word from a coprocessor register.

Description: Register *r* of the coprocessor identified by *uid* is stored in the aligned word at the effective address. The offset is formed as the sum of a base register, *b*, and either an index register, *x* (Format 40), or a displacement *d* (Format 42.) The displacement is encoded into the immediate field. Optional base modification can also be performed.

The completer, *cmplt*, determines whether the offset is the base register, or the base register plus the index register or displacement. The completer also specifies base register modification, optional index prescaling, and ordering constraints (see Table H-3 on page H-8, and Table H-1 on page H-4 for the assembly language completer mnemonics.) The completer, *cc*, specifies the cache control hint (see Table 6-8 on page 6-10.)

For short displacements, a one in the *m* field specifies base modification, and the *a* field encodes whether pre-modification (*a*=1), or post-modification (*a*=0) is performed. For indexed stores, a one in the *m* field specifies base modification, and a one in the *u* field specifies index prescaling.

Operation: if (indexed_store)   /* indexed (Format 40)*/

```
            switch (cmplt) {
                case S:
                case SM:        dx ← lshift(GR[x],2);
                                break;

                case M:
                default:        dx ← GR[x];
                                break;

            }
        } else                                          /* short displacement */
            dx ← low_sign_ext(im5,5);                   /* (Format 42) */
        space ← space_select(s,GR[b],format);
        if (cmplt == O)
            enforce_ordered_store;
        switch (cmplt) {
            case MB:        offset ← GR[b] + dx;
                            GR[b] ← GR[b] + dx;
                            break;

            case MA:
            case M:
            case SM:        offset ← GR[b];
                            GR[b] ← GR[b] + dx;
                            break;

            default:        offset ← GR[b] + dx;
                            break;

        }
        send_to_copr(uid,r);
         mem_store(space,offset,0,31,cc,CPR[uid][r]);
```

Exceptions:

Assist exception trap	TLB dirty bit trap
Data TLB miss fault/data page fault	Page reference trap
Data memory access rights trap	Unaligned data reference trap
Data memory protection ID trap	Assist emulation trap

Restrictions: If the completer _O_ is specified, the displacement must be 0.

Format: DCOR,cmplt,cond   r,t

(8)

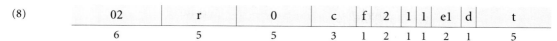

02	r	0	c	f	2	1	1	e1	d	t
6	5	5	3	1	2	1	1	2	1	5

Purpose: To separately correct the 16 BCD digits of the result of an addition or subtraction.

Description: A decimal correction value, computed from the 4-bit carries in the PSW C/B bits, is combined with GR r, and the result is placed in GR t. The correction can be either an intermediate correction (*cmplt* == I), which leaves the result pre-biased, or a final correction (no *cmplt*), which removes the pre-bias. This is encoded in the *e1* field (*e1*=3 for intermediate correction, *e1*=2 for final correction.)

For intermediate correction, every digit of GR r corresponding to a bit which is 1 in the PSW C/B-bits has 6 added to it. For final correction, every digit of GR r corresponding to a bit which is 0 in the PSW C/B-bits has 6 subtracted from it.

The following instruction is nullified if the result of the operation satisfies the specified condition *cond*. The condition is encoded in the *c*, *d*, and *f* fields of the instruction.

Conditions: The condition *cond* is any of the 32-bit unit conditions shown in Table D-11 on page D-8 or any of the 64-bit unit conditions shown in Table D-12 on page D-8. When a condition completer is not specified, the "never" condition is used. The boolean variable "cond_satisfied" in the operation section is set when the result of the operation satisfies the specified condition.

Operation: if (cmplt == I)

        GR[t] ← GR[r] + cat(
           0x6*PSW[C/B]{0}, 0x6*PSW[C/B]{1},
           0x6*PSW[C/B]{2}, 0x6*PSW[C/B]{3},
           0x6*PSW[C/B]{4}, 0x6*PSW[C/B]{5},
           0x6*PSW[C/B]{6}, 0x6*PSW[C/B]{7},
           0x6*PSW[C/B]{8}, 0x6*PSW[C/B]{9},
           0x6*PSW[C/B]{10}, 0x6*PSW[C/B]{11},
           0x6*PSW[C/B]{12}, 0x6*PSW[C/B]{13},
           0x6*PSW[C/B]{14}, 0x6*PSW[C/B]{15});

    else

        GR[t] ← GR[r] - cat(
           0x6*(1 - PSW[C/B]{0}), 0x6*(1 - PSW[C/B]{1}),
           0x6*(1 - PSW[C/B]{2}), 0x6*(1 - PSW[C/B]{3}),
           0x6*(1 - PSW[C/B]{4}), 0x6*(1 - PSW[C/B]{5}),
           0x6*(1 - PSW[C/B]{6}), 0x6*(1 - PSW[C/B]{7}),
           0x6*(1 - PSW[C/B]{8}), 0x6*(1 - PSW[C/B]{9}),
           0x6*(1 - PSW[C/B]{10}), 0x6*(1 - PSW[C/B]{11}),
           0x6*(1 - PSW[C/B]{12}), 0x6*(1 - PSW[C/B]{13}),
           0x6*(1 - PSW[C/B]{14}), 0x6*(1 - PSW[C/B]{15}));

    if (cond_satisfied) PSW[N] ← 1;

Exceptions: None

Programming Note

DECIMAL CORRECT can be used to take the sum of 64-bit BCD values. *ra*, *rb*, *rc*, and *rd* each contain a 64-bit BCD value and *rt* will hold the result at the end of the sequence. The UADDCM operation is used to pre-bias the value in *ra* in order to perform BCD arithmetic. The DCOR,I operations between the ADD operations are used to re-adjust the BCD bias of the result. The final DCOR operation is used to remove the bias and leave the value in *rt* in BCD format. For the following example, the register *nines* contains the value 0x99999999 99999999.

UADDCM	ra,nines,rt	; pre-bias first operand
ADD	rt,rb,rt	; add in the next value
DCOR,I	rt,rt	; correct result, retaining bias
ADD	rt,rc,rt	; add in the next value
DCOR,I	rt,rt	; correct result, retaining bias
ADD	rt,rd,rt	; add in the next value
DCOR	rt,rt	; final correction

Format: DEPD,cmplt,cond   r,pos,len,t

(13)

35	t	r	c	0	nz	1	cl	0	clen
6	5	5	3	2	1	1	1	3	5

(16)

3C	t	r	c	cl	cp	nz	cpos	clen
6	5	5	3	1	1	1	5	5

Purpose: To deposit a value into a register at a fixed or variable position, and conditionally nullify the following instruction.

Description: A right-justified field from GR *r* is deposited (merged) into GR *t*. The field begins at the bit position given by *pos* and extends *len* bits to the left. The remainder of GR *t* is optionally zeroed or left unchanged.

The bit position, *pos*, can either be a constant (specifying a fixed deposit), or can be SAR, the Shift Amount Register (CR 11) (specifying a variable deposit.) Format 13 is used for variable deposits; Format 16 is used for fixed deposits. For variable deposits, if the deposited field extends beyond the leftmost bit, it is truncated and the higher bits are ignored. For fixed deposits, it is an undefined operation for the field to extend beyond the leftmost bit.

The completer, *cmplt*, determines whether or not the target register is zeroed before the field is deposited into it. (Table 7-1 defines the assembly language completer mnemonics.) This is encoded in the *nz* field of the instruction, with 0 indicating that the register is zeroed and 1 indicating that it is not.

Table 7-1. Deposit Instruction Completers

cmplt	Description	nz
<none>	value is deposited into the old value of the target register	1
Z	value is deposited into a field of zeros	0

The following diagram illustrates a fixed deposit of a 50-bit field at bit position 56. The instruction is: DEPD   r,56,50,t.

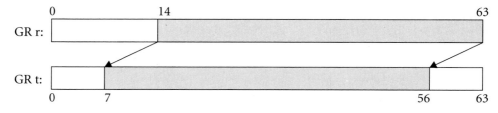

The length *len* in the assembly language format is encoded into the *cl* and *clen* fields. For fixed deposits, the bit position *pos* in the assembly language format is represented by cat(*cp*,*cpos*) in the machine instruction, whose value is 63–*pos*.

The following instruction is nullified if the result of the operation satisfies the specified condition, *cond*. The condition is encoded in the *c* field of the instruction.

Conditions: The condition is any of the 64-bit extract/deposit conditions shown in Table D-14 on page D-9. When a condition completer is not specified, the "never" condition is used. The boolean variable "cond_satisfied" in the operation section is set when the result of the operation satisfies the specified condition.

Operation:
```
len ← assemble_6(cl,clen)
if (fixed_deposit) {                                          /* (Format 16) */
      if (pos >= len–1)
            tpos ← pos;
      else
            undefined;
} else                                                        /* (Format 13) */
      tpos ← CR[11];
if (cmplt == Z)                                              /* nz=0 */
    GR[t] ← 0;
if (tpos–len+1< 0)                          /* field extends beyond leftmost bit */
    GR[t]{0..tpos} ← GR[r]{63–tpos..63};
else
    GR[t]{tpos–len+1..tpos} ← GR[r]{64–len..63};
if (cond_satisfied) PSW[N] ← 1;
```

Exceptions: None

Restrictions: Since for fixed deposits, the deposited field is fully specified by *len* and *pos*, it is an undefined operation if the field extends beyond the leftmost bit.

Notes: The SHLD,cond r,sa,t pseudo-operation generates a DEPD,Z,cond r,63-sa,64-sa,t instruction to perform a shift left by sa bits on the doubleword in general register r.

Format: DEPDI,cmplt,cond   i,pos,len,t

(13)

35	t	im5	c	2	nz	1	cl	0	clen
6	5	5	3	2	1	1	1	3	5

(16)

3D	t	im5	c	cl	cp	nz	cpos	clen
6	5	5	3	1	1	1	5	5

Purpose: To deposit an immediate value into a register at a fixed or variable position, and conditionally nullify the following instruction.

Description: A right-justified field from the sign-extended immediate *i* is deposited (merged) into GR *t*. The field begins at the bit position given by *pos* and extends *len* bits to the left. The remainder of GR *t* is optionally zeroed or left unchanged.

The bit position, *pos*, can either be a constant (specifying a fixed deposit), or can be SAR, the Shift Amount Register (CR 11) (specifying a variable deposit.) Format 13 is used for variable deposits; Format 16 is used for fixed deposits. For variable deposits, if the deposited field extends beyond the leftmost bit, it is truncated and the higher bits are ignored. For fixed deposits, it is an undefined operation for the field to extend beyond the leftmost bit.

The completer, *cmplt*, determines whether or not the target register is zeroed before the field is deposited into it (see Table 7-1 on page 7-37 for the assembly language completer mnemonics.) This is encoded in the *nz* field of the instruction, with 0 indicating that the register is zeroed and 1indicating that it is not.

The following diagram illustrates a fixed deposit of the value 0x9 into a 50-bit field at bit position 56. The instruction is: DEPDI   0x9,56,50,t.

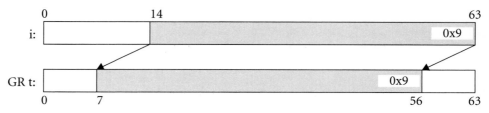

The length *len* in the assembly language format is encoded into the *cl* and *clen* fields. For fixed deposits, the bit position *pos* in the assembly language format is represented by cat(*cp,cpos*) in the machine instruction, whose value is 63–*pos*. The immediate is encoded in the *im5* field of the instruction.

The following instruction is nullified if the result of the operation satisfies the specified condition, *cond*. The condition is encoded in the *c* field of the instruction.

Conditions: The condition is any of the 64-bit extract/deposit conditions shown in Table D-14 on page D-9. When a condition completer is not specified, the "never" condition is used. The boolean variable "cond_satisfied" in the operation section is set when the result of the operation satisfies the specified condition.

Operation:

```
len  ← assemble_6(cl,clen)
ival ← low_sign_ext(im5,5);
if (fixed_deposit) {                                          /* (Format 16) */
     if (pos >= len–1)
          tpos  ← pos;
     else
          undefined;
} else                                                         /* (Format 13) */
     tpos  ← CR[11];
if (cmplt == Z)                                                /* nz=0 */
     GR[t]  ← 0;
if (tpos–len+1< 0)                              /* field extends beyond leftmost bit */
     GR[t]{0..tpos}  ← ival{63–tpos..63};
else
     GR[t]{tpos–len+1..tpos}  ← ival{64–len..63};
if (cond_satisfied) PSW[N]  ← 1;
```

Exceptions: None

Restrictions: Since for fixed deposits, the deposited field is fully specified by *len* and *pos*, it is an undefined operation if the field extends beyond the leftmost bit.

Format: DEPW,cmplt,cond   r,pos,len,t

(13)

35	t	r	c	0	nz	0	0	0	clen
6	5	5	3	2	1	1	1	3	5

(16)

35	t	r	c	0	1	nz	cpos	clen
6	5	5	3	1	1	1	5	5

Purpose: To deposit a value into the rightmost 32 bits of a register at a fixed or variable position, and conditionally nullify the following instruction.

Description: A right-justified field from GR r is deposited (merged) into the rightmost 32 bits of GR t. The field begins at the bit position given by $pos+32$ and extends len bits to the left. The remainder of GR t is optionally zeroed or left unchanged. The leftmost 32 bits of GR t are undefined.

The bit position, pos, can either be a constant (specifying a fixed deposit), or can be SAR, the Shift Amount Register (CR 11) (specifying a variable deposit.) Format 13 is used for variable deposits; Format 16 is used for fixed deposits. For variable deposits, the leftmost bit of the SAR is ignored, and 32 is added to the value in the lower 5 bits. For fixed deposits, 32 is added to the pos value in the instruction. For variable deposits, if the deposited field extends beyond the leftmost bit (of the rightmost 32), it is truncated and the higher bits are ignored. For fixed deposits, it is an undefined operation for the field to extend beyond the leftmost bit (of the rightmost 32.)

The completer, $cmplt$, determines whether or not the target register is zeroed before the field is deposited into it (see Table 7-1 on page 7-37 for the assembly language completer mnemonics.) This is encoded in the nz field of the instruction, with 0 indicating that the register is zeroed and 1indicating that it is not.

The following diagram illustrates a deposit of a 10-bit field when the Shift Amount Register contains the value 24. The instruction is: DEPW   r,sar,10,t.

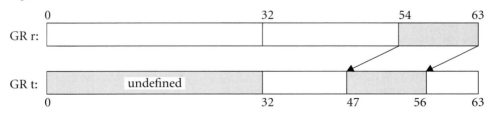

The length len in the assembly language format is encoded into the $clen$ field. For fixed deposits, the bit position pos in the assembly language format is represented by $cpos$ in the machine instruction, whose value is $31-pos$.

The following instruction is nullified if the result of the operation satisfies the specified condition, *cond*. The condition is encoded in the *c* field of the instruction.

Conditions: The condition is any of the 32-bit extract/deposit conditions shown in Table D-13 on page D-9. When a condition completer is not specified, the "never" condition is used. The boolean variable "cond_satisfied" in the operation section is set when the result of the operation satisfies the specified condition.

Operation:
```
len ← assemble_6(0,clen);
if (fixed_deposit) {                                          /* (Format 16) */
    if (pos >= len−1)
        tpos ← pos + 32;
    else
        undefined;
} else                                                        /* (Format 13) */
    tpos ← CR[11]{1..5} + 32;
if (cmplt == Z)                                               /* nz=0 */
    GR[t]{32..63} ← 0;
if (tpos−len+1< 32)                       /* field extends beyond leftmost bit */
    GR[t]{32..tpos} ← GR[r]{95−tpos..63};
else
    GR[t]{tpos−len+1..tpos} ← GR[r]{64−len..63};
GR[t]{0..31} ← undefined;
if (cond_satisfied) PSW[N] ← 1;
```

Exceptions: None

Restrictions: Since for fixed deposits, the deposited field is fully specified by *len* and *pos*, it is an undefined operation if the field extends beyond the leftmost bit (of the rightmost 32.)

Notes: The SHLW,cond r,sa,t pseudo-operation generates a DEPW,Z,cond r,31-sa,32-sa,t instruction to perform a shift left by sa bits on the word in general register r.

Format: DEPWI,cmplt,cond   i,pos,len,t

(13)

35	t	im5	c	2	nz	0	0	0	clen
6	5	5	3	2	1	1	1	3	5

(16)

35	t	im5	c	1	1	nz	cpos	clen
6	5	5	3	1	1	1	5	5

Purpose: To deposit an immediate value into the rightmost 32 bits of a register at a fixed or variable position, and conditionally nullify the following instruction.

Description: A right-justified field from the sign-extended immediate *i* is deposited (merged) into the rightmost 32 bits of GR *t*. The field begins at the bit position given by *pos*+32 and extends *len* bits to the left. The remainder of GR *t* is optionally zeroed or left unchanged. The leftmost 32 bits of GR *t* are undefined.

The bit position, *pos*, can either be a constant (specifying a fixed deposit), or can be SAR, the Shift Amount Register (CR 11) (specifying a variable deposit.) Format 13 is used for variable deposits; Format 16 is used for fixed deposits. For variable deposits, the leftmost bit of the SAR is ignored, and 32 is added to the value in the lower 5 bits. For fixed deposits, 32 is added to the *pos* value in the instruction. For variable deposits, if the deposited field extends beyond the leftmost bit (of the rightmost 32), it is truncated and the higher bits are ignored. For fixed deposits, it is an undefined operation for the field to extend beyond the leftmost bit (of the rightmost 32.)

The completer, *cmplt*, determines whether or not the target register is zeroed before the field is deposited into it (Table 7-1 on page 7-37 for the assembly language completer mnemonics.) This is encoded in the *nz* field of the instruction, with 0 indicating that the register is zeroed and 1indicating that it is not.

The following diagram illustrates a deposit of the value 0x9 into a 10-bit field when the Shift Amount Register contains the value 24. The instruction is: DEPWI   0x9,sar,10,t.

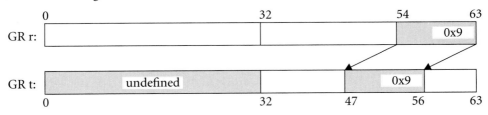

The length *len* in the assembly language format is encoded into the *clen* field. For fixed deposits, the bit position *pos* in the assembly language format is represented by *cpos* in the machine instruction, whose value is 31–*pos*. The immediate is encoded in the *im5* field of the instruction.

The following instruction is nullified if the result of the operation satisfies the specified condition, *cond*. The condition is encoded in the *c* field of the instruction.

Conditions: The condition is any of the 32-bit extract/deposit conditions shown in Table D-13 on page D-9. When a condition completer is not specified, the "never" condition is used. The boolean variable "cond_satisfied" in the operation section is set when the result of the operation satisfies the specified condition.

Operation:
```
len ← assemble_6(0,clen);
ival ← low_sign_ext(im5,5);
if (fixed_deposit) {              /* (Format 16) */
    if (pos >= len−1)
        tpos ← pos + 32;
    else
        undefined;
} else                                                    /* (Format 13) */
    tpos ← CR[11]{1..5} + 32;
if (cmplt == Z)                                           /* nz=0 */
    GR[t]{32..63} ← 0;
if (tpos−len+1< 32)                       /* field extends beyond leftmost bit */
    GR[t]{32..tpos} ← ival{95−tpos..63};
else
    GR[t]{tpos−len+1..tpos} ← ival{64−len..63};
GR[t]{0..31} ← undefined;
if (cond_satisfied) PSW[N] ← 1;
```

Exceptions: None

Restrictions: Since for fixed deposits, the deposited field is fully specified by *len* and *pos*, it is an undefined operation if the field extends beyond the leftmost bit (of the rightmost 32.)

Format: DIAG   i

(28)	05	im26
	6	26

Purpose: To provide implementation-dependent operations for system initialization, reconfiguration, and diagnostic purposes.

Description: The immediate value in the assembly language is encoded in the *im26* field of the instruction. Refer to the hardware reference manual for the definition on a particular machine implementation.

Operation: if (priv != 0)
         privileged_operation_trap;
      else
         implementation_dependent;

Exceptions: Privileged operation trap
      Implementation-dependent.

Restrictions: This instruction may be executed only at the most privileged level.

Notes: Since the DIAG instruction is privileged, a privileged operation trap will result from unprivileged diagnostic software executing DIAG. The trap could invoke an emulator which would allow the unprivileged software access to the required unprivileged implementation-dependent resources.

Divide Step   DS

Format: DS,cond   r1,r2,t

(8)	02	r2	r1	c	f	1	0	0	1	0	t
	6	5	5	3	1	2	1	1	2	1	5

Purpose: To provide the primitive operation for integer division.

Description: This instruction performs a single-bit non-restoring divide step and produces a set of result conditions. It calculates one bit of the quotient when a 32-bit value in GR *r1* is divided by a 32-bit value in GR *r2* and leaves the partial remainder in GR *t*. The quotient bit is PSW C/B{8}. The carry/borrow bits in the PSW are updated. The variable "carry_borrows" in the operation section captures the 4-bit carries resulting from the single-bit divide operation.

The following instruction is nullified if the result of the operation satisfies the specified condition, *cond*. The condition is encoded in the *c* and *f* fields of the instruction.

For this instruction, signed overflow condition means that the bit shifted out of the lower 32 bits differs from the leftmost bit of the lower 32 bits following the shift or an ordinary 32-bit signed overflow occurred during the addition or subtraction. Unsigned overflow means that the bit shifted out of the lower 32 bits is 1 or that an ordinary 32-bit unsigned overflow occurred during the addition or subtraction. The conditions take on special interpretations since the shift operation participates in overflow determination.

Conditions: The condition is any of the 32-bit compare or subtract conditions shown in Table D-3 on page D-4. When a condition completer is not specified, the "never" condition is used. The boolean variable "cond_satisfied" in the operation section is set when the result of the operation satisfies the specified condition.

Operation: if (PSW[V])
        GR[t] ← cat(lshift(GR[r1],1),PSW[C/B]{8}) + ~GR[r2] + 1;
else
        GR[t] ← cat(lshift(GR[r1],1),PSW[C/B]{8}) + GR[r2];
PSW[C/B] ← carry_borrows;
PSW[V] ← xor(carry_borrows{8},GR[r2]{32});
if (cond_satisfied) PSW[N] ← 1;

Exceptions: None

Format: EXTRD,cmplt,cond   r,pos,len,t

(12)

34	r	t	c	2	se	1	cl	0	clen
6	5	5	3	2	1	1	1	3	5

(15)

36	r	t	c	cl	p	se	pos	clen
6	5	5	3	1	1	1	5	5

Purpose: To extract any 64-bit or shorter field from a fixed or variable position, and conditionally nullify the following instruction.

Description: A field is extracted from GR *r*, zero or sign extended and placed right-justified in GR *t*. The field begins at the bit position given by *pos* and extends *len* bits to the left.

The bit position, *pos*, can either be a constant (specifying a fixed extract), or can be SAR, the Shift Amount Register (CR 11) (specifying a variable extract.) Format 12 is used for variable extracts; Format 15 is used for fixed extracts. For variable extracts, if the extracted field extends beyond the leftmost bit, it is zero or sign extended. For fixed extracts, it is an undefined operation for the field to extend beyond the leftmost bit.

The completer, *cmplt*, determines whether the extracted field is zero extended or sign extended. (Table 7-2 defines the assembly language completer mnemonics.) This is encoded in the *se* field of the instruction, with 1 indicating sign extension and 0 indicating zero extension.

Table 7-2. Extract Instruction Completers

cmplt	Description	se
<none> or S	extracted value is sign extended	1
U	extracted value is zero extended	0

The following diagram illustrates a fixed extract of a 50-bit field at bit position 56. The instruction is: EXTRD,U   r,56,50,t.

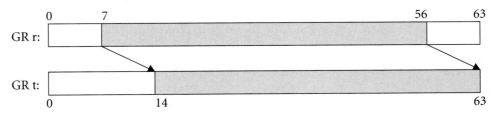

The length *len* in the assembly language format is encoded into the *cl* and *clen* fields. For fixed extracts, the bit position *pos* in the assembly language format is represented in the machine instruction by cat(*p,pos*.)

The following instruction is nullified if the result of the operation satisfies the specified condition, *cond*. The condition is encoded in the *c* field of the instruction.

Conditions: The condition is any of the 64-bit extract/deposit conditions shown in Table D-14 on page D-9. When a condition completer is not specified, the "never" condition is used. The boolean variable "cond_satisfied" in the operation section is set when the result of the operation satisfies the specified condition.

Operation:
```
len ← assemble_6(cl,clen)
if (variable_extract) {                                    /* (Format 12) */
    pos ← CR[11];
shamt ← 63 – pos;
if (pos >= len–1)
    tlen ← len;
else
    if (variable_extract)                                  /* (Format 12) */
        tlen ← pos + 1;
    else                                                   /* (Format 15) */
        undefined;
if (cmplt == U)                                            /* se=0 */
    GR[t] ← zero_ext(rshift(GR[r],shamt),tlen);
else                                                       /* se=1 */
    GR[t] ← sign_ext(rshift(GR[r],shamt),tlen);
if (cond_satisfied) PSW[N] ← 1;
```

Exceptions: None

Restrictions: Since for fixed extracts, the extracted field is fully specified by *len* and *pos*, it is an undefined operation if the field extends beyond the leftmost bit.

Programming Note

An arithmetic right shift of a 64-bit value in GR *r* by a variable amount contained in GR *p* leaving the result in GR *t* may be done by the following sequence:

```
MTSARCM   p
EXTRD,S   r,sar,64,t
```

Notes: The SHRD,S,cond r,sa,t pseudo-operation generates a EXTRD,S,cond r,63-sa,64-sa,t instruction to perform a signed shift right by sa bits on the doubleword in general register r.

The SHRD,U,cond r,sa,t pseudo-operation generates a EXTRD,S,cond r,63-sa,64-sa,t instruction to perform an unsigned shift right by sa bits on the doubleword in general register r.

Format: EXTRW,cmplt,cond   r,pos,len,t

(12)

34	r	t	c	2	se	0	0	0	clen
6	5	5	3	2	1	1	1	3	5

(15)

34	r	t	c	1	1	se	pos	clen
6	5	5	3	1	1	1	5	5

Purpose: To extract any 32-bit or shorter field from a fixed or variable position, and conditionally nullify the following instruction.

Description: A field is extracted from the rightmost 32 bits of GR r, zero or sign extended and placed right-justified in GR t. The field begins at the bit position given by $pos+32$ and extends len bits to the left. The leftmost 32 bits of GR t are undefined.

The bit position, pos, can either be a constant (specifying a fixed extract), or can be SAR, the Shift Amount Register (CR 11) (specifying a variable extract.) Format 12 is used for variable extracts; Format 15 is used for fixed extracts. For variable extracts, the leftmost bit of the SAR is ignored, and 32 is added to the value in the lower 5 bits. For fixed extracts, 32 is added to the pos value in the instruction. For variable extracts, if the extracted field extends beyond the leftmost bit (of the rightmost 32), it is zero or sign extended. For fixed extracts, it is an undefined operation for the field to extend beyond the leftmost bit (of the rightmost 32.)

The completer, $cmplt$, determines whether the extracted field is zero extended or sign extended (see Table 7-2 on page 7-47 for the assembly language completer mnemonics.) This is encoded in the se field of the instruction, with 1 indicating sign extension and 0 indicating zero extension.

The following diagram illustrates a variable extract of a 10-bit field when the Shift Amount Register contains the value 24. The instruction is: EXTRW,U   r,sar,10,t.

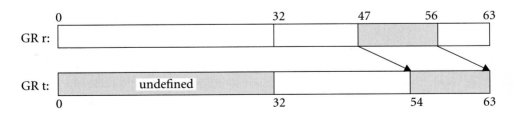

The length len in the assembly language format is encoded into the $clen$ field.

The following instruction is nullified if the result of the operation satisfies the specified condition, $cond$. The condition is encoded in the c field of the instruction.

Conditions: The condition is any of the 32-bit extract/deposit conditions shown in Table D-13 on page D-9. When a condition completer is not specified, the "never" condition is used. The boolean variable "cond_satisfied" in the operation section is set when the result of the operation satisfies the specified condition.

Operation:
```
len ← assemble_6(0,clen);
if (variable_extract) {                                          /* (Format 12) */
     pos ← CR[11]{1..5};
shamt ← 31 – pos;
if (pos >= len–1)
     tlen ← len;
else
     if (variable_extract)                                       /* (Format 12) */
          tlen ← pos + 1;
     else                                                        /* (Format 15) */
          undefined;
if (cmplt == U)                                                  /* se=0 */
     GR[t]{32..63} ← zero_ext(rshift(GR[r],shamt),tlen){32..63};
else                                                             /* se=1 */
     GR[t]{32..63} ← sign_ext(rshift(GR[r],shamt),tlen){32..63};
GR[t]{0..31} ← undefined;
if (cond_satisfied) PSW[N] ← 1;
```

Exceptions: None

Restrictions: Since for fixed extracts, the extracted field is fully specified by *len* and *pos*, it is an undefined operation if the field extends beyond the leftmost bit (of the rightmost 32.)

Programming Note

An arithmetic right shift of a 32-bit value in GR *r* by a variable amount contained in GR *p* leaving the result in GR *t* may be done by the following sequence:

```
MTSARCM    p
EXTRW,S    r,sar,32,t
```

Notes: The SHRW,S,cond r,sa,t pseudo-operation generates a EXTRD,S,cond r,31-sa,32-sa,t instruction to perform a signed shift right by sa bits on the word in general register r.

The SHRW,U,cond r,sa,t pseudo-operation generates a EXTRD,S,cond r,31-sa,32-sa,t instruction to perform an unsigned shift right by sa bits on the word in general register r.

Format: FDC,cmplt   x(s,b)
                  FDC d(s,b)

(24)

01	b	x	s	4A	m	rv
6	5	5	2	8	1	5

(25)

01	b	im5	s	CA	0	rv
6	5	5	2	8	1	5

Purpose: To invalidate a data cache line and write it back to memory if it is dirty.

Description: The data cache line (if present) specified by the effective address generated by the instruction is written back to memory, if and only if it is dirty, and then invalidated from the data cache. The offset is formed as the sum of a base register, *b*, and either an index register, *x* (Format 24), or a displacement *d* (Format 25.) The displacement is encoded into the *im5* field. Optional base modification can also be performed with the indexed form.

The completer, *cmplt*, determines whether the offset is the base register, or the base register plus the index register or displacement. The completer, encoded in the *m*-field of the instruction, also specifies base register modification. (Table 7-3 defines the assembly language completer mnemonics.)

Table 7-3. System Control Instruction Completers

cmplt	Description	m
<none>	don't modify base register	0
M	Modify base register	1

The PSW D-bit (Data address translation enable) determines whether a virtual or absolute address is used.

A cache line is called *dirty* if any byte has been written to since it was read from memory or if a STBY,E to the leftmost byte of a word has been performed.

In a multiprocessor system, a flush request is broadcast to all data and combined caches.

Operation: space ← space_select(s,GR[b],format);
            if (indexed_load)   /* indexed (Format 24)*/
                switch (cmplt) {
                    case M: offset ← GR[b];
                                    GR[b] ← GR[b] + GR[x];
                                      break;
                    default: offset ← GR[b] + GR[x];
                                    break;
                }

```
        else                                              /* short displacement (Format 25)*/
             offset ← GR[b] + low_sign_ext(im5,5);                            /* (new) */
        Dcache_flush(space,offset);
```

Exceptions: Non-access data TLB miss fault

Notes: For systems that do not have a cache, this instruction executes as a null instruction.

In systems with a combined cache, this instruction may be used to flush both data and instruction lines from the cache.

This instruction may be executed out of sequence but must satisfy the instruction ordering constraints. The SYNC instruction enforces program order with respect to the instructions following the SYNC.

It is an undefined operation to execute an FDC with a nonzero s-field at a nonzero privilege level when the PSW W-bit is 1.

Format: FDCE,cmplt x(s,b)

(24)	01	b	x	s	4B	m	rv
	6	5	5	2	8	1	5

Purpose: To provide for flushing the entire data or combined cache by causing zero or more cache lines to be invalidated.

Description: Zero or more cache lines specified by an implementation-dependent function of the effective address are written back to main memory, if and only if they are dirty, and are invalidated in the data or combined cache. The completer, *cmplt*, determines if the offset is the base register, *b*, or the base register plus the index register *x*. The completer, encoded in the *m*-field of the instruction, specifies base register modification. No address translation is performed (see Table 7-3 on page 7-51 for the assembly language completer mnemonics.)

When this instruction is used in an architecturally defined cache flush loop, the entire data or combined cache will be flushed upon completion of the loop.

Operation:
```
space ← space_select(s,GR[b],INDEXED);
switch (cmplt) {
    case M:  offset ← GR[b];                    /*m=1*/
             GR[b] ← GR[b] + GR[x];
             break;
    default: offset ← GR[b] + GR[x];            /*m=0*/
             break;
}
Dcache_flush_entries(space,offset);
```

Exceptions: None

Notes: In a multiprocessor system, this instruction is not broadcast to other processors. This instruction does not necessarily flush the entry specified by "space" and "offset".

For systems that do not have a cache, this instruction executes as a null instruction.

It is an undefined operation to execute an FDCE with a nonzero *s*-field at a nonzero privilege level when the PSW W-bit is 1.

Format: FIC,cmplt   x(s|sr,b)

(26)

01	b	x	s	0A	m	rv
6	5	5	3	7	1	5

(24)

01	b	x	s	4F	m	0
6	5	5	2	8	1	5

Purpose: To invalidate an instruction cache line.

Description: The instruction cache line (if any) specified by the effective address generated by the instruction is invalidated in the instruction cache. The completer, *cmplt*, determines if the offset is the base register, *b*, or the base register plus the index register *x*. The completer, encoded in the *m*-field of the instruction, also specifies base register modification (see Table 7-3 on page 7-51 for the assembly language completer mnemonics.)

The space register, *sr*, is explicitly encoded in the 3-bit *s* field of the instruction (Format 26) or is implicitly specified by the 2-bit *s* field of the instruction (Format 24.)

The PSW D-bit (Data address translation enable) determines whether a virtual or absolute address is used.

Either the instruction TLB or the data TLB can be used to perform the address translation for the address to be flushed. If the data TLB is used, a TLB miss fault is reported using a non-access data TLB miss fault.

In a multiprocessor system, a flush request is broadcast to all instruction and combined caches.

Operation:
```
if (explicit_pointer)                                       /*(Format 26)*/
     space ← SR[assemble_3(s)];
else                                                        /*(Format 24)*/
     space ← space_select(s,GR[b],INDEXED);
switch (cmplt) {
     case M:  offset ← GR[b];                               /*m=1*/
              GR[b] ← GR[b] + GR[x];
              break;
     default: offset ← GR[b] + GR[x];                       /*m=0*/
              break;
}
Icache_flush(space,offset);
```

Exceptions: Non-access instruction TLB miss fault   Non-access data TLB miss fault

Notes: For systems that do not have a cache, this instruction executes as a null instruction.

In systems with a combined cache, this instruction may be used to flush both instruction and data lines from the cache, including writing them back to main memory, if they are dirty.

This instruction may be executed out of sequence but must satisfy the instruction ordering constraints. The SYNC instruction enforces program order with respect to the instructions following the SYNC.

It is an undefined operation to execute an implicit-pointer FIC with a nonzero s-field at a nonzero privilege level when the PSW W-bit is 1.

Format: FICE,cmplt   x(sr,b)

(26)	01	b	x	s	0B	m	rv
	6	5	5	3	7	1	5

Purpose: To provide for flushing the entire instruction or combined cache by causing zero or more cache lines to be invalidated.

Description: Zero or more cache lines specified by an implementation-dependent function of the effective address are invalidated in the instruction or combined cache. For implementations with a combined cache, the cache lines are written back to main memory, if and only if they are dirty, and are invalidated. The completer, *cmplt*, determines if the offset is the base register, *b*, or the base register plus the index register *x*. The completer, encoded in the *m*-field of the instruction, specifies base register modification. No address translation is performed (see Table 7-3 on page 7-51 for the assembly language completer mnemonics.) The space register, *sr*, is encoded in the *s* field of the instruction.

When this instruction is used in an architecturally defined cache flush loop, the entire instruction or combined cache will be flushed upon completion of the loop (all the contents of the instruction cache, except the loop itself, prior to the beginning of the flush loop must be flushed.)

Operation:
```
switch (cmplt) {
      case M:  offset ← GR[b];                                          /*m=1*/
               GR[b] ← GR[b] + GR[x];
               break;
      default: offset ← GR[b] + GR[x];                                  /*m=0*/
               break;
}
space ← SR[assemble_3(s)];
Icache_flush_entries(space,offset);
```

Exceptions: None

Notes: In a multiprocessor system, this instruction is not broadcast to other processors. This instruction does not necessarily flush the entry specified by "space" and "offset".

For systems which do not have a cache, this instruction executes as a null instruction.

Format: HADD,cmplt   r1,r2,t

(8)	02	r2	r1	0	0	0	1	1	sat	0	t
	6	5	5	3	1	2	1	1	2	1	5

Purpose: To add multiple halfwords in parallel with optional saturation.

Description: The corresponding halfwords of GR *r1* and GR *r2* are added together in parallel. Optional saturation is performed, which forces each halfword result to either the maximum or the minimum value, if the result would have been out of the range of the target format. The halfword results are placed in GR *t*.

The completer, *cmplt*, determines whether modular, signed-saturation, or unsigned-saturation arithmetic is performed. The completer is encoded in the *sat* field of the instruction. (Table 7-4 defines the assembly language completer mnemonics.) For signed saturation, all operands are treated as signed numbers, and the results are signed numbers. For unsigned saturation, the first operands, from GR *r1*, are treated as unsigned numbers, the second operands, from GR *r2*, are treated as signed numbers, and the results are unsigned numbers.

Table 7-4. Halfword Arithmetic Completers

cmplt	Description	sat
<none>	modular arithmetic	3
SS	Signed Saturation	1
US	Unsigned Saturation	0

Operation: parallel for (start ← 0; start <= 48; start += 16) {
         end ← start + 15;
         GR[t]{start..end} ← (GR[r1]{start..end} + GR[r2]{start..end});
         switch (cmplt) {
             case SS: if (maximum_signed_saturation)   /*sat=1*/
                                 GR[t]{start..end} ← 0x7FFF;
                        else if(minimum_signed_saturation)
                                 GR[t]{start..end} ← 0x8000;
                        break;
             case US: if (maximum_unsigned_saturation)   /*sat=0*/
                                   GR[t]{start..end} ← 0xFFFF;
                        else if(minimum_unsigned_saturation)
                                 GR[t]{start..end} ← 0x0000;
                        break;
             default: /*sat=3*/
                        break;
         }
         }

Exceptions: None.

Format: HAVG   r1,r2,t

(8)	02	r2	r1	0	0	0	1	0	3	0	t
	6	5	5	3	1	2	1	1	2	1	5

Purpose: To average multiple halfwords in parallel.

Description: The corresponding halfwords of GR *r1* and GR *r2* are averaged in parallel. The average is obtained by adding the corresponding halfwords, and shifting the result right by one bit, to perform a divide by 2, with the halfword carry bit from the addition shifted back into the leftmost position of each result. The halfword results are placed in GR *t*.

Unbiased rounding is performed on the results to reduce the accumulation of rounding errors with cascaded operations.

Operation: parallel for (start ← 0; start <= 48; start += 16){
       end ← start + 15;
       sum ← GR[r1]{start..end} + GR[r2]{start..end};
       new_lsb ← sum{14} | sum{15};   /*unbiased rounding*/
       GR[t]{start..end} ← cat(carry,sum{0..13},new_lsb);
    }

Exceptions: None

Format: HSHL r,sa,t

(10)	3E	0	r	1	0	0	2	sa	0	t
	6	5	5	1	2	1	2	4	1	5

Purpose: To perform multiple parallel halfword shift left operations.

Description: Each of the halfwords in GR r is shifted left sa bits. The shift amount is between 0 and 15, and is encoded in the sa field in the instruction. The halfword results are placed in GR t.

Operation: parallel for (start ← 0; start <= 48; start += 16) {
                      end ← start + 15;
                      GR[t]{start..end} ← lshift(GR[r1]{start..end},sa);
                  }

Exceptions: None.

Format: HSHLADD   r1,sa,r2,t

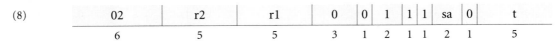

(8)	02	r2	r1	0	0	1	1	1	sa	0	t
	6	5	5	3	1	2	1	1	2	1	5

Purpose: To perform multiple halfword shift left and add operations in parallel with saturation.

Description: Each halfword of GR *r1* is shifted left by *sa* bits, and then added to the corresponding halfword of GR *r2*. Signed saturation is performed, which forces each halfword result to either the maximum or the minimum value, if the result would have been out of range. The halfword results are placed in GR *t*. The shift amount is either 1, 2, or 3, and is encoded in the *sa* field of the instruction.

All operands are treated as signed numbers, and the results are signed numbers. Signed saturation is performed.

For this instruction, signed saturation is based both on the shift operation and the add operation. That is, if the result of the shift operation is not representable in 16 bits, signed saturation occurs. If GR *r1* was positive, maximum saturation occurs. If GR *r2* was negative, minimum saturation occurs. If the result of the shift operation is representable in 16 bits, then saturation is determined by the add operation in the normal fashion.

Operation:
```
parallel for (start ← 0; start <= 48; start += 16) {
        end ← start + 15;
        GR[t]{start..end} ← lshift(GR[r1]{start..end},sa) + GR[r2]{start..end};
        if (maximum_signed_saturation)
            GR[t]{start..end} ← 0x7FFF;
        else if(minimum_signed_saturation)
            GR[t]{start..end} ← 0x8000;
}
```

Exceptions: None

Format: HSHR,cmplt   r,sa,t

(10)	3E	r	0	1	2	0	se	sa	0	t
	6	5	5	1	2	1	2	4	1	5

Purpose: To perform multiple parallel halfword signed or unsigned shift right operations.

Description: Each of the halfwords in GR *r* is shifted right *sa* bits. The completer, *cmplt*, determines whether a signed or unsigned shift is performed. The completer is encoded in the *se* field of the instruction. (Table 7-5 defines the assembly language completer mnemonics.) The shift amount is between 0 and 15, and is encoded in the *sa* field in the instruction. The halfword results are placed in GR *t*.

Table 7-5. Halfword Parallel Shift Right Completers

cmplt	Description	se
U	Unsigned Shift	2
<none> or S	Signed Shift	3

Operation:
```
parallel for (start ← 0; start <= 48; start += 16) {
        end ← start + 15;
        if (cmplt == U)                                         /*se=2 (unsigned)*/
                GR[t]{start..end} ← rshift(GR[r1]{start..end},sa);
        else                                                    /*se=3 (signed)*/
                GR[t]{start..end} ← sign_ext_16(rshift(GR[r1]{start..end},sa),16–sa);
}
```

Exceptions: None.

Format: HSHRADD   r1,sa,r2,t

(8)	02	r2	r1	0	0	1	0	1	sa	0	t
	6	5	5	3	1	2	1	1	2	1	5

Purpose: To perform multiple halfword shift right and add operations in parallel with saturation.

Description: Each halfword of GR *r1* is shifted right by *sa* bits, and then added to the corresponding halfword of GR *r2*. The bits shifted in equal the sign bit for each halfword. Signed saturation is performed, which forces each halfword result to either the maximum or the minimum value, if the result would have been out of range. The halfword results are placed in GR *t*. The shift amount is either 1, 2, or 3, and is encoded in the *sa* field of the instruction.

All operands are treated as signed numbers, and the results are signed numbers. Signed saturation is performed.

Operation: parallel for (start ← 0; start <= 48; start += 16) {
        end ← start + 15;
        GR[t]{start..end} ← sign_ext_16(rshift(GR[r1]{start..end},sa),16–sa) +
                            GR[r2]{start..end};
        if (maximum_signed_saturation)
            GR[t]{start..end} ← 0x7FFF;
        else if(minimum_signed_saturation)
            GR[t]{start..end} ← 0x8000;
        }

Exceptions: None.

Format: HSUB,cmplt   r1,r2,t

(8)

02	r2	r1	0	0	0	0	1	sat	0	t
6	5	5	3	1	2	1	1	2	1	5

Purpose: To subtract multiple halfwords in parallel with optional saturation.

Description: The corresponding halfwords of GR *r2* are subtracted from the halfwords of GR *r1* in parallel. Optional saturation is performed, which forces each halfword result to either the maximum or the minimum value, if the result would have been out of the range of the target format. The halfword results are placed in GR *t*.

The completer, *cmplt*, determines whether modular, signed-saturation, or unsigned-saturation arithmetic is performed. The completer is encoded in the *sat* field of the instruction (see Table 7-4 on page 7-57 for the assembly language completer mnemonics.) For signed saturation, all operands are treated as signed numbers, and the results are signed numbers. For unsigned saturation, the first operands, from GR *r1*, are treated as unsigned numbers, the second operands, from GR *r2*, are treated as signed numbers, and the results are unsigned numbers.

Operation: parallel for (start ← 0; start <= 48; start += 16) {
        end ← start + 15;
        GR[t]{start..end} ← (GR[r1]{start..end} + ~GR[r2]{start..end} + 1);
        switch (cmplt) {
            case SS: if (maximum_signed_saturation)   /*sat=1*/
                        GR[t]{start..end} ← 0x7FFF;
                    else if(minimum_signed_saturation)
                        GR[t]{start..end} ← 0x8000;
                    break;
            case US: if (maximum_unsigned_saturation)   /*sat=0*/
                        GR[t]{start..end} ← 0xFFFF;
                    else if(minimum_unsigned_saturation)
                        GR[t]{start..end} ← 0x0000;
                    break;
            default: /*sat=3*/
                    break;
        }
    }

Exceptions: None.

Format: IDTLBT r1,r2

(26)

01	r2	r1	0	60	0	0
6	5	5	3	7	1	5

Purpose: To add an entry to the data TLB.

Description: A slot is found in the data or combined TLB and the new translation is placed there. If the data or combined TLB already contains one or more entries whose virtual address ranges overlap the virtual address range of the new translation, the old entries are removed. The virtual address is specified by the IOR and ISR control registers. The contents of the ISR are concatenated with the lower 32 bits of the IOR to form the virtual address. The upper 32-bits of the IOR are ignored.

The physical address and the page size for the translation are specified by GR *r1*. The flags and access control bits are specified by GR *r2*.

Operation: if (priv != 0)
                privileged_operation_trap;
            else {
                space ← ISR;
                offset ← cat(ISR{32..63},IOR{32..63});
                page_size ← (GR[r1]{60..63} + 1) * 4096;
                for (i ← 0; i < page_size/4096; i++) {
                    if (entry ← DTLB_search(space, offset + i*4096))
                        DTLB_purge_local(entry);
                }
                entry ← DTLB_alloc(space,offset);
                DTLB[entry].VIRTUAL_ADDR ← (space<<32) | (offset);
                DTLB[entry].PHY_PAGE_NO ← GR[r1]{7..58};
                DTLB[entry].PAGE_SIZE ← GR[r1]{60..63};
                DTLB[entry].ACCESS_RIGHTS ← GR[r2]{5..11};
                DTLB[entry].ACCESS_ID ← GR[r2]{32..62};
                DTLB[entry].T ← GR[r2]{2}
                DTLB[entry].D ← GR[r2]{3}
                DTLB[entry].B ← GR[r2]{4}
                DTLB[entry].U ← GR[r2]{12}
                DTLB[entry].O ← GR[r2]{13}
                if (combined_TLB) {
                    ITLB[entry].P ← GR[r2]{14}
                }
            }

Exceptions: Privileged operation trap

Restrictions: This instruction may be executed only at the most privileged level.

Notes: This instruction may be used to insert both instruction entries and data entries into a combined TLB. The P bit is set to the appropriate bit of GR r in that case.

Note that no OR function is performed in creating the virtual address, since the IIA queue already contains a global address.

If smaller than 31-bit access IDs are implemented, only the appropriate number of the rightmost bits of GR[r]{32..62} are stored in the TLB.

Format: IITLBT r1,r2

(26)	01	r2	r1	0	20	0	0
	6	5	5	3	7	1	5

Purpose: To add an entry to the instruction TLB.

Description: A slot is found in the instruction or combined TLB and the new translation is placed there. If the instruction or combined TLB already contains one or more entries whose virtual address ranges overlap the virtual address range of the new translation, the old entries are removed. The virtual address is specified by the front entry in the IIA queue. The contents of the front element of the IIASQ are concatenated with the lower 32 bits of the front element of the IIAOQ to form the virtual address. The upper 32-bits of the IIAOQ are ignored.

The physical address and the page size for the translation are specified by GR $r1$. The flags and access control bits are specified by GR $r2$.

Operation:
```
if (priv != 0)
        privileged_operation_trap;
else {
        space ← IIASQ_Front;
        offset ← cat(IIASQ_Front{32..63},IIAOQ_Front{32..63});
        page_size ← (GR[r1]{60..63} + 1) * 4096;
        for (i ← 0; i < page_size/4096; i++) {
                if (entry ← ITLB_search(space, offset + i*4096))
                        ITLB_purge_local(entry);
        }
        entry ← ITLB_alloc(space,offset);
        ITLB[entry].VIRTUAL_ADDR ← (space<<32) | (offset);
        ITLB[entry].PHY_PAGE_NO ← GR[r1]{7..58};
        ITLB[entry].PAGE_SIZE ← GR[r1]{60..63};
        ITLB[entry].ACCESS_RIGHTS ← GR[r2]{5..11};
        ITLB[entry].ACCESS_ID ← GR[r2]{32..62};
        ITLB[entry].P ← GR[r2]{14}
if (combined_TLB) {
        ITLB[entry].T ← GR[r2]{2}
        ITLB[entry].D ← GR[r2]{3}
        ITLB[entry].B ← GR[r2]{4}
        ITLB[entry].U ← GR[r2]{12}
        ITLB[entry].O ← GR[r2]{13}
        }
}
```

Exceptions: Privileged operation trap

Restrictions: This instruction may be executed only at the most privileged level.

Notes: This instruction may be used to insert both instruction entries and data entries into a combined TLB. The T, D, B, U, and O bits are set to the appropriate bits of GR *r* in that case.

Note that no OR function is performed in creating the virtual address, since the IIA queue already contains a global address.

If smaller than 31-bit access IDs are implemented, only the appropriate number of the rightmost bits of GR[r]{32..62} are stored in the TLB.

Load Coherence Index   LCI

Format: LCI   x(s,b),t

(24)	01	b	x	s	4C	0	t
	6	5	5	2	8	1	5

Purpose: To determine the coherence index corresponding to a virtual address.

Description: The effective address is calculated. GR *t* receives the coherence index corresponding to the given virtual address.

In systems with separate data and instruction caches, the coherence index is obtained from the data cache.

The coherence index function is independent of the state of the PSW D-bit.

Operation:
```
if (priv != 0)
        privileged_operation_trap;
else {
    space ← space_select(s,GR[b],INDEXED);
    offset ← GR[b] + GR[x];
    GR[t] ← coherence_index(space,offset);
}
```

Exceptions: Privileged operation trap

Restrictions: This instruction may be executed only at the most privileged level.

Notes: All addresses within a page have the same coherence index.

The coherence index corresponding to a physical address can be determined by performing LCI on the equivalently-mapped virtual address. Also, in order to allow I/O modules to have coherent access to equivalently-mapped addresses without knowing the coherence index, the coherence index for equivalently-mapped addresses must be an implementation-defined function of the physical address bits only.

Two virtual addresses having the same coherence index are not guaranteed to alias unless they also meet the virtual aliasing rules.

For systems that do not have a cache, the target register receives an undefined value.

For system that do not support coherent I/O, this instruction is undefined.

Format: LDB,cmplt,cc   x|d(s,b),t

(1)

10	b	t	s	im14
6	5	5	2	14

(5)

03	b	im5	s	a	1	cc	0	m	t
6	5	5	2	1	1	2	4	1	5

(4)

03	b	x	s	u	0	cc	0	m	t
6	5	5	2	1	1	2	4	1	5

Purpose: To load a byte into a general register.

Description: The byte at the effective address is zero-extended and loaded into GR t. The offset is formed as the sum of a base register, b, and either an index register, x (Format 4), or a displacement d. The displacement can be either long (Format 1) or short (Format 5.) The displacement is encoded into the immediate field. Optional base modification can also be performed.

The completer, *cmplt*, determines whether the offset is the base register, or the base register plus the index register or displacement. The completer also specifies base register modification, optional index prescaling, and ordering constraints (see Table H-1 on page H-4, and Table H-3 on page H-8 for the assembly language completer mnemonics.) The completer, *cc*, specifies the cache control hint (see Table 6-7 on page 6-10.)

For short displacements, a one in the m field specifies base modification, and the a field encodes whether pre-modification ($a=1$), or post-modification ($a=0$) is performed. For indexed loads, a one in the m field specifies base modification, and a one in the u field specifies index prescaling.

If base register modification is specified and $b = t$, GR t receives the aligned byte at the effective address.

Operation:
```
if (indexed_load)                                        /* indexed (Format 4)*/
        dx ← GR[x];
else if (d > 15 || d < -16) {                            /* long displacement */
        dx ← sign_ext(assemble_16(s,im14),16);               /* (Format 1) */
        cc ← NO_HINT;
} else                                                   /* short displacement */
        dx ← low_sign_ext(im5,5);                            /* (Format 5) */
space ← space_select(s,GR[b],format);
switch (cmplt) {
        case MB:        offset ← GR[b] + dx;
                        GR[b] ← GR[b] + dx;
                        break;
        case MA:
        case M:
        case SM:        offset ← GR[b];
                        GR[b] ← GR[b] + dx;
                        break;
        default:        offset ← GR[b] + dx;
                        break;
}
GR[t] ← zero_ext(mem_load(space,offset,0,17,cc),8);
if (cmplt == O)
        enforce_ordered_load;
```

Exceptions: Data TLB miss fault/data page fault   Page reference trap
Data memory access rights trap
Data memory protection ID trap

Restrictions: If the completer O is specified, the displacement must be 0.

Format: LDCD,cmplt,cc   xld(s,b),t

(5)

03	b	im5	s	a	1	cc	5	m	t
6	5	5	2	1	1	2	4	1	5

(4)

03	b	x	s	u	0	cc	5	m	t
6	5	5	2	1	1	2	4	1	5

Purpose: To read and lock a doubleword semaphore in main memory.

Description: The effective address is calculated. The offset is formed as the sum of a base register, *b*, and either an index register, *x* (Format 4), or a displacement *d* (Format 5.) The displacement is encoded into the immediate field. Optional base modification can also be performed.

The completer, *cmplt*, determines whether the offset is the base register, or the base register plus the index register or displacement. The completer also specifies base register modification, and optional index prescaling'(see Table H-1 on page H-4, and Table H-3 on page H-8 for the assembly language completer mnemonics.) The completer, *cc*, specifies the cache control hint (see Table 6-9 on page 6-11.)

For short displacements, a one in the *m* field specifies base modification, and the *a* field encodes whether pre-modification (*a*=1), or post-modification (*a*=0) is performed. For indexed loads, a one in the *m* field specifies base modification, and a one in the *u* field specifies index prescaling. If base register modification is specified and *b* = *t*, the value loaded is the aligned doubleword at the effective address.

The address must be 16-byte aligned. If the address is unaligned, the operation of the instruction is undefined.

The remaining steps of the instruction are indivisible and non-interruptible. The semaphore operation is strongly ordered.

If a cache control hint is not specified, the instruction is performed as follows:

- If the cache line containing the effective address is not present in the cache or is present but not dirty, and the system is not fully coherent, the line is flushed, the addressed doubleword is copied into GR *t*, and then set to zero in memory. If the line is retained in the cache, it must not be marked as dirty.
- If the cache line containing the effective address is present in the cache and is dirty, or the system is fully coherent, the semaphore operation may be handled as above or may be optimized by copying the addressed doubleword into GR *t* and then setting the addressed doubleword to zero in the cache.

If a cache control hint is specified, the semaphore operation may be handled as if a cache control hint had not been specified, or, preferably, the addressed doubleword is copied into GR *t* and then the addressed doubleword is set to zero in the cache. The cleared doubleword need not be flushed to memory.

Operation: if (indexed_load)   /* indexed (Format 4)*/

```
        switch (cmplt) {
            case S:
            case SM:        dx ← lshift(GR[x],3);
                            break;
            case M:
            default:        dx ← GR[x];
                            break;
        }
    else                                                /* short displacement */
        dx ← low_sign_ext(im5,5);                       /* (Format 5) */
    space ← space_select(s,GR[b],format);
    switch (cmplt) {
        case MB:        offset ← GR[b] + dx;
                        GR[b] ← GR[b] + dx;
                        break;
        case MA:
        case M:
        case SM:        offset ← GR[b];
                        GR[b] ← GR[b] + dx;
                        break;
        default:        offset ← GR[b] + dx;
                        break;
    }
    (indivisible)
```

> if (cache line is present and dirty || coherent_system || cc != 0) {
>   GR[t] ← mem_load(space,offset,0,63,NO_HINT);
>   mem_store(space,offset,0,63,NO_HINT,0);
> } else {
>   Dcache_flush(space, offset);
>   GR[t] ← mem_load(space,offset,0,63,NO_HINT);
>   store_in_memory(space,offset,0,63,NO_HINT,0);
> }

Exceptions: Data TLB miss fault/data page fault   TLB dirty bit trap
                     Data memory access rights trap   Page reference trap
                     Data memory protection ID trap
                     Data memory break trap

Restrictions: All software users of a semaphore must access the semaphore using the same cache control hint. Sharing a semaphore using different cache control hints is undefined.

Format: LDCW,cmplt,cc   xld(s,b),t

(5)

03	b	im5	s	a	1	cc	7	m	t
6	5	5	2	1	1	2	4	1	5

(4)

03	b	x	s	u	0	cc	7	m	t
6	5	5	2	1	1	2	4	1	5

Purpose: To read and lock a word semaphore in main memory.

Description: The effective address is calculated. The offset is formed as the sum of a base register, b, and either an index register, x (Format 4), or a displacement d (Format 5.) The displacement is encoded into the immediate field. Optional base modification can also be performed.

The completer, *cmplt*, determines whether the offset is the base register, or the base register plus the index register or displacement. The completer also specifies base register modification, and optional index prescaling (see Table H-1 on page H-4, and Table H-3 on page H-8 for the assembly language completer mnemonics.) The completer, *cc*, specifies the cache control hint (see Table 6-9 on page 6-11.)

For short displacements, a one in the m field specifies base modification, and the a field encodes whether pre-modification ($a=1$), or post-modification ($a=0$) is performed. For indexed loads, a one in the m field specifies base modification, and a one in the u field specifies index prescaling. If base register modification is specified and $b = t$, the value loaded is the aligned word at the effective address.

The address must be 16-byte aligned. If the address is unaligned, the operation of the instruction is undefined.

The remaining steps of the instruction are indivisible and non-interruptible. The semaphore operation is strongly ordered.

If a cache control hint is not specified, the instruction is performed as follows:

- If the cache line containing the effective address is not present in the cache or is present but not dirty, and the system is not fully coherent, the line is flushed, the addressed word is zero extended and copied into GR t, and then set to zero in memory. If the line is retained in the cache, it must not be marked as dirty.
- If the cache line containing the effective address is present in the cache and is dirty, or the system is fully coherent, the semaphore operation may be handled as above or may be optimized by copying the addressed word into GR t (zero extended) and then setting the addressed word to zero in the cache.

If a cache control hint is specified, the semaphore operation may be handled as if a cache control hint had not been specified, or, preferably, the addressed word is zero extended and copied into GR t and then the addressed word is set to zero in the cache. The cleared word need not be flushed to memory.

Operation: if (indexed_load)   /* indexed (Format 4)*/

```
            switch (cmplt) {
                case S:
                case SM:     dx ← lshift(GR[x],3);
                             break;
                case M:
                default:     dx ← GR[x];
                             break;
            }
        else                                              /* short displacement */
            dx ← low_sign_ext(im5,5);                     /* (Format 5) */
        space ← space_select(s,GR[b],format);
        switch (cmplt) {
            case MB:     offset ← GR[b] + dx;
                         GR[b] ← GR[b] + dx;
                         break;
            case MA:
            case M:
            case SM:     offset ← GR[b];
                         GR[b] ← GR[b] + dx;
                         break;
            default:     offset ← GR[b] + dx;
                         break;
        }
        (indivisible)
```

```
if (cache line is present and dirty || coherent_system || cc != 0) {
  GR[t] ← zero_ext(mem_load(space,offset,0,31,NO_HINT),32);
  mem_store(space,offset,0,31,NO_HINT,0);
} else {
  Dcache_flush(space, offset);
  GR[t] ← zero_ext(mem_load(space,offset,0,31,NO_HINT),32);
  store_in_memory(space,offset,0,31,NO_HINT,0);
}
```

Exceptions: Data TLB miss fault/data page fault   TLB dirty bit trap

                 Data memory access rights trap   Page reference trap

                 Data memory protection ID trap

                 Data memory break trap

Restrictions: All software users of a semaphore must access the semaphore using the same cache control hint. Sharing a semaphore using different cache control hints is undefined.

Notes: Note that the "index shift" option for this instruction shifts by three, not two.

Format: LDD,cmplt,cc xld(s,b),t

(3)

14	b	t	s	im10a	m	a	0	i
6	5	5	2	10	1	1	1	1

(5)

03	b	im5	s	a	1	cc	3	m	t
6	5	5	2	1	1	2	4	1	5

(4)

03	b	x	s	u	0	cc	3	m	t
6	5	5	2	1	1	2	4	1	5

Purpose: To load a doubleword into a general register.

Description: The aligned doubleword, at the effective address, is loaded into GR t from the effective address. The offset is formed as the sum of a base register, b, and either an index register, x (Format 4), or a displacement d. The displacement can be either long (Format 3) or short (Format 5.) The displacement is encoded into the immediate field. Optional base modification can also be performed.

The completer, *cmplt*, determines whether the offset is the base register, or the base register plus the index register or displacement. The completer also specifies base register modification, optional index prescaling, and ordering constraints (see Table H-1 on page H-4, and Table H-3 on page H-8 for the assembly language completer mnemonics.) The completer, *cc*, specifies the cache control hint (see Table 6-7 on page 6-10.)

For long and short displacements, a one in the m field specifies base modification, and the a field encodes whether pre-modification ($a=1$), or post-modification ($a=0$) is performed. For indexed loads, a one in the m field specifies base modification, and a one in the u field specifies index prescaling.

If base register modification is specified and $b = t$, GR t receives the aligned doubleword at the effective address.

Operation: if (indexed_load)   /* indexed (Format 4)*/
                  switch (cmplt) {
                      case S:
                      case SM: dx ← lshift(GR[x],3);
                                     break;
                      case M:
                      default: dx ← GR[x];
                                     break;
                  }
              else if (d > 15 || d < -16) {   /* long displacement */
                  dx ← sign_ext(assemble_16a(s,cat(im10a,0),i),16);   /* (Format 3) */
                  cc ← NO_HINT;
              } else   /* short displacement */
                  dx ← low_sign_ext(im5,5);   /* (Format 5) */
              space ← space_select(s,GR[b],format);
              switch (cmplt) {
                  case MB: offset ← GR[b] + dx;
                                 GR[b] ← GR[b] + dx;
                                 break;
                  case MA:
                  case M:
                  case SM: offset ← GR[b];
                                 GR[b] ← GR[b] + dx;
                                 break;
                  default: offset ← GR[b] + dx;
                                 break;
              }
              GR[t] ← mem_load(space,offset,0,63,cc);
              if (cmplt == O)
                  enforce_ordered_load;

Exceptions: Data TLB miss fault/data page fault   Unaligned data reference trap
                  Data memory access rights trap   Page reference trap
                  Data memory protection ID trap

Restrictions: For long displacements (Format 3), only displacements which are multiples of eight may
                  be used.

                  If the completer O is specified, the displacement must be 0.

Format: LDDA,cmplt,cc   xld(b),t

(5)

03	b	im5	0	a	1	cc	4	m	t
6	5	5	2	1	1	2	4	1	5

(4)

03	b	x	0	u	0	cc	4	m	t
6	5	5	2	1	1	2	4	1	5

Purpose: To load a doubleword into a general register from an absolute address.

Description: The aligned doubleword at the effective absolute address is loaded into GR t. The offset is formed as the sum of a base register, b, and either an index register, x (Format 4), or a displacement d (Format 5.) The displacement is encoded into the immediate field. Optional base modification can also be performed.

The completer, *cmplt*, determines whether the offset is the base register, or the base register plus the index register or displacement. The completer also specifies base register modification, optional index prescaling, and ordering constraints (see Table H-1 on page H-4, and Table H-3 on page H-8 for the assembly language completer mnemonics.) The completer, *cc*, specifies the cache control hint (see Table 6-7 on page 6-10.)

For short displacements, a one in the m field specifies base modification, and the a field encodes whether pre-modification ($a=1$), or post-modification ($a=0$) is performed. For indexed loads, a one in the m field specifies base modification, and a one in the u field specifies index prescaling.

If base register modification is specified and $b = t$, GR t receives the aligned doubleword at the effective address. Protection is not checked when this instruction is executed. This operation is only defined if the address is aligned on an 8-byte boundary.

Operation: if (priv != 0)
                      privileged_operation_trap;
                else {
                    if (indexed_load)   /* indexed (Format 4)*/
                        switch (cmplt) {
                            case S:
                            case SM: dx ← lshift(GR[x],3);
                                            break;

                            case M:
                            default: dx ← GR[x];
                                            break;
                        }
                    else   /* short displacement */
                        dx ← low_sign_ext(im5,5);   /* (Format 5) */
                    switch (cmplt) {
                        case MB: offset ← GR[b] + dx;
                                        GR[b] ← GR[b] + dx;
                                        break;
                        case MA:
                        case M:
                        case SM: offset ← GR[b];
                                        GR[b] ← GR[b] + dx;
                                        break;
                        default: offset ← GR[b] + dx;
                                        break;
                    }
                    GR[t] ← phys_mem_load(offset,0,63,cc);
                    if (cmplt == O)
                        enforce_ordered_load;
                }

Exceptions: Privileged operation trap

Restrictions: This instruction may be executed only at the most privileged level. If the completer O is specified, the displacement must be 0.

Format: LDH,cmplt,cc   x|d(s,b),t

(1)

11	b	t	s	im14
6	5	5	2	14

(5)

03	b	im5	s	a	1	cc	1	m	t
6	5	5	2	1	1	2	4	1	5

(4)

03	b	x	s	u	0	cc	1	m	t
6	5	5	2	1	1	2	4	1	5

Purpose: To load a halfword into a general register.

Description: The aligned halfword, at the effective address, is zero-extended and loaded into GR t from the effective address. The offset is formed as the sum of a base register, b, and either an index register, x (Format 4), or a displacement d. The displacement can be either long (Format 1) or short (Format 5.) The displacement is encoded into the immediate field. Optional base modification can also be performed.

The completer, *cmplt*, determines whether the offset is the base register, or the base register plus the index register or displacement. The completer also specifies base register modification, optional index prescaling, and ordering constraints (see Table H-1 on page H-4, and Table H-3 on page H-8 for the assembly language completer mnemonics.) The completer, *cc*, specifies the cache control hint (see Table 6-7 on page 6-10.)

For short displacements, a one in the m field specifies base modification, and the a field encodes whether pre-modification ($a=1$), or post-modification ($a=0$) is performed. For indexed loads, a one in the m field specifies base modification, and a one in the u field specifies index prescaling.

If base register modification is specified and $b = t$, GR t receives the aligned halfword at the effective address.

Operation: if (indexed_load)   /* indexed (Format 4)*/
         switch (cmplt) {
            case S:
            case SM: dx ← lshift(GR[x],1);
                      break;
            case M:
            default: dx ← GR[x];
                      break;
         }
      else if (d > 15 || d < -16) {   /* long displacement */
         dx ← sign_ext(assemble_16(s,im14),16);   /* (Format 1) */
         cc ← NO_HINT;
      } else   /* short displacement */
         dx ← low_sign_ext(im5,5);   /* (Format 5) */
      space ← space_select(s,GR[b],format);
      switch (cmplt) {
            case MB: offset ← GR[b] + dx;
                      GR[b] ← GR[b] + dx;
                      break;
            case MA:
            case M:
            case SM: offset ← GR[b];
                      GR[b] ← GR[b] + dx;
                      break;
            default: offset ← GR[b] + dx;
                      break;
      }
      GR[t] ← zero_ext(mem_load(space,offset,0,15,cc),16);
      if (cmplt == O)
         enforce_ordered_load;

Exceptions: Data TLB miss fault/data page fault   Unaligned data reference trap
             Data memory access rights trap   Page reference trap
             Data memory protection ID trap

Restrictions: If the completer O is specified, the displacement must be 0.

Format: LDIL   i,t

(7)	08	t	im21
	6	5	21

Purpose: To load the upper portion of a 32-bit immediate value into a general register.

Description: The 21-bit immediate value, *i*, is assembled, shifted left 11 bits, sign extended, and placed in GR *t*.

Operation: $GR[t] \leftarrow sign\_ext(lshift(assemble\_21(im21),11),32);$

Exceptions: None

Notes: Memory is not referenced.

Programming Note

LOAD IMMEDIATE LEFT can be used to generate a 32-bit literal in an arbitrary general register *t* by the following sequence of assembly language code:

```
LDIL    l%literal,GRt
LDO     r%literal(GRt),GRt
```

Format: LDO   d(b),t

(1)

0D	b	t	i	im14
6	5	5	2	14

Purpose: To load an offset into a general register.

Description: The effective address is calculated, and its offset part is loaded into GR t. The displacement d is encoded into the immediate field.

Operation: GR[t] $\leftarrow$ GR[b] + sign_ext(assemble_16(i,im14),16);

Exceptions: None

Notes: Memory is not referenced.

              The LDI i,t pseudo-operation generates an LDO i(0),t instruction to load an immediate value into a register.

              The COPY pseudo-operation allows for the movement of data from one register to another by generating the instruction LDO 0(r),t.

Load Space Identifier

Format: LDSID   (s,b),t

00	b	rv	s	0	85	t
6	5	5	2	1	8	5

Purpose: To calculate the space register number referenced by an implicit pointer and copy the space register into a general register.

Description: If *s* is zero, the space identifier referenced by GR *b* is copied into GR *t*. If *s* is not zero, SR *s* is copied into GR *t*.

Operation: GR[t] ← space_select(s,GR[b],INDEXED);

Exceptions: None

Notes: Unimplemented space register bits must read as zero.

The target register receives an undefined value if LDSID with a nonzero *s*-field is executed at a nonzero privilege level when the PSW W-bit is 1.

This instruction provides no useful function when the PSW W-bit is 1, since the operating system is free to change the space register contents at any time.

Format: LDW,cmplt,cc   x|d(s,b),t

(1)

12/13	b	t	s	im14
6	5	5	2	14

(2)

17	b	t	s	im11a	2	i
6	5	5	2	11	2	1

(5)

03	b	im5	s	a	1	cc	2	m	t
6	5	5	2	1	1	2	4	1	5

(4)

03	b	x	s	u	0	cc	2	m	t
6	5	5	2	1	1	2	4	1	5

Purpose: To load a word into a general register.

Description: The aligned word, at the effective address, is zero-extended and loaded into GR t from the effective address. The offset is formed as the sum of a base register, b, and either an index register, x (Format 4), or a displacement d. The displacement can be either long (Formats 1 and 2) or short (Format 5.) The displacement is encoded into the immediate field. Optional base modification can also be performed.

The completer, *cmplt*, determines whether the offset is the base register, or the base register plus the index register or displacement. The completer also specifies base register modification, optional index prescaling, and ordering constraints (see Table H-1 on page H-4, and Table H-3 on page H-8 for the assembly language completer mnemonics.) The completer, *cc*, specifies the cache control hint (see Table 6-7 on page 6-10.)

For long displacements with pre-decrement or post-increment, Format 1 (opcode 13) is used. For long displacements with post-decrement or pre-increment, Format 2 is used. For long displacements with no base modification, Format 1 (opcode 12) is used.

For short displacements, a one in the m field specifies base modification, and the a field encodes whether pre-modification (a=1), or post-modification (a=0) is performed. For indexed loads, a one in the m field specifies base modification, and a one in the u field specifies index prescaling.

If base register modification is specified and $b = t$, GR t receives the aligned word at the effective address.

Operation: if (indexed_load)   /* indexed (Format 4)*/
                switch (cmplt) {
                        case S:
                        case SM: dx ← lshift(GR[x],2);
                                        break;
                        case M:
                        default: dx ← GR[x];
                                        break;
                }
        else if (d > 15 || d < -16) {   /* long displacement */
                if ((cmplt == MB && d >= 0) || (cmplt == MA && d < 0))
                        dx ← sign_ext(assemble_16a(s,im11a,i),16);   /* (Format 2) */
                else
                        dx ← sign_ext(assemble_16(s,im14),16);   /* (Format 1) */
                cc ← NO_HINT;
        } else   /* short displacement */
                dx ← low_sign_ext(im5,5);   /* (Format 5) */
        space ← space_select(s,GR[b],format);
        switch (cmplt) {
                case MB: offset ← GR[b] + dx;
                                GR[b] ← GR[b] + dx;
                                break;
                case MA:
                case M:
                case SM: offset ← GR[b];
                                GR[b] ← GR[b] + dx;
                                break;
                default: offset ← GR[b] + dx;
                                break;
        }
        GR[t] ← zero_ext(mem_load(space,offset,0,31,cc),32);
        if (cmplt == O)
                enforce_ordered_load;

Exceptions: Data TLB miss fault/data page fault   Unaligned data reference trap
                Data memory access rights trap   Page reference trap
                Data memory protection ID trap

Restrictions: For post-decrement and pre-increment with long displacements (Format 2), only
                displacements which are multiples of four may be used.

                If the completer O is specified, the displacement must be 0.

Format: LDWA,cmplt,cc   x|d(b),t

(5)

03	b	im5	0	a	1	cc	6	m	t
6	5	5	2	1	1	2	4	1	5

(4)

03	b	x	0	u	0	cc	6	m	t
6	5	5	2	1	1	2	4	1	5

Purpose: To load a word into a general register from an absolute address.

Description: The aligned word at the effective absolute address is zero-extended and loaded into GR t.
The offset is formed as the sum of a base register, b, and either an index register, x (Format
4), or a displacement d (Format 5.) The displacement is encoded into the immediate field.
Optional base modification can also be performed.

The completer, *cmplt*, determines whether the offset is the base register, or the base register
plus the index register or displacement. The completer also specifies base register
modification, optional index prescaling, and ordering constraints (see Table H-1 on
page H-4, and Table H-3 on page H-8 for the assembly language completer mnemonics.)
The completer, *cc*, specifies the cache control hint (see Table 6-7 on page 6-10.)

For short displacements, a one in the m field specifies base modification, and the a field
encodes whether pre-modification ($a=1$), or post-modification ($a=0$) is performed. For
indexed loads, a one in the m field specifies base modification, and a one in the u field
specifies index prescaling.

If base register modification is specified and $b = t$, GR t receives the aligned word at the
effective address. Protection is not checked when this instruction is executed. This
operation is only defined if the address is aligned on a 4-byte boundary.

Operation: if (priv != 0)
                privileged_operation_trap;
           else {
                if (indexed_load)   /* indexed (Format 4)*/
                    switch (cmplt) {
                        case S:
                        case SM: dx ← lshift(GR[x],2);
                                        break;
                        case M:
                        default: dx ← GR[x];
                                        break;
                  }
                else   /* short displacement */
                    dx ← low_sign_ext(im5,5);   /* (Format 5) */
                switch (cmplt) {
                    case MB: offset ← GR[b] + dx;
                                    GR[b] ← GR[b] + dx;
                                    break;
                    case MA:
                    case M:
                    case SM: offset ← GR[b];
                                    GR[b] ← GR[b] + dx;
                                    break;
                    default: offset ← GR[b] + dx;
                                    break;
                }
                GR[t] ← zero_ext(phys_mem_load(offset,0,31,cc),32);
                if (cmplt == O)
                    enforce_ordered_load;
           }

Exceptions: Privileged operation trap

Restrictions: This instruction may be executed only at the most privileged level. If the completer O is specified, the displacement must be 0.

Format: LPA,cmplt   x(s,b),t

(24)

01	b	x	s	4D	m	t
6	5	5	2	8	1	5

Purpose: To determine the absolute address of a mapped virtual page.

Description: The effective address is calculated. The completer, *cmplt*, determines if the offset is the base register, *b*, or the base register plus index register *x*. The completer, encoded in the *m* field of the instruction, also specifies base register modification (see Table 7-3 on page 7-51 for the assembly language completer mnemonics.) GR *t* receives the absolute address corresponding to the given virtual address. If the page is not present, a fault is taken and software sets the target register to 0. If base register modification is specified and $b = t$, the value loaded is the absolute address of the item indicated by the effective address.

In systems with separate data and instruction TLBs, the absolute address is obtained from the data TLB. This instruction performs data address translation regardless of the state of the PSW D-bit.

Operation:
```
if (priv != 0)
        privileged_operation_trap;
else {
        space ← space_select(s,GR[b],INDEXED);
        switch (cmplt) {
            case M:  offset ← GR[b];                        /*m=1*/
                     GR[b] ← GR[b] + GR[x];
                     break;
            default: offset ← GR[b] + GR[x];                /*m=0*/
                     break;
        }
        if (DTLB_search(space,offset))
            GR[t] ← absolute_address(space,offset);
        else
            non-access_data_TLB_miss_fault();
}
```

Exceptions: Non-access data TLB miss fault   Privileged operation trap

Restrictions: The result of LPA is ambiguous for an address which maps to absolute address 0. This instruction may be executed only at the most privileged level.

Notes: If this instruction causes a non-access data TLB miss fault/non-access data page fault, the operating system's handler is required to search its page tables for the given address. If found, it does the appropriate TLB insert and returns to the interrupting instruction. If not found, the handler must decode the target field of the instruction, set that GR to 0, set the IPSW[N] bit to 1, and return to the interrupting instruction.

Format: MFCTL   r,t
              MFCTL,W   cr11,t

(32)	00	r	0	rv	e	rv	45	t
	6	5	5	1	1	1	8	5

Purpose: To move a value to a general register from a control register.

Description: CR r is copied into GR t.

Operation:
```
if (r >= 1 && r <= 7)
     undefined;
else if (priv != 0 && !(r == 11 || r == 26 || r == 27 || (r == 16 && !PSW[S])))
     privileged_register_trap;
else if (r >= 17 && r <= 22)
     if (PSW[Q])
          undefined;
     else
          GR[t] ← CR[r];                              /* IA Queues, IPRs */
else if (r == 0)
     if (PSW[R])
          undefined;
     else
          GR[t] ← CR[r];                              /* Recovery Counter */
else if (r == 11)
     if (cmplt == W)                                  /*e=1*/
          GR[t] ← CR[r];
     else                                             /*e=0*/
          GR[t] ← CR[r]{1..5};                        /* SAR */
else if (r >= 8)
     GR[t] ← CR[r];                                   /* other control registers */
```

Exceptions: Privileged register trap

Restrictions: System control registers other than the Shift Amount Register (CR 11), the Interval Timer (CR 16), and temporary registers CR 26 and CR 27, may be read only at the most privileged level. CR 11, CR 26, and CR 27 may be read at any privilege level. CR 16 may be read at any privilege level only if the PSW S-bit is 0; otherwise, CR 16 may be read only at the most privileged level. The Interruption Instruction Address Queues (CRs 17 and 18) and Interruption Parameter Registers (CRs 19, 20, and 21) and the Interruption Processor Status Word (CR 22) may be read reliably only when the PSW[Q] bit is 0.

If the completer *W* is specified, the control register source must specify CR11 (SAR).

Move From Instruction Address

MFIA

Format: MFIA t

(32)	00	rv	0	rv	A5	t
	6	5	5	3	8	5

Purpose: To move the current instruction address to a general register.

Description: IAOQ_FRONT is copied into GR t. The rightmost two bits of GR t, corresponding to the privilege level are zeroed.

Operation: GR[t] ← cat(IAOQ_FRONT{0..61},0{62..63});

Exceptions: None

Move From Space Register **MFSP**

Format: MFSP   sr,t

(29)	00	rv	0	s	25	t
	6	5	5	3	8	5

Purpose: To move a value to a general register from a space register.

Description: SR *sr* (which is assembled from the *s* field in the instruction) is copied into GR *t*.

Operation: sr ← assemble_3(s);
                  GR[t] ← SR[sr];

Exceptions: None

Notes: Unimplemented space register bits must read as zero.

Format: MIXH,cmplt   r1,r2,t

(10)

3E	r2	r1	1	ea	0	1	0	0	t
6	5	5	1	2	1	2	4	1	5

Purpose: To combine four halfwords from two source registers, and merge them in a result register.

Description: Two halfwords from GR *r1* are merged with two halfwords from GR *r2* and the result is placed in GR *t*.

The completer, *cmplt*, determines which halfwords are selected. The completer is encoded in the *ea* field of the instruction. (Table 7-6 defines the assembly language completer mnemonics.)

Table 7-6. Mix Instruction Completers

cmplt	Description	ea
L	Left Halfwords/Words are combined	0
R	Right Halfwords/Words are combined	2

If *cmplt* is "L", the left halfword of each of the four input words is merged into the result. If *cmplt* is "R", the right halfword of each of the four input words is merged into the result. The two cases are shown in the following diagram:

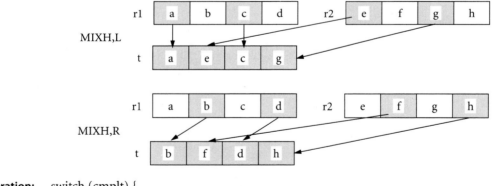

Operation: switch (cmplt) {
           case L: GR[t] ← cat(GR[r1]{0..15},GR[r2]{0..15},   /*ea=0*/
                             GR[r1]{32..47},GR[r2]{32..47});
                    break;
           case R: GR[t] ← cat(GR[r1]{16..31},GR[r2]{16..31},   /*ea=2*/
                             GR[r1]{48..63}, GR[r2]{48..63});
                    break;
       }

Exceptions: None.

Format: MIXW,cmplt   r1,r2,t

(10)

3E	r2	r1	1	ea	0	0	0	0	t
6	5	5	1	2	1	2	4	1	5

Purpose: To combine two words from two source registers, and merge them in a result register.

Description: A word from GR *r1* is merged with a word from GR *r2* and the result is placed in GR *t*.

                  The completer, *cmplt*, determines which words are selected. The completer is encoded in the *ea* field of the instruction (see Table 7-6 on page 7-92 for the assembly language completer mnemonics.) If *cmplt* is "L", the left word of each of the two input doublewords is merged into the result. If *cmplt* is "R", the right word of each of the two input doublewords is merged into the result. The two cases are shown in the following diagram:

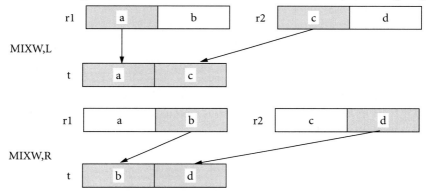

Operation: switch (cmplt) {
                 case L: GR[t] ← cat(GR[r1]{0..31},GR[r2]{0..31});   /*ea=0*/
                                     break;
                 case R: GR[t] ← cat(GR[r1]{32..63},GR[r2]{32..63});   /*ea=2*/
                                       break;
         }

Exceptions: None.

Format: MOVB,cond,n   r1,r2,target

(17)

32	r2	r1	c	w1	n	w
6	5	5	3	11	1	1

Purpose: To copy one register to another and perform an IA-relative branch conditionally based on the value moved.

Description: GR *r1* is copied into GR *r2*. If the value moved satisfies the specified condition, *cond*, the word displacement is assembled from the *w* and *w1* fields, sign extended, and added to the current instruction offset plus 8 to form the target offset. The condition is encoded in the *c* field of the instruction. The branch target, *target*, in the assembly language format is encoded in the *w* and *w1* fields.

If nullification is not specified, the following instruction is not nullified. If nullification is specified, the instruction following a taken forward branch or a failing backward branch is nullified. The ,N completer, encoded in the *n* field of the instruction, specifies nullification.

Conditions: The condition, *cond*, is any of the extract/deposit 32-bit conditions shown in Table D-13 on page D-9 (never, =, <, OD, TR, <>, >=, EV.) When a condition completer is not specified, the "never" condition is used. The boolean variable "cond_satisfied" in the operation section is set to 1 when the value moved satisfies the specified condition and set to 0 otherwise.

Operation:
GR[r2] ← GR[r1];
disp ← lshift(sign_ext(assemble_12(w1,w),12),2);
if (cond_satisfied)
    IAOQ_Next ← IAOQ_Front + disp + 8;
if (n)
    if (disp < 0)
        PSW[N] ← !cond_satisfied;
    else
        PSW[N] ← cond_satisfied;

Exceptions: Taken branch trap

Format: MOVIB,cond,n i,r,target

(17)

33	r	im5	c	w1	n	w
6	5	5	3	11	1	1

Purpose: To copy an immediate value into a register and perform an IA-relative branch conditionally based on the value moved.

Description: The immediate value *im5* is sign extended and copied into GR *r*. If the value moved satisfies the specified condition, *cond*, the word displacement is assembled from the *w* and *w1* fields, sign extended, and added to the current instruction offset plus 8 to form the target offset. The condition is encoded in the *c* field of the instruction. The branch target, *target*, in the assembly language format is encoded in the *w* and *w1* fields.

If nullification is not specified, the following instruction is not nullified. If nullification is specified, the instruction following a taken forward branch or a failing backward branch is nullified. The ,N completer, encoded in the *n* field of the instruction, specifies nullification.

Conditions: The condition, *cond*, is any of the extract/deposit 32-bit conditions shown in Table D-13 on page D-9 (never, =, <, OD, TR, <>, >=, EV.) When a condition completer is not specified, the "never" condition is used. The boolean variable "cond_satisfied" in the operation section is set to 1 when the value moved satisfies the specified condition and set to 0 otherwise.

Operation:
GR[r] ← low_sign_ext(im5,5);
disp ← lshift(sign_ext(assemble_12(w1,w),12),2);
if (cond_satisfied)
    IAOQ_Next ← IAOQ_Front + disp + 8;
if (n)
    if (disp < 0)
        PSW[N] ← !cond_satisfied;
    else
        PSW[N] ← cond_satisfied;

Exceptions: Taken branch trap

Programming Note

Since *i* is known at the time a MOVE IMMEDIATE AND BRANCH instruction is written, conditions other than always and never (the ,TR and <none> completers) are of no use.

Format: MTCTL   r,t

(31)	00	t	r	rv	C2	0
	6	5	5	3	8	5

Purpose: To move a value from a general register to a control register.

Description: GR *r* is copied into CR *t*. If CR 23 is specified, then the value is first complemented and ANDed with the original value.

Notes: The MTSAR r pseudo-operation generates an MTCTL r,%SAR instruction to copy a general register to the Shift Amount Register.

Operation: if (t >= 1 && t <= 7)
                 undefined;
             else if (t != 11 && priv != 0)
                 privileged_register_trap;
             else
                 switch(t) {
                     case 0:   if (PSW[R])
                                       undefined;
                                   else
                                       CR[t] ← GR[r]{32..63};   /* Recovery Counter */
                                   break;
                     case 14: case 15: case 16: case 24: case 25: case 26:
                     case 27: case 28: case 29: case 30: case 31:
                                       CR[t] ← GR[r];   /* other control registers */
                                   break;
                     case 17: case 18: case 20: case 21: case 22:
                                   if (PSW[Q])
                                       undefined;
                                   else
                                       CR[t] ← GR[r];   /* IIA Queues, IOR, ISR */
                                   break;
                     case 23:   CR[23] ← CR[23] & ~GR[r];   /* EIRR */
                                   break;
                     case 10:   CR[10] ← GR[r]{48..63};   /* CCR, SCR */
                                   break;
                     case 11:   CR[11] ← GR[r]{26..31};   /* SAR */
                                   break;
                     case 8: case 9: case 12: case 13:
                                       CR[t] ← GR[r];   /* Protection Identifiers */
                                   break;
                     case 19:
                                   undefined;   /* IIR */
                                   break;
                 }

Exceptions: Privileged register trap

Restrictions: System control registers other than the Shift Amount Register (CR 11) may be written only at the most privileged level. CR 11 may be written at any privilege level. The Recovery Counter (CR 0) may be written reliably only when the PSW[R] bit is 0. Writing into the Interruption Instruction Register (CR 19) is an undefined operation. Writing into the Interruption Instruction Address Queues (CRs 17 and 18), the Interruption Processor Status Word (CR 22), the Interruption Offset Register (CR 21) or the Interruption Space Register (CR 20) when the PSW[Q] bit is 1 is an undefined operation.

Notes: The MTSAR pseudo-operation generates an MTCTL r,CR11 to copy a general register to the Shift Amount Register (CR 11.)

Format: MTSARCM   r

(31)

00	B	r	rv	C6	0
6	5	5	3	8	5

Purpose: To take the one's complement of a value from a general register and move it to the Shift Amount Register (CR11.)

Description: The one's complement of GR *r* is copied into CR[11].

Operation: CR[11] ← ~ GR[r]{26..31};

Exceptions: None.

Notes: The upper bits of the SAR are non-existent and so on a MFCTL instruction with the SAR as the specified register, hardware can return either 0's or what was last written for the upper 58 bits. If hardware returns what was last written, the value written by a MTSARCM instruction must be the complement of GR[r].

Format: MTSM   r

(33)

00	0	r	0	C3	0
6	5	5	3	8	5

Purpose: To set PSW system mask bits to a value from a register.

Description: Bits 36, 37 and 56..63 of GR *r* replace the system mask, PSW{36,37,56..63}. Setting the PSW Q-bit, PSW{60}, to 1 with this instruction, if it was not already 1, is an undefined operation.

Operation: if (priv != 0)
                     privileged_operation_trap;
                 else {
                    if ((PSW[Q] == 0) && (GR[r]{60} == 1))
                        undefined;
                    else {
                        PSW[W]← GR[r]{36};
                        PSW[E] ← GR[r]{37};
                        PSW[O] ← GR[r]{56};
                        PSW[G] ← GR[r]{57};
                        PSW[F] ← GR[r]{58};
                        PSW[R] ← GR[r]{59};
                        PSW[Q] ← GR[r]{60};
                        PSW[P] ← GR[r]{61};
                        PSW[D]← GR[r]{62};
                        PSW[I] ← GR[r]{63};
                    }
                 }

Exceptions: Privileged operation trap

Restrictions: This instruction may be executed only at the most privileged level.

Notes: The state of the IPRs, IIA queues, and the IPSW is undefined when this instruction is used to set the Q-bit to 0, if it was not already 0.

Format: MTSP   r,sr

(29)

00	rv	r	s	C1	0
6	5	5	3	8	5

Purpose: To move a value from a general register to a space register.

Description: GR r is copied into SR sr (which is assembled from the s field in the instruction.)

Operation: sr $\leftarrow$ assemble_3(s);
if (sr >= 5 && priv != 0)
     privileged_register_trap;
else
     if (PSW[W])
         SR[sr] $\leftarrow$ GR[r];
     else
         SR[sr]{32..63} $\leftarrow$ GR[r]{32..63};

Exceptions: Privileged register trap

Restrictions: SRs 5, 6 and 7 may be changed only by software running at the most privileged level.

Notes: The values written to unimplemented space register bits must be ignored.

Bits 0..31 of the target space register, if implemented, are unchanged by this instruction if the PSW W-bit is 0.

Format: OR,cond   r1,r2,t

(8)	02	r2	r1	c	f	0	1	0	1	d	t
	6	5	5	3	1	2	1	1	2	1	5

Purpose: To do a 64-bit, bitwise inclusive OR.

Description: GR *r1* and GR *r2* are ORed and the result is placed in GR *t*. The following instruction is nullified if the values ORed satisfy the specified condition, *cond*. The condition is encoded in the *c*, *d*, and *f* fields of the instruction.

Conditions: The condition is any of the 32-bit logical conditions shown in Table D-9 on page D-7 or any of the 64-bit logical conditions shown in Table D-10 on page D-7. When a condition completer is not specified, the "never" condition is used. The boolean variable "cond_satisfied" in the operation section is set when the values ORed satisfy the specified condition.

Operation: GR[t] ← GR[r1] | GR[r2];
if (cond_satisfied) PSW[N] ← 1;

Exceptions: None

Notes: The NOP pseudo-operation generates the instruction OR 0,0,0.

Format: PDC,cmplt   x(s,b)

(24)	01	b	x	s	4E	m	0
	6	5	5	2	8	1	5

Purpose: To invalidate a data cache line.

Description: The cache line (if present) specified by the effective address generated by the instruction is invalidated from the data cache. If the privilege level is non-zero and the cache line is dirty then it is written back to memory before being invalidated. If the privilege level is zero and the line is dirty then the implementation may optionally write back the line to memory.

The completer, *cmplt*, determines if the offset is the base register, *b*, or the base register plus the index register *x*. The completer, encoded in the *m* field of the instruction, specifies base register modification (see Table 7-3 on page 7-51 for the assembly language completer mnemonics.)

If a cache purge operation is performed, write access to the data is required and a special access rights check is performed. See "Access Control" on page 3-11. The PSW D-bit (Data address translation enable) determines whether a virtual or absolute address is used.

In a multiprocessor system, a purge or flush request is broadcast to all data and combined caches.

Operation: space ← space_select(s,GR[b],INDEXED);
switch (cmplt) {
      case M: offset ← GR[b];   /*m=1*/
              GR[b] ← GR[b] + GR[x];
              break;
      default: offset ← GR[b] + GR[x];   /*m=0*/
              break;
}
if (priv != 0)
    Dcache_flush(space,offset);
else
    Dcache_flush_or_purge(space,offset);

Exceptions: Non-access data TLB miss fault   Data memory break trap
Data memory access rights trap
Data memory protection ID trap

Notes: For systems that do not have a cache, this instruction executes as a null instruction.

At privilege level zero, implementations are encouraged to purge the cache line for performance reasons.

This instruction may be executed out of sequence but must satisfy the instruction ordering constraints. The SYNC instruction enforces program order with respect to the instructions following the SYNC.

It is an undefined operation to execute a PDC with a nonzero *s*-field at a nonzero privilege level when the PSW W-bit is 1.

Format: PDTLB,scope,cmplt   x(s,b)

(24)

01	b	x	s	2	e1	8	m	rv
6	5	5	2	3	1	4	1	5

Purpose: To invalidate a data TLB entry.

Description: The data or combined TLB entries (if any) which match the effective address generated by the instruction are removed. The completer, *scope*, encoded in the *e1* field of the instruction, specifies whether the purge is global to all processors in a multiprocessor system (no completer, *e1*=0) or limited to the local processor (,L completer, *e1*=1.) The completer, *cmplt*, encoded in the *m* field of the instruction, determines if the offset is the base register, *b*, or the base register plus index register, *x*, and whether base register modification is performed (see Table 7-3 on page 7-51 for the assembly language completer mnemonics.)

TLB purges are strongly ordered. In a multiprocessor system, a global TLB purge causes a purge request to be broadcast to all data and combined TLBs. The other processors must remove all matching entries before the issuing processor continues.

Operation:
```
if (priv != 0)
        privileged_operation_trap;
else {
        space ← space_select(s,GR[b],INDEXED);
        switch (cmplt) {
            case M:  offset ← GR[b];                          /*m=1*/
                     GR[b] ← GR[b] + GR[x];
                     break;
            default:  offset ← GR[b] + GR[x];                 /*m=0*/
                     break;
        }
        page_size ← (GR[b]{60..63} + 1) * 4096;
        for (i ← 0; i < page_size/4096; i++) {
            if (entry ← DTLB_search(space, offset + i*4096))
                DTLB_purge_local(entry);
        }
        if (scope != L)
                DTLB_purge_broadcast(space,offset,page_size);
}
```

Exceptions: Privileged operation trap.

Restrictions: This instruction may be executed only at the most privileged level.

Notes: This instruction may be used to purge both instruction entries and data entries from a combined TLB.

Purge Data TLB Entry

PDTLBE

Format: PDTLBE,cmplt   x(s,b)

(24)	01	b	x	s	49	m	rv
	6	5	5	2	8	1	5

Purpose: To invalidate a data TLB entry without matching the address portion.

Description: The data or combined TLB entries (if any) specified by an implementation-dependent function of the effective address generated by the instruction are removed. All the fields of these entries may be changed to arbitrary values as long as these entries do not validate any subsequent accesses. The completer, *cmplt*, determines if the offset is the base register, *b*, or the base register plus the index register *x*. The completer, encoded in the *m* field of the instruction, specifies base register modification (see Table 7-3 on page 7-51 for the assembly language completer mnemonics.)

This is an implementation-dependent instruction that can be used to purge the entire data TLB without knowing the translations in the TLB. No broadcast occurs in a multiprocessor system.

Operation: if (priv != 0)
             privileged_operation_trap;
          else {
             space ← space_select(s,GR[b],INDEXED);
             switch (cmplt) {
                case M: offset ← GR[b];   /*m=1*/
                          GR[b] ← GR[b] + GR[x];
                          break;
                default: offset ← GR[b] + GR[x];   /*m=0*/
                          break;
             }
             DTLB_purge_entries(space,offset);
          }

Exceptions: Privileged operation trap

Restrictions: This instruction may be executed only at the most privileged level.

Notes: This instruction may be used to purge both instruction entries and data entries from a combined TLB. This instruction does not necessarily purge the entry specified by "space" and "offset".

Format: PERMH,c   r,t

(10)

3E	r	r	0	c0	0	c1	c2	c3	0	t
6	5	5	1	2	1	2	2	2	1	5

Purpose: To select any combination of four halfwords from a source register, and place that combination in a result register.

Description: The source register, GR r, is treated as four 16-bit fields. A 64-bit result is generated, consisting of four 16-bit fields. Each field in the result is independently selected from one of the fields in GR r. The result is placed in GR t.

The choice of which fields are selected for each result field is specified by the completer c, which is given as a four-digit number, where each digit is either 0, 1, 2, or 3. Each digit controls the selection for one result field. For example, a digit value of 0 specifies that the result field receives the value from the leftmost source field, and a digit value of 2 selects the next-to-rightmost source field. c is encoded in the $c0$, $c1$, $c2$, and $c3$ fields of the instruction. $c0$ encodes the first digit, $c1$ the second, etc. Thus, $c0$ encodes which source field will appear in the leftmost result field, $c1$ which source field will appear in the next-to-leftmost result field, etc.

The array of boolean variables "c[]" in the operation section represent the completer c. The variable "c[0]" represents the first digit in c, "c[1]" the second digit in c, etc.

Any combination or permutation of the four source fields can be generated.

Operation:
```
parallel for (i ← 0; i <= 3; i++) {
        start ← 16 * i;
        end ← start + 15;
        field_select ← c[i];
        switch (field_select) {
            case 0:   GR[t]{start..end} ← GR[r]{0..15};
                      break;
            case 1:   GR[t]{start..end} ← GR[r]{16..31};
                      break;
            case 2:   GR[t]{start..end} ← GR[r]{32..47};
                      break;
            case 3:   GR[t]{start..end} ← GR[r]{48..63};
                      break;
        }
    }
```

Exceptions: None.

Notes: The source register specifier, r, must appear in both source operand fields of the instruction, as shown in the format. If it does not, the operation is undefined.

Programming Note

The following figures illustrate examples of how the source fields are specified and how the result is generated.

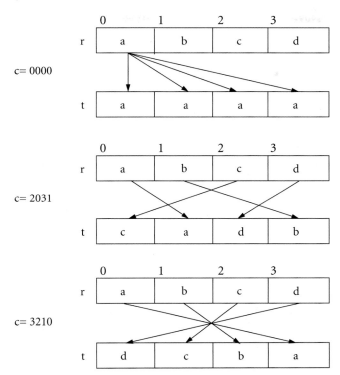

Format: PITLB,scope,cmplt   x(sr,b)

(26)

01	b	x	s	0	e1	8	m	rv
6	5	5	3	2	1	4	1	5

Purpose: To invalidate an instruction TLB entry.

Description: The instruction or combined TLB entry (if any) for the page specified by the effective address generated by the instruction is removed. The completer, *scope*, encoded in the *e1* field of the instruction, specifies whether the purge is global to all processors in a multiprocessor system (no completer, *e1*=0) or limited to the local processor (,L completer, *e1*=1.) The completer, *cmplt*, encoded in the *m* field of the instruction, determines if the offset is the base register, *b*, or the base register plus index register, *x*, and whether base register modification is performed (see Table 7-3 on page 7-51 for the assembly language completer mnemonics.)

TLB purges are strongly ordered. In a multiprocessor system, a global TLB purge causes a purge request to be broadcast to all instruction and combined TLBs. The other processors must remove the entry before the issuing processor continues.

Operation: if (priv != 0)
          privileged_operation_trap;
      else {
          space ← SR[assemble_3(s)];
          switch (cmplt) {
              case M: offset ← GR[b];   /*m=1*/
                       GR[b] ← GR[b] + GR[x];
                       break;
              default: offset ← GR[b] + GR[x];   /*m=0*/
                       break;
          }
          page_size ← (GR[b]{60..63} + 1) * 4096;
          for (i ← 0; i < page_size/4096; i++) {
              if (entry ← ITLB_search(space, offset + i*4096))
                  ITLB_purge_local(entry);
          }
          if (scope != L)
              ITLB_purge_broadcast(space,offset,page_size);
      }

Exceptions: Privileged operation trap

Restrictions: This instruction may be executed only at the most privileged level.

Notes: This instruction may be used to purge both instruction entries and data entries from a combined TLB.

Format: PITLBE,cmplt   x(sr,b)

(26)	01	b	x	s	09	m	rv
	6	5	5	3	7	1	5

Purpose: To invalidate an instruction TLB entry without matching the address portion.

Description: The instruction or combined TLB entries (if any) specified by an implementation-dependent function of the effective address generated by the instruction are removed. All the fields of these entries may be changed to arbitrary values as long as these entries do not validate any subsequent accesses. The completer, *cmplt*, determines if the offset is the base register, *b*, or the base register plus the index register *x*. The completer, encoded in the *m* field of the instruction, specifies base register modification (see Table 7-3 on page 7-51 for the assembly language completer mnemonics.) The space register, *sr*, is encoded in the *s* field of the instruction.

This is an implementation-dependent instruction that can be used to purge the entire instruction TLB without knowing the translations in the TLB. No broadcast occurs in a multiprocessor system.

Operation:
```
if (priv != 0)
        privileged_operation_trap;
else {
        space  ←  SR[assemble_3(s)];
        switch (cmplt) {
            case M:  offset  ←  GR[b];                          /*m=1*/
                     GR[b]  ←  GR[b] + GR[x];
                     break;
            default: offset  ←  GR[b] + GR[x];                  /*m=0*/
                     break;
        }
        ITLB_purge_entries(space,offset);
}
```

Exceptions: Privileged operation trap

Restrictions: This instruction may be executed only at the most privileged level.

Notes: This instruction may be used to purge both instruction entries and data entries from a combined TLB. This instruction does not necessarily purge the entry specified by "space" and "offset".

Format: POPBTS   i

(23)

3A	0	0	2	0	i	1	0	1
6	5	5	3	1	9	1	1	1

Purpose: To pop one or more entries off the branch target stack.

Description: The top i entries of the branch target stack are popped.

If this instruction is nullified, the results are undefined.

This instruction is executed as a NOP on machines that do not implement the branch target stack.

Operation: for (j=i; j>0; j--) {
            pop_from_BTS();
        }

Exceptions: None

Format: PROBE,cmplt   (s,b),r,t

(24)

01	b	r	s	23	e1	0	t
6	5	5	2	7	1	1	5

Purpose: To determine whether read or write access to a given address is allowed.

Description: A test is performed to determine if access to the address computed by the instruction is
permitted at the privilege level given by the two rightmost bits of the GR r. GR t is set to 1 if
the test succeeds and 0 otherwise.

The completer, *cmplt*, encoded in the sub-operation field *e1*, specifies whether the
instruction checks for read (*cmplt* ==R) or write (*cmplt* ==W) access (*e1*=0: check for read
access, *e1*=1: check for write access.) If the PSW P-bit is 1, the protection IDs are also
checked. The instruction performs data address translation regardless of the state of the
PSW D-bit.

Operation: space ← space_select(s,GR[b],INDEXED);
offset ← GR[b];
if (DTLB_search(space,offset))
    switch (cmplt) {
        case W: if (write_access_allowed(space,offset,GR[r]))   /*e1=1*/
                GR[t] ← 1;
            else
                GR[t] ← 0;
            break;
        case R:
        default: if (read_access_allowed(space,offset,GR[r]))   /*e1=0*/
                GR[t] ← 1;
            else
                GR[t] ← 0;
            break;
    }
else
    non-access_data_TLB_miss_fault();

Exceptions: Non-access data TLB miss fault/non-access data page fault

Notes: If this instruction causes a non-access data TLB miss fault/non-access data page fault, the
operating system's handler is required to search its page tables for the given address. If
found, it does the appropriate TLB insert and returns to the interrupting instruction. If not
found, the handler must decode the target field of the instruction, set that GR to 0, set the
IPSW[N] bit to 1, and return to the interrupting instruction.

It is an undefined operation to execute a PROBE with a nonzero *s*-field at a nonzero
privilege level when the PSW W-bit is 1.

Format: PROBEI,cmplt   (s,b),i,t

(24)

01	b	i	s	63	e1	0	t
6	5	5	2	7	1	1	5

Purpose: To determine whether read or write access to a given address is allowed.

Description: A test is performed to determine if access to the address computed by the instruction is permitted at the privilege level given by the two rightmost bits of the immediate value *i*. GR *t* is set to 1 if the test succeeds and 0 otherwise.

The completer, *cmplt*, encoded in the sub-operation field *e1*, specifies whether the instruction checks for read (*cmplt* ==R) or write (*cmplt* ==W) access (*e1*=0: check for read access, *e1*=1: check for write access.) If the PSW P-bit is 1, the protection IDs are also checked. This instruction performs data address translation regardless of the state of the PSW D-bit.

Operation: space ← space_select(s,GR[b],INDEXED);
offset ← GR[b];
if (DTLB_search(space,offset))
    switch (cmplt) {
        case W: if (write_access_allowed(space,offset,i))   /*e1=1*/
                  GR[t] ← 1;
            else
                  GR[t] ← 0;
            break;
        case R:
        default: if (read_access_allowed(space,offset,i))   /*e1=0*/
                  GR[t] ← 1;
            else
                  GR[t] ← 0;
            break;
    }
else
    non-access_data_TLB_miss_fault();

Exceptions: Non-access data TLB miss fault/non-access data page fault

Notes: If this instruction causes a non-access data TLB miss fault/non-access data page fault, the operating system's handler is required to search its page tables for the given address. If found, it does the appropriate TLB insert and returns to the interrupting instruction. If not found, the handler must decode the target field of the instruction, set that GR to 0, set the IPSW[N] bit to 1, and return to the interrupting instruction.

It is an undefined operation to execute a PROBEI with a nonzero s-field at a nonzero privilege level when the PSW W-bit is 1.

Push Branch Target Stack   PUSHBTS

Format: PUSHBTS   r

(23)

3A	0	r	2	0	0	0	0	1
6	5	5	3	1	9	1	1	1

Purpose: To push a value from a GR onto the branch target stack.

Description: Either the value in GR *r*, or an "invalid" value is pushed onto the branch target stack.

If this instruction is nullified, the results are undefined.

This instruction is executed as a NOP on machines that do not implement the branch target stack.

Operation: push_onto_BTS(GR[b]{0..61});

Exceptions: None.

Format: PUSHNOM

(23)

3A	0	0	2	0	0	0	0	1
6	5	5	3	1	9	1	1	1

Purpose: To push the currently nominated address onto the branch target stack.

Description: If there is a current nominated value, it is pushed onto the branch target stack. Otherwise, an "invalid" value is pushed.

If this instruction is nullified, the results are undefined.

This instruction is executed as a NOP on machines that do not implement the branch target stack.

Operation: push_onto_BTS(BNR);

Exceptions: None.

Format: RFI,cmplt

(33)

00	rv	rv	rv	6	e1	0
6	5	5	3	4	4	5

Purpose: To restore processor state and restart execution of an interrupted instruction stream and optionally restore GRs 1, 8, 9, 16, 17, 24, and 25 from the shadow registers.

Description: The PSW register contents are restored from the IPSW register but are not modified by this instruction. The IA queues are restored from the IIA queues. Execution continues at the locations loaded into the IA queues.

The completer, *cmplt*, encoded in the sub-operation field *e1*, specifies whether the contents of GRs 1, 8, 9, 16, 17, 24, and 25 are restored from the shadow registers (*e1*=5: restore from shadow registers, *e1*=0: GRs are unchanged.) Execution of an RFI with the ,R completer when the contents of the shadow registers are undefined leaves the contents of GRs 1, 8, 9, 16, 17, 24, and 25 undefined. After execution of an RFI with the ,R completer, the SHRs are undefined.

Execution of an RFI with the IPSW Q-bit equal to 0 returns to the location specified by the IIA queues, but leaves the IIAOQ, IIASQ, and IPRs undefined. Software is responsible for avoiding interruptions during the execution of an RFI. Execution of an RFI instruction when any of the PSW Q, I, or R bits are ones is an undefined operation. Execution of an RFI instruction when the PSW L-bit is a one is an undefined operation if the new privilege level after execution of the RFI is non zero.

Operation: if (priv != 0)
                          privileged_operation_trap;
                     else {
                          if (cmplt == R) {
                               GR[1]   ←   SHR[0];   /*e1=5*/
                               GR[8]   ←   SHR[1];
                               GR[9]   ←   SHR[2];
                               GR[16]   ←   SHR[3];
                               GR[17]   ←   SHR[4];
                               GR[24]   ←   SHR[5];
                               GR[25]   ←   SHR[6];
                          } else
                               ;   /* do nothing */   /*e1=0*/
                          PSW   ←   IPSW;
                          IAOQ_Back   ←   IIAOQ_Back;
                          IAOQ_Front   ←   IIAOQ_Front;
                          if (!level_0) {
                               IASQ_Back   ←   IIASQ_Back & ~zero_ext(IIAOQ_Back{0..31},32);
                               IASQ_Front   ←   IIASQ_Front & ~zero_ext(IIAOQ_Front{0..31},32);
                          }
                     }

Exceptions: Privileged operation trap

Restrictions: This instruction may be executed only at the most privileged level.

Because this instruction restores the state of the execution pipeline, it is possible for software to place the processor in states which could not result from the execution of any sequence of instructions not involving interruptions. For example, it could set the PSW B-bit to 0 even though the addresses in the IA queues are not contiguous. The operation of the machine is undefined in such cases, and it is the responsibility of software to avoid them.

To avoid improper processor states, software must not set the PSW B-bit to 0 with different privilege levels in the IAOQ.

Notes: When this instruction returns to an instruction which executes at a lower privilege level, a lower-privilege transfer trap is not taken.

This instruction is the only instruction that can set the PSW Q-bit to 1.

Format: RSM   i,t

(33)	00	i	0	73	t
	6	10	3	8	5

Purpose: To selectively reset bits in the system mask to 0.

Description: The current value of the system mask, PSW{36,37,56..63}, is saved in GR t and then the complement of the immediate value i is ANDed with the system mask.

Operation:
```
if (priv != 0)
        privileged_operation_trap;
else {
    GR[t]         ←   0;
    GR[t]{36}     ←   PSW[W];
    GR[t]{37}     ←   PSW[E];
    GR[t]{56}     ←   PSW[O];
    GR[t]{57}     ←   PSW[G];
    GR[t]{58}     ←   PSW[F];
    GR[t]{59}     ←   PSW[R];
    GR[t]{60}     ←   PSW[Q];
    GR[t]{61}     ←   PSW[P];
    GR[t]{62}     ←   PSW[D];
    GR[t]{63}     ←   PSW[I];
    PSW[W]←   PSW[W] & (~i{0});
    PSW[E] ←   PSW[E] & (~i{1});
    PSW[O] ←   PSW[O] & (~i{2});
    PSW[G] ←   PSW[G] & (~i{3});
    PSW[F] ←   PSW[F] & (~i{4});
    PSW[R] ←   PSW[R] & (~i{5});
    PSW[Q] ←   PSW[Q] & (~i{6});
    PSW[P] ←   PSW[P] & (~i{7});
    PSW[D] ←   PSW[D] & (~i{8});
    PSW[I] ←   PSW[I] & (~i{9});
}
```

Exceptions: Privileged operation trap

Restrictions: This instruction may be executed only at the most privileged level.

Notes: The state of the IPRs, IIA queues, and the IPSW is undefined when this instruction is used to set the Q-bit to 0, if it was not already 0.

Format: SHLADD,cmplt,cond   r1,sa,r2,t

(8)

02	r2	r1	c	f	e1	1	0	sa	d	t
6	5	5	3	1	2	1	1	2	1	5

Purpose: To provide a primitive operation for multiplication.

Description: GR $r1$ is shifted left sa bit positions and added to GR $r2$. If no trap occurs, the result is placed in GR t. The variable "carry_borrows" in the operation section captures the 4-bit carries resulting from the add operation. The completer, *cmplt*, encoded in the $e1$ field, specifies whether the carry/borrow bits in the PSW are updated and whether a trap is taken on signed overflow as shown in the table below. The shift amount is either 1, 2, or 3, and is encoded in the sa field of the instruction.

Completer	Description	e1
<none>	Shift left and add	1
L	Shift left and add logical	2
TSV	Shift left and add and trap on signed overflow	3

The following instruction is nullified if the values added satisfy the specified condition, *cond*. The condition is encoded in the c, d, and f fields of the instruction. The boolean variable "overflow" in the operation section is set if the operation results in a 32-bit signed overflow ($d=0$) or a 64-bit signed overflow ($d=1$.) For addition with carry in, the d field encodes whether the word carry (PSW C/B{8}, $d=0$), or the doubleword carry (PSW C/B{0}, $d=1$) is used.

For this instruction, signed overflow condition means that either the bit(s) shifted out differ from the leftmost bit following the shift or an ordinary signed overflow occurred during the addition. Unsigned overflow means that one or more of the bit(s) shifted out are 1 or an ordinary unsigned overflow occurred during the addition. For 32-bit overflows, it is the bits shifted out of the lower word that are checked. The conditions take on special interpretations since the shift operation participates in overflow determination.

The $e1$ field encodes whether the carry/borrow bits in the PSW are updated and whether a trap is taken on overflow ($e1=1$: carries updated, no trap, $e1=2$: carries not updated, no trap, $e1=3$: carries updated, trap on overflow.)

Conditions: The condition is any of the 32-bit add conditions shown in Table D-6 on page D-5 or any of the 64-bit add conditions shown in Table D-7 on page D-6. When a condition completer is not specified, the "never" condition is used. The boolean variable "cond_satisfied" in the operation section is set when the values added satisfy the specified condition.

Operation: res ← lshift(GR[r1],sa) + GR[r2];
if (cmplt == TSV && overflow)
        overflow_trap;
else {
        GR[t] ← res;
        if (cmplt != 'L')
                PSW[C/B] ← carry_borrows;
        if (cond_satisfied) PSW[N] ← 1;
}

Exceptions: Overflow trap

Notes: When the ,L completer is specified, no trapping on overflow is available.

Format: SHRPD,cond   r1,r2,sa,t

(11)

34	r2	r1	c	0	0	1	0	t
6	5	5	3	2	1	1	4	5

(14)

34	r2	r1	c	0	cp	1	cpos	t
6	5	5	3	1	1	1	5	5

Purpose: To shift a pair of registers by a fixed or variable amount and conditionally nullify the following instruction.

Description: The rightmost 63 bits of GR $r1$ are concatenated with the 64 bits of GR $r2$ and shifted right the number of bits given by the shift amount, sa. The rightmost 64 bits of the result are placed in GR t.

The shift amount, sa, can either be a constant (specifying a fixed shift), or can be SAR, the Shift Amount Register (CR 11) (specifying a variable shift.) Format 11 is used for variable shifts; Format 14 is used for fixed shifts. For fixed shifts, the shift amount sa in the assembly language format is represented by cat($cp,cpos$) in the machine instruction, whose value is 63–sa.

The following instruction is nullified if the result of the operation satisfies the specified condition, $cond$. The condition is encoded in the c field of the instruction.

Conditions: The condition is any of the 64-bit extract/deposit conditions shown in Table D-14 on page D-9. When a condition completer is not specified, the "never" condition is used. The boolean variable "cond_satisfied" in the operation section is set when the result of the operation satisfies the specified condition.

Operation: if (fixed_shift)   /* (Format 14) */
          shamt ← sa;
     else   /* (Format 11) */
          shamt ← CR[11];
     GR[t] ← rshift(cat(GR[r1]{1..63},GR[r2]),shamt){63..126};
     if (cond_satisfied) PSW[N] ← 1;

Exceptions: None.

Programming Note

A logical right shift of GR *r* by a variable amount contained in GR *p* leaving the result in GR *t* may be done by the following sequence:

```
MTSAR    p
SHRPD    0,r,sar,t
```

An arithmetic right shift can be done with an extract instruction. See EXTRACT DOUBLEWORD for an example.

If *r1* and *r2* name the same register, its contents are rotated and placed in GR *t*. For example, the following rotates the contents of *ra* right by 8 bits:

```
SHRPD    ra,ra,8,ra
```

Format: SHRPW,cond   r1,r2,sa,t

(11)

34	r2	r1	c	0	0	0	0	t
6	5	5	3	2	1	1	4	5

(14)

34	r2	r1	c	0	1	0	cpos	t
6	5	5	3	1	1	1	5	5

Purpose: To shift the rightmost 32 bits of a pair of registers by a fixed or variable amount and conditionally nullify the following instruction.

Description: The rightmost 31 bits of GR $r1$ are concatenated with the rightmost 32 bits of GR $r2$ and shifted right the number of bits given by the shift amount, sa. The rightmost 32 bits of the result are placed in GR t. The leftmost 32 bits of GR t are undefined.

The shift amount, sa, can either be a constant (specifying a fixed shift), or can be SAR, the Shift Amount Register (CR 11) (specifying a variable shift.) Format 11 is used for variable shifts; Format 14 is used for fixed shifts. For variable shifts, the leftmost bit of the SAR is ignored, so the shift amount is between 0 and 31. For fixed shifts, the shift amount sa in the assembly language format is represented by $cpos$ in the machine instruction, whose value is $31-sa$.

The following instruction is nullified if the result of the operation satisfies the specified condition, $cond$. The condition is encoded in the c field of the instruction.

Conditions: The condition is any of the 32-bit extract/deposit conditions shown in Table D-13 on page D-9. When a condition completer is not specified, the "never" condition is used. The boolean variable "cond_satisfied" in the operation section is set when the result of the operation satisfies the specified condition.

Operation:
```
if (fixed_shift)                                         /* (Format 14) */
        shamt ← sa;
else                                                     /* (Format 11) */
        shamt ← CR[11]{1..5};
GR[t]{32..63}  ←  rshift(cat(GR[r1]{33..63},GR[r2]{32..63}),shamt){31..62};
GR[t]{0..31}  ←  undefined;
if (cond_satisfied) PSW[N]  ←  1;
```

Exceptions: None.

Programming Note

A logical right shift of GR *r* by a variable amount contained in GR *p* leaving the result in GR *t* may be done by the following sequence:

```
MTSAR    p
SHRPW    0,r,sar,t
```

An arithmetic right shift can be done with an extract instruction. See EXTRACT WORD for an example.

If *r1* and *r2* name the same register, its contents are rotated and placed in GR *t*. For example, the following rotates the contents of *ra* right by 8 bits:

```
SHRPW    ra,ra,8,ra
```

Format: SPOP0,sfu,sop,n

(34)

04	sop1	0	sfu	n	sop2
6	15	2	3	1	5

Purpose: To invoke a special function unit operation.

Description: The SFU identified by *sfu* is directed to perform the operation specified by the information supplied to it. If nullification is specified, the SFU also computes a 1-bit condition that causes the following instruction to be nullified if the condition is satisfied.

The *sop* field in the assembly language format is the concatenation of the *sop1* and *sop2* fields in the machine instruction, sop = cat(sop1,sop2.)

Operation: sfu_operation0(cat(sop1,sfu,n,sop2),IAOQ_Front{30..31});
if (n && sfu_condition0(cat(sop1,sfu,n,sop2),IAOQ_Front{30..31}))
      PSW[N] ← 1;

Exceptions: Assist emulation trap   Assist exception trap

Format: SPOP1,sfu,sop,n   t

(35)

04	sop	1	sfu	n	t
6	15	2	3	1	5

Purpose: To copy a special function unit register or a result to a general register.

Description: A single word is sent from the SFU identified by *sfu* to GR *t*. The SFU uses its internal state and the instruction fields supplied to it to compute or select the result. If nullification is specified, the SFU also computes a 1-bit condition that causes the following instruction to be nullified if the condition is satisfied.

Operation: GR[t] ← sfu_operation1(cat(sop,sfu,n),IAOQ_Front{30..31});
    if (n && sfu_condition1(cat(sop,sfu,n),IAOQ_Front{30..31}))
       PSW[N] ← 1;

Exceptions: Assist emulation trap   Assist exception trap

Notes: The SPECIAL OPERATION ONE instruction is used to implement the IDENTIFY SFU pseudo-operation. This operation returns a 32-bit identification number from the special function unit *sfu* to general register *t*. The value returned is implementation dependent and is useful for configuration, diagnostics, and error recovery. The state of the SFU is undefined after this instruction.

Each implementation must choose an identification number that identifies the version of the SFU. The values all zeros and all ones are reserved. The assist emulation trap handler returns zero when executing this instruction. An assist exception trap is not allowed and this instruction must be implemented by all SFUs. The IDENTIFY SFU pseudo-operation is coded as: SPOP1,sfu,0   t

Format: SPOP2,sfu,sop,n   r

(36)

04	r	sop1	2	sfu	n	sop2
6	5	10	2	3	1	5

Purpose: To perform a parameterized special function unit operation.

Description: GR *r* is passed to the SFU identified by *sfu*. The SFU uses its internal state, the contents of the register, and the instruction fields supplied to it to compute a result. If nullification is specified, the SFU also computes a 1-bit condition that causes the following instruction to be nullified if the condition is satisfied.

The *sop* field in the assembly language format is the concatenation of the *sop1* and *sop2* fields in the machine instruction, sop = cat(sop1,sop2.)

Operation: sfu_operation2(cat(sop1,sfu,n,sop2),IAOQ_Front{30..31},GR[r]);
if (n && sfu_condition2(cat(sop1,sfu,n,sop2),IAOQ_Front{30..31},GR[r]))
    PSW[N] ← 1;

Exceptions: Assist emulation trap   Assist exception trap

Format: SPOP3,sfu,sop,n   r1,r2

(37)

04	r2	r1	sop1	3	sfu	n	sop2
6	5	5	5	2	3	1	5

Purpose: To perform a parameterized special function unit operation.

Description: GR *r1* and GR *r2* are passed to the SFU identified by *sfu*. The SFU uses its internal state, the contents of the two registers, and the instruction fields supplied to it to compute a result. If nullification is specified, the SFU also computes a 1-bit condition that causes the following instruction to be nullified if the condition is satisfied.

The *sop* field in the assembly language format is the concatenation of the *sop1* and *sop2* fields in the machine instruction, sop = cat(sop1,sop2.)

Operation: sfu_operation3(cat(sop1,sfu,n,sop2),IAOQ_Front{30..31},GR[r1],GR[r2]);
if (n && sfu_condition3(cat(sop1,sfu,n,sop2),IAOQ_Front{30..31},GR[r1],GR[r2]))
        PSW[N] ← 1;

Exceptions: Assist emulation trap   Assist exception trap

Format: SSM   i,t

(33)

00	i	0	6B	t
6	10	3	8	5

Purpose: To selectively set bits in the system mask to 1.

Description: The current value of the system mask, PSW{36,37,56..63}, is saved in GR t and then the immediate value i is ORed with the system mask. Setting the PSW Q-bit, PSW{60}, to 1 with this instruction, if it was not already 1, is an undefined operation.

Operation:

```
if (priv != 0)
        privileged_operation_trap;
else {
    if ((PSW[Q] == 0) && (i{6}))
        undefined;
    else {
        GR[t]        ←   0;
        GR[t]{36}    ←   PSW[W];
        GR[t]{37}    ←   PSW[E];
        GR[t]{56}    ←   PSW[O];
        GR[t]{57}    ←   PSW[G];
        GR[t]{58}    ←   PSW[F];
        GR[t]{59}    ←   PSW[R];
        GR[t]{60}    ←   PSW[Q];
        GR[t]{61}    ←   PSW[P];
        GR[t]{62}    ←   PSW[D];
        GR[t]{63}    ←   PSW[I];
        PSW[W]←   PSW[W] I i{0};
        PSW[E] ←   PSW[E] I i{1};
        PSW[O] ←   PSW[O] I i{2};
        PSW[G] ←   PSW[G] I i{3};
        PSW[F] ←   PSW[F] I i{4};
        PSW[R] ←   PSW[R] I i{5};
        PSW[P] ←   PSW[P] I i{7};
        PSW[D] ←   PSW[D] I i{8};
        PSW[I] ←   PSW[I] I i{9};
    }
}
```

Exceptions: Privileged operation trap

Restrictions: This instruction may be executed only at the most privileged level.

Format: STB,cmplt,cc   r,d(s,b)

(1)

18	b	r	s	im14
6	5	5	2	14

(6)

03	b	r	s	a	1	cc	8	m	im5
6	5	5	2	1	1	2	4	1	5

Purpose: To store a byte from a general register.

Description: The rightmost byte in GR r is stored in the aligned byte at the effective address. The offset is formed as the sum of a base register, b, and a displacement d. The displacement can be either long (Format 1) or short (Format 6.) The displacement is encoded into the immediate field. Optional base modification can also be performed.

The completer, *cmplt*, determines whether the offset is the base register, or the base register plus the displacement. The completer also specifies base register modification and ordering constraints (see Table H-1 on page H-4, and Table H-3 on page H-8 for the assembly language completer mnemonics.) The completer, *cc*, specifies the cache control hint (see Table 6-8 on page 6-10.)

For short displacements, a one in the m field specifies base modification, and the a field encodes whether pre-modification ($a=1$), or post-modification ($a=0$) is performed.

If base register modification is specified and $b = r$, the value stored at the effective address is the byte from the source register before modification.

Operation: if (d > 15 || d < -16) {   /* long displacement */
                        dx ← sign_ext(assemble_16(s,im14),16);   /* (Format 1) */
                        cc ← NO_HINT;
                 } else   /* short displacement */
                        dx ← low_sign_ext(im5,5);   /* (Format 6) */
                 space ← space_select(s,GR[b],format);
                 if (cmplt == O)
                        enforce_ordered_store;
                 switch (cmplt) {
                        case MB: offset ← GR[b] + dx;
                                      mem_store(space,offset,0,7,cc,GR[r]{56..63});
                                      GR[b] ← GR[b] + dx;
                                      break;
                        case MA: offset ← GR[b];
                                      mem_store(space,offset,0,7,cc,GR[r]{56..63});
                                      GR[b] ← GR[b] + dx;
                                      break;
                        default: offset ← GR[b] + dx;
                                      mem_store(space,offset,0,7,cc,GR[r]{56..63});
                                      break;
                 }

Exceptions: Data TLB miss fault/data page fault   TLB dirty bit trap
                  Data memory access rights trap   Page reference trap
                  Data memory protection ID trap
                  Data memory break trap

Restrictions: If the completer *O* is specified, the displacement must be 0.

Format: STBY,cmplt,cc   r,d(s,b)

(6)

03	b	r	s	a	1	cc	C	m	im5
6	5	5	2	1	1	2	4	1	5

Purpose: To implement the beginning, middle, and ending cases for fast byte moves with unaligned sources and destinations.

Description: If the PSW E-bit is 0 and begin (modifier ",B" corresponding to $a = 0$) is specified, the rightmost bytes of GR r are stored in memory starting at the byte whose address is given by the effective address. The number of bytes stored is sufficient to fill out the word containing the byte addressed by the effective address.

If the PSW E-bit is 0 and end (modifier ",E" corresponding to $a = 1$) is specified, the leftmost bytes of the rightmost word of GR r are stored in memory starting at the leftmost byte in the word specified by the effective address, and continuing until (but not including) the byte specified by the effective address. When the effective address specifies the leftmost byte in a word, nothing is stored, but protection is checked and the cache line is marked as *dirty*.

If the PSW E-bit is 1 and begin (modifier ",B" corresponding to $a = 0$) is specified, the leftmost bytes of the rightmost word of GR r are stored in memory starting at the byte whose address is given by the effective address. The number of bytes stored is sufficient to fill out the word containing the byte addressed by the effective address.

If the PSW E-bit is 1 and end (modifier ",E" corresponding to $a = 1$) is specified, the rightmost bytes of GR r are stored in memory starting at the leftmost byte in the word specified by the effective address, and continuing until (but not including) the byte specified by the effective address. When the effective address specifies the leftmost byte in a word, nothing is stored, but protection is checked and the cache line is marked as *dirty*.

If base register modification is specified through completer ",M", GR b is updated and then truncated to a word address. (Table 7-7 defines the assembly language completer mnemonics.) If base register modification is specified and $b = r$, the value stored at the effective address is the bytes from the source register before modification.

Table 7-7. Store Bytes Instruction Completers

cmplt	Description	a	m
<none> or B	Beginning case, don't modify base register	0	0
B,M	Beginning case, Modify base register	0	1
E	Ending case, don't modify base register	1	0
E,M	Ending case, Modify base register	1	1

The completer, *cc*, specifies the cache control hint (see Table 6-8 on page 6-10.) If the first byte of the addressed cache line is not written to, the processor must perform the store as if the cache control hint had not been specified.

Operation: space ← space_select(s,GR[b],format);
dx ← low_sign_ext(im5,5);
if (cmplt == B,M)   /*a=0, m=1*/
    offset ← GR[b];
else
    offset ← GR[b] + dx;
pos ← 8*(offset & 0x3);
offset ← offset & ~0x3;   /* word aligned */
switch (cmplt) {
    case B: /*a=0, m=0*/
        if (PSW[E] == 0)
            mem_store(space,offset,pos,31,cc,GR[r]{pos+32..63});
        else
            mem_store(space,offset,pos,31,cc,GR[r]{32..63-pos});
        break;
    case E: /*a=1, m=0*/
        if (PSW[E] == 0)
            mem_store(space,offset,0,pos-1,cc,GR[r]{32..pos+31});
        else
            mem_store(space,offset,0,pos-1,cc,GR[r]{64-pos..63});
        break;
    case B,M: /*a=0, m=1*/
        if (PSW[E] == 0)
            mem_store(space,offset,pos,31,cc,GR[r]{pos+32..63});
        else
            mem_store(space,offset,pos,31,cc,GR[r]{32..63-pos});
        GR[b] ← (GR[b] + dx) & ~0x3;
        break;
    case E,M: /*a=1, m=1*/
        if (PSW[E] == 0)
            mem_store(space,offset,0,pos-1,cc,GR[r]{32..pos+31});
        else
            mem_store(space,offset,0,pos-1,cc,GR[r]{64-pos..63});
        GR[b] ← (GR[b] + dx) & ~0x3;
        break;
}

Exceptions: Data TLB miss fault/data page fault   TLB dirty bit trap
Data memory access rights trap   Page reference trap
Data memory protection ID trap   Data memory break trap

Notes: All bits of the original virtual offset are saved, unmasked, to IOR (CR21) if this instruction traps.

For this instruction, the low 2 bits of the virtual offset are masked to 0 when comparing against the contents of the data breakpoint address offset registers.

Programming Note

The STBY instruction with the ',E' completer and the effective address specifying the leftmost byte of the word may be used to implement a memory scrubbing operation. This is possible because the line is marked *dirty* but the contents are not modified.

Format: STD,cmplt,cc   r,d(s,b)

(3)

1C	b	r	s	im10a	m	a	0	i
6	5	5	2	10	1	1	1	1

(6)

03	b	r	s	a	1	cc	B	m	im5
6	5	5	2	1	1	2	4	1	5

Purpose: To store a doubleword from a general register.

Description: GR r is stored in the aligned doubleword at the effective address. The offset is formed as the sum of a base register, b, and a displacement d. The displacement can be either long (Format 3) or short (Format 6.) The displacement is encoded into the immediate field. Optional base modification can also be performed.

The completer, *cmplt*, determines whether the offset is the base register, or the base register plus the displacement. The completer also specifies base register modification and ordering constraints (see Table H-1 on page H-4, and Table H-3 on page H-8 for the assembly language completer mnemonics.) The completer, *cc*, specifies the cache control hint (see Table 6-8 on page 6-10.)

For long and short displacements, a one in the m field specifies base modification, and the a field encodes whether pre-modification ($a=1$), or post-modification ($a=0$) is performed.

If base register modification is specified and $b = r$, the value stored at the effective address is the word from the source register before modification.

Operation: if (d > 15 || d < -16) {   /* long displacement */
              dx ← sign_ext(assemble_16a(s,cat(im10a,0),i),16);   /* (Format 3) */
              cc ← NO_HINT;
          } else   /* short displacement */
              dx ← low_sign_ext(im5,5);   /* (Format 6) */
          space ← space_select(s,GR[b],format);
          if (cmplt == O)
              enforce_ordered_store;
          switch (cmplt) {
              case MB: offset ← GR[b] + dx;
                            mem_store(space,offset,0,63,cc,GR[r]);
                            GR[b] ← GR[b] + dx;
                            break;
              case MA: offset ← GR[b];
                            mem_store(space,offset,0,63,cc,GR[r]);
                            GR[b] ← GR[b] + dx;
                            break;
              default: offset ← GR[b] + dx;
                            mem_store(space,offset,0,63,cc,GR[r]);
                            break;
          }

Exceptions: Data TLB miss fault/data page fault   Data memory break trap
                 Data memory access rights trap   TLB dirty bit trap
                 Data memory protection ID trap   Page reference trap
                 Unaligned data reference trap

Restrictions: For long displacements (Format 3), only displacements which are multiples of eight may be used.

If the completer O is specified, the displacement must be 0.

Store Doubleword Absolute

STDA

Format: STDA,cmplt,cc   r,d(b)

(6)	03	b	r	0	a	1	cc	F	m	im5
	6	5	5	2	1	1	2	4	1	5

Purpose: To store a doubleword from a general register to an absolute address.

Description: GR r is stored in the aligned doubleword at the effective absolute address. The offset is formed as the sum of a base register, b, and a displacement d. The displacement is encoded into the immediate field. Optional base modification can also be performed.

The completer, *cmplt*, determines whether the offset is the base register, or the base register plus the displacement. The completer also specifies base register modification and ordering constraints (see Table H-1 on page H-4 for the assembly language completer mnemonics.) The completer, *cc*, specifies the cache control hint (see Table 6-8 on page 6-10.)

If base register modification is specified and b = r, the value stored at the effective address is the doubleword from the source register before modification. Protection is not checked when this instruction is executed. This operation is only defined if the address is aligned on an 8-byte boundary.

Operation:
```
if (priv != 0)
        privileged_operation_trap;
else {
        dx ← low_sign_ext(im5,5);
        if (cmplt == O)
            enforce_ordered_store;
        switch (cmplt) {
            case MB:    offset ← GR[b] + dx;
                        phys_mem_store(offset,0,63,cc,GR[r]);
                        GR[b] ← GR[b] + dx;
                        break;
            case MA:    offset ← GR[b];
                        phys_mem_store(offset,0,63,cc,GR[r]);
                        GR[b] ← GR[b] + dx;
                        break;
            default:    offset ← GR[b] + dx;
                        phys_mem_store(offset,0,63,cc,GR[r]);
                        break;
        }
}
```

Exceptions: Privileged operation trap

Restrictions: This instruction may be executed only at the most privileged level. If the completer O is specified, the displacement must be 0.

Format: STDBY,cmplt,cc   r,d(s,b)

(6)	03	b	r	s	a	1	cc	D	m	im5
	6	5	5	2	1	1	2	4	1	5

Purpose: To implement the beginning, middle, and ending cases for fast byte moves with unaligned sources and destinations.

Description: If the PSW E-bit is 0 and begin (modifier ",B" corresponding to $a = 0$) is specified, the rightmost bytes of GR r are stored in memory starting at the byte whose address is given by the effective address. The number of bytes stored is sufficient to fill out the doubleword containing the byte addressed by the effective address.

If the PSW E-bit is 0 and end (modifier ",E" corresponding to $a = 1$) is specified, the leftmost bytes of GR r are stored in memory starting at the leftmost byte in the doubleword specified by the effective address, and continuing until (but not including) the byte specified by the effective address. When the effective address specifies the leftmost byte in a doubleword, nothing is stored, but protection is checked and the cache line is marked as *dirty*.

If the PSW E-bit is 1 and begin (modifier ",B" corresponding to $a = 0$) is specified, the leftmost bytes of GR r are stored in memory starting at the byte whose address is given by the effective address. The number of bytes stored is sufficient to fill out the doubleword containing the byte addressed by the effective address.

If the PSW E-bit is 1 and end (modifier ",E" corresponding to $a = 1$) is specified, the rightmost bytes of GR r are stored in memory starting at the leftmost byte in the doubleword specified by the effective address, and continuing until (but not including) the byte specified by the effective address. When the effective address specifies the leftmost byte in a doubleword, nothing is stored, but protection is checked and the cache line is marked as *dirty*.

If base register modification is specified through completer ",M", GR b is updated and then truncated to a doubleword address (see Table 7-7 on page 7-131 for the assembly language completer mnemonics.) If base register modification is specified and $b = r$, the value stored at the effective address is the bytes from the source register before modification.

The completer, cc, specifies the cache control hint (see Table 6-8 on page 6-10.) If the first byte of the addressed cache line is not written to, the processor must perform the store as if the cache control hint had not been specified.

Operation: space ← space_select(s,GR[b],format);
dx ← low_sign_ext(im5,5);
if (cmplt == B,M)   /*a=0, m=1*/
    offset ← GR[b];
else
    offset ← GR[b] + dx;
pos ← 8*(offset & 0x7);
offset ← offset & ~0x7;   /* doubleword aligned */
switch (cmplt) {
    case B: /*a=0, m=0*/
                if (PSW[E] == 0)
                    mem_store(space,offset,pos,63,cc,GR[r]{pos..63});
                else
                    mem_store(space,offset,pos,63,cc,GR[r]{0..63-pos});
                break;
    case E: /*a=1, m=0*/
                if (PSW[E] == 0)
                    mem_store(space,offset,0,pos-1,cc,GR[r]{0..pos-1});
                else
                    mem_store(space,offset,0,pos-1,cc,GR[r]{64-pos..63});
                break;
    case B,M: /*a=0, m=1*/
                if (PSW[E] == 0)
                    mem_store(space,offset,pos,63,cc,GR[r]{pos..63});
                else
                    mem_store(space,offset,pos,63,cc,GR[r]{0..63-pos});
                GR[b] ← (GR[b] + dx) & ~0x7;
                break;
    case E,M: /*a=1, m=1*/
                if (PSW[E] == 0)
                    mem_store(space,offset,0,pos-1,cc,GR[r]{0..pos-1});
                else
                    mem_store(space,offset,0,pos-1,cc,GR[r]{64-pos..63});
                GR[b] ← (GR[b] + dx) & ~0x7;
                break;
    }

Exceptions: Data TLB miss fault/data page fault   TLB dirty bit trap
Data memory access rights trap   Page reference trap
Data memory protection ID trap
Data memory break trap

Notes: All bits of the original virtual offset are saved, unmasked, to IOR (CR21) if this instruction traps.

For this instruction, the low 3 bits of the virtual offset are masked to 0 when comparing against the contents of the data breakpoint address offset registers.

Programming Note

The STDBY instruction with the ',E' completer and the effective address specifying the leftmost byte of the doubleword may be used to implement a memory scrubbing operation. This is possible because the line is marked *dirty* but the contents are not modified.

Format: STH,cmplt,cc   r,d(s,b)

(1)

19	b	r	s	im14
6	5	5	2	14

(6)

03	b	r	s	a	1	cc	9	m	im5
6	5	5	2	1	1	2	4	1	5

Purpose: To store a halfword from a general register.

Description: The rightmost halfword in GR r is stored in the aligned halfword at the effective address. The offset is formed as the sum of a base register, b, and a displacement d. The displacement can be either long (Format 1) or short (Format 6.) The displacement is encoded into the immediate field. Optional base modification can also be performed.

The completer, *cmplt*, determines whether the offset is the base register, or the base register plus the displacement. The completer also specifies base register modification and ordering constraints (see Table H-1 on page H-4, and Table H-3 on page H-8 for the assembly language completer mnemonics.) The completer, *cc*, specifies the cache control hint (see Table 6-8 on page 6-10.)

For short displacements, a one in the m field specifies base modification, and the a field encodes whether pre-modification (a=1), or post-modification (a=0) is performed.

If base register modification is specified and $b = r$, the value stored at the effective address is the halfword from the source register before modification.

Operation: if (d > 15 || d < -16) {   /* long displacement */

                dx ← sign_ext(assemble_16(s,im14),16);   /* (Format 1) */

                cc ← NO_HINT;

        } else   /* short displacement */

                dx ← low_sign_ext(im5,5);   /* (Format 6) */

        space ← space_select(s,GR[b],format);

        if (cmplt == O)

                enforce_ordered_store;

        switch (cmplt) {

                case MB: offset ← GR[b] + dx;

                                mem_store(space,offset,0,15,cc,GR[r]{48..63});

                                GR[b] ← GR[b] + dx;

                                break;

                case MA: offset ← GR[b];

                                mem_store(space,offset,0,15,cc,GR[r]{48..63});

                                GR[b] ← GR[b] + dx;

                                break;

                default: offset ← GR[b] + dx;

                                mem_store(space,offset,0,15,cc,GR[r]{48..63});

                                break;

        }

Exceptions: Data TLB miss fault/data page fault   Data memory break trap

              Data memory access rights trap   TLB dirty bit trap

              Data memory protection ID trap   Page reference trap

              Unaligned data reference trap

Restrictions: If the completer O is specified, the displacement must be 0.

Format: STW,cmplt,cc   r,d(s,b)

(1)

1A/1B	b	r	s	im14
6	5	5	2	14

(2)

1F	b	r	s	im11a	2	i
6	5	5	2	11	2	1

(6)

03	b	r	s	a	1	cc	A	m	im5
6	5	5	2	1	1	2	4	1	5

Purpose: To store a word from a general register.

Description: The rightmost word in GR r is stored in the aligned word at the effective address. The offset is formed as the sum of a base register, b, and a displacement d. The displacement can be either long (Formats 1 and 2) or short (Format 6.) The displacement is encoded into the immediate field. Optional base modification can also be performed.

The completer, *cmplt*, determines whether the offset is the base register, or the base register plus the displacement. The completer also specifies base register modification and ordering constraints (see Table H-1 on page H-4, and Table H-3 on page H-8 for the assembly language completer mnemonics.) The completer, *cc*, specifies the cache control hint (see Table 6-8 on page 6-10.)

For long displacements with pre-decrement or post-increment, Format 1 (opcode 1B) is used. For long displacements with post-decrement or pre-increment, Format 2 is used. For long displacements with no base modification, Format 1 (opcode 1A) is used.

For short displacements, a one in the m field specifies base modification, and the a field encodes whether pre-modification (a=1), or post-modification (a=0) is performed.

If base register modification is specified and $b = r$, the value stored at the effective address is the word from the source register before modification.

Operation: if (d > 15 || d < -16) {   /* long displacement */
            if ((cmplt==MB && d>=0) || (cmplt==MA && d<0))
                dx ← sign_ext(assemble_16a(s,im11a,i),16);   /* (Format 2) */
            else
                dx ← sign_ext(assemble_16(s,im14),16);   /* (Format 1) */
            cc ← NO_HINT;
        } else   /* short displacement */
            dx ← low_sign_ext(im5,5);   /* (Format 6) */
        space ← space_select(s,GR[b],format);
        if (cmplt == O)
            enforce_ordered_store;
        switch (cmplt) {
            case MB: offset ← GR[b] + dx;
                           mem_store(space,offset,0,31,cc,GR[r]{32..63});
                           GR[b] ← GR[b] + dx;
                           break;
            case MA: offset ← GR[b];
                           mem_store(space,offset,0,31,cc,GR[r]{32..63});
                           GR[b] ← GR[b] + dx;
                           break;
            default: offset ← GR[b] + dx;
                           mem_store(space,offset,0,31,cc,GR[r]{32..63});
                           break;
        }

Exceptions: Data TLB miss fault/data page fault   Data memory break trap
        Data memory access rights trap   TLB dirty bit trap
        Data memory protection ID trap   Page reference trap
        Unaligned data reference trap

Restrictions: For post-decrement and pre-increment with long displacements (Format 2), only displacements which are multiples of four may be used.

    If the completer O is specified, the displacement must be 0.

Format: STWA,cmplt,cc   r,d(b)

(6)

03	b	r	0	a	1	cc	E	m	im5
6	5	5	2	1	1	2	4	1	5

Purpose: To store a word from a general register to an absolute address.

Description: The rightmost word in GR *r* is stored in the aligned word at the effective absolute address. The offset is formed as the sum of a base register, *b*, and a displacement *d*. The displacement is encoded into the immediate field. Optional base modification can also be performed.

The completer, *cmplt*, determines whether the offset is the base register, or the base register plus the displacement. The completer also specifies base register modification and ordering constraints (see Table H-1 on page H-4 for the assembly language completer mnemonics.) The completer, *cc*, specifies the cache control hint (see Table 6-8 on page 6-10.)

If base register modification is specified and *b* = *r*, the value stored at the effective address is the word from the source register before modification. Protection is not checked when this instruction is executed. This operation is only defined if the address is aligned on a 4-byte boundary.

Operation: if (priv != 0)
                    privileged_operation_trap;
               else {
                    dx ← low_sign_ext(im5,5);
                    if (cmplt == O)
                        enforce_ordered_store;
                    switch (cmplt) {
                        case MB: offset ← GR[b] + dx;
                                     phys_mem_store(offset,0,31,cc,GR[r]{32..63});
                                     GR[b] ← GR[b] + dx;
                                     break;
                        case MA: offset ← GR[b];
                                     phys_mem_store(offset,0,31,cc,GR[r]{32..63});
                                     GR[b] ← GR[b] + dx;
                                     break;
                        default: offset ← GR[b] + dx;
                                     phys_mem_store(offset,0,31,cc,GR[r]{32..63});
                                     break;
                    }
               }

Exceptions: Privileged operation trap

Restrictions: This instruction may be executed only at the most privileged level. If the completer O is specified, the displacement must be 0.

Subtract

SUB

Format: SUB,cmplt,borrow,trapc,cond   r1,r2,t

(8)

02	r2	r1	c	f	e1	0	e2	e3	d	t
6	5	5	3	1	2	1	1	2	1	5

Purpose: To do 64-bit integer subtraction, and conditionally nullify the following instruction.

Description: GR $r2$ is subtracted from GR $r1$. If no trap occurs, the result is placed in GR t and the carry/borrow bits in the PSW are updated. The variable "carry_borrows" in the operation section captures the 4-bit carries resulting from the subtract operation. The completer, *cmplt*, encoded in the *e1* field, specifies whether a trap is taken on signed overflow. The completer, *borrow*, encoded in the *e2* field, specifies whether the subtraction is done with borrow. The completer, *trapc*, encoded in the *e3* field, specifies whether a trap is taken if the values subtracted satisfy the condition specified.

The following instruction is nullified if the values subtracted satisfy the specified condition, *cond*. The condition is encoded in the c, d, and f fields of the instruction. The boolean variable "overflow" in the operation section is set if the operation results in a 32-bit signed overflow ($d=0$) or a 64-bit signed overflow ($d=1$.) For subtraction with borrow, the d field encodes whether the word borrow (PSW C/B{8}, $d=0$), or the doubleword borrow (PSW C/B{0}, $d=1$) is used.

The *e1* field encodes whether the a trap is taken on overflow (*e1*=1: no trap, *e1*=3: trap on overflow.) The *e2* field encodes whether subtraction with borrow in is performed (*e2*=0: no borrow, *e2*=1: subtraction performed with borrow.) The *e3* field encodes whether to trap if the values subtracted satisfy the specified condition (*e3*=0: no trap, *e3*=3: trap on condition.) The following table shows the allowed combinations:

Completer	Description	e1	e2	e3
<none>	Subtract	1	0	0
TC	Subtract and trap on condition	1	0	3
B or DB	Subtract with borrow/doubleword borrow	1	1	0
TSV	Subtract and trap on signed overflow	3	0	0
TSV,TC	Subtract and trap on signed overflow or condition	3	0	3
B,TSV or DB,TSV	Subtract with borrow/doubleword borrow and trap on signed overflow	3	1	0

Conditions: The condition is any of the 32-bit compare or subtract conditions shown in Table D-3 on page D-4 or any of the 64-bit compare or subtract conditions shown in Table D-4 on page D-4. When a condition completer is not specified, the "never" condition is used. The boolean variable "cond_satisfied" in the operation section is set when the values subtracted satisfy the specified condition.

Operation: switch (borrow) {
          case B: res ← GR[r1] + ~GR[r2] + PSW[C/B]{8};
                         break;
          case DB: res ← GR[r1] + ~GR[r2] + PSW[C/B]{0};
                         break;
          default: res ← GR[r1] + ~GR[r2] + 1;
                         break;
          }
          if (cmplt == TSV && overflow)
               overflow_trap;
          else if (trapc == TC && cond_satisfied)
               conditional_trap;
          else {
               GR[t] ← res;
               PSW[C/B] ← carry_borrows;
               if (cond_satisfied) PSW[N] ← 1;
          }

Exceptions: Overflow trap
                  Conditional trap

Notes: When the ,B completer is specified, only 32-bit conditions are available. When the ,DB completer is specified, only 64-bit conditions are available.

Format: SUBI,cmplt,cond   i,r,t

(9)

25	r	t	c	f	e1	im11
6	5	5	3	1	1	11

Purpose: To subtract a register from an immediate value and conditionally nullify the following instruction.

Description: GR r is subtracted from the sign-extended immediate value i. If no trap occurs, the result is placed in GR t and the carry/borrow bits in the PSW are updated. The immediate value is encoded into the *im11* field. The variable "carry_borrows" in the operation section captures the 4-bit carries resulting from the subtract operation.

The completer, *cmplt*, encoded in the *e1* field, specifies whether a trap is taken on a 32-bit signed overflow (*e1*=0: no trap, no *cmplt*, *e1*=1: trap on 32-bit signed overflow, *cmplt*==TSV.)

The following instruction is nullified if the values subtracted satisfy the specified condition, *cond*. The condition is encoded in the *c* and *f* fields of the instruction. The boolean variable "overflow" in the operation section is set if the operation results in a 32-bit signed overflow.

Conditions: The condition is any of the 32-bit compare or subtract conditions shown in Table D-3 on page D-4. When a condition completer is not specified, the "never" condition is used. The boolean variable "cond_satisfied" in the operation section is set when the values subtracted satisfy the specified condition.

Operation: res $\leftarrow$ low_sign_ext(im11,11) + ~GR[r] + 1;
if (cmplt == TSV && overflow)
     overflow_trap;
else {
     GR[t] $\leftarrow$ res;
     PSW[C/B] $\leftarrow$ carry_borrows;
     if (cond_satisfied) PSW[N] $\leftarrow$ 1;
}

Exceptions: Overflow trap

Programming Note

SUBTRACT FROM IMMEDIATE can be used to perform a logical NOT operation when coded as follows:

     SUBI   -1,r,t   /* GR[t] $\leftarrow$ ~GR[r]
                             all PSW[C/B] are set to ones */

Format: SYNC

(33)

00	rv	0	rv	0	20	0
6	5	1	4	3	8	5

Purpose: To enforce program order of instruction execution.

Description: Any load, store, semaphore, cache flush, or cache purge instructions that follow the SYNC instruction get executed only after all such instructions prior to the SYNC instruction have completed executing. On implementations which execute such instructions out of sequence, this instruction enforces program ordering.

Operation: Enforce program order of memory references

Exceptions: None

Notes: In systems in which all memory references are performed in order, this instruction executes as a null instruction.

Programming Note

The minimum spacing that is guaranteed to work for "self-modifying code" is shown in the code segment below. Since instruction prefetching is permitted, any data cache flushes must be separated from any instruction cache flushes by a SYNC. This will ensure that the "new" instruction will be written to memory prior to any attempts at prefetching it as an instruction.

```
        LDIL    l%newinstr,rnew
        LDW     r%newinstr(0,rnew),temp
        LDIL    l%instr,rinstr
        STW     temp,r%instr(0,rinstr)
        FDC     r%instr(0,rinstr)
        SYNC
        FIC     r%instr(rinstr)
        SYNC
        (at least seven instructions)
instr   ...
```

This sequence assumes a uniprocessor system. In a multiprocessor system, software must ensure no processor is executing code which is in the process of being modified.

Format: SYNCDMA

(33)

00	rv	1	rv	0	20	0
6	5	1	4	3	8	5

Purpose: To enforce DMA completion order.

Description: On implementations which can signal DMA completion prior to achieving cache coherence, this instruction enforces ordering. All cache coherence actions which are outstanding as a consequence of prior DMA operations must be completed before the next memory access is performed.

Operation: Enforce DMA completion order

Exceptions: None

Notes: In systems in which all DMA operations are performed in order, this instruction executes as a null instruction.

Format: UADDCM,trapc,cond   r1,r2,t

(8)	02	r2	r1	c	f	2	0	1	e1	d	t
	6	5	5	3	1	2	1	1	2	1	5

Purpose: To individually compare corresponding sub-units of a doubleword for a greater-than or less-than-or-equal a relation.

Description: GR *r1* is added to the one's complement of GR *r2*. If no trap occurs, the result is placed in GR *t*. The following instruction is nullified if the values added satisfy the specified condition, *cond*. The completer, *trapc*, encoded in the *e1* field, specifies whether a trap is taken if the condition, *cond*, is satisfied by the values added (*e1*=2: no trap, no *cmplt*, *e1*=3: trap on condition, *cmplt*==TC.) The condition is encoded in the *c*, *d*, and *f* fields of the instruction.

Conditions: The condition *cond* is any of the 32-bit unit conditions shown in Table D-11 on page D-8 or any of the 64-bit conditions shown in Table D-12 on page D-8. When a condition completer is not specified, the "never" condition is used. The boolean variable "cond_satisfied" in the operation section is set when the values added satisfy the specified condition.

Operation:
```
res ← GR[r1] + ~GR[r2];
if (trapc == TC && cond_satisfied)
    conditional_trap;
else {
    GR[t] ← res;
    if (cond_satisfied) PSW[N] ← 1;
}
```

Exceptions: Conditional trap

Programming Note

UNIT ADD COMPLEMENT can be used to perform a logical NOT operation when coded as follows:

         UADDCM   0,r,t   /* GR[t] ← ~GR[r] */

UNIT ADD COMPLEMENT with the TC (Trap on Condition) completer can be used to check decimal validity and to pre-bias decimal numbers. *ra* contains the number to be checked and *rt* will contain the number plus the bias as result of the UADDCM operation.

```
NINES        .equ              X'99999999
             LDIL              l%NINES,nines
             LDO               r%NINES(nines),nines
             UADDCM,TC,SDC  ra,nines,rt
```

Format: UXOR,cond   r1,r2,t

(8)	02	r2	r1	c	f	0	1	1	2	d	t
	6	5	5	3	1	2	1	1	2	1	5

Purpose: To individually compare corresponding sub-units of two doublewords for equality.

Description: GR *r1* and GR *r2* are XORed and the result is placed in GR *t*. This instruction generates unit conditions unlike XOR which generates logical conditions. The following instruction is nullified if the values XORed satisfy the specified condition, *cond*. The condition is encoded in the *c*, *d*, and *f* fields of the instruction.

Conditions: The condition, *cond*, is any of the 32-bit unit conditions not involving carries shown in Table D-11 on page D-8 ("never", SBZ, SHZ, TR, NBZ, NHZ) or any of the 64-bit unit conditions not involving carries shown in Table D-12 on page D-8 (*, *SBZ, *SHZ, *SWZ, *TR, *NBZ, *NHZ, *NWZ.) When a condition completer is not specified, the "never" condition is used. The boolean variable "cond_satisfied" in the operation section is set when the values XORed satisfy the specified condition.

Operation: GR[t] ← xor(GR[r1], GR[r2]);
                   if (cond_satisfied) PSW[N] ← 1;

Exceptions: None

Format: XOR,cond   r1,r2,t

(8)

02	r2	r1	c	f	0	1	0	2	d	t
6	5	5	3	1	2	1	1	2	1	5

Purpose: To do a 64-bit, bitwise exclusive OR.

Description: GR *r1* and GR *r2* are XORed and the result is placed in GR *t*. The following instruction is nullified if the values XORed satisfy the specified condition, *cond*. The condition is encoded in the *c*, *d*, and *f* fields of the instruction.

Conditions: The condition is any of the 32-bit logical conditions shown in Table D-9 on page D-7 or any of the 64-bit logical conditions shown in Table D-10 on page D-7. The boolean variable "cond_satisfied" in the operation section is set when the values XORed satisfy the specified condition.

Operation: GR[t] ← xor(GR[r1], GR[r2]);
if (cond_satisfied) PSW[N] ← 1;

Exceptions: None

8   Floating-point Coprocessor

The PA-RISC floating-point coprocessor is an assist processor that is added to a system to improve the system's performance on floating-point operations. The floating-point coprocessor contains a register file which is independent of the processor's register file. The floating-point coprocessor executes floating-point instructions to perform arithmetic on this register file and to move data between the register file and memory. The architecture permits pipelined execution of floating-point instructions, further increasing the system's performance.

Floating-point instructions are implementations of the more general coprocessor instructions described previously in Chapter 6, "Instruction Set Overview". The floating-point coprocessor responds to coprocessor instructions with a coprocessor id equal to 0 and 1.

While the floating-point coprocessor is not required to execute instructions sequentially, the coprocessor and processor must ensure that the instructions appear sequentially executed to the software. At any one time, the processor and coprocessor may be operating on a number of instructions. For purposes of this chapter, the **current instruction** is the instruction pointed to by the IA queues. The term **pending instructions** refers to instructions which have entered and left the IA queues, but which the coprocessor is still executing.

The IEEE Standard

When used in this chapter, the term **IEEE standard** or simply **the standard**, refers to the *IEEE Standard for Binary Floating-Point Arithmetic, ANSI/IEEE Std 754-1985*. PA-RISC fully conforms to the requirements of the IEEE floating-point standard and permits implementation of all IEEE floating-point recommendations. Where hardware is unable to fully implement the standard, software completes the implementation.

Though this chapter uses quotes from the IEEE standard as architecture, knowledge of the standard is not necessary to understand the architecture. Whenever a quote of the standard contains a reference to another part of the standard, the quote also contains an equivalent reference to a section of this document. In these quotes, a reference to the IEEE standard is enclosed in parentheses, and the equivalent reference to this document is enclosed in square brackets.

The Instruction Set

The floating-point instruction set consists of load and store instructions, and operations. Floating-point load and store instructions copy both single-word and double-word data between memory and the floating-point registers. Floating-point operations do arithmetic on the floating-point registers and copy data between floating-point registers.

The floating-point coprocessor operates on single-word and double-word IEEE floating-point numbers, as well as quad-word numbers, which are an implementation of the IEEE double-extended format. Each type of floating-point number may represent one of the following: a normalized number, a denormalized number, a zero, an infinity, or a NaN (Not a Number). These floating-point formats consist of a sign bit, an exponent, and a fraction.

The instruction set also has operations that convert among the three formats of floating-point numbers and between floating-point numbers and single-word, double-word, and quad-word unsigned and two's complement integers, as well as an instruction which multiplies two 32-bit unsigned integers with a 64-bit unsigned integer result.

Coprocessor Registers

The coprocessor contains thirty-two 64-bit floating-point registers. These same 32 locations can be used as sixty-four 32-bit locations or as sixteen 128-bit locations. Instructions executing at any privilege level may read or write the floating-point registers. Double-word load/store operations access the entire 64-bit register; single-word load/stores access either the left portion of a 64-bit register, bits 0 to 31, or the right portion of a 64-bit register, bits 32 to 63.

By convention, a 32-bit floating-point register is identified by appending a suffix to the identifier of the 64-bit register within which it is contained. The suffix for the left hand side 32-bit register is 'L'; the use of this suffix is optional. The suffix for the right hand side 32-bit register is 'R'; its use is **not** optional. Thus, for example, the left half of double-word register 13 (bits 0 to 31) would be referred to as either 13 or 13L; the right half of double-word register 13 (bits 32 to 63) would be referred to as 13R. The specification 'L' or 'R' for each register is encoded in the instructions that access these registers.

Table 8-1 illustrates the specification of single-word registers and Table 8-2 illustrates the specification of double-word registers.

Table 8-1. Single-Word Floating-Point Registers

Register	Purpose	
0	Status Register	Undefined
1	Undefined	Undefined
2	Undefined	Undefined
3	Undefined	Undefined
4	Floating-point register 4L	Floating-point register 4R
5	Floating-point register 5L	Floating-point register 5R
6	Floating-point register 6L	Floating-point register 6R
7	Floating-point register 7L	Floating-point register 7R
8	Floating-point register 8L	Floating-point register 8R
9	Floating-point register 9L	Floating-point register 9R
10	Floating-point register 10L	Floating-point register 10R
11	Floating-point register 11L	Floating-point register 11R
12	Floating-point register 12L	Floating-point register 12R
13	Floating-point register 13L	Floating-point register 13R
14	Floating-point register 14L	Floating-point register 14R
15	Floating-point register 15L	Floating-point register 15R
16	Floating-point register 16L	Floating-point register 16R
17	Floating-point register 17L	Floating-point register 17R
18	Floating-point register 18L	Floating-point register 18R
19	Floating-point register 19L	Floating-point register 19R
20	Floating-point register 20L	Floating-point register 20R
21	Floating-point register 21L	Floating-point register 21R
22	Floating-point register 22L	Floating-point register 22R
23	Floating-point register 23L	Floating-point register 23R
24	Floating-point register 24L	Floating-point register 24R
25	Floating-point register 25L	Floating-point register 25R
26	Floating-point register 26L	Floating-point register 26R
27	Floating-point register 27L	Floating-point register 27R
28	Floating-point register 28L	Floating-point register 28R
29	Floating-point register 29L	Floating-point register 29R
30	Floating-point register 30L	Floating-point register 30R
31	Floating-point register 31L	Floating-point register 31R

Table 8-2. Double-Word Floating-Point Registers

Register	Purpose	
0	Status Register	Exception Register 1
1	Exception Register 2	Exception Register 3
2	Exception Register 4	Exception Register 5
3	Exception Register 6	Exception Register 7
4	Floating-point register 4	
5	Floating-point register 5	
6	Floating-point register 6	
7	Floating-point register 7	
8	Floating-point register 8	
9	Floating-point register 9	
10	Floating-point register 10	
11	Floating-point register 11	
12	Floating-point register 12	
13	Floating-point register 13	
14	Floating-point register 14	
15	Floating-point register 15	
16	Floating-point register 16	
17	Floating-point register 17	
18	Floating-point register 18	
19	Floating-point register 19	
20	Floating-point register 20	
21	Floating-point register 21	
22	Floating-point register 22	
23	Floating-point register 23	
24	Floating-point register 24	
25	Floating-point register 25	
26	Floating-point register 26	
27	Floating-point register 27	
28	Floating-point register 28	
29	Floating-point register 29	
30	Floating-point register 30	
31	Floating-point register 31	

Single-word register 0 contains the Status Register. Double-word registers 0 - 3 contain the Status Register and the Exception Registers. Double-word registers 4 - 31 and single-word registers 4R - 31R and 4L - 31L are data registers.

Registers 0 - 3 are partitioned into eight 32-bit registers. Bits 0 to 31 of double-word register 0 contain the Status Register, which holds information on rounding, compares, and exceptions. Bits 32 to 63 of double-word register 0 contain Exception Register 1. Specifying Floating-point Register 0 in a non-load/store operation encodes a floating-point +0 or a fixed-point 0, whichever is appropriate, when used as a source and is an undefined operation when used as a destination.

Double-word registers 1 to 3 contain the remaining exception registers. The exception registers form a queue of instructions which could not normally complete and thus complete with a trapping exception. The exception registers are accessed using double-word load and store instructions. Single-word loads and stores of exception registers are undefined operations. Specifying an exception register as a source or destination of a non-load/store operation is undefined.

The entire state of the floating-point coprocessor is contained in the register file. Saving the entire register file is sufficient for a context switch. A special instruction sequence allows the saving and restoring of this state without an interruption. This sequence ensures that context switches and other operations which affect the state of the coprocessor do not affect a process.

Data Registers

Floating-point registers 4 - 31 contain the 64-bit data registers which instructions use as operands. Software may access these registers with single-word or double-word load and store instructions.

Each of the floating-point data registers may contain values in a number of formats. The fields in these formats are packed into words, double-words, or quad-words so that load and store operations do not require field-shuffling or tag bits.

Single-word formats occupy either the left half (bits 0 to 31, suffix 'L'), or the right half (bits 32 to 63, suffix 'R') of a register as shown in Figure 8-1.

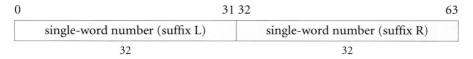

Figure 8-1. Single-word Data Format

Double-word formats fill one register as shown in Figure 8-2.

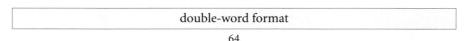

Figure 8-2. Double-word Data Format

Quad-word formats (128 bits) are packed into adjacent even-odd pairs of registers. An instruction which references a register containing a quad-word value must name an even numbered register. An operation which specifies an odd numbered register for a quad-word format is an undefined operation. Quad formats are assembled in register pairs as shown in Figure 8-3.

even # register	most significant bits
odd # register	least significant bits

64

Figure 8-3. Quad-word Data Format

Data Formats

Two data types are defined for floating-point coprocessor operations: floating-point formats and fixed-point formats.

Floating-point Formats

Numbers in the single, double, and quad binary floating-point formats are composed of three fields:

1. A 1-bit sign, s.

2. A biased exponent, $e = E + bias$.

3. A fraction, $f = .b_1 b_2 ... b_{p-1}$.

Note that adding the *bias* to the unbiased exponent E produces the biased exponent e. The number e is always non-negative. Also, p is the precision of the number, and is equal to one plus the number of fraction bits. Figure 8-4 shows the positions of these fields in the registers.

Single Binary Floating-point

s	e	fraction
1	8	23

Double Binary Floating-point

s	e	fraction
1	11	52

Quad Binary Floating-point

s	e	high fraction
1	15	48

low fraction

64

Figure 8-4. Floating-point Formats

For each floating-point format, a number may either be a normalized number, a denormalized number, an infinity, a zero, or a NaN (Not a Number). Each representable nonzero numerical value has just one encoding. Use the format parameters listed in Table 8-3 and the equations which follow to determine the representation and value, v, of a floating-point number.

Zero: If $E = E_{min} - 1$ and $f = 0$, then $v = (-1)^s 0$.

Denormalized: If $E = E_{min} - 1$ and $f \neq 0$, then $v = (-1)^s 2^{E_{min}} (0.f)$.

Normalized: If $E_{min} \leq E \leq E_{max}$, then $v = (-1)^s 2^E (1.f)$.

Infinity: If $E = E_{max} + 1$ and $f = 0$, then $v = (-1)^s \infty$.

NaN: If $E = E_{max} + 1$ and $f \neq 0$, then v is a NaN, regardless of s.

If the number is a NaN, then the leftmost bit in the fraction, b_1, determines whether the NaN is signaling or quiet. If b_1 is 1, the NaN is a signaling NaN. If b_1 is 0, it is a quiet NaN.

Table 8-3. Floating-Point Format Parameters

Parameter	Format		
	Single	Double	Quad
p (precision)	24	53	113
E_{max}	+127	+1023	+16383
E_{min}	−126	−1022	−16382
exponent *bias*	+127	+1023	+16383
under/overflow *bias*-adjustment	192	1536	24576
exponent width in bits	8	11	15
format width in bits	32	64	128

NaNs are not ordered; neither the fraction nor the sign bits have any significance.

Fixed-Point Formats

Fixed-point values are held in the formats shown in Figure 8-5.

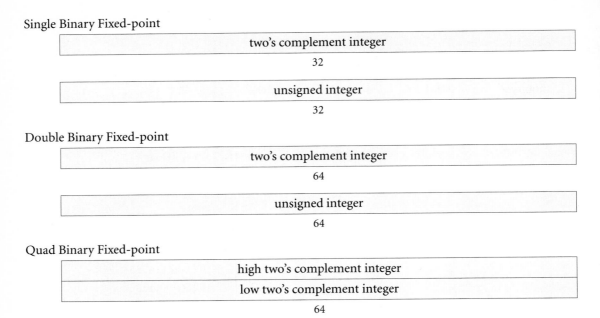

Single Binary Fixed-point

two's complement integer
32

unsigned integer
32

Double Binary Fixed-point

two's complement integer
64

unsigned integer
64

Quad Binary Fixed-point

high two's complement integer
low two's complement integer

64

Figure 8-5. Fixed-point Formats

Floating-Point Status Register

The Status Register controls the arithmetic rounding mode, enables user-level traps, indicates exceptions that have occurred, indicates the results of comparisons, and contains information to identify the implementation of the coprocessor. The Status Register is located in bits 0 to 31 of Floating-point Register 0, and is accessed by specifying Floating-point Register 0 with single-word or double-word load and store instructions.

Non-load/store instructions do not access the Status Register. Specifying Floating-point Register 0 in a non-load/store operation, encodes a floating-point +0 or a fixed-point 0, whichever is appropriate, when used as a source and is an undefined operation when used as a destination.

Figure 8-6 shows the three formats of the Status Register. The first format is valid when the FLOATING-POINT COMPARE and FLOATING-POINT TEST instructions are being used to generate and test a queue of comparison results. The second format is valid when the FLOATING-POINT COMPARE and FLOATING-POINT TEST instructions are being used to generate and test individual comparison bits. The third format is only valid immediately after the execution of a FLOATING-POINT IDENTIFY instruction. This format remains valid until a floating-point instruction is executed which is not a double-word store of Floating-point Register 0. The first or second format is valid thereafter. See the description of the FLOATING-POINT IDENTIFY instruction on page 9-9 for more information.

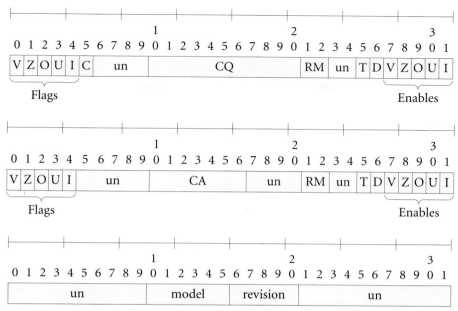

Figure 8-6. Floating-Point Status Register

Field	Description
RM	The rounding mode for all floating-point operations. The values corresponding to each rounding mode are listed in Table 8-4.

Table 8-4. Floating-Point Rounding Modes

Rounding mode	Description
0	Round to nearest
1	Round toward zero
2	Round toward $+\infty$
3	Round toward $-\infty$

Field	Description
Enables	The exception trap enables. An enable bit is associated with each IEEE exception. When an enable bit equals 1, the corresponding trap is enabled. An instruction completes with a delayed trap when the instruction causes an exception whose corresponding enable bit equals 1. If an enable bit equals 0, the corresponding IEEE exception usually sets the corresponding exception flag to 1 instead of causing a trap. However, see "Unimplemented Exception" on page 10-8, "Overflow Exception" on page 10-11, and "Underflow Exception" on page 10-12 for cases when a trap is taken even when the trap is not enabled. Table 8-5 lists the bits that correspond to each IEEE exception.
Flags	The exception flags. A flag bit is associated with each IEEE exception. The coprocessor sets an exception flag to 1 when the corresponding exception occurs but does not cause a trap. An implementation may also choose to set a flag bit to 1 when the corresponding exception

occurs and causes a trap. An exception flag is never set to 0 as a side effect of floating-point operations, but it may be set to either 1 or 0 by a load instruction. Table 8-5 lists the bits that correspond to each IEEE exception.

Table 8-5. IEEE Exceptions

Bit Name	Description
V	Invalid operation
Z	Division-by-zero
O	Overflow
U	Underflow
I	Inexact result

C   The Compare bit. The C-bit contains the result of the most recent queued compare instruction. This bit is set to 1 if the result of the most recent queued compare is true, and 0 if false. The C-bit is undefined following a targeted compare. No other non-load/store instruction affects this bit, but it may be set to 1 or 0 by load instructions.

CQ   The Compare Queue. The CQ field contains the results of the second-most recent queued compare (in CQ{0}) through the twelfth-most recent queued compare (in CQ{10}). Every queued compare instruction shifts the CQ field right by one bit (discarding the rightmost bit) and the C-bit from the previous queued compare is copied into CQ{0}. The CQ field is undefined following a targeted compare. No other non-load/store instruction affects this field, but it may be set to any value by load instructions.

CA   The Compare Array. The CA field is an array of seven independent compare bits, each of which contains the result of the most recent compare instruction targeting that bit. Any compare targeting a particular bit sets that bit to 1 if the result of the compare is true, and 0 if false. The CA field is undefined following a queued compare. No other non-load/store instruction affects this field, but it may be set to any value by load instructions.

T   The Delayed Trap bit. The coprocessor sets this bit to 1 when an IEEE exception occurs that is signalled with a trap or when an unimplemented exception occurs. When this bit is 1, the coprocessor is armed to trap, and the next floating-point instruction forces the processor to take an assist exception trap. No non-load/store instructions affect this bit, but load instructions may set this bit to 1 or 0, and double-word stores of the Status Register set this bit to 0 after completion of the store. Also, save and restore software uses this bit to record the state of traps. See "Saving and Restoring State" on page 10-13 for information on state swapping and "Interruptions and Exceptions" on page 10-4 for a detailed discussion of the T-bit's operation.

D   The Denormalized As Zero bit.   The D-bit provides the arithmetic floating-point instructions a "fast mode" handling of denormalized operands and tiny results. When the D-bit is 1, any of these instructions may optionally produce a correctly signed zero when the result, before or after rounding, lies between $\pm 2^{E_{min}}$, and may optionally treat any denormalized operand as an equivalently signed zero. When the D-bit is 1, and an arithmetic instruction treats an operand as a zero, or produces a zero result as described above, the values of the Underflow and Inexact flags become undefined. When the D-bit is 0, all denformalized operands and tiny results must be handled as described in the remainder of this chapter.

Implementation of the D-bit is optional; if not implemented, it is a nonexistent bit.

model   The implementation-dependent model number. Model number zero (0) is reserved for the software emulation routines.

revision The implementation-dependent revision number.

un   Undefined bits.

Floating-Point Instruction Set

The floating-point instruction set consists of load and store instructions, and floating-point operations. All these instructions are part of the PA-RISC standard instruction set. When the instruction specifies a register for double precision and 64-bit fixed-point values, a 5-bit encoding maps directly into the associated floating-point register. When the instruction specifies a register for single-precision or 32-bit fixed-point values, a 6-bit encoding maps into the appropriate 'L' or 'R' single-word floating-point register.

Instruction Validity

Table 8-6 shows which floating-point instructions are defined, undefined, or will take an Assist Emulation Trap for various values of the uid field and the Coprocessor Configuration Register.

Table 8-6. Floating-Point Instruction Validity

Opcode	CCR{0..1}		
	0	1, 2	3
0B/0C	trap	undefined	uid=0: defined uid=1: undefined
06/09/0E/26	trap	undefined	defined

Load and Store Instructions

The floating-point load and store instructions are implementations of the PA-RISC coprocessor load and store instructions described in "Coprocessor Instructions" on page 6-22. Table 8-7 shows the floating-point load and store instructions.

Table 8-7. Floating-Point Load and Store Instructions

Mnemonic	Description
FLDW	Load word
FLDD	Load doubleword
FSTW	Store word
FSTD	Store doubleword

The load and store instructions transfer data between the floating-point registers and memory. These instructions transfer aligned words or aligned double-words, and form an effective address using a base register plus either a short displacement value, a long displacement value, or the value of an index register. They also have completers that specify base register modification, ordering, and cache control hints.

Single-word loads and stores access either bits 0 to 31 (suffix 'L') or bits 32 to 63 (suffix 'R') of a register. The ability to specify more than 32 locations is accomplished by the use of bit 25 of the instruction. A 0 in this bit specifies an access of bits 0 to 31 (left half of the register); a 1 specifies an access of bits 32 to 63 (the right half of the register). However, single-word loads and stores of floating-point registers 0R (the right half of floating-point register 0), 1, 2, and 3 are undefined operations.

Double-word loads and stores can access any of the floating-point registers and may be used to load or store a pair of single-word values in the left and right halves of a register.

A single-word or double-word load or store of Floating-point Register 0 forces the coprocessor to complete all pending floating-point instructions and signal all floating-point exceptions for those instructions. Additionally, a double-word store of Floating-point Register 0 cancels traps due to all previous instructions and, after completion of the store, sets the Status Register T-bit to 0.

Single-word stores of register 0 do not cancel traps. Also, single-word loads of register 0 that set the Status Register T-bit to 1 are undefined operations.

Load and store instructions may cause a number of memory reference traps. They are not arithmetic instructions and do not cause IEEE exceptions.

Load and store instructions that access the I/O address space are defined operations.

Floating-point Operations

There are three categories of floating-point operation instructions. Each instruction in the first category performs a single operation. Instructions in the second category perform fused operations. Instructions in the third category perform multiple operations.

Single-operation Instructions

This section describes the single-operation floating-point instructions. Single-operation floating-point instructions are encoded using two major opcodes - 0C and 0E. Most of the functions in the 0C opcode are also duplicated in the 0E opcode with the following exceptions:

- Instructions using the 0E opcode can address both the left and right halves of the floating-point register set whereas the instructions using the 0C opcode can only address the left halves of the floating-point register set.

- The FLOATING-POINT IDENTIFY and FLOATING-POINT TEST instructions are available only in the 0C opcode.

- The format completer for the quad-word data type is available only in the 0C opcode.

- The FIXED-POINT MULTIPLY UNSIGNED instruction is available only in the 0E opcode.

There are four classes of operations:

- **Class 0** contains single source, single destination operations and includes the non-arithmetic operations.
- **Class 1** consists of the conversion operations.
- **Class 2** operations provide mechanisms to compare two operands.
- **Class 3** consists of the arithmetic operations with two sources and one destination.

Figure 8-7 shows the format of these operations.

Floating-point operation class zero: 1 source, 1 destination*

0C	r	0	sub	fmt	0	0	0	t
6	5	5	3	2	2	3	1	5

0E	r	0	sub	0	f	0	0	r	t	0	t
6	5	5	3	1	1	2	1	1	1	1	5

Floating-point operation class one: 1 source, 1 destination

0C	r	0	sub	df	sf	1	0	0	t
6	5	3	3	2	2	2	3	1	5

0E	r	0	sub	0	df	0	sf	1	0	r	t	0	t
6	5	3	3	1	1	1	1	2	1	1	1	1	5

Floating-point operation class two: 2 sources, no destination*

0C	r1	r2	sub	fmt	2	0	n	c
6	5	5	3	2	2	3	1	5

0E	r1	r2	sub	r2	f	2	0	r1	0	0	c
6	5	5	3	1	1	2	1	1	1	1	5

Floating-point operation class three: 2 sources, 1 destination†

0C	r1	r2	sub	fmt	3	0	0	t
6	5	5	3	2	2	3	1	5

0E	r1	r2	sub	r2	f	3	x	r1	t	0	t
6	5	5	3	1	1	2	1	1	1	1	5

*   The FLOATING-POINT IDENTIFY and FLOATING-POINT TEST instructions have no source or destination operands, and no format specifiers, so the register and format fields equal 0.

†   The FIXED-POINT MULTIPLY UNSIGNED instruction has no format specifier, so the format field equals 0.

Figure 8-7. Single-operation Instruction Formats

Whenever single-precision operands are specified for the 0E opcode, the *t* at bit position 25 of class zero, one, and three instructions represents a sixth bit of the *t* field, and the *r* or *r1* at bit position 24 represents a sixth bit of the *r* or *r1* field. Similarly, the *r2* at bit position 19 represents a sixth bit of the *r2* field. These bits specify the left side single-word register, bits 0 to 31, when 0, and the right side single-word register, bits 32 to 63, when 1. The *x* at bit position 23 of a class three instruction indicates, when 1, that the sub-opcode is to be interpreted as a fixed-point operation.

Table 8-8 shows the floating-point operations, their mnemonics, classes, and sub-opcodes.

Table 8-8. Floating-Point Operations

Opcode	Sub-op	Class	Mnemonic	Operation
0C	0		FID	Identify coprocessor
0E	0			undefined
0C/0E	1			undefined
0C/0E	2		FCPY	Copy
0C/0E	3	0	FABS	Absolute value
0C/0E	4		FSQRT	Square root
0C/0E	5		FRND	Round to integer
0C/0E	6		FNEG	Negate
0C/0E	7		FNEGABS	Negate absolute value
0C/0E	0			Convert from floating-point to floating-point
0C/0E	1			Convert from fixed-point to floating-point
0C/0E	2			Convert from floating-point to fixed-point
0C/0E	3			Convert from floating-point to fixed-point with explicit round to zero rounding
0C/0E	4	1	FCNV	undefined
0C/0E	5			Convert from unsigned fixed-point to floating-point
0C/0E	6			Convert from floating-point to unsigned fixed-point
0C/0E	7			Convert from floating-point to unsigned fixed-point with explicit round to zero rounding
0C/0E	y	2	FCMP	Arithmetic compare ($n = 0$)
0C	y		FTEST	Test condition bit ($n = 1$)
0C/0E	0		FADD	Add
0C/0E	1		FSUB	Subtract
0C/0E	2		FMPY	Multiply ($x = 0$)
0C/0E	3	3	FDIV	Divide
0C	4			reserved
0E	4			undefined
0C/0E	5-6			reserved
0C/0E	7			undefined

While the coprocessor may simultaneously operate on more than one instruction, the coprocessor is restricted by the number of exception registers to executing no more than seven floating-point operations at one time.

All the operations which have at least one floating-point operand are considered arithmetic instructions and will generate an invalid exception when operating on a signaling NaN, except for the FLOATING-POINT NEGATE, FLOATING-POINT NEGATE ABSOLUTE VALUE, FLOATING-POINT COPY, and FLOATING-POINT ABSOLUTE VALUE instructions, which are considered non-arithmetic and never generate any IEEE exceptions.

The FLOATING-POINT IDENTIFY and FLOATING-POINT TEST instructions do not cause exceptions.

Table 8-9 shows the only fixed-point operation, its mnemonic, class and sub-opcode.

Table 8-9. Fixed-Point Operations

Opcode	Sub-op	x-bit	Class	Mnemonic	Operation
0E	2	1	3	XMPYU	Fixed-point Multiply Unsigned

Operand Format Completers

For class 0, 2 and 3 operations, except for FIXED-POINT MULTIPLY UNSIGNED, the source and destination widths are the same and the instructions operate only on floating-point numbers. Except for the FLOATING-POINT IDENTIFY, FLOATING-POINT TEST, and FIXED-POINT MULTIPLY UNSIGNED operations, each has an accompanying completer which specifies the data width the operation is using.

Table 8-10 shows the instruction completers and their corresponding format codes for the 0C and 0E opcodes.

Table 8-10. Single-Operation Instruction Format Completers

Opcode	Mnemonic	Code	Description	Data Size
0C/0E	<none>	0	single-word number	32 bits
0C/0E	SGL	0	single-word number	32 bits
0C/0E	DBL	1	double-word number	64 bits
0C	QUAD	3	quad-word number	128 bits
0C		2	undefined	

The *Code* field above indicates the encoding corresponding to each completer. The absence of a completer specifies a single-word number. An operation with a *Code* value of 2 is an undefined operation. In the 0E opcode, only *Code* values 0 and 1 can be specified.

The operations in class 1 (the conversion instructions) have two completers which specify the source and destination formats independently. However, the floating-point to floating-point conversions single-to-single and double-to-double in the 0C and 0E opcodes are undefined operations; In addition, in the 0C opcode, quad-to-quad floating-point conversion is an undefined operation (quad precision cannot be specified in the 0E opcode). Table 8-11 shows the conversion instruction completers and their corresponding format codes.

Table 8-11. Conversion Instruction Format Completers

Opcode	Mnemonic	Code	Description	Data Size
0C/0E	SGL W UW	0	single-word floating-point single-word signed integer single-word unsigned integer	32 bits
0C/0E	DBL DW UDW	1	double-word floating-point double-word signed integer double-word unsigned integer	64 bits
0C	QUAD QW UQW	3	quad-word floating-point quad-word signed integer quad-word unsigned integer	128 bits
0C		2	undefined	

The *Code* field above indicates the encoding corresponding to each completer, which appears in the *sf* and *df* fields of the instruction. An operation with a *Code* value of 2 is an undefined operation. In the 0E opcode, only *Code* values 0 and 1 can be specified.

Comparison Conditions

The FLOATING-POINT COMPARE instruction has an additional completer which indicates the condition being tested. These conditions are listed in Table 8-12 which is derived from the IEEE standard.

Table 8-12. Floating-Point Compare Instruction Conditions

Condition	Relations				Code	Condition	Relations				Code
	>	<	=	unordered			>	<	=	unordered	
false?	F	F	F	F	0	!?<=	T	F	F	F	16
false	F	F	F	F *	1	>	T	F	F	F *	17
?	F	F	F	T	2	?>	T	F	F	T	18
!<=>	F	F	F	T *	3	!<=	T	F	F	T *	19
=	F	F	T	F	4	!?<	T	F	T	F	20
=T	F	F	T	F *	5	>=	T	F	T	F *	21
?=	F	F	T	T	6	?>=	T	F	T	T	22
!<>	F	F	T	T *	7	!<	T	F	T	T *	23
!?>=	F	T	F	F	8	!?=	T	T	F	F	24
<	F	T	F	F *	9	<>	T	T	F	F *	25
?<	F	T	F	T	10	!=	T	T	F	T	26
!>=	F	T	F	T *	11	!=T	T	T	F	T *	27
!?>	F	T	T	F	12	!?	T	T	T	F	28
<=	F	T	T	F *	13	<=>	T	T	T	F *	29
?<=	F	T	T	T	14	true?	T	T	T	T	30
!>	F	T	T	T *	15	true	T	T	T	T *	31

Comparisons are exact and neither overflow or underflow. Between any two operands, one of four mutually exclusive relations is possible: **less than**, **equal**, **greater than**, and **unordered**. The last case arises when at least one operand is a NaN. Every NaN compares unordered with every operand, including itself. Comparisons ignore the sign of zero, so +0 is equal to -0.

In the table above, *Condition* is the condition mnemonic used in the assembly language and *Code* is the machine language encoding.

There are two types of floating-point compare instructions – targeted compares and queued compares.

- A targeted compare targets a specific bit of the compare array (CA) in the floating-point Status Register (see the second format in Figure 8-6 on page 8-9). The CA-bit specified by the instruction is set to the result in the appropriate relations column, 1 for a true result, 0 for false.

- A queued compare updates the compare queue (CQ) in the floating-point Status Register (see the first format in Figure 8-6 on page 8-9). The CQ field in the floating-point Status Register is shifted right by one bit (discarding the rightmost bit) and the C-bit is copied into CQ{0}. Then, the C-bit in the floating-point Status Register is set to the result in the appropriate relations column, 1 for a true result, 0 for false.

The asterisk (*) indicates that the instruction causes an invalid operation exception if its operands are unordered. However, if at least one operand is a signaling NaN, the compare instruction always causes an invalid operation exception.

Test Conditions

There are two types of FLOATING-POINT TEST instructions – targeted tests and queue tests.

- A targeted test tests a specific bit of the compare array (CA) in the floating-point Status Register (see the second format in Figure 8-6 on page 8-9). If the CA-bit specified by the instruction is 1, the PSW[N] bit is set to 1. No condition may be specified for a targeted test.

- A queue test tests for a specific condition in the C-bit and compare queue (CQ) in the floating-point Status Register (see the first format in Figure 8-6 on page 8-9). Each queue test instruction has an additional completer which indicates the condition being tested. These conditions are listed in Table 8-13. If the condition being tested is true, the PSW[N] bit is set to 1.

Table 8-13. Floating-Point Test Instruction Conditions

Completer	Description	Condition	Code
<none>	Simple Test	C == 1	0
ACC	Graphics (12-bit) Trivial Accept	C == 0 && CQ{0..10} == 0	1
ACC8	Graphics 8-bit Trivial Accept	C == 0 && CQ{0..6} == 0	5
ACC6	Graphics 6-bit Trivial Accept	C == 0 && CQ{0..4} == 0	9
ACC4	Graphics 4-bit Trivial Accept	C == 0 && CQ{0..2} == 0	13
ACC2	Graphics 2-bit Trivial Accept	C == 0 && CQ{0} == 0	17
REJ	Graphics (12-bit) Trivial Reject	C == 1 && CQ{5} == 1 || CQ{0} == 1 && CQ{6} == 1 || CQ{1} == 1 && CQ{7} == 1 || CQ{2} == 1 && CQ{8} == 1 || CQ{3} == 1 && CQ{9} == 1 || CQ{4} == 1 && CQ{10} == 1	2
REJ8	Graphics 8-bit Trivial Reject	C == 1 && CQ{3} == 1 || CQ{0} == 1 && CQ{4} == 1 || CQ{1} == 1 && CQ{5} == 1 || CQ{2} == 1 && CQ{6} == 1	6

Fused-Operation Instructions

The floating-point instruction set includes instructions which perform a fused floating-point multiply and add operation. Fused-operation instructions are four-operand instructions which perform a two-input multiply whose intermediate result is optionally negated and is then added to the third input operand. This final result is then rounded and placed in the destination register. That is: dest ← ±(op1 * op2) + op3. These instructions are encoded using the 2E opcode.

The format of the fused-operation instructions is as follows:

2E	rm1	rm2	ra	r2	f	ra	r1	t	e	t
6	5	5	3	1	1	3	1	1	1	5

Figure 8-8. Fused-Operation Instruction Format

The *rm1*, *rm2*, and *t* fields specify the two source operands for the multiply and the destination operand for the final result. These fields occupy the same positions within the instruction word as the operands of a class 3 single-operation floating-point instruction. The *ra* field specifies the source operand for the add operation.

Table 8-14 lists the two fused-operation instructions, their mnemonics and sub-ops (encoded in the *e* field).

Table 8-14. Fused-Operation Instructions

Sub-op	Mnemonic	Operation
0	FMPYFADD	Multiply Fused Add
1	FMPYNFADD	Multiply Negate Fused Add

The *f* field in the floating-point fused-operation instructions is the operand format completer. Only single-word and double-word formats are supported. The interpretation of the format completer is the same as for the single-operation 0E opcode instructions as given in Table 8-10 on page 8-15.

Multiple-Operation Instructions

The floating-point instruction set includes instructions which perform more than one independent floating-point operation. Multiple-operation instructions are five-operand instructions which combine a three-operand multiply with a two-operand operation (ADD or SUB) of the form: dest ← dest <op> source. These instructions are encoded using the 06 and 26 opcodes.

The format of the multiple-operation instructions is as follows:

op	rm1	rm2	ta	ra	f	tm
6	5	5	5	5	1	5

Figure 8-9. Multiple-Operation Instruction Format

The *rm1*, *rm2*, and *tm* fields specify the two source operands and the destination operand for the multiply operation. These fields occupy the same positions within the instruction word as the operands of a class 3 single-operation floating-point instruction. The *ra* and *ta* fields specify source and destination operands for the ALU operation.

The behavior of the multiple-operation instructions is undefined if *ra* specifies the same register as *tm*, or if *ta* specifies the same register as any of *rm1*, *rm2*, or *tm*. The behavior of these instructions is also undefined if *ra* specifies double-precision register 0 or single-precision register 16L.

Table 8-15 lists the two multiple-operation instructions, their mnemonics and opcodes.

Table 8-15. Multiple-Operation Instructions

Opcode	Mnemonic	Operation
06	FMPYADD	Multiply/Add
26	FMPYSUB	Multiply/Subtract

The *f* field in the floating-point multiple-operation instructions is the operand format completer. Only single-word and double-word formats are supported. The interpretation of the format completer is given in Table 8-16.

Table 8-16. Multiple-Operation Instruction Format Completers

Mnemonic	Code	Description	Data Size
<none> or SGL	1	single-word number	32 bits
DBL	0	double-word number	64 bits

NOTE

Note that the instruction format completers for the multiple-operation instructions do not follow the same pattern as those for the single-operation and fused-operation instructions.

Because the floating-point multiple-operation instructions have only five-bit operand specifiers, these instructions operate on only 32 locations, even when the single-word data format is specified. When double-word data is specified, the interpretation of these operand specifiers is the same as for the single-operation instructions. For single-word data, however, the operand specifiers are restricted to the top 16 registers (32 locations). The details of the interpretation of the operand specifier field in the instruction are shown in Table 8-17.

Table 8-17. Single-Precision Operand Specifier Use in Multi-Operation Instructions

Register specifier field in instruction	Register selected
0	16L*
16	16R
1	17L
17	17R
2	18L
18	18R
3	19L
19	19R
4	20L
20	20R
5	21L
21	21R
6	22L
22	22R
7	23L
23	23R
8	24L
24	24R
9	25L
25	25R
10	26L
26	26R
11	27L
27	27R
12	28L
28	28R
13	29L
29	29R
14	30L
30	30R
15	31L
31	31R

*not allowed

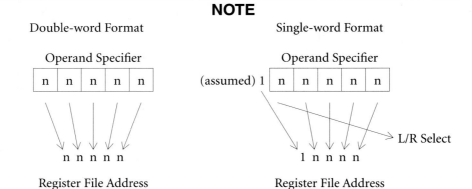

NOTE

Double-word Format

Single-word Format

Operand Specifier

| n | n | n | n | n |

Register File Address

n n n n

Operand Specifier

(assumed) 1 | n | n | n | n | n |

→ L/R Select

1 n n n n

Register File Address

The L/R Select bit in the single-word format specifies the suffix 'L' single-word register, bits 0 to 31, when 0, and the suffix 'R' single-word register, bits 32 to 63, when 1.

Rounding

The specification for the rounding operation from the IEEE standard is:

Rounding takes a number regarded as infinitely precise and, if necessary, modifies it to fit in the destination's format while signaling the inexact exception (7.5) [see "Inexact Exception" on page 10-10]. Except for binary-decimal conversion (whose weaker conditions are specified in 5.6 [not included]), every operation specified in Section 5 [see "Floating-point Operations" on page 8-12] shall be performed as if it first produced an intermediate result correct to infinite precision and with unbounded range, and then rounded that result according to one of the modes in this section.

The rounding modes affect all arithmetic operations except comparison. The rounding modes may affect the signs of zero sums (6.3) [see "Sign Bit" on page 8-24], and do affect the thresholds beyond which overflow (7.3) [see "Overflow Exception" on page 10-11] and underflow (7.4) [see "Underflow Exception" on page 10-12] may be signaled.

[§]**4.1 Round to nearest.** An implementation of this standard shall provide round to nearest as the default rounding mode. In this mode the representable value nearest to the infinitely precise result shall be delivered; if the two nearest representable values are equally near, the one with its least-significant bit zero shall be delivered. However, an infinitely precise result with magnitude at least $2^{E_{max}}(2 - 2^{-p})$ shall round to ∞ with no change in sign; here E_{max} and p are determined by the destination format (§3) [see "Floating-point Formats" on page 8-6] unless overridden by a rounding precision mode (4.3) [not possible in PA-RISC].

[§]**4.2 Directed Roundings.** An implementation shall also provide three user-selectable directed rounding modes: round toward +∞, round toward −∞, and round toward 0. When rounding toward +∞, the result shall be the format's value (possibly +∞) closest to and no less than the infinitely precise result. When rounding toward −∞, the result shall be the format's value (possibly $-\infty$) closest to and no greater than the infinitely precise result. When rounding toward 0, the result shall be the format's value closest to and no greater in magnitude than the infinitely precise result.

The *RM* field in the Status Register determines the rounding mode.

While the above IEEE quote describes the process of rounding, an operation does not always return a rounded result. The result of an operation may be affected if the operation causes an exception.

Infinity Arithmetic

From the standard:

> [§]6.1 Infinity Arithmetic. Infinity arithmetic shall be construed as the limiting case of real arithmetic with operands of arbitrarily large magnitude, when such a limit exists. Infinities shall be interpreted in the affine sense, that is:
>
> $$-\infty < (\text{every finite number}) < +\infty$$

Arithmetic with an infinite operand is always exact and can only signal invalid and unimplemented exceptions. An infinite result is created from finite operands only by a non-trapping overflow exception or a non-trapping division-by-zero exception.

Operations With NaNs

From the standard:

> [§]6.2 Operations with NaNs. Two different kinds of NaN, signaling and quiet, shall be supported in all operations. Signaling NaNs afford values for uninitialized variables and arithmetic-like enhancements (such as complex-affine infinities or extremely wide range) that are not the subject of the standard. Quiet NaNs should, by means left to the implementor's discretion, afford retrospective diagnostic information inherited from invalid or unavailable data and results. Propagation of the diagnostic information requires that information contained in the NaNs be preserved through arithmetic operations and floating-point format conversions.

An operation causes an invalid exception when at least one operand is a signaling NaN and the operation is any arithmetic operation. Also, certain compare operations cause an invalid exception if an operand is a quiet NaN. See "Comparison Conditions" on page 8-16 for more detail.

Converting either a quiet or a signaling NaN to an integer format causes an invalid exception.

A NaN is created in two ways. Any operation that causes a non-trapping invalid exception returns a quiet NaN. Otherwise, an operation returns a quiet NaN when at least one of its operands is a quiet NaN, and the operation is any arithmetic operation.

An operation converts a signaling NaN to a quiet NaN when the operation causes a non-trapping invalid exception and one of its operands is a signaling NaN. If both operands are signaling NaNs, the operation converts the contents of the first operand (the *r1* register).

An operation which converts a signaling NaN to a quiet NaN sets the first bit of the fraction (b_1) to 0. If the remaining bits in the fraction are all zeros ($b_2 \ldots b_{p-1} = 0$), the operation must set the second bit in the fraction to 1. Otherwise, if the remainder of the fraction is not 0, an implementation has the option of setting the second bit in the fraction to 1, or leaving it unchanged. Only the first and second bits in the fraction may change when creating a quiet NaN from a signaling NaN. The remaining fraction bits are copied from the signaling NaN.

When one of its operands is a quiet NaN, but neither operand is a signaling NaN, an operation copies the quiet NaN to the destination. If both operands are quiet NaNs, the *r1* register is copied to the destination.

The creation of a quiet NaN when neither input is a NaN sets the second fraction bit (b_2) to 1 and sets each of the remaining fraction bits to 0.

A conversion operation which does not trap, and which converts a NaN to a smaller floating-point format, preserves the most-significant portion of the fraction while returning a quiet NaN. But if the most-significant portion of the fraction is all zeros, the second bit of the fraction must be set to 1 to prevent the number from becoming an infinity. A conversion which does not trap, and which converts a NaN to a larger floating-point format, augments the fraction with zeros to the right of the smaller fraction while returning a quiet NaN.

Load and store instructions, as well as the FLOATING-POINT NEGATE, FLOATING-POINT NEGATE ABSOLUTE VALUE, FLOATING-POINT COPY, and FLOATING-POINT ABSOLUTE VALUE instructions, are not arithmetic and do not signal an invalid operation exception.

Sign Bit

From the standard:

> [§]6.3 **The sign bit.** This standard does not interpret the sign of a NaN. Otherwise the sign of a product or quotient is the exclusive OR of the operands' signs; and the sign of the sum, or of a difference $x - y$ regarded as a sum $x + (-y)$, differs from at most one of the addends' signs. These rules shall apply even when operands or results are zero or infinite.
>
> When the sum of two operands with opposite signs (or the difference of two operands with like signs) is exactly zero, the sign of that sum (or difference) shall be "+" in all rounding modes except round toward $-\infty$, in which mode the sign shall be "−". However, $x + x = x - (-x)$ retains the same sign as x even when x is zero.
>
> Except that $\sqrt{-0}$ shall be "−0", every valid square root shall have positive sign.

9   Floating-Point Instruction Set

This chapter provides a description of each of the instructions supported by the floating-point coprocessor. The instructions are listed in alphabetical order, according to the name of the instruction - as opposed to the instruction mnemonic.

The *Description* section of each non-load/store instruction contains a list of the Floating-Point Exceptions which the instruction may cause. Each instruction description has an *Exceptions* section which lists the processor interruptions that may occur while the instruction is pointed to by the front of the IA queues.

In the following pages, the notation, FPR, refers to floating-point coprocessor registers 0 through 31. FPSR refers to the Floating-point Status Register. Refer to "Instruction Notations" on page -xviii for the explanation of the operation section. The mem_load and the mem_store descriptions are located in "Memory Reference Instructions" on page 6-6.

Format: FABS,fmt   r,t

(49)

0E	r	0	3	0	f	0	0	r	t	0	t
6	5	5	3	1	1	2	1	1	1	1	5

(45)

0C	r	0	3	fmt	0	0	0	t
6	5	5	3	2	2	3	1	5

Purpose: To perform a floating-point absolute value.

Description: The floating-point register specified by *r* is copied to the floating-point register specified by *t* with the sign bit set to 0. This instruction is non-arithmetic and does not cause an invalid operation exception when the sign of a NaN is set to 0.

Floating-point exceptions:
- Unimplemented

Operation: FPR[t]{all_bits_except_sign} ← FPR[r]{all_bits_except_sign};
FPR[t]{sign_bit} ← 0;

Exceptions: Assist emulation trap
Assist exception trap

Format: FADD,fmt   r1,r2,t

(52)

0E	r1	r2	0	r2	f	3	0	r1	t	0	t
6	5	5	3	1	1	2	1	1	1	1	5

(48)

0C	r1	r2	0	fmt	3	0	0	t
6	5	5	3	2	2	3	1	5

Purpose: To perform a floating-point addition.

Description: The floating-point registers specified by *r1* and *r2* are interpreted in the specified format and arithmetically added. The result is calculated to infinite precision and then rounded to the specified format according to the current rounding mode. The result is placed in the floating-point register specified by *t*.

Floating-point exceptions:

- Unimplemented
- Invalid operation
- Overflow
- Underflow
- Inexact

Operation: $FPR[t] \leftarrow FPR[r1] + FPR[r2];$

Exceptions: Assist emulation trap
Assist exception trap

Floating-Point Compare   FCMP

Format: FCMP,fmt,cond   r1,r2,cbit   /*targeted compare*/
              FCMP,fmt,cond   r1,r2   /*queued compare*/

(51)

0E	r1	r2	y	r2	f	2	0	r1	0	0	c
6	5	5	3	1	1	2	1	1	1	1	5

(47)

0C	r1	r2	y	fmt	2	0	0	c
6	5	5	3	2	2	3	1	5

Purpose: To perform a floating-point comparison.

Description: The floating-point registers specified by $r1$ and $r2$ are interpreted in the specified format and arithmetically compared. A result is determined based on the comparison and the condition, *cond*. The condition is encoded in the c field of the instruction.

There are two types of floating-point compare instructions – targeted compares and queued compares.

- A targeted compare targets a specific bit of the compare array (CA) in the floating-point Status Register (see the second format in Figure 8-6 on page 8-9.) The CA-bit specified by *cbit* is set to 1 if the comparison result is true, or set to 0 otherwise. The CA-bit to set is encoded in the y field of the instruction as *cbit* + 1.
- A queued compare updates the compare queue (CQ) in the floating-point Status Register (see the first format in Figure 8-6 on page 8-9) and is specified by omitting the *cbit* operand. The CQ field in the floating-point Status Register is shifted right by one bit (discarding the rightmost bit) and the C-bit is copied into CQ{0}. Then, if the comparison result is true, the C-bit in the floating-point Status Register is set to 1, otherwise the C-bit is set to 0. A queued compare is encoded with a y field of 0.

If at least one of the values is a signaling NaN, or if at least one of the values is a NaN and the low-order bit of the condition is 1, an invalid operation exception is signaled.

For unimplemented and trapped invalid operation exceptions, the state of the C-bit and CA field is unchanged, and the CQ field is not shifted.

For untrapped invalid operation exceptions, the state of the C-bit, or the CA-bit specified by the instruction is the AND of the unordered relation (which is true) and bit 3 of the c field.

Comparisons are exact and neither overflow nor underflow. Four mutually exclusive relations are possible results: *less than*, *equal*, *greater than*, and *unordered*. The last case arises when at least one operand is a NaN. Every NaN compares *unordered* with everything, including itself. Comparisons ignore the sign of zero, so +0 = −0 .

Floating-point exceptions:
- Unimplemented
- Invalid operation

Operation: if (NaN(FPR[r1]) || NaN(FPR[r2]))
        if (c{4})
            invalid_operation_exception;
        else {
            greater_than ← false;
            less_than ← false;
            equal_to ← false;
            unordered ← true;
        }
    else {
        greater_than ← FPR[r1] > FPR[r2];
        less_than ← FPR[r1] < FPR[r2];
        equal_to ← FPR[r1] = FPR[r2];
        unordered ← false;
    }
    if (y) {   /*targeted compare*/
        FPSR[CA{y–1}] ← (((c{0} == 1) && greater_than) ||
                      ((c{1} == 1) && less_than) ||
                      ((c{2} == 1) && equal_to) ||
                      ((c{3} == 1) && unordered));
    } else {   /*queued compare*/
        FPSR[CQ] ← rshift(FPSR[CQ],1);
        FPSR[CQ{0}] ← FPSR[C];
        FPSR[C] ← (((c{0} == 1) && greater_than) ||
                ((c{1} == 1) && less_than) ||
                ((c{2} == 1) && equal_to) ||
                ((c{3} == 1) && unordered));
    }

Exceptions: Assist emulation trap
Assist exception trap

Floating-Point Convert

Format: FCNV,sf,df   r,t
               FCNV,t,sf,df   r,t

(50)

0E	r	0	sub	0	df	0	sf	1	0	r	t	0	t
6	5	3	3	1	1	1	1	2	1	1	1	1	5

(46)

0C	r	0	sub	df	sf	1	0	0	t
6	5	3	3	2	2	2	3	1	5

Purpose: To change the value in a floating-point register from one format to a different format.

Description: The floating-point register specified by *r* is interpreted in the specified source format, *sf*, and arithmetically converted to the specified destination format, *df*. The result is placed in the floating-point register specified by *t*.

The *sf* and *df* completers specify both the type of conversion and the size of the source and destination formats, and are encoded in the *sub*, *sf*, and *df* fields of the instruction (see Table 8-8 on page 8-14 and Table 8-11 on page 8-16.)

If the ",t" (truncate) completer is specified, the current rounding mode is ignored and the result is rounded toward zero. Otherwise, rounding occurs according to the currently specified rounding mode.

Floating-point exceptions:

- Unimplemented
- Invalid operation
- Overflow[*]
- Underflow[*]
- Inexact

[*] Not reported unless both source and destination formats are floating-point formats.

Operation: if (truncate)
           FPR[t] ← convert(FPR[r],sf,df,ROUND_TOWARD_ZERO);
    else
           FPR[t] ← convert(FPR[r],sf,df,FPSR[RM]);

Exceptions: Assist emulation trap
               Assist exception trap

Restrictions: The",t" completer may only be specified with a fixed-point destination format.

Specifying the same source and destination format is an undefined operation.

Specifying any quadword format in the 0E opcode is an undefined operation.

Format: FCPY,fmt   r,t

(49)

0E	r	0	2	0	f	0	0	r	t	0	t
6	5	5	3	1	1	2	1	1	1	1	5

(45)

0C	r	0	2	fmt	0	0	0	t
6	5	5	3	2	2	3	1	5

Purpose: To copy a floating-point value to another floating-point register.

Description: The floating-point register specified by r is copied into the floating-point register specified by t. This operation is non-arithmetic and does not cause an invalid operation exception when a NaN is copied.

Floating-point exceptions:

- Unimplemented

Operation: $FPR[t] \leftarrow FPR[r];$

Exceptions: Assist emulation trap
Assist exception trap

Format: FDIV,fmt r1,r2,t

(52)

0E	r1	r2	3	r2	f	3	0	r1	t	0	t
6	5	5	3	1	1	2	1	1	1	1	5

(48)

0C	r1	r2	3	fmt	3	0	0	t
6	5	5	3	2	2	3	1	5

Purpose: To perform a floating-point division.

Description: The floating-point registers specified by *r1* and *r2* are interpreted in the specified format and arithmetically divided. The result is calculated to infinite precision and then rounded to the specified format according to the current rounding mode. The result is placed in the floating-point register specified by *t*.

Floating-point exceptions:

- Unimplemented
- Invalid operation
- Division-by-zero
- Overflow
- Underflow
- Inexact

Operation: FPR[t] ← FPR[r1] / FPR[r2];

Exceptions: Assist emulation trap
Assist exception trap

Format: FID

(45)

0C	0	0	0	0	0	0	0	0
6	5	5	3	2	2	3	1	5

Purpose: To validate fields in the Status Register which identify the floating-point coprocessor.

Description: The *model* and *revision* fields in the Status Register become defined. The contents of the other fields in the Status Register are undefined after the execution of this instruction. The *model* and *revision* fields remain defined until a floating-point instruction is executed which is not a double-word store of register 0.

Floating-point exceptions:

- None

Operation: FPSR[model] ← *implementation-dependent model number*;
FPSR[revision] ← *implementation-dependent revision number*;

Exceptions: Assist emulation trap

Notes: This instruction must be implemented. Software may use the following sequence to obtain the *model* and *revision* fields in the Status Register:

```
        .CODE

        LDIL      L%fpreg0,r2        ; load address of
        LDO       R%fpreg0(r2),r2    ; fp reg0 save area
        FSTD      fr0,0(r2)          ; save fp reg0, cancel exception traps

        FID                          ; identify coprocessor

        LDIL      L%version,r2       ; load address of
        LDO       R%version(r2),r2   ; model/rev save area
        FSTD      fr0,0(r2)          ; store coprocessor id, cancel
                                     ; exception traps

        .DATA

fpreg0  .DOUBLE   0
version .DOUBLE   0
```

For the FID instruction to work correctly, the floating-point instructions immediately preceding and following it must be double-word stores of Floating-Point Register 0. If not, the instruction is an undefined operation.

The sequence described will work in user mode. For example, if a context switch occurs just prior to FID but after the first FSTD 0,0(2) instruction, the floating-point state save and state restore sequence will restore the state of the Status Register ("T" bit off, cancel trap) just prior to the execution of FID.

Format: FLDD,cmplt,cc   xld(s,b),t

(3)

14	b	t	s	im10a	m	a	1	i
6	5	5	2	10	1	1	1	1

(41)

0B	b	im5	s	a	1	cc	0	0	0	m	t
6	5	5	2	1	1	2	1	2	1	1	5

(39)

0B	b	x	s	u	0	cc	0	0	0	m	t
6	5	5	2	1	1	2	1	2	1	1	5

Purpose: To load a doubleword into a floating-point coprocessor register.

Description: The aligned doubleword at the effective address is loaded into floating-point register t. The offset is formed as the sum of a base register, b, and either an index register, x (Format 39), or a displacement d. The displacement can be either long (Format 3) or short (Format 41.) The displacement is encoded into the immediate field. Optional base modification can also be performed.

The completer, *cmplt*, determines whether the offset is the base register, or the base register plus the index register or displacement. The completer also specifies base register modification, optional index prescaling, and ordering constraints (see Table H-1 on page H-4, and Table H-3 on page H-8 for the assembly language completer mnemonics.) The completer, *cc*, specifies the cache control hint (see Table 6-7 on page 6-10.)

For long and short displacements, a one in the m field specifies base modification, and the a field encodes whether pre-modification (a=1), or post-modification (a=0) is performed. For indexed loads, a one in the m field specifies base modification, and a one in the u field specifies index prescaling.

Specifying Floating-Point Register 0 forces the coprocessor to complete all previous floating-point instructions.

Operation: if (indexed_load)   /* indexed (Format 39)*/
                  switch (cmplt) {
                      case S:
                      case SM: dx ← lshift(GR[x],3);
                                      break;
                      case M:
                      default: dx ← GR[x];
                                      break;
                  }
              else if (d > 15 || d < -16) {   /* long displacement */
                  dx ← sign_ext(assemble_16a(s,cat(im10a,0),i),16);   /* (Format 3) */
                  cc ← NO_HINT;
              } else   /* short displacement */
                  dx ← low_sign_ext(im5,5);   /* (Format 41) */
              space ← space_select(s,GR[b],format);
              switch (cmplt) {
                  case MB: offset ← GR[b] + dx;
                                  GR[b] ← GR[b] + dx;
                                  break;
                  case MA:
                  case M:
                  case SM: offset ← GR[b];
                                  GR[b] ← GR[b] + dx;
                                  break;
                  default: offset ← GR[b] + dx;
                                  break;
              }
              FPR[t] ← mem_load(space,offset,0,63,cc);
              if (cmplt == O)
                  enforce_ordered_load;

Exceptions: Assist exception trap   Unaligned data reference trap
                  Data TLB miss fault/data page fault   Page reference trap
                  Data memory access rights trap   Assist emulation trap
                  Data memory protection ID trap

Restrictions: For loads with long displacements (Format 3), only displacements which are multiples of eight may be used.

                  If the completer O is specified, the displacement must be 0.

Format: FLDW,cmplt,cc xld(s,b),t

(43)

17	b	t	s	im11a	0	t	i
6	5	5	2	11	1	1	1

(44)

16	b	t	s	im11a	a	t	i
6	5	5	2	11	1	1	1

(41)

09	b	im5	s	a	1	cc	0	0	t	m	t
6	5	5	2	1	1	2	1	2	1	1	5

(39)

09	b	x	s	u	0	cc	0	0	t	m	t
6	5	5	2	1	1	2	1	2	1	1	5

Purpose: To load a word into a floating-point coprocessor register.

Description: The aligned word at the effective address is loaded into floating-point register t. The offset is formed as the sum of a base register, b, and either an index register, x (Format 39), or a displacement d. The displacement can be either long (Formats 43 and 44) or short (Format 41.) The displacement is encoded into the immediate field. Optional base modification can also be performed.

The completer, *cmplt*, determines whether the offset is the base register, or the base register plus the index register or displacement. This completer also specifies base register modification, optional index prescaling, and ordering constraints (see Table H-1 on page H-4, and Table H-3 on page H-8 for the assembly language completer mnemonics.) The completer, *cc*, specifies the cache control hint (see Table 6-7 on page 6-10.)

For long displacements with base modification, Format 44 is used, and the a field encodes whether pre-modification ($a=1$), or post-modification ($a=0$) is performed. For long displacements with no base modification, Format 43 is used.

For short displacements, a one in the m field specifies base modification, and the a field encodes whether pre-modification ($a=1$), or post-modification ($a=0$) is performed. For indexed loads, a one in the m field specifies base modification, and a one in the u field specifies index prescaling.

Specifying floating-point registers 0R, 1L, 1R, 2L, 2R, 3L, or 3R is an undefined operation. Specifying Floating-Point Register 0L forces the coprocessor to complete all previous floating-point instructions. However, loading Floating-Point Register 0L with a value that sets the Status Register T-bit to 1 is an undefined operation.

Operation: if (indexed_load)   /* indexed (Format 39)*/
                switch (cmplt) {
                    case S:
                    case SM: dx ← lshift(GR[x],2);
                                      break;
                    case M:
                    default: dx ← GR[x];
                                      break;
                }
        else if (d > 15 || d < -16) {   /* long displacement */
                dx ← sign_ext(assemble_16a(s,im11a,i),16);   /* (Formats 43 and 44) */
                cc ← NO_HINT;
        } else   /* short displacement */
                dx ← low_sign_ext(im5,5);   /* (Format 41) */
        space ← space_select(s,GR[b],format);
        switch (cmplt) {
                case MB: offset ← GR[b] + dx;
                                GR[b] ← GR[b] + dx;
                                break;
                case MA:
                case M:
                case SM: offset ← GR[b];
                                GR[b] ← GR[b] + dx;
                                break;
                default: offset ← GR[b] + dx;
                                break;
        }
        FPR[t] ← mem_load(space,offset,0,31,cc);
        if (cmplt == O)
                enforce_ordered_load;

Exceptions: Assist exception trap   Unaligned data reference trap
               Data TLB miss fault/data page fault   Page reference trap
               Data memory access rights trap   Assist emulation trap
               Data memory protection ID trap

Restrictions: For loads with long displacements (Formats 43 and 44), only displacements which are multiples of four may be used.

If the completer O is specified, the displacement must be 0.

Format: FMPY,fmt   r1,r2,t

(52)

0E	r1	r2	2	r2	f	3	0	r1	t	0	t
6	5	5	3	1	1	2	1	1	1	1	5

(48)

0C	r1	r2	2	fmt	3	0	0	t
6	5	5	3	2	2	3	1	5

Purpose: To perform a floating-point multiply.

Description: The floating-point registers specified by *r1* and *r2* are interpreted in the specified format and arithmetically multiplied. The result is calculated to infinite precision and then rounded to the specified format according to the current rounding mode. The result is placed in the floating-point register specified by *t*.

Floating-point exceptions:

- Unimplemented
- Invalid operation
- Overflow
- Underflow
- Inexact

Operation: FPR[t] ← FPR[r1] * FPR[r2];

Exceptions: Assist emulation trap
Assist exception trap

Format: FMPYADD,fmt   rm1,rm2,tm,ra,ta

(53)

06	rm1	rm2	ta	ra	f	tm
6	5	5	5	5	1	5

Purpose: To perform a floating-point multiply and a floating-point add.

Description: The floating-point registers specified by *rm1* and *rm2* are interpreted in the specified format and arithmetically multiplied. The result is calculated to infinite precision and then rounded to the specified format according to the current rounding mode. The result is placed in the floating-point register specified by *tm*.

The floating-point registers specified by *ta* and *ra* are interpreted in the specified format and arithmetically added. The result is calculated to infinite precision and then rounded to the specified format according to the current rounding mode. The result is placed in the floating-point register specified by *ta*.

The behavior of this instruction is undefined if *ra* specifies the same register as *tm*, or if *ta* specifies the same register as any of *rm1*, *rm2*, or *tm*. The behavior of this instruction is also undefined if *ra* specifies double-precision register 0 or single-precision register 16L.

Floating-point exceptions:

- Unimplemented
- Invalid operation
- Overflow
- Underflow
- Inexact

Operation: FPR[tm] ← FPR[rm1] * FPR[rm2];
FPR[ta] ← FPR[ta] + FPR[ra];

Exceptions: Assist emulation trap
Assist exception trap

Notes: When operating on single-precision operands, each register field specifies one of registers 16L through 31L, or one of 16R through 31R. See Table 8-17 on page 8-21 for the register specifier encodings.

This instruction can be decomposed into FMPY and FADD and then the full set of floating-point exceptions can be reported.

Format: FMPYFADD,fmt   rm1,rm2,ra,t

(54)

2E	rm1	rm2	ra	r2	f	ra	r1	t	0	t
6	5	5	3	1	1	3	1	1	1	5

Purpose: To perform a floating-point multiply and fused add.

Description: The floating-point registers specified by *rm1* and *rm2* are interpreted in the specified format and arithmetically multiplied. The intermediate result is calculated to infinite precision with an unbounded exponent (and is not rounded.) The floating-point register specified by *ra* is interpreted in the specified format, arithmetically added to the result obtained by the multiply operation and then rounded to the specified format according to the current rounding mode. The result is placed in the floating-point register specified by *t*.

Floating-point exceptions:

  • Unimplemented
  • Invalid operation
  • Overflow
  • Underflow
  • Inexact

Operation: FPR[t] ← (FPR[rm1] * FPR[rm2]) + FPR[ra];

Exceptions: Assist emulation trap
                  Assist exception trap

Format: FMPYNFADD,fmt   rm1,rm2,ra,t

(54)

2E	rm1	rm2	ra	r2	f	ra	r1	t	1	t
6	5	5	3	1	1	3	1	1	1	5

Purpose: To perform a floating-point multiply, negate, and fused add.

Description: The floating-point registers specified by *rm1* and *rm2* are interpreted in the specified format and arithmetically multiplied. The intermediate result is calculated to infinite precision with an unbounded exponent (and is not rounded.) The floating-point register specified by *ra* is interpreted in the specified format, arithmetically added to the negated result obtained by the multiply operation and then rounded to the specified format according to the current rounding mode. The result is placed in the floating-point register specified by *t*.

Floating-point exceptions:

- Unimplemented
- Invalid operation
- Overflow
- Underflow
- Inexact

Operation: FPR[t] ← −(FPR[rm1] * FPR[rm2]) + FPR[ra];

Exceptions: Assist emulation trap
Assist exception trap

Format: FMPYSUB,fmt   rm1,rm2,tm,ra,ta

(53)

26	rm1	rm2	ta	ra	f	tm
6	5	5	5	5	1	5

Purpose: To perform a floating-point multiply and a floating-point subtract.

Description: The floating-point registers specified by *rm1* and *rm2* are interpreted in the specified format and arithmetically multiplied. The result is calculated to infinite precision and then rounded to the specified format according to the current rounding mode. The result is placed in the floating-point register specified by *tm*.

The floating-point registers specified by *ta* and *ra* are interpreted in the specified format and arithmetically subtracted. The result is calculated to infinite precision and then rounded to the specified format according to the current rounding mode. The result is placed in the floating-point register specified by *ta*.

The behavior of this instruction is undefined if *ra* specifies the same register as *tm*, or if *ta* specifies the same register as any of *rm1*, *rm2*, or *tm*. The behavior of this instruction is also undefined if *ra* specifies double-precision register 0 or single-precision register 16L.

Floating-point exceptions:

- Unimplemented
- Invalid operation
- Overflow
- Underflow
- Inexact

Operation: FPR[tm] ← FPR[rm1] * FPR[rm2];
FPR[ta] ← FPR[ta] - FPR[ra];

Exceptions: Assist emulation trap
Assist exception trap

Notes: When operating on single-precision operands, each register field specifies one of registers 16L through 31L, or one of 16R through 31R. See Table 8-17 on page 8-21 for the register specifier encodings.

This instruction can be decomposed into FMPY and FSUB and then the full set of floating-point exceptions can be reported.

Floating-Point Negate

Format: FNEG,fmt   r,t

(49)

0E	r	0	6	0	f	0	0	r	t	0	t
6	5	5	3	1	1	2	1	1	1	1	5

(45)

0C	r	0	6	fmt	0	0	0	t
6	5	5	3	2	2	3	1	5

Purpose: To negate a floating-point value.

Description: The floating-point register specified by *r* is copied into the floating-point register specified by *t* and negated. This operation is non-arithmetic and does not cause an invalid operation exception when a NaN is negated.

Floating-point exceptions:

  • Unimplemented

Operation: FPR[t]{all_bits_except_sign} ← FPR[r]{all_bits_except_sign};
              FPR[t]{sign_bit} ← ~FPR[r]{sign_bit};

Exceptions: Assist emulation trap
                Assist exception trap

PA-RISC 2.0 Architecture   Floating-Point Instruction Set   **9-19**

Format: FNEGABS,fmt   r,t

(49)	0E	r	0	7	0	f	0	0	r	t	0	t
	6	5	5	3	1	1	2	1	1	1	1	5

(45)	0C	r	0	7	fmt	0	0	0	t
	6	5	5	3	2	2	3	1	5

Purpose: To negate a floating-point absolute value.

Description: The floating-point register specified by *r* is copied into the floating-point register specified by *t* with the sign bit set to 1. This operation is non-arithmetic and does not cause an invalid operation exception when the sign of a NaN is set to 1.

Floating-point exceptions:

- Unimplemented

Operation: FPR[t]{all_bits_except_sign} ← FPR[r]{all_bits_except_sign};
FPR[t]{sign_bit} ← 1;

Exceptions: Assist emulation trap
Assist exception trap

Floating-Point Round to Integer

Format: FRND,fmt   r,t

(49)

0E	r	0	5	0	f	0	0	r	t	0	t
6	5	5	3	1	1	2	1	1	1	1	5

(45)

0C	r	0	5	fmt	0	0	0	t
6	5	5	3	2	2	3	1	5

Purpose: To round a floating-point value to an integral value.

Description: The floating-point register specified by r is interpreted in the specified format and arithmetically rounded to an integral value. This result remains a floating-point number. Results are rounded according to the current rounding mode with the proviso that when rounding to nearest, if the difference between the unrounded operand and the rounded result is exactly one half, the rounded result is even. The result is placed in the floating-point register specified by t. An inexact exception is signaled when the result and source are not the same.

Floating-point exceptions:

- Unimplemented
- Invalid operation
- Inexact

Operation: FPR[t] ← floating_point_round(FPR[r]);

Exceptions: Assist emulation trap
Assist exception trap

Format: FSQRT,fmt   r,t

(49)

0E	r	0	4	0	f	0	0	r	t	0	t
6	5	5	3	1	1	2	1	1	1	1	5

(45)

0C	r	0	4	fmt	0	0	0	t
6	5	5	3	2	2	3	1	5

Purpose: To perform a floating-point square root.

Description: The floating-point register specified by *r* is interpreted in the specified format and the positive arithmetic square root is taken. The result is calculated to infinite precision and then rounded to the specified format according to the current rounding mode. If the source register contains -0, the result will be -0. The result is placed in the floating-point register specified by *t*.

Floating-point exceptions:

- Unimplemented
- Invalid operation
- Inexact

Operation: FPR[t] ← square_root(FPR[r]);

Exceptions: Assist emulation trap
                   Assist exception trap

Format: FSTD,cmplt,cc   r,xld(s,b)

(3)

1C	b	t	s	im10a	m	a	l	i
6	5	5	2	10	1	1	1	1

(42)

0B	b	im5	s	a	1	cc	1	0	0	m	r
6	5	5	2	1	1	2	1	2	1	1	5

(40)

0B	b	x	s	u	0	cc	1	0	0	m	r
6	5	5	2	1	1	2	1	2	1	1	5

Purpose: To store a doubleword from a floating-point coprocessor register.

Description: Floating-point register r is stored in the aligned doubleword at the effective address. The offset is formed as the sum of a base register, b, and either an index register, x (Format 40), or a displacement d. The displacement can be either long (Format 3) or short (Format 42.) The displacement is encoded into the immediate field. Optional base modification can also be performed.

The completer, *cmplt*, determines whether the offset is the base register, or the base register plus the index register or displacement. This completer also specifies base register modification, optional index prescaling, and ordering constraints (see Table H-1 on page H-4, and Table H-3 on page H-8 for the assembly language completer mnemonics.) The completer, *cc*, specifies the cache control hint (see Table 6-8 on page 6-10.)

For long and short displacements, a one in the m field specifies base modification, and the a field encodes whether pre-modification ($a=1$), or post-modification ($a=0$) is performed. For indexed stores, a one in the m field specifies base modification, and a one in the u field specifies index prescaling.

Specifying Floating-Point Register 0 forces the coprocessor to complete all previous floating-point instructions and sets the Status Register T-bit to 0 following completion of the store.

Operation: if (indexed_store)   /* indexed (Format 40)*/
       switch (cmplt) {
          case S:
          case SM: dx ← lshift(GR[x],3);
                      break;
          case M:
          default: dx ← GR[x];
                      break;
       }
    else if (d > 15 || d < -16) {   /* long displacement */
       dx ← sign_ext(assemble_16a(s,cat(im10a,0),i),16);   /* (Format 3) */
       cc ← NO_HINT;
    } else   /* short displacement */
       dx ← low_sign_ext(im5,5);   /* (Format 42) */
    space ← space_select(s,GR[b],format);
    if (cmplt == O)
       enforce_ordered_store;
    switch (cmplt) {
       case MB: offset ← GR[b] + dx;
                 GR[b] ← GR[b] + dx;
                 break;
       case MA:
       case M:
       case SM: offset ← GR[b];
                 GR[b] ← GR[b] + dx;
                 break;
       default: offset ← GR[b] + dx;
                 break;
    }
    mem_store(space,offset,0,63,cc,FPR[r]);

Exceptions:

Assist exception trap	Data memory break trap
Data TLB miss fault/data page fault	TLB dirty bit trap
Data memory access rights trap	Page reference trap
Data memory protection ID trap	Assist emulation trap
Unaligned data reference trap	

Restrictions: For stores with long displacements (Format 3), only displacements which are multiples of eight may be used.

If the completer O is specified, the displacement must be 0.

Format: FSTW,cmplt,cc   r,x|d($_s$,b)

(43)

1F	b	r	s	im11a	0	r	i
6	5	5	2	11	1	1	1

(44)

1E	b	r	s	im11a	a	r	i
6	5	5	2	11	1	1	1

(42)

09	b	im5	s	a	1	cc	1	0	r	m	r
6	5	5	2	1	1	2	1	2	1	1	5

(40)

09	b	x	s	u	0	cc	1	0	r	m	r
6	5	5	2	1	1	2	1	2	1	1	5

Purpose: To store a word from a floating-point coprocessor register.

Description: Floating-point register *r* is stored in the aligned word at the effective address. The offset is formed as the sum of a base register, *b*, and either an index register, *x* (Format 40), or a displacement *d*. The displacement can be either long (Formats 43 and 44) or short (Format 42.) The displacement is encoded into the immediate field. Optional base modification can also be performed.

The completer, *cmplt*, determines whether the offset is the base register, or the base register plus the index register or displacement. This completer also specifies base register modification, optional index prescaling, and ordering constraints (see Table H-1 on page H-4, and Table H-3 on page H-8 for the assembly language completer mnemonics.) The completer, *cc*, specifies the cache control hint (see Table 6-8 on page 6-10.)

For long displacements with base modification, Format 44 is used, and the *a* field encodes whether pre-modification (*a*=1), or post-modification (*a*=0) is performed. For long displacements with no base modification, Format 43 is used.

For short displacements, a one in the *m* field specifies base modification, and the *a* field encodes whether pre-modification (*a*=1), or post-modification (*a*=0) is performed. For indexed stores, a one in the *m* field specifies base modification, and a one in the *u* field specifies index prescaling.

Specifying floating-point registers 0R, 1L, 1R, 2L, 2R, 3L, or 3R is an undefined operation. Specifying Floating-Point Register 0L forces the coprocessor to complete all previous floating-point instructions.

Operation: if (indexed_store)   /* indexed (Format 40)*/
                    switch (cmplt) {
                        case S:
                        case SM: dx ← lshift(GR[x],2);
                                          break;
                        case M:
                        default: dx ← GR[x];
                                          break;
                    }
                else if (d > 15 || d < -16) {   /* long displacement */
                    dx ← sign_ext(assemble_16a(s,im11a,i),16);   /* (Formats 43 and 44) */
                    cc ← NO_HINT;
                } else   /* short displacement */
                    dx ← low_sign_ext(im5,5);   /* (Format 42) */
                space ← space_select(s,GR[b],format);
                if (cmplt == O)
                    enforce_ordered_store;
                switch (cmplt) {
                    case MB: offset ← GR[b] + dx;
                                      GR[b] ← GR[b] + dx;
                                      break;
                    case MA:
                    case M:
                    case SM: offset ← GR[b];
                                      GR[b] ← GR[b] + dx;
                                      break;
                    default: offset ← GR[b] + dx;
                                      break;
                }
                mem_store(space,offset,0,31,cc,FPR[r]);

Exceptions: Assist exception trap   Data memory break trap
                  Data TLB miss fault/data page fault   TLB dirty bit trap
                  Data memory access rights trap   Page reference trap
                  Data memory protection ID trap   Assist emulation trap
                  Unaligned data reference trap

Restrictions: For stores with long displacements (Formats 43 and 44), only displacements which are multiples of four may be used.

                  If the completer O is specified, the displacement must be 0.

Format: FSUB,fmt   r1,r2,t

(52)

0E	r1	r2	1	r2	f	3	0	r1	t	0	t
6	5	5	3	1	1	2	1	1	1	1	5

(48)

0C	r1	r2	1	fmt	3	0	0	t
6	5	5	3	2	2	3	1	5

Purpose: To perform a floating-point subtraction.

Description: The floating-point registers specified by *r1* and *r2* are interpreted in the specified format and arithmetically subtracted. The result is calculated to infinite precision and then rounded to the specified format according to the current rounding mode. The result is placed in the floating-point register specified by *t*.

Floating-point exceptions:
- Unimplemented
- Invalid operation
- Overflow
- Underflow
- Inexact

Operation: FPR[t] ← FPR[r1] − FPR[r2];

Exceptions: Assist emulation trap
Assist exception trap

Format: FTEST   cbit   /*targeted test*/
                 FTEST,cond   /*queue test*/

(47)

0C	0	0	y	0	2	0	1	c
6	5	5	3	2	2	3	1	5

Purpose: To test the results of one or more earlier comparisons.

Description: The specified condition in the floating-point Status Register is tested. The condition, *cond*, is encoded in the *c* field of the instruction. If the condition is satisfied, then the following instruction is nullified.

There are two types of floating-point test instructions – targeted tests and queue tests.

- A targeted test tests a specific bit of the compare array (CA) in the floating-point Status Register (see the second format in Figure 8-6 on page 8-9.) If the CA-bit specified by *cbit* is 1, the PSW[N] bit is set to 1. The CA-bit to test is encoded in the *y* field of the instruction as xor(*cbit*+1,1.) No condition may be specified for a targeted test and the *c* field must be 0.

- A queue test tests for a specific condition in the C-bit and compare queue (CQ) in the floating-point Status Register (see the first format in Figure 8-6 on page 8-9) and is specified by omitting the *cbit* operand. A queue test is encoded with a *y* field of 1.

Floating-point exceptions:

- None

Conditions: For targeted tests, no condition may be specified. For queue tests, the condition is any of the conditions shown in Table 8-13 on page 8-18. When a condition completer is not specified, the "Simple Test" (C == 1) condition is used. The boolean variable "cond_satisfied" in the operation section is set when the specified condition is satisfied.

Operation: if (y == 1) {   /*queue test*/
                   if (cond_satisfied)
                         PSW[N] ← 1;
                 } else {   /*targeted test*/
                   if (FPSR[CA{xor(y,1)–1}]) {   /*test CA{cbit}*/
                       PSW[N] ← 1
                 }

Exceptions: Assist emulation trap
                 Assist exception trap

Restrictions: It is an undefined operation to mix targeted FCMP instructions with queue FTEST instructions or to mix queue FCMPs with targeted FTESTs. For a targeted FTEST to be defined, an FCMP to the same CA bit must precede it without any intervening queued FCMP. For a queue FTEST to be defined, enough queued FCMPs must be executed to define the CQ bits being tested without any intervening targeted FCMPs. Any FTEST may follow a load of the FPSR, because the load defines all of the C-, CA-, and CQ-bits.

Notes: This instruction must be implemented, may not be queued and may not cause any assist exception traps. However, any assist exception traps caused by previous instructions may be taken while this instruction is in the IA queue.

Format: XMPYU   r1,r2,t

(52)

0E	r1	r2	2	r2	0	3	1	r1	0	0	t
6	5	5	3	1	1	2	1	1	1	1	5

Purpose: To perform unsigned fixed-point multiplication.

Description: The floating-point registers specified by *r1* and *r2* are interpreted as unsigned 32-bit integers and arithmetically multiplied. The unsigned 64-bit result is placed in the floating-point register specified by *t*.

Floating-point exceptions:

- Unimplemented

Operation: FPR[t] ← FPR[r1] * FPR[r2];

Exceptions: Assist emulation trap
                 Assist exception trap

10   Floating-Point Exceptions

Floating-point instructions may cause an interruption in the processor, an exception in the coprocessor, or both. Interruptions are described in Chapter 5, "Interruptions" and always force the processor to branch to a location in the Interruption Vector Table. Floating-point coprocessor exceptions may or may not force the processor to trap (that is, force the processor to take an interruption). In this chapter, an instruction which causes a floating-point exception is called an **excepting instruction**.

Floating-point exceptions are divided into immediate trapping exceptions and delayed trapping exceptions. Immediate trapping exceptions always force the processor to trap. Delayed trapping exceptions are further divided into exceptions that always trap, and exceptions that will trap only when the corresponding trap is enabled. An immediate trapping exception forces the processor to signal an assist exception trap when the excepting instruction is the current instruction being executed. A delayed trapping exception forces the processor to signal an assist exception trap when the current instruction is a floating-point instruction, and the excepting instruction is a pending instruction.

The only immediate trapping exception is the reserved-op exception. This exception cannot be disabled.

The only delayed trapping exception that cannot be disabled is the unimplemented exception. The other delayed trapping exceptions are the IEEE exceptions. Each has a corresponding bit in the Status Register which enables and disables the delayed trap. The IEEE exceptions are the following: invalid operation, division-by-zero, overflow, underflow, and inexact.

Exception Registers

The exception registers contain information on floating-point operations that have completed execution and have caused a delayed trapping exception. All the registers must be present and storage provided for loads and stores even if an implementation never uses a particular register to record exception state.

The exception registers are accessed with double-word load and store instructions. Single-word loads and stores of registers 0R, 1L, 1R, 2L, 2R, 3L, and 3R are undefined. Specifying an exception register as a source or destination of a non-load/store operation is undefined.

For single-operation instructions, an exception register contains a modified copy of an excepting instruction that traps. The coprocessor replaces the field that normally contains the instruction opcode with a code that indicates the type of exception detected. The remaining fields are duplicates from the original instruction.

The fused-operation instructions (FLOATING-POINT MULTIPLY FUSED ADD and FLOATING-POINT MULTIPLY NEGATE FUSED ADD) cannot directly cause trapping IEEE exceptions, because the exception state cannot be represented in the exception registers. When one of these instructions would cause a trapping IEEE exception, the implementation causes, instead, an unimplemented exception. The fused-operation instruction is placed in an exception register along with the appropriate unimplemented exception code.

The multiple-operation instructions (FLOATING-POINT MULTIPLY/ADD and FLOATING-POINT MULTIPLY/SUBTRACT) cannot directly cause trapping IEEE exceptions, because the exception state cannot be represented in the exception registers. When one of these instructions would cause a trapping IEEE exception, the implementation does one of the following:

- Cause, instead, an unimplemented exception. The multiple-operation instruction is placed in an exception register along with the appropriate unimplemented exception code. Or,

- Treat the multiple-operation instruction as two separate single-operation instructions. In this case, an instruction pattern is fabricated for the portion of the instruction that caused the trapping exception (e.g., the instruction pattern for a FLOATING-POINT ADD if the add operation caused the exception), and this pattern, along with the appropriate exception code, is placed in an exception register. The other operation, if it does not also cause a trapping exception, completes normally. If both operations cause trapping IEEE exceptions, then two instruction patterns are fabricated and placed in two exception registers. These two instructions have the same ordering constraints with respect to other instructions as for other single-operation instructions as described in the next section.

Figure 10-1 shows the format of the exception registers. The exception and ei fields are explained in the paragraphs that follow.

exception	ei
6	26

Figure 10-1. Floating-Point Exception Register Format

exception   The exception code corresponding to the exception detected as shown in Table 10-1. Exception codes not listed are reserved.

Table 10-1. Floating-Point Exception Codes

Exception code	Opcode	Description
000000	0C/0E	No exception
100000	0C/0E	Invalid operation
010000	0C/0E	Division-by-zero
001000	0C/0E	Overflow
pp0100	0C/0E	Underflow
000010	0C/0E	Inexact
000001	0C/0E	Unimplemented
001010	0C/0E	Inexact & Overflow
pp0110	0C/0E	Inexact & Underflow
001001	0C	Unimplemented
001011	0E	Unimplemented
000011	06	Unimplemented
100011	26	Unimplemented
101011	2E	Unimplemented
pp1100	2E	Underflow
010010	2E	Inexact
pp1110	2E	Underflow and Inexact
011000	2E	Overflow
011010	2E	Overflow and Inexact
110000	2E	Invalid

The two bits labeled 'pp' in the exception code contain information regarding the parameters for the underflow exceptions. See "Underflow Exception" on page 10-12 for a detailed description of this field.

ei   All bits other than the major opcode, copied from the excepting instruction. This field is undefined if the exception code is set to 'no exception'.

Exception Register Operation

When all pending instructions are forced to complete, all operations which complete with a trapping exception are placed in the exception registers together with their corresponding exception codes. In order to complete an operation, the coprocessor may place the operation in an exception register and mark it with an unimplemented exception.

The coprocessor places the excepting instruction that first entered the IA queues in any of Exception Registers 1 through 7. Other instructions which complete with a trap are placed in any of the other available Exception Registers (those which are not already occupied by excepting instructions). Excepting instructions may be placed in the Exception Registers 1 through 7 in any order as long as the data dependencies are preserved (the order need not be the order in which they were fetched but must be ordered for the data dependencies). If an instruction completes without a trapping exception, no record of that instruction appears in the exception registers. The exception queue need not be packed.

Once software has processed the exception registers, it must clear the exception registers by setting them all to zeros before non-load/store instructions can be executed.

If the T-bit equals 0 and any exception register has an exception field not equal to "no exception", execution of any non-load/store floating-point instruction is an undefined operation.

Interruptions and Exceptions

Floating-point instructions may cause interruptions in the processor, exceptions in the coprocessor, or both. Coprocessor exceptions are divided into immediate trapping exceptions and delayed trapping exceptions. The only immediate trapping exception is the reserved-op exception. The delayed trapping exceptions consist of the unimplemented exception and the IEEE exceptions.

The IEEE exceptions are the following:

- invalid operation
- division-by-zero
- inexact
- overflow
- underflow

While the unimplemented and reserved-op exceptions must always trap, the IEEE exception traps may be disabled.

Each IEEE exception has a corresponding enable bit in the Status Register. When an enable bit is 1, the corresponding trap is enabled, and if the corresponding exception occurs, a delayed trap is taken. However, on the overflow and underflow exceptions, an implementation may choose to ignore the enable bit and always trap on the exception. In such implementations, the corresponding trap is always enabled.

Immediate Trapping

Floating-point instructions may cause three types of immediate trapping interruptions: memory reference interruptions, the assist emulation trap, and the reserved-op exception. Immediate trapping exceptions and interruptions always cause a trap or fault when the front of the IA queues points to the interrupting instruction. An interrupting instruction must not alter its operands.

As described in Chapter 4, "Control Flow", when the processor detects a memory reference problem, a memory reference fault or trap occurs. Only load and store instructions cause memory reference interruptions. The memory reference interruptions associated with floating-point instructions are the following:

- Data TLB miss fault/Data page fault
- Data memory access rights trap
- Data memory protection ID trap

- Unaligned data reference trap

- Data memory break trap

- TLB dirty bit trap

- Page reference trap

- Data debug trap

As described in "Coprocessor Configuration Register" on page 6-22, the Coprocessor Configuration Register (CCR) in the processor controls the assist emulation trap. Software may set this register to force an assist emulation trap on every occurrence of a floating-point instruction. See "Coprocessor Instructions" on page 6-22 for more information.

Finally, attempting an instruction with a reserved sub-opcode may cause an immediate assist exception trap. See "Reserved-op Exception" on page 10-8 for details.

Delayed Trapping

Delayed traps report an exception when the excepting instruction is a pending instruction but is not in the IA queues. The following descriptions indicate when the processor and coprocessor may take a delayed trap and must take a delayed trap. Normally, a delayed trap forces the processor to take an assist exception trap. However, if the current instruction is a double-word store of Floating-point Register 0, all the floating-point registers are set normally as if a trap occurred, but the processor does not take the assist exception trap.

The coprocessor may signal a delayed trap when at least one of the following occurs:

- A pending instruction caused an unimplemented exception and the current instruction is a floating-point instruction, or

- A pending instruction caused an IEEE exception, the corresponding exception trap is enabled, and the current instruction is a floating-point instruction.

A delayed trap must occur when at least one of the following conditions exist:

- The T-bit is 1 and the current instruction is any floating-point instruction.

- The exception queue is full and the current instruction is any floating-point instruction.

- A pending instruction causes a trapping exception and the current instruction is a load or store of Floating-point Register 0.

- The current instruction is a load or store of an exception register that will be set by a pending instruction.

- The current instruction is a load or store of the destination register of a pending, trapping instruction or an operation which depends on a pending, trapping instruction.

- The current instruction is a load of the source register of a pending, trapping instruction or an operation which depends on a pending, trapping instruction.

- The current instruction is a FLOATING-POINT TEST instruction and the previous FLOATING-POINT COMPARE either is pending and caused a trapping exception or depends on a pending, trapping instruction.

An instruction depends on a previous instruction whenever it must wait for the previous instruction to complete in order to ensure that the instructions appear sequentially executed to software. Instruction dependency is transitive. For example, if the exception queue is full, and every instruction in the queue depends on the instruction immediately preceding it, then each instruction in the queue depends on all the instructions preceding it.

When a delayed trap occurs, the following happens:

1. The coprocessor completes all pending floating-point instructions.

2. The coprocessor sets the exception registers as described in "Exception Register Operation" on page 10-3.

3. The coprocessor sets the Status Register T-bit to 1.

4. For each pending instruction that completes with a trapping IEEE exception, the corresponding exception flag may either be set to 1, or left unchanged, but cannot be set to 0.

5. If the current instruction is any floating-point instruction except a double-word store of Floating-point Register 0, the processor takes an assist exception trap. Otherwise, if the current instruction is a double-word store of Floating-point Register 0, the store completes, no trap occurs, the T-bit is set to 0 and execution proceeds normally.

Any pending instruction which depends on a pending, trapping instruction must complete with an unimplemented exception.

Table 10-2 specifies the status of the source and destination registers when an instruction causes a delayed trap. When the table indicates the original operand values are preserved, and if the destination register is not one of the source registers, the contents of the destination register are undefined.

Table 10-2. Delayed Trap Results

Exception type	Trapped result
Invalid operation	original operand values preserved
Division-by-zero	original operand values preserved
Overflow	rounded bias-adjusted result in destination
Underflow	rounded bias-adjusted result in destination
Inexact	rounded result in destination
Unimplemented	original operand values preserved

As indicated in the table, trapping overflow exceptions and underflow exceptions return a rounded bias-adjusted result. A bias-adjusted result is obtained by dividing (in the case of overflow) or multiplying (in the case of underflow) the infinitely precise result by 2^a and then rounding. The bias adjustment, a, is 192 for single-word numbers, 1536 for double-word numbers, and 24576 for quad-word numbers.

Non-trapping Exceptions

If an IEEE exception occurs, but the corresponding trap is disabled, then the coprocessor sets the corresponding flag bit in the Status Register to 1. Table 10-3 lists the results returned by an operation which completes with a non-trapping exception with a floating point destination format.

Table 10-3. Non-trapped Exception Results

Exception type	Non-trapped result
Invalid operation	quiet NaN in destination
Division-by-zero	properly signed ∞ in destination
Overflow	rounded result in destination
Underflow	rounded result in destination
Inexact	rounded result in destination

Multiple Exceptions

If the current instruction causes a reserved-op exception, and at the same time the coprocessor signals a delayed trap caused by a previous exception, the delayed trap occurs. Software then retries the instruction to handle the reserved-op exception.

The only other exceptions which may both occur on the same instruction are one of the following:

- inexact and overflow exceptions
- inexact and underflow exceptions

When one of these two cases occur, the action taken is as follows:

1. If both traps are enabled when the coprocessor takes a delayed trap, the implementation may set either or both corresponding status flags to 1, or leave them unchanged. The coprocessor sets the exception field in the corresponding exception register to the value that indicates both exceptions occurred.

2. If only one trap is enabled when the coprocessor takes a delayed trap, the coprocessor sets the corresponding exception field to the value that indicates the enabled trap. The implementation may either set the flag bit that corresponds to the enabled trap to 1, or leave it unchanged. The coprocessor sets the flag bit that corresponds to the disabled trap to 1.

3. If neither trap is enabled, the coprocessor sets both corresponding status flags to 1.

If the overflow or underflow exception caused a trap on the instruction, a rounded bias-adjusted result is returned. Otherwise, a rounded result is returned.

Trap Handlers

Programming Note

The IEEE standard strongly recommends that users be allowed to specify a trap handler for any of the five standard exceptions. The mechanisms to accomplish this are programming language and operating system dependent.

Since the coprocessor continues to trap if the Status Register T-bit is 1, the trap handler must first set the bit to 0 by executing a double-word store of register 0. The trap handler may then emulate any of the instructions in the exception queue beginning with the instruction in Exception Register 1 and proceeding sequentially to the end.

The trap handler must clear all the exception registers. If the trap handler chooses not to emulate all the instructions, it must reset the T-bit to 1 before returning to the trapped process.

To emulate an instruction, the trap handler computes or specifies a substitute result to be placed in the destination register of the operation. The trap handler may determine what operation was being performed and what exceptions occurred during the operation by examining the corresponding exception register. On overflow, underflow, and inexact exceptions, the trap handler has access to the correctly rounded result by examining the destination register of the operation. On unimplemented, invalid operation, and divide-by-zero exceptions, the trap handler has access to the operand values by examining the source registers of the instruction.

Reserved-op Exception

When a non-load/store instruction has a reserved sub-opcode, an implementation signals either a reserved-op exception or an unimplemented exception.

A reserved-op exception always forces the processor to take an immediate assist exception trap. It does not set the exception registers or the T-bit, and does not change any of the flag bits in the Status Register. The reserved-op exception cannot be disabled.

Programming Note

Trapping is immediate for reserved-op exceptions. The trap handler must check for a Status Register T-bit equal to 0 to determine that the trap was caused by a reserved-op exception. When a reserved-op exception occurs, software interprets the contents of the IIR, nullifies the instruction pointed to by the front of the IIA queues, and returns control to the trapping process.

Unimplemented Exception

If an implementation chooses not to execute an instruction, the instruction signals an unimplemented exception. An unimplemented exception always causes a delayed trap on a later floating-point instruction. It does not change the Status Register Flag bits and cannot be disabled. When a non-load/store floating-point operation references a reserved sub-opcode, an implementation signals either an unimplemented exception or a reserved-op exception.

An implementation may signal an unimplemented exception on any floating-point instruction except the FLOATING-POINT TEST instruction, the FLOATING-POINT IDENTIFY instruction, a load instruction, or a store instruction.

When a trap forces the coprocessor to complete all pending instructions, implementations may put uncompleted instructions in the exception registers and set the corresponding *exception* field to the appropriate unimplemented exception code.

A conversion to a floating-point format always causes an unimplemented exception when the result overflows, the result lies too far outside the range for the exponent to be bias-adjusted, and the overflow trap is enabled. Table 10-4 shows the result values which produce an unimplemented exception; a is the bias-adjustment value for the destination format, p is the precision, and v is the source value.

Table 10-4. Overflow Results Causing Unimplemented Exception

Rounding Mode	Ranges	
nearest	$-\infty < v \leq -2^{(E_{max}+a)}(2-2^{-p})$	$2^{(E_{max}+a)}(2-2^{-p}) \leq v < +\infty$
to 0	$-\infty < v \leq -2^{(E_{max}+a+1)}$	$2^{(E_{max}+a+1)} \leq v < +\infty$
to $+\infty$	$-\infty < v \leq -2^{(E_{max}+a+1)}$	$2^{(E_{max}+a)}(2-2^{-(p-1)}) < v < +\infty$
to $-\infty$	$-\infty < v < -2^{(E_{max}+a)}(2-2^{-(p-1)})$	$2^{(E_{max}+a+1)} \leq v < +\infty$

Similarly, an unimplemented exception is always caused by a conversion to a floating-point format that underflows, lies too far outside the range for the exponent to be bias-adjusted, and the underflow trap is enabled. Table 10-5 shows the floating-point underflow results which cause an unimplemented exception; a is the bias-adjustment value for the destination format, p is the precision, and v is the source value.

Reporting these overflows and underflows as unimplemented exceptions allows a trap handler the ability to inspect the source operands. Source operands are not preserved on overflow or underflow trapping exceptions.

Table 10-5. Underflow Results Causing Unimplemented Exception

Rounding Mode	Range
nearest	$-2^{(E_{min}-a)}(1-2^{-(p+1)}) < v < 2^{(E_{min}-a)}(1-2^{-(p+1)})$
to 0	$-2^{(E_{min}-a)} < v < 2^{(E_{min}-a)}$
to $+\infty$	$-2^{(E_{min}-a)} < v \leq 2^{(E_{min}-a)}(1-2^{-p})$
to $-\infty$	$-2^{(E_{min}-a)}(1-2^{-p}) \leq v < 2^{(E_{min}-a)}$

Finally, the unimplemented exception is always signaled when the operand of a conversion to an integer format is a NaN. Low-level trap handlers may choose to silently deliver a result or convert it to an invalid exception.

Invalid Operation Exception

An instruction signals the invalid operation exception if an operand is invalid for the operation to be performed. When the exception occurs without a trap and a floating-point formated result is delivered, the coprocessor delivers a quiet NaN to the destination register. If an integer result is delivered, then the closest integer is delivered. For example, a signed conversion of an infinity will deliver the appropriately signed largest integer. Unsigned conversions will deliver either a zero or the maximum integer.

If the exception causes a trap, the coprocessor leaves the operands unchanged.

The invalid operations are:

1. Any arithmetic operation on a signaling NaN except for conversions to integer formats.

2. Magnitude subtraction of infinities like $(+\infty) + (-\infty)$ or $(+\infty) - (+\infty)$;

3. The multiplication of 0 and ∞;

4. The division operations $0/0$ and ∞/∞ ;

5. Square root if the operand is less than zero;

6. Comparison using conditions involving a "T" or conditions involving "<", ">", "true", or "false" without a "?", when the operands are unordered. See "Comparison Conditions" on page 8-16.

7. Conversion to an integer format of an ∞, or when the result overflows. Table 10-6 shows the results which produce an integer overflow. In the table, I_{max} is the most positive integer representable by the destination format, I_{min} is the most negative (zero for unsigned integers), and v is the source value.

Table 10-6. Integer Results Causing Invalid Exception

Rounding Mode	Ranges	
nearest	$v < I_{min} - 1/2$	$v \geq I_{max} + 1/2$
to 0	$v \leq I_{min} - 1$	$v \geq I_{max} + 1$
to $+\infty$	$v \leq I_{min} - 1$	$v > I_{max}$
to $-\infty$	$v < I_{min}$	$v \geq I_{max} + 1$

Integer overflow is determined after rounding as if the result has infinite width. For example, an unsigned conversion of -0.25 is zero (and inexact) in all rounding modes except $-\infty$. In rounding mode $-\infty$, the operation results in an invalid exception.

Division-by-zero Exception

From the standard:

[§]7.2 Division by zero. If the divisor is zero and the dividend is a finite nonzero number, then the division by zero exception is signaled. The result, when no trap occurs, is a correctly signed ∞ (6.3) [see "Sign Bit" on page 8-24].

When a trap occurs, the operands must be left unchanged.

Inexact Exception

From the standard:

[§]7.5 Inexact. If the rounded result of an operation is not exact or if it overflows without an overflow trap, then the inexact exception shall be signaled. The rounded or overflowed result shall be delivered to the destination or, if an inexact trap occurs, to the trap handler [the destination register in this architecture].

A conversion to a fixed-point format also signals the inexact exception when the result is not exact.

Overflow Exception

To determine overflow on an operation, the coprocessor uses the result that would have occurred had the result been computed and rounded as if the destination's exponent range were unbounded. On all operations except converts, the coprocessor signals an overflow exception when the magnitude of this result exceeds the destination format's largest finite number. The same is true of conversion operations, except that when this result is beyond the range of bias-adjusted numbers and the overflow trap is enabled, the instruction causes an unimplemented exception.

An instruction cannot cause an overflow exception when at least one operand is a NaN or infinity.

Table 10-7 summarizes the result values that cause an overflow exception. In the table, E_{max} is the maximum exponent value for the destination format, p is the precision of the format, and v is the value of the exact result before rounding.

Table 10-7. Results Causing Overflow Exception

Rounding Mode	Ranges	
nearest	$2^{E_{max}}(2-2^{-p}) \leq v < +\infty^*$	$-\infty^* < v \leq -2^{E_{max}}(2-2^{-p})$
to 0	$2^{(E_{max}+1)} \leq v < +\infty^*$	$-\infty^* < v \leq -2^{(E_{max}+1)}$
to $+\infty$	$2^{E_{max}}(2-2^{-(p-1)}) < v < +\infty^*$	$-\infty^* < v \leq -2^{(E_{max}+1)}$
to $-\infty$	$2^{(E_{max}+1)} \leq v < +\infty^*$	$-\infty^* < v < -2^{E_{max}}(2-2^{-(p-1)})$

*   When the overflow trap is enabled and the operation is a conversion to a floating-point format, this bound is limited to bias-adjusted numbers. See "Unimplemented Exception" on page 10-8.

When no trap occurs, the result of an overflow exception is one of the following:

1. Round to nearest carries all overflows to ∞ with no change in sign.

2. Round toward 0 carries all overflows to the format's largest finite number with no change in sign.

3. Round toward $-\infty$ carries positive overflows to the format's largest finite number, and carries negative overflows to $-\infty$.

4. Round toward $+\infty$ carries negative overflows to the format's most negative finite number, and carries positive overflows to $+\infty$.

When an overflow exception causes a trap, the excepting operation returns a bias-adjusted number to the destination register.

The overflow exception is not signaled for integer results. The coprocessor signals integer overflows with an unimplemented exception.

Underflow Exception

From the standard:

[§]7.4 Underflow. Two correlated events contribute to underflow. One is the creation of a tiny nonzero result between $\pm 2^{E_{min}}$ which, because it is tiny, may cause some other exception later such as overflow upon division. The other is extraordinary loss of accuracy during the approximation of such tiny numbers by denormalized numbers.

Tininess is detected on a nonzero result which lies strictly between $\pm 2^{E_{min}}$, when the result is rounded as if the exponent range were unbounded. Note that rounding for detection of tininess and rounding to determine a result are distinct. In certain cases, the coprocessor signals an underflow exception even though it returns a normalized result to the destination register.

Table 10-8 shows the range of exact results which will cause detection of tininess. In the table, E_{min} is the minimum exponent value for the destination format, p is the precision of the format, and v is the value of the exact result before rounding.

Table 10-8. Results Causing Tininess

Rounding Mode	Range
nearest	$-2^{E_{min}}(1 - 2^{-(p+1)}) < v < 2^{E_{min}}(1 - 2^{-(p+1)})$
to 0	$-2^{E_{min}} < v < 2^{E_{min}}$
to $+\infty$	$-2^{E_{min}} < v \leq 2^{E_{min}}(1 - 2^{-p})$
to $-\infty$	$-2^{E_{min}}(1 - 2^{-p}) \leq v < 2^{E_{min}}$

Loss of accuracy occurs when the coprocessor detects an inexact result, where the result returned after rounding differs from what the result would have been if the destination had infinite precision and unbounded range.

An instruction causes an underflow exception when the underflow trap is enabled and tininess occurs. An instruction also causes an underflow exception when the underflow trap is disabled and both tininess and loss of accuracy occur.

An operation which causes a non-trapping underflow exception may return a zero, denormalized number, or $\pm 2^{E_{min}}$.

Trapped underflows on all operations except conversions deliver a bias-adjusted result to the destination register. Trapped underflow on conversions to a floating-point format delivers a bias-adjusted result when the result can be represented by a bias-adjusted number. If not, an unimplemented exception is signaled instead of an underflow exception.

Conversion to an integer format cannot underflow. The result when the magnitude of the source operand is less than 1 is either 0, +1, or −1 depending on the rounding mode and the sign of the source operand.

When an instruction causes a trapping underflow exception and the trap enable bit equals 0, the leftmost two bits in the corresponding exception register's *exception* field are set (see Figure 10-2). The first parameter bit, the round away (RA) bit, is set to 1 whenever the result is rounded away from zero. The second is the inexact (I) bit which is set to 1 if the rounded bias-adjusted result is not the infinitely precise result. The trap handler uses this information to denormalize the result and prevent errors caused by rounding twice.

RA	I	0	1	0/1	0
1	1	1	1	1	1

Figure 10-2. Exception Field Underflow Parameters

Saving and Restoring State

To save state, software first performs a double-word store of register 0, then double-word stores of registers 1, 2, and 3, and a sufficient number of double-word stores to save registers needed at a later time. Thirty-two double-word coprocessor stores are sufficient to save the entire state of the floating-point coprocessor.

A double-word store of register 0 cancels all pending traps, forces the completion of all previous instructions, suppresses any ensuing trap, completes the store, and sets the Status Register T-bit to 0. When the store cancels a trap, the value written to memory has the bit corresponding to the Status Register T-bit set to 1; otherwise, this bit is set to 0. This special treatment of a double-word store lets the save routine be nested, does not require the assistance of a trap handler, and need not have the IIA queues enabled.

To restore state, software performs double-word loads of all required registers, followed by a double-word load of Floating-point Register 0. Thirty-two double-word loads are sufficient to restore the entire state of the coprocessor. A double-word load of Floating-point Register 0 which sets the Status Register T-bit to 1 re-arms a trap. The next floating-point instruction will cause a trap (apart from a double-word store of Floating-point Register 0).

The following sequences save and restore the entire state of the coprocessor.

; enter with SaveAreaPtr pointing at the first double-word of the save area			
	Instruction		Comment
SAVEFPU			
	FSTD,MA	FPR0,8(SaveAreaPtr)	;quiescent, cancel trap
	FSTD,MA	FPR1,8(SaveAreaPtr)	;save exception register
	FSTD,MA	FPR2,8(SaveAreaPtr)	;save exception register
	FSTD,MA	FPR3,8(SaveAreaPtr)	;save exception register
	FSTD,MA	FPR4,8(SaveAreaPtr)	;save data register
	FSTD,MA	FPR5,8(SaveAreaPtr)	;save data register
	•		
	•		
	•		
	FSTD,MA	FPR30,8(SaveAreaPtr)	;save data register
	FSTD	FPR31,0(SaveAreaPtr)	;save last data register

; enter with SaveAreaPtr pointing at the last double-word of the save area.			
RSTFPU	Instruction		Comment
	FLDD	0(SaveAreaPtr),FPR31	;restore data register
	FLDD,MB	-8(SaveAreaPtr),FPR30	;restore data register
	•		
	•		
	•		
	FLDD,MB	-8(SaveAreaPtr),FPR4	;restore data register
	FLDD,MB	-8(SaveAreaPtr),FPR3	;restore exception register
	FLDD,MB	-8(SaveAreaPtr),FPR2	;restore exception register
	FLDD,MB	-8(SaveAreaPtr),FPR1	;restore exception register
	FLDD,MB	-8(SaveAreaPtr),FPR0	;restore exception register ;potentially re-arm trap

The only required ordering in these sequences is that Floating-point Register 0 must be saved first and restored last.

11   Performance Monitor Coprocessor

The performance monitor coprocessor is an optional, implementation-dependent coprocessor which provides a minimal common software interface to implementation-dependent performance monitor hardware.

The performance monitor coprocessor responds to coprocessor instructions with a *uid* equal to 2.

Performance Monitor Instructions

The performance monitor instruction set consists of two instructions, PERFORMANCE MONITOR ENABLE (PMENB) and PERFORMANCE MONITOR DISABLE (PMDIS), which provide a common software interface to enable and disable the implementation-dependent performance monitor features.

The following figure shows the format of these operations and Table 11-1 shows the operations, their mnemonics, and sub-opcodes:

0C	rv	sub	2	n	rv
6	12	5	3	1	5

Table 11-1. Performance Monitor Operations

Opcode	Sub-op	Mnemonic	Operation
0C	1	PMDIS	Disable performance monitor
0C	3	PMENB	Enable performance monitor
0C	0,2,4..F		undefined
0C	10..1F		reserved

The performance monitor coprocessor instructions are described at the end of this chapter.

When a performance monitor coprocessor instruction is executed and CCR{2} is 0, the coprocessor instruction causes an assist emulation trap. It is an undefined operation to set CCR{2} to 1 if the performance monitor coprocessor is nonexistent.

Performance Monitor Interruptions

Interruption vector number 29 in interruption group 2 is defined as the performance monitor coprocessor interrupt for implementation-dependent use by the performance monitor coprocessor. The interrupt is unmasked when the PSW F-bit is 1, and is masked when the PSW F-bit is 0. See Chapter 5, "Interruptions" for additional details.

Reserved Sub-Opcode Exception

When a performance monitor coprocessor instruction has a reserved sub-opcode, the implementation must signal a reserved-op exception by taking an assist exception trap.

Monitor Units

The monitor units are hardware units used to collect the necessary information during performance monitoring. The number of the monitor units and their hardware types are implementation dependent.

If a monitor unit provides counters, the most significant bit of the counter is required to be an overflow indicator. The bit must be set when the counter overflows and must remain set until explicitly reset by software. When the overflow indicator is set the remaining bits of the counter are undefined.

NOTE

If counters are used to implement the measurement units, it is recommended that the counters be at least 32 bits wide.

Format: PMDIS,n

(55)

0C	rv	1	2	n	rv
6	12	5	3	1	5

Purpose: To disable the implementation-dependent performance monitor coprocessor, and conditionally nullify the following instruction.

Description: Disable all measurement units, after the current instruction. The following instruction is nullified if measurement is enabled and the ,N completer is specified. The completer is encoded in the *n* field of the instruction.

Operation: if (n && measurement_enabled)
                         PSW[N] ← 1;
                 measurement_enabled ← 0;

Exceptions: Assist emulation trap

Format: PMENB

(55)	0C	rv	3	2	0	rv
	6	12	5	3	1	5

Purpose: To enable the implementation-dependent performance monitor coprocessor.

Description: Enable the measurement units, starting with the next instruction.

Operation: measurement_enabled ← 1;

Exceptions: Assist emulation trap

A   Glossary

Absolute Address

See Physical Address.

Access Rights

A function of virtual address translation that controls access to each page through privilege levels for read, write, execute, and gateway. The TLB contains, within each entry, information used to determine who may have access to that page. This information is divided into two groups: (1) page access (access ID) which is used to determine if a process or user may access a page; and (2) the access rights field that is combined with the user's privilege level and the WD bit of the PID register to determine if the type of access the user is requesting will be allowed.

Address

PA-RISC is a byte-addressable system which uses both virtual and absolute addresses. A virtual address can be split into two parts: the high-order bits which are the space identifier and the low-order bits that give the offset within the space. Absolute addresses do not have space identifiers; only a 64-bit offset. Doublewords, words, and halfwords are always located at addresses which are aligned to their size (in bytes). Quadwords are aligned on doubleword boundaries.

Address Translation

For a virtual memory system, the process whereby the virtual (logical) address of data or instructions is translated to its absolute address in physical memory.

Aliasing

The condition when the same physical memory location is accessed by different virtual addresses or by both an absolute and a virtual address.

Alter

The action of setting the E-bit of a TLB entry to 0 and modifying some portion of the physical page number field. Altered entries in the TLB are still visible to software through the insert TLB protection instructions.

Architecture

Refers to the time-independent functional appearance of a computer system. An implementation of an architecture is an ensemble of hardware, firmware, and software that provides all the functions as defined in the architecture.

Arithmetic and Logical Unit (ALU)

The part of a PA-RISC processor that performs arithmetic and logic operations on its inputs, producing output and status information.

Assist Processor

A processor which may be added to the basic PA-RISC system to enhance performance or functionality for algorithms which experience substantial gains from the use of specialized hardware. Assist processors are differentiated by the level at which they interface with the memory hierarchy. (See special function units and coprocessors).

B-bit (Taken Branch in Previous Cycle)

A bit in the PSW that is 1 if the previous instruction was a taken branch.

Base Register

A register that holds the numeric value that is used as a base value in the calculation of addresses. Displacements or index values are added to this base value.

Base-Relative Branch

When a general register is used as the base offset to obtain the target address, the branch is called base relative.

Biased Exponent

The exponent field for a floating-point number. It consists of the true exponent plus the bias.

Binary Floating-point Number

A number format consisting of the three components: sign, exponent, and significand.

Block TLB

A block TLB provides fixed address translations which map address ranges larger than a page.

Byte

A group of eight contiguous bits which is the smallest addressable unit on a PA-RISC system.

C-bit (Code Address Translation Enable)

A bit in the PSW that specifies whether virtual address translation of the instruction address is to be performed.

Cache

A high-speed buffer unit between main memory and the CPU. The cache is continually updated to contain recently accessed contents of main memory to reduce access time. When a program makes a memory request, the CPU first checks to see if the data is in the cache so that it can be retrieved without accessing memory. There may be one cache for both instructions and data or separate caches for each.

Cache Coherence

The property of multiple caches whereby they provide identical shared memory images. Processors in a multiprocessor system are said to be cache coherent if they provide the image of single cache.

Cache Control Hint

A 2-bit field in some memory reference instructions which provides a hint to the processor on how to resolve cache coherence. The processor may disregard the hint without compromising system integrity, but performance may be enhanced by following the hint.

Cache Miss

A cache miss occurs when the cache does not contain a copy of the cache line being requested by the address. The cache is updated with data and re-accessed.

Carry/Borrow Bits

A 16-bit field in the PSW that indicates if a carry or borrow occurred from the corresponding nibble (4 bits) as a result of the previous arithmetic operation.

Central Processing Unit (CPU)

The part of a PA-RISC processor that fetches and executes instructions.

Check

The interruption condition when the processor detects an internal or external malfunction. Checks may be either synchronous or asynchronous with respect to the instruction stream.

Coherence Check

An action taken by hardware to insure coherence.

Combined TLB

Some systems have a TLB which provides address translation for both instruction and data references.

Compatibility

The ability for software developed for one machine type to execute on another machine type. PA-RISC provides compatible execution of application programs written for earlier-generation Hewlett-Packard computer systems.

Completer

A machine instruction field used to specify instruction options. Typical options include address modification, address indexing, precision of operands, and conditions to be tested to determine whether to nullify the following instruction.

Condition

The state of a value or a relationship between values used in determining whether an instruction is to branch, nullify, or trap.

Control Register (CR)

A register which contains system state information used for memory access protection, interruption control, and processor state control. A PA-RISC processor contains 25 control registers (7 more are reserved).

Coprocessor

A type of assist processor which interfaces to the memory hierarchy at the level of the cache. Coprocessors are special purpose units that work with the main processor to speed up specialized operations such as floating-point arithmetic and graphics processing. Coprocessors generally have their own internal state and hardware evaluation mechanism.

Coprocessor Configuration Register (CCR)

The CCR (in CR 10) is an 8-bit register which records the presence and usability of coprocessors. Each bit position (0-7) corresponds to the coprocessor with the same unit number. Setting a bit in the CCR to 1 enables the use of the corresponding coprocessor, if present and operational. If a CCR bit is 0, the corresponding coprocessor, if present, is logically decoupled and an attempt to reference the coprocessor causes an assist emulation trap.

Current Instruction

The instruction whose address is in the front element of the instruction address queues (IASQ and IAOQ).

D-bit (Data Address Translation Enable)

A bit in the PSW that specifies whether virtual address translation of data addresses is to be performed.

Data Cache (D-cache)

A high-speed storage device which contains data items that have been recently accessed from main memory. The D-cache can be accessed independently of the instruction cache (I-cache) and no synchronization is performed.

Data TLB (DTLB)

A separate TLB which does address translation only for data memory references.

Denormalized Numbers

Any non-zero floating-point number with the exponent field all zeros. Denormalized numbers are distinguished from normal numbers in that the value of the "hidden" bit to the left of the implied binary point is zero.

Dirty

A block of memory (commonly a cache line or a page) which has been written to is referred to as dirty.

Disabling an Interrupt

A disabled interrupt is prevented from occurring. The interruption does not wait until re-enabled and it is not kept pending.

Displacement

The amount that is added to a base register to form an offset in the virtual address computation.

Dynamic Displacement

If the displacement value is computed during the course of program execution and is obtained from a general register, it is called dynamic.

E-bit (Little Endian Memory Access Enable)

A bit in the PSW which determines whether memory references assume big endian or little endian byte ordering.

Effective Address

The address of the operand for the current instruction, derived by applying specific address building rules.

Equivalently Aliased

A condition when two virtual addresses map to the same physical address, and where the two addresses are identical in the following bits: Offset bits 12 through 31. If the use of space bits in generating the cache index is enabled, the addresses must also be identical in these bits: Space Identifier bits 36 through 39, 44 through 47, and 52 through 63.

Equivalently Mapped

A condition when a virtual address is equal to its absolute address.

Exponent

The part of a binary floating-point number that normally signifies the integer power to which two is raised in determining the value of the represented number.

External Branch Instructions

The target of these instructions may lie in a different address space than that of the instruction. The external branch instructions are: BE and BLE.

External Interrupt Enable Mask (EIEM)

The EIEM (CR 15) is a 64-bit register containing one bit for each external interrupt class. When set to 0, bits in the EIEM mask interruptions pending for the external interrupts corresponding to those bit positions.

External Interrupt Request Register (EIR)

The EIR register (CR 23) is a 64-bit register containing one bit for each external interrupt. When set to 1, a bit designates that an interruption is pending for the corresponding external interrupt.

F-bit (Performance Monitor Interruption Unmask)

A bit in the PSW used to unmask the performance monitor interruption.

Fault

The interruption condition when the current instruction requests a legitimate action which cannot be carried out due to a system problem such as the absence of a main memory page. After the system problem is cleared, the faulting instruction will execute normally. Faults are synchronous with respect to the instruction stream.

Floating-point Register (FPR)

A storage unit which constitutes the basic resource of the floating-point coprocessor. Floating-point registers are at the highest level of memory hierarchy and are used to load data from and store data to memory and hold operands and results of the floating-point coprocessor. The floating-point coprocessor contains 32 double-precision (64-bit) floating-point registers which may also be accessed as 64 single-precision (32-bit), or 16 quad-precision (128-bit) registers.

Following Instruction

The instruction whose address is in the back element of the instruction address queues (IASQ and IAOQ). This instruction will be executed after the current instruction. This instruction is not necessarily the next instruction in the linear code space.

Fraction

The portion of the significand explicitly contained in a binary floating-point number. The rest of the significand is the "hidden" bit to the left of the implied binary point. The "hidden" bit normally has the value one.

G-bit (Debug Trap Enable)

A bit in the PSW used to enable data and instruction debug traps.

General Register (GR)

A storage unit which constitutes the basic resource of the CPU. General registers are at the highest level of memory hierarchy and are used to load data from and store data to memory and hold operands and results from the ALU. A PA-RISC processor contains 32 general registers.

H-bit (Higher Privilege Transfer Trap Enable)

A bit in the PSW that enables an interruption whenever the following instruction will execute at a higher privilege level.

High-Priority Machine Check (HPMC)

An interruption which occurs when a hardware error has been detected which requires immediate attention.

I-bit (External, Power Failure, and LPMC Interruption Unmask)

A bit in the PSW used to unmask external interrupts, power failure interrupts, and low-priority machine check interruptions.

IAOQ (Instruction Address Offset Queue)

A two-element queue of 64-bit registers that is used to hold the Instruction Address offset (IA offset). The first element is IAOQ_Front and holds the IA offset of the current instruction. The other element is IAOQ_Back and holds the IA offset of the following instruction.

IA-Relative Branches

When a displacement is added to the current Instruction Address offset (IA offset) to obtain the target address, the branch is called IA relative.

IASQ (Instruction Address Space Queue)

A two-element queue of up to 64-bit registers that is used to hold the Instruction Address space (IA space). The first element is IASQ_Front and holds the IA space of the current instruction. The other element is IASQ_Back and holds the IA space of the following instruction.

IIAOQ (Interruption Instruction Address Offset Queue)

A two-element queue of 64-bit registers that is used to save the Instruction Address offset for use in processing interruptions.

IIASQ (Interruption Instruction Address Space Queue)

A two-element queue of up to 64-bit registers that is used to save the Instruction Address space for use in processing interruptions.

Infinity

The binary floating-point numbers that have all ones in the exponent and all zeros in the fraction. The values of these two numbers are distinguished only by the sign. Thus, they are $+\infty$ and $-\infty$.

Instruction Cache (I-cache)

A high-speed storage device that contains instructions that have been recently accessed from main memory. The I-cache can be accessed independently of the data cache (D-cache) and no synchronization is performed.

Instruction TLB (ITLB)

A separate TLB which does address translation only for instructions.

Interrupt

The interruption condition when an external entity (such as an I/O device or the power supply) requires attention. Interrupts are asynchronous with respect to the instruction stream.

Interruption

An event that changes the instruction stream to handle exceptional conditions including traps, checks, faults, and interrupts.

Interruption Instruction Register (IIR)

The IIR (CR 19) is used by the hardware to store the instruction that caused the interruption or the instruction that was in progress at the time the interruption occurred.

Interruption Offset Register (IOR)

The IOR (CR 21) receives a copy of the offset portion of a virtual address at the time of an interruption whenever the PSW Q-bit is 1. The value copied is dependent upon the type of interruption.

Interruption Parameter Registers (IPRs)

The Interruption Instruction Register or IIR (CR 19), Interruption Space Register or ISR (CR 20), and Interruption Offset Register or IOR (CR 21) are collectively termed the Interruption Parameter Registers or IPRs. They are used to pass the interrupted instruction and a virtual address to an interruption handler. These registers are set (or frozen) at the time of an interruption when the PSW Q-bit is 1. The IPRs can be read reliably only when the PSW Q-bit is 0. The values saved in these registers are dependent upon the type of interruption.

Interruption Processor Status Word (IPSW)

The IPSW (CR 22) receives the value of the PSW when an interruption occurs. The layout of IPSW is identical to that of PSW and it always reflects the machine state at the point of interruption.

Interruption Space Register (ISR)

The ISR (CR 20) receives a copy of the space portion of a virtual address at the time of an interruption whenever the PSW Q-bit is 1. The value copied is dependent upon the type of interruption.

Interruption Vector Address (IVA)

The IVA (CR 14) contains the absolute address of an array of service procedures assigned to interruptions.

Interspace Branches

When the target of the branch lies in a different address space as that of the branch instruction, it is referred to as an interspace branch.

Intraspace Branches

When the target of the branch lies in the same address space as that of the branch instruction, it is referred to as an intraspace branch.

Interval Timer

Two internal registers which are both accessed through Control Register 16. The Interval Timer is a free-running counter that signals an interruption when equal to a comparison value.

Invalidate

The action of setting the E-bit of a TLB entry to a 0, leaving the virtual page number and physical page number fields unchanged. Invalid entries in the TLB are still visible to software through insert TLB protection instructions.

L-bit (Lower Privilege Transfer Trap Enable)

A bit in the PSW that enables an interruption whenever the following instruction will execute at a lower privilege level.

Local Branch Instructions

The target of these instructions always lie in the same address space as that of the instruction.

Low-Priority Machine Check (LPMC)

An interruption which occurs when a recoverable hardware error has been detected.

M-bit (High-Priority Machine Check Mask)

A bit in the PSW that disables the recognition of an HPMC.

Many-Reader/One-Writer Non-Equivalent Aliasing

A condition where multiple virtual addresses are non-equivalent aliases. Generally, before enabling a write-capable translation, any non-equivalent read-only aliases must be disabled, and the affected address range flushed from the cache. Similarly, before re-enabling the read translation(s), the write-capable translation must be disabled, and the affected address range flushed from the cache.

Masking an Interrupt

A masked interrupt can still be recognized as a pending event but occurrence of the interrupt is delayed until it is unmasked.

Memory

A device capable of storing information in binary form. The term "memory" typically refers to main memory.

Memory Address Space

The memory address space consists of absolute addresses in the range 0x0000000000000000 through 0xEFFFFFFFFFFFFFFF.

Memory-mapped I/O

Control of input and output through load and store instructions to particular virtual or physical addresses.

Move-in

The action of bringing data or instructions into a cache.

Multiprocessor

A computer with multiple processors.

NaN

The binary floating-point numbers that have all ones in the exponent and a non-zero fraction. NaN is the term used for a binary floating-point number that has no value (i.e., "Not a Number"). The two types of NaNs, quiet and signaling, are distinguished by the value of the most significant bit in the fraction field. A zero indicates a quiet NaN and a one indicates a signaling NaN.

Non-Equivalently Aliased

A condition when two virtual addresses map to the same physical address, but do not meet the requirements for equivalently aliased addresses. (See "Equivalently Aliased" on page A-5.)

Nullify

To nullify an instruction is equivalent to skipping over that instruction. A nullified instruction has no effect on the machine state (except that the IA queues advance and the PSW B, N, X, Y, and Z bits are set to 0). The current instruction is nullified when the PSW N-bit is 1.

P-bit (Protection Identifier Validation Enable)

A bit in the PSW that is used as a protection identifier validation enable bit. If the P-bit is 1, the Protection Identifiers in control registers 8, 9, 12, and 13 are used to enforce protection.

Page

Virtual memory is partitioned into pages which can be resident in matching size blocks (called page frames) in memory. The smallest page size is 4096 bytes (4 Kbytes).

Page Group

Eight contiguous pages, with the first of these pages beginning on a 32-Kbyte boundary.

Physical Address

The address that is the result of the virtual address translation or any address that is not translated. A physical address is the concatenation of the physical page number and the offset. Physical addresses are also referred to as absolute addresses.

Privilege Level

The PA-RISC access control mechanisms are based on 4 privilege levels numbered from 0 to 3, with 0 being the most privileged. The current privilege level is maintained in the front element of the Instruction Address Offset Queue (IAOQ_Front).

Processor Status Word (PSW)

A 64-bit register which contains information about the processor state.

Q-bit (Interruption State Collection Enable)

A bit in the PSW that, when set to 1, enables collection of the machine state at the instant of interruption (IIASQ, IIAOQ, IIR, ISR, and IOR).

R-bit (Recovery Counter Enable)

A bit in the PSW that enables recovery counter trapping and decrementing of the Recovery Counter.

Read-Only Non-Equivalent Aliasing

A condition where multiple virtual addresses map to the same physical address, and where each virtual address has a read-only translation.

Recovery Counter

The Recovery Counter (CR 0) counts down by 1 during execution of each non-nullified instruction for which the PSW R-bit is 1.

Remove

The action of taking a TLB entry out of the TLB. Insertion of translations into the TLB, for example, causes other entries to be removed.

S-bit (Secure Interval Timer)

A bit in the PSW that, when set to 1, allows the Interval Timer to be read only by code executing at the most privileged level.

SFU Configuration Register (SCR)

The SCR (in CR 10) is an 8-bit register which records the presence and usability of SFUs (Special Function Units), Each bit position (0-7) corresponds to the SFU with the same unit number. Setting a bit in the SCR to 1 enables the use of the corresponding SFU if present and operational. If a SCR bit is 0, the corresponding SFU if present, is logically decoupled and an attempt to reference the SFU causes an assist emulation trap.

Shadow Register (SHR)

A register into which the contents of a general register are copied upon interruptions. A PA-RISC processor contains 7 shadow registers which receive the contents of GRs 1, 8, 9, 16, 17, 24, and 25. The contents of the shadow registers are copied back to these GRs by the RETURN FROM INTERRUPTION AND RESTORE instruction.

Shift Amount Register (SAR)

The SAR (CR 11) is used by the variable shift, extract, deposit, and branch on bit instructions. It specifies the number of bits or the ending bit position of a quantity that is to be shifted, extracted or deposited.

Sign

A one bit field in which one indicates a negative value and zero indicates a positive value.

Significand

The component of a binary floating-point number that consists of the implicit (or "hidden") leading bit to the left of the implied binary point together with the fraction field to its right.

Space Identifier (Space ID)

An up to 64-bit value which combines with the offset to form the upper portion of a virtual address.

Space Register (SR)

A register used to specify the space identifier for virtual addressing. A PA-RISC processor contains 8 space registers.

Special Function Unit (SFU)

A type of assist processor which interfaces to the memory hierarchy at the general register level. It acts as an alternate ALU for the main processor and may have its own internal state.

Static Displacement

If the displacement is a fixed value that is known at compile time, it is called static.

Strong Ordering

The property that accesses to storage, such as loads and stores, appear to software to be done in program order. In multiprocessing systems, strong ordering means that accesses by a given processor appear to that processor as well as to all other processors in the system, to be done in program order.

System Mask

The W, E, O, G, F, R, Q, P, D, and I bits of the PSW are known as the system mask. Each of these bits, with the exception of the Q-bit, may be set to 1, set to 0, written, and read by the system control instructions that manipulate the system mask.

T-bit (Taken Branch Trap Enable)

A bit in the PSW that enables the taken branch trap.

Taken Branch

Conditional branches are considered to be "taken" if the specified condition is met. Unconditional branches are always "taken".

TLB Entry

A virtual to physical address translation, either valid or invalid, which is present in the TLB. Entries are visible to software through either references (such as loads, stores, and semaphores) or insert TLB protection instructions (IITLBP and IDTLBP).

TLB Miss Handling

The action taken, either by hardware or software, on a TLB miss. This involves inserting the missing translation into the proper TLB.

TLB Miss

The condition when there is no entry in the TLB matching the current virtual page number. In this case, the TLB is updated either by software or by hardware.

TLB Slot

A hardware resource in the TLB which holds a TLB entry.

Translation Lookaside Buffer (TLB)

A hardware unit which serves as a cache for virtual-to-absolute memory address mapping. When a memory reference is made to a given virtual address, the virtual page number is passed to the TLB and the TLB is searched for an entry matching the virtual page number. If the entry exists, the absolute page number (contained in the entry) is concatenated with the page offset from the original virtual address to form an absolute address.

Trap

The interruption condition when either (1) the function requested by the current instruction cannot or should not be carried out, or (2) system intervention is requested by the user before or after the instruction is executed.

Virtual Addressing

A capability that eliminates the need to assign programs to fixed locations in main memory. Addresses supplied by a program are treated as logical addresses which are translated to absolute addresses when physical memory is addressed.

Write Disable (WD) Bit

The low-order bit of each of the four protection identifiers (PIDs) which, when 1, disables the use of that PID for validating write accesses.

X-bit (Data Memory Break Disable)

A bit in the PSW that disables the data memory break trap if equal to 1. A data memory break trap happens if a write is attempted to a page whose TLB B-bit is 1.

Y-bit (Data Debug Trap Disable)

A bit in the PSW that disables the data debug trap if equal to 1. A data debug trap happens if a memory reference is performed to an address which matches an enabled data breakpoint.

Z-bit (Instruction Debug Trap Disable)

A bit in the PSW that disables the instruction debug trap if equal to 1. An instruction debug trap happens if an attempt is made to execute an instruction at an address which matches an enabled instruction breakpoint.

The PA-RISC instruction formats are shown below. The most general form of each format is given. Individual instructions in each class may have reserved or zero fields in place of one or more of the fields shown. Refer to Table B-1 at the end of this appendix for a description of the field names used in the following instruction formats.

1. Loads and Stores, Load and Store Word Modify, Load Offset

op	b	t/r	s	im14
6	5	5	2	14

2. Load and Store Word Modify (Complement)

op	b	t/r	s	im11a	2	i
6	5	5	2	11	2	1

3. Load and Store Doubleword

op	b	t/r	s	im10a	m	a	e	i
6	5	5	2	10	1	1	1	1

4. Indexed Loads

op	b	x	s	u	0	cc	ext4	m	t
6	5	5	2	1	1	2	4	1	5

5. Short Displacement Loads

op	b	im5	s	a	1	cc	ext4	m	t
6	5	5	2	1	1	2	4	1	5

6. Short Displacement Stores

op	b	r	s	a	1	cc	ext4	m	im5
6	5	5	2	1	1	2	4	1	5

7. Long Immediates

op	t/r	im21
6	5	21

8. Arithmetic/Logical

op	r2	r1	c	f	ea	eb	ec	ed	d	t
6	5	5	3	1	2	1	1	2	1	5

9. Arithmetic Immediate

op	r	t	c	f	e1	im11
6	5	5	3	1	1	11

10. Rearrangement/Halfword Shift

op	r2	r1	e	ea	0	eb	sa	0	t
6	5	5	1	2	1	2	4	1	5

11. Variable Shift Pair

op	r2	r1	c	ext2	0	d	0	t
6	5	5	3	2	1	1	4	5

12. Variable Extract

op	r	t	c	ext2	se	d	cl	0	clen
6	5	5	3	2	1	1	1	3	5

13. Variable Deposit

op	t	r/im5	c	ext2	nz	d	cl	0	clen
6	5	5	3	2	1	1	1	3	5

14. Fixed Shift Pair

op	r2	r1	c	0	cp	d	cpos	t
6	5	5	3	1	1	1	5	5

15. Fixed Extract

op	r	t	c	cl	p	se	pos	clen
6	5	5	3	1	1	1	5	5

16. Fixed Deposit

op	t	r/im5	c	cl	cp	nz	cpos	clen
6	5	5	3	1	1	1	5	5

17. Conditional Branch

op	r/r2	r1/im5	c	w1	n	w
6	5	5	3	11	1	1

18. Branch on Bit

op	p	r	c	cp	w1	n	w
6	5	5	3	1	11	1	1

19. Branch External

op	b	w1	s	w2	n	w
6	5	5	3	11	1	1

20. Branch, Branch and Link

op	t/w3	w1	ext3	w2	n	w
6	5	5	3	11	1	1

21. Branch and Link Register, Branch Vectored

op	t/b	x	ext3	0	n	0
6	5	5	3	11	1	1

22. Branch Vectored External

op	b	0	ext3	1	0	n	p
6	5	5	3	1	10	1	1

23. Branch Target Stack

op	0	r	ext3	0	i	e	0	1
6	5	5	3	1	9	1	1	1

24. Data Memory Management, Probe

op	b	r/x	s	ext8	m	t
6	5	5	2	8	1	5

25. Short Displacement, Flush Data Cache

op	b	im5	s	ext8	m	t
6	5	5	2	8	1	5

26. Instruction Memory Management

op	b	r/x/im5	s	ext7	m	0
6	5	5	3	7	1	5

27. Break

op	im13	ext8	im5
6	13	8	5

28. Diagnose

op	im26
6	26

29. Move to/from Space Register

op	rv	r	s	ext8	t
6	5	5	3	8	5

30. Load Space ID

op	b	rv	s	0	ext8	t
6	5	5	2	1	8	5

31. Move to Control Register

op	t	r	rv	ext8	0
6	5	5	3	8	5

32. Move from Control Register

op	r	0	rv	e	rv	ext8	t
6	5	5	1	1	1	8	5

33. System Control

op	b/im5	r/im5	0	ext8	t
6	5	5	3	8	5

34. Special Operation Zero

op	sop1	0	sfu	n	sop2
6	15	2	3	1	5

35. Special Operation One

op	sop	1	sfu	n	t
6	15	2	3	1	5

36. Special Operation Two

op	r	sop1	2	sfu	n	sop2
6	5	10	2	3	1	5

37. Special Operation Three

op	r2	r1	sop1	3	sfu	n	sop2
6	5	5	5	2	3	1	5

38. Coprocessor Operation

op	sop1	uid	n	sop2
6	17	3	1	5

39. Coprocessor Indexed Loads

op	b	x	s	u	0	cc	0	uid	m	t
6	5	5	2	1	1	2	1	3	1	5

40. Coprocessor Indexed Stores

op	b	x	s	u	0	cc	1	uid	m	r
6	5	5	2	1	1	2	1	3	1	5

41. Coprocessor Short Displacement Loads

op	b	im5	s	a	1	cc	0	uid	m	t
6	5	5	2	1	1	2	1	3	1	5

42. Coprocessor Short Displacement Stores

op	b	im5	s	a	1	cc	1	uid	m	r
6	5	5	2	1	1	2	1	3	1	5

43. Floating-point Load and Store Word

op	b	t/r	s	im11a	e	h	i
6	5	5	2	11	1	1	1

44. Floating-point Load and Store Word Modify

op	b	t/r	s	im11a	a	h	i
6	5	5	2	11	1	1	1

45. Floating-point Operation Zero, Major Opcode 0C

op	r	0	sop	fmt	0	0	0	t
6	5	5	3	2	2	3	1	5

46. Floating-point Operation One, Major Opcode 0C

op	r	0	sop	df	sf	1	0	0	t
6	5	3	3	2	2	2	3	1	5

47. Floating-point Operation Two, Major Opcode 0C

op	r1	r2	sop	fmt	2	0	n	c
6	5	5	3	2	2	3	1	5

48. Floating-point Operation Three, Major Opcode 0C

op	r1	r2	sop	fmt	3	0	0	t
6	5	5	3	2	2	3	1	5

49. Floating-point Operation Zero, Major Opcode 0E

op	r	0	sop	0	f	0	0	r	t	0	t
6	5	5	3	1	1	2	1	1	1	1	5

50. Floating-point Operation One, Major Opcode 0E

op	r	0	sop	0	df	0	sf	1	0	r	t	0	t
6	5	3	3	1	1	1	1	2	1	1	1	1	5

51. Floating-point Operation Two, Major Opcode 0E

op	r1	r2	sop	r2	f	2	0	r1	0	0	c
6	5	5	3	1	1	2	1	1	1	1	5

52. Floating-point Operation Three, Major Opcode 0E

op	r1	r2	sop	r2	f	3	x	r1	t	0	t
6	5	5	3	1	1	2	1	1	1	1	5

53. Floating-point Multiple-operation

op	rm1	rm2	ta	ra	f	tm
6	5	5	5	5	1	5

54. Floating-point Fused-operation

op	rm1	rm2	ra	r2	f	ra	r1	t	e	t
6	5	5	3	1	1	3	1	1	1	5

55. Performance Monitor

op	rv	sub	2	n	rv
6	12	5	3	1	5

The field names used in the previous instruction format layouts are described in Table B-1. Some of the field names may be followed by one or two digits. Those digits indicate the length of the field. An example of a field name may be *im5* which indicates the field is a 5-bit immediate value. But names, such as *r1*, which refers to the first source register field, are the actual field names.

Table B-1. Field Names for Instruction Formats

Field	Description
a	modify before/after bit
b	base register
c	condition specifier
cc	cache control hint
cl, clen	complement of extract/deposit length
cp, cpos	complement of deposit/shift bit position
d	word/doubleword bit
df	floating-point destination format
e, ea, eb, ec, ed, or ext	operation code extension
f	condition negation bit
f or fmt	floating-point data format
h	floating-point register half
im	immediate value
m	modify bit
n	nullify bit
nz	deposit zero/not zero bit
op	operation code
p	extract/deposit/shift bit position
pos	extract bit position
r, r1, or r2	source register
ra, rm1, or rm2	floating-point source register
rv	reserved instruction field
s	2 or 3 bit space register
sa	shift amount
se	extract sign-extend bit
sf	floating-point source format
sfu	special function unit number
sop, sop1, or sop2	special function unit or coprocessor operation
t, ta, or tm	target register
u	shift index bit
uid	coprocessor unit identifier
w, w1, w2, or w3	word offset/word offset part
x	index register

C   Operation Codes

This appendix provides a complete description of all of the PA-RISC 2.0 instruction operation codes.

Major Opcode Assignments

The major opcode assignments are listed in Table C-1. Instructions are shown in uppercase. Instruction classes are capitalized. Extensions of the major opcodes can be found in the tables indicated, where applicable. In the following discussions of opcode extensions the major opcode class names are shown in parentheses.

Table C-1. Major Opcode Assignments

bits 2:5	bits 0:1			
	0	1	2	3
0	System_op (Table C-2)	LDB	CMPB (true)	BB (sar)
1	Mem_Mgmt (Tables C-3 and C-4)	LDH	CMPIB (true)	BB
2	Arith/Log (Table C-5)	LDW	CMPB (false)	MOVB
3	Index_Mem (Table C-6)	LDW (mod)	CMPIB (false)	MOVIB
4	SPOPn (Table C-15)	Load_dw (Table C-7)	CMPICLR	Sh_Ex_Dep (Tables C-10 and C-11)
5	DIAG	—	Subi (Table C-9)	Sh_Ex_Dep (Tables C-10 and C-11)
6	FMPYADD	FLDW (mod)	FMPYSUB	Sh_Ex_Dep (Table C-10)
7	—	Load_w (Table C-8)	CMPB (dw true)	—
8	LDIL	STB	ADDB (true)	BE
9	Copr_w (Table C-14)	STH	ADDIB (true)	BE,L
A	ADDIL	STW	ADDB (false)	Branch (Table C-13)
B	Copr_dw (Table C-14)	STW (mod)	ADDIB (false)	CMPIB (dw)
C	COPR	Store_dw (Table C-7)	Addi (Table C-9)	Sh_Ex_Dep (Table C-10)
D	LDO	—	Addi (Table C-9)	Sh_Ex_Dep (Table C-10)
E	Float (Tables C-20 through C-24)	FSTW (mod)	Fp_fused (Table C-25)	Multimedia (Table C-12)
F	Product Specific	Store_w (Table C-8)	CMPB (dw false)	—

Opcode Extension Assignments

Many instructions require both a major opcode and an opcode extension to be uniquely identified. The extension can be one to nine bits, depending on the major opcode.

System Control Instructions (System_op)

Figure C-1 shows the format of the system control instructions (major opcode 00) and Table C-2 lists the opcode extensions. Bits 19:21 encode the source of the operation and bits 24:26 encode the destination.

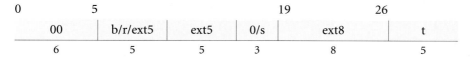

Figure C-1. Format for System Control Instructions

Table C-2. System Control Instructions

Instruction	Opcode	Extension						
	hex		binary				hex	
	bits 0:5	bit 17	bits 19:21	bits 22:23	bits 24:26		bits 19:26	bits 11:15
BREAK	00	–	000	00	000		00	im5
SYNC	00	0	001	00	000		20	0
SYNCDMA	00	0	001	00	000		20	10
RFI	00	rv	011	00	000		60	rv
RFI,R	00	rv	011	00	101		65	rv
SSM	00	0	011	01	011		6B	i
RSM	00	0	011	10	011		73	i
MTSM	00	0	110	00	011		C3	r
LDSID	00	–	100	00	101		85	rv
MTSP	00	–	110	00	001		C1	r
MFSP	00	–	001	00	101		25	0
MFIA	00	rv	101	00	101		A5	0
MTCTL	00	rv	110	00	010		C2	r
MTSARCM	00	rv	110	00	110		C6	r
MFCTL	00	0	010	00	101		45	0
MFCTL,W	00	1	010	00	101		45	0

Bits	Value	Description
19:21 / 24:26	000	no source / no destination
	001	system resource
	010	control register
	011	PSW system mask
	100	space register
	101	general register destination
	110	general register source
22:23	01	encodes SSM
	10	encodes RSM

Memory Management Instructions (Mem_Mgmt)

Figure C-2 shows the format of the memory management instructions (major opcode 01). The opcode extensions (bits 19:26) for instruction memory management instructions are listed in Table C-3. The opcode extensions (bits 18:26) for data memory management instructions are listed in Table C-4 on page C-6. This group includes instructions that access the translation lookaside buffers and the caches.

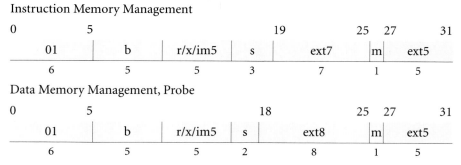

Instruction Memory Management

Data Memory Management, Probe

Figure C-2. Formats for Memory Management Instructions

Table C-3. Instruction Memory Management Instructions

Instruction	Opcode	Extension							Modify
	hex	binary					hex		binary
	bits 0:5	bit 19	bits 20:21	bits 22:24	bit 25	bits 19:25	bits 27:31		bit 26
IITLBT	01	0	10	000	0	20	0		0
PITLB	01	0	00	100	0	08	rv		m
PITLBE	01	0	00	100	1	09	rv		m
PITLB,L	01	0	01	100	0	18	rv		m
FIC,0A	01	0	00	101	0	0A	rv		m
FICE	01	0	00	101	1	0B	rv		m

Bits	Value	Description
19	0	instruction memory management
22:24	000	insert instruction
	100	purge TLB instruction
	101	flush instruction
22	1	modify (bit 26) enable
24	1	nonprivileged instruction
26	m	modification is allowed for this instruction

Table C-4. Data Memory Management Instructions

Instruction	Opcode hex bits 0:5	Extension binary bit 18	Extension binary bit 19	Extension binary bits 20:21	Extension binary bits 22:24	Extension binary bit 25	Extension hex bits 18:25	Extension hex bits 27:31	Modify binary bit 26
IDTLBT	01	0	1	10	000	0	60	0	0
PDTLB	01	0	1	00	100	0	48	rv	m
PDTLBE	01	0	1	00	100	1	49	rv	m
PDTLB,L	01	0	1	01	100	0	58	rv	m
FDC (index)	01	0	1	00	101	0	4A	rv	m
FDC (imm)	01	1	1	00	101	0	CA	rv	0
FDCE	01	0	1	00	101	1	4B	rv	m
PDC	01	0	1	00	111	0	4E	0	m
FIC,4F	01	0	1	00	111	1	4F	0	m
PROBE,R	01	0	1	00	011	0	46	t	0
PROBEI,R	01	1	1	00	011	0	C6	t	0
PROBE,W	01	0	1	00	011	1	47	t	0
PROBEI,W	01	1	1	00	011	1	C7	t	0
LPA	01	0	1	00	110	1	4D	t	m
LCI	01	0	1	00	110	0	4C	t	0

Bits	Value	Description
18	0	non-immediate value
	1	immediate value
19	1	data memory management
22:24	000	insert instruction
	011	probe instruction
	100	purge TLB instruction
	101	flush instruction
	110	load instruction
	111	purge cache instruction
22	1	modify (bit 26) enable
23	1	store result
24	1	nonprivileged instruction
26	m	modification is allowed for this instruction

Arithmetic/Logical Instructions (Arith/Log)

Figure C-3 shows the format of the arithmetic/logical instructions. The opcode extensions for the arithmetic/logical instructions (major opcode 02) are listed in Table C-5.

Figure C-3. Format for Arithmetic/Logical Instructions

Table C-5. Arithmetic/Logical Instructions

Instruction	Opcode hex bits 0:5	Extension binary bits 20:21	Extension binary bits 22:25	Extension hex bits 20:25
ADD	02	01	1000	18
ADD,L	02	10	1000	28
ADD,TSV	02	11	1000	38
ADD,C	02	01	1100	1C
ADD,C,TSV	02	11	1100	3C
SHLADD (1)	02	01	1001	19
SHLADD,L (1)	02	10	1001	29
SHLADD,TSV (1)	02	11	1001	39
SHLADD (2)	02	01	1010	1A
SHLADD,L (2)	02	10	1010	2A
SHLADD,TSV (2)	02	11	1010	3A
SHLADD (3)	02	01	1011	1B
SHLADD,L (3)	02	10	1011	2B
SHLADD,TSV (3)	02	11	1011	3B
SUB	02	01	0000	10
SUB,TSV	02	11	0000	30
SUB,TC	02	01	0011	13
SUB,TSV,TC	02	11	0011	33
SUB,B	02	01	0100	14
SUB,B,TSV	02	11	0100	34
DS	02	01	0001	11
ANDCM	02	00	0000	00
AND	02	00	1000	08
OR	02	00	1001	09
XOR	02	00	1010	0A
UXOR	02	00	1110	0E
CMPCLR	02	10	0010	22
UADDCM	02	10	0110	26
UADDCM,TC	02	10	0111	27

Table C-5. Arithmetic/Logical Instructions (Continued)

Instruction	Opcode hex bits 0:5	Extension binary bits 20:21	Extension binary bits 22:25	Extension hex bits 20:25
DCOR	02	10	1110	2E
DCOR,I	02	10	1111	2F
HADD	02	00	1111	0F
HADD,SS	02	00	1101	0D
HADD,US	02	00	1100	0C
HSUB	02	00	0111	07
HSUB,SS	02	00	0101	05
HSUB,US	02	00	0100	04
HAVG	02	00	1011	0B
HSHLADD (1)	02	01	1101	1D
HSHLADD (2)	02	01	1110	1E
HSHLADD (3)	02	01	1111	1F
HSHRADD (1)	02	01	0101	15
HSHRADD (2)	02	01	0110	16
HSHRADD (3)	02	01	0111	17

Bits	Value	Description
20:21	00	unit/logical; do not set carry/borrow bits.
	01	arithmetic; set carry/borrow bits; do not trap.
	10	unit/logical; do not set carry/borrow bits.
	11	arithmetic; set carry/borrow bits; trap on overflow.

Indexed and Short Displacement Load/Store Instructions (Index_Mem)

Figure C-4 shows the formats of the indexed and short displacement load and store instructions. The opcode extensions (bits 22:25) for indexed and short displacement memory reference instructions (major opcode 03) are listed in Table C-6. The short displacement forms are distinguished from the indexed instructions by bit 19 (0=indexed, 1=short).

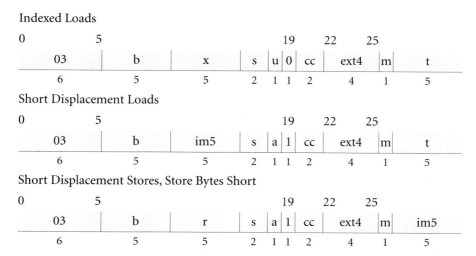

Figure C-4. Formats for Indexed and Short Displacement Load/Store Instructions

Table C-6. Indexed and Short Displacement Load/Store Instructions

Instruction	Opcode	Extension			
	hex		binary		hex
	bits 0:5	bit 19	bits 22:23	bits 24:25	bits 22:25
LDB (index)	03	0	00	00	0
LDH (index)	03	0	00	01	1
LDW (index)	03	0	00	10	2
LDD (index)	03	0	00	11	3
LDDA (index)	03	0	01	00	4
LDCD (index)	03	0	01	01	5
LDWA (index)	03	0	01	10	6
LDCW (index)	03	0	01	11	7
LDB (short)	03	1	00	00	0
LDH (short)	03	1	00	01	1
LDW (short)	03	1	00	10	2
LDD (short)	03	1	00	11	3
LDDA (short)	03	1	01	00	4
LDCD (short)	03	1	01	01	5
LDWA (short)	03	1	01	10	6
LDCW (short)	03	1	01	11	7
STB (short)	03	1	10	00	8
STH (short)	03	1	10	01	9
STW (short)	03	1	10	10	A
STD (short)	03	1	10	11	B
STBY (short)	03	1	11	00	C
STDBY (short)	03	1	11	01	D
STWA (short)	03	1	11	10	E
STDA (short)	03	1	11	11	F

Load/Store Doubleword Instructions (Load_dw and Store_dw)

Figure C-5 shows the formats of the long displacement load and store doubleword instructions. The opcode extensions (bit 30) for long displacement load and store doubleword instructions (major opcodes 14 and 1C) are listed in Table C-7.

Figure C-5. Format for Load/Store Doubleword Instructions

Table C-7. Load/Store Doubleword Instructions

Instruction	Opcode hex bits 0:5	Extension binary bit 30
LDD (long)	14	0
STD (long)	1C	0
FLDD (long)	14	1
FSTD (long)	1C	1

Load/Store Word Instructions (Load_w and Store_w)

Figure C-6 shows the formats of the long displacement load and store word instructions. The opcode extensions (bit 29) for long displacement load and store word instructions (major opcodes 17 and 1F) are listed in Table C-8.

Floating-Point Load/Store Word

Load/Store Word and Modify (Complement)

Figure C-6. Format for Load/Store Word Instructions

Table C-8. Load/Store Word Instructions

Instruction	Opcode hex bits 0:5	Extension binary bit 29
FLDW (long)	17	0
FSTW (long)	1F	0
LDW (mod comp)	17	1
STW (mod comp)	1F	1

Arithmetic Immediate Instructions (Addi, Subi)

Figure C-7 shows the format of the arithmetic immediate instructions. The opcode extensions (bit 20) for the arithmetic immediate instructions (major opcodes 25, 2C, and 2D) are listed in Table C-9. The extension field, e, determines whether or not the instruction traps on overflow.

Figure C-7. Format for Arithmetic Immediate Instructions

Table C-9. Arithmetic Immediate Instructions

Instruction	Opcode hex bits 0:5	Extension binary bit 20
ADDI	2D	0
ADDI,TC	2C	0
SUBI	25	0
ADDI,TSV	2D	1
ADDI,TSV,TC	2C	1
SUBI,TSV	25	1

Shift, Extract, and Deposit Instructions (Sh_Ex_Dep)

Figure C-8 shows the formats of the shift, extract, and deposit instructions. The opcode extensions (bits 19:21) for the fixed shift, extract, and deposit instructions (major opcodes 34, 35, 36, 3C, and 3D) are listed in Table C-10. The opcode extensions (bits 19:22) for the variable shift, extract, and deposit instructions (major opcodes 34 and 35) are listed in Table C-11.

Variable Shift Pair

op	r2	r1	c	ext2	0	d	0	t
6	5	5	3	2	1	1	4	5

(bits 19:20, 22)

Variable Extract

op	r	t	c	ext2	se	d	cl	0	clen
6	5	5	3	2	1	1	1	3	5

(bits 19:20, 22)

Variable Deposit

op	t	r/im5	c	ext2	nz	d	cl	0	clen
6	5	5	3	2	1	1	1	3	5

(bits 19:20, 22)

Fixed Shift Pair

op	r2	r1	c	0	cp	d	cpos	t
6	5	5	3	1	1	1	5	5

(bit 21)

Fixed Extract

op	r	t	c	cl	p	se	pos	clen
6	5	5	3	1	1	1	5	5

(bit 21)

Fixed Deposit

op	t	r/im5	c	cl	cp	nz	cpos	clen
6	5	5	3	1	1	1	5	5

(bit 21)

Figure C-8. Formats for Shift, Extract, and Deposit Instructions

Table C-10. Fixed Shift/Extract/Deposit Instructions

Instruction	Opcode	Extension		
	hex	binary	binary	binary
	bits 0:5	bit 19	bit 20	bit 21
SHRPD	34	0	p	1
SHRPW	34	0	1	0
EXTRD	36	cl	p	se
EXTRW	34	1	1	se
DEPD	3C	cl	cp	nz
DEPDI	3D	cl	cp	nz
DEPW	35	0	1	nz
DEPWI	35	1	1	nz

Table C-11. Variable Shift/Extract/Deposit Instructions

Instruction	Opcode	Extension			
	hex	binary	hex	binary	binary
	bits 0:5	bits 19:20	bits 19:20	bit 21	bit 22
SHRPD	34	00	0	0	1
SHRPW	34	00	0	0	0
EXTRD	34	10	2	se	1
EXTRW	34	10	2	se	0
DEPD	35	00	0	nz	1
DEPDI	35	10	2	nz	1
DEPW	35	00	0	nz	0
DEPWI	35	10	2	nz	0

Multimedia Instructions (Multimedia)

Figure C-9 shows the formats of the multimedia instructions. The opcode extensions (bits 16, 17:18, and 20:21) for the multimedia instructions (major opcode 3E) are listed in Table C-12

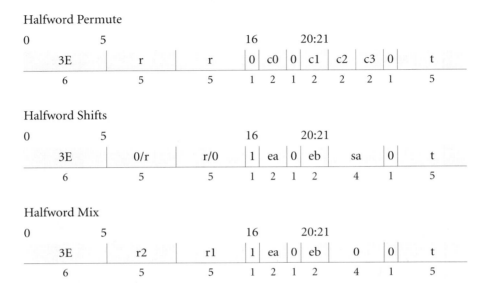

Figure C-9. Formats for Multimedia Instructions

Table C-12. Multimedia Instructions

Instruction	Opcode	Extension				
	hex		binary		hex	
	bits 0:5	bit 16	bits 17:18	bits 20:21	bits 17:18	bits 20:21
PERMH	3E	0	—	—	—	—
HSHL	3E	1	00	10	0	2
HSHR,U	3E	1	10	10	2	2
HSHR,S	3E	1	10	11	2	3
MIXW,L	3E	1	00	00	0	0
MIXW,R	3E	1	10	00	2	0
MIXH,L	3E	1	00	01	0	1
MIXH,R	3E	1	10	01	2	1

Unconditional Branch Instructions (Branch)

Figure C-10 shows the formats of the unconditional branch instructions. The opcode extensions (bits 16:18 and 31) for the unconditional branch instructions (major opcode 3A) are listed in Table C-13.

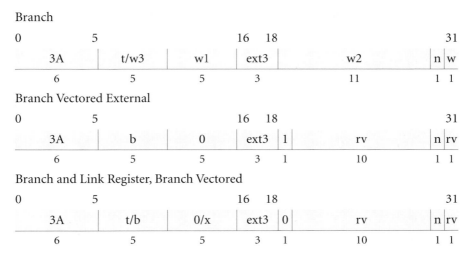

Figure C-10. Formats for Unconditional Branch Instructions

Table C-13. Unconditional Branch Instructions

Instruction	Opcode		Extension	
	hex	binary	hex	binary
	bits 0:5	bits 16:18	bits 16:18	bit 19
B,L	3A	000	0	–
B,GATE	3A	001	1	–
B,L,PUSH	3A	100	4	–
B,L (long)	3A	101	5	–
BLR	3A	010	2	0
BV	3A	110	6	0
BVE	3A	110	6	1
BVE,L	3A	111	7	1

Coprocessor Loads and Stores (Copr_w and Copr_dw)

Figure C-11 shows the formats of the coprocessor load and store instructions. The opcode extensions for the coprocessor memory reference instructions (major opcodes 09 and 0B) are listed in Table C-14. Opcode 09 indicates the instruction operates on word data (Copr_w). Opcode 0B indicates the instruction operates on doubleword data (Copr_dw). The short displacement forms are distinguished from the indexed instructions by bit 19 (0 = indexed; 1 = short) and loads from stores by bit 22 (0 = load; 1 = store).

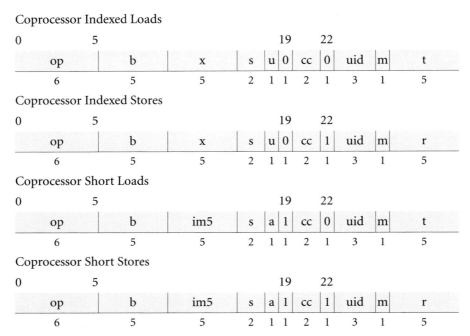

Figure C-11. Formats for Coprocessor Load/Store Instructions

Table C-14. Coprocessor Load and Store Instructions

Instruction	Opcode hex bits 0:5	Extension binary bit 19	Extension binary bit 22
CLDW (index)	09	0	0
CLDD (index)	0B	0	0
CSTW (index)	09	0	1
CSTD (index)	0B	0	1
CLDW (short)	09	1	0
CLDD (short)	0B	1	0
CSTW (short)	09	1	1
CSTD (short)	0B	1	1

Special Function Unit Instructions

Figure C-12 shows the formats of the special function unit instructions. The opcode extensions for the special function unit instructions (major opcode 04) are listed in Table C-15.

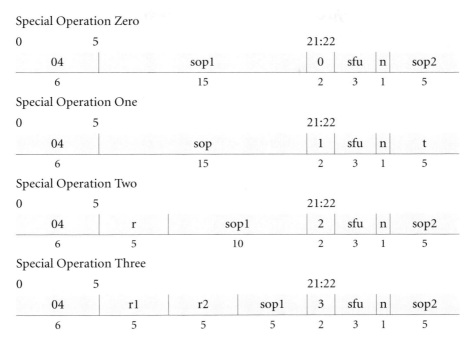

Figure C-12. Formats for Special Function Unit (SFU) Instructions

Table C-15. Special Function Unit (SFU) Instructions

Instruction	Opcode hex bits 0:5	Extension binary bits 21:22	Extension hex bits 21:22
SPOP0	04	00	0
SPOP1	04	01	1
SPOP2	04	10	2
SPOP3	04	11	3

Floating-Point Coprocessor Operation Instructions

Figures C-13, C-14, and C-15 show the formats of the floating-point coprocessor operation instructions. The opcode extensions for the floating-point coprocessor operation instructions (major opcode 0C, uid 0, major opcode 0E, and major opcode 2E) are listed in Tables C-16 through C-24.

Major Opcode 0C

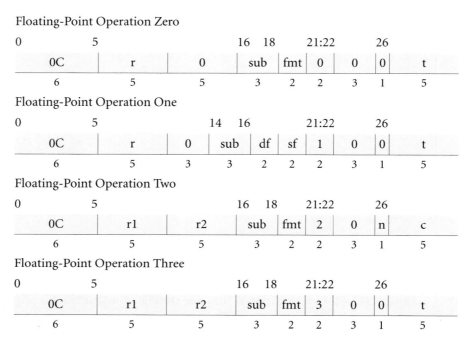

Figure C-13. Formats for Floating-Point Operations - Major Opcode 0C

Table C-16. Floating-Point Class Zero - Major Opcode 0C Instructions

Instruction	Opcode	Uid	Class	Sub-Op	Cond/Targ	Nullify
	hex	hex	hex	hex	hex	binary
	bits 0:5	bits 23:25	bits 21:22	bits 16:18	bits 27:31	bit 26
FID	0C	0	0	0	0	0
FCPY	0C	0	0	2	t	0
FABS	0C	0	0	3	t	0
FSQRT	0C	0	0	4	t	0
FRND	0C	0	0	5	t	0
FNEG	0C	0	0	6	t	0
FNEGABS	0C	0	0	7	t	0

Table C-17. Floating-Point Class One - Major Opcode 0C Instructions

Instruction	Opcode	Uid	Class	Sub-Op	Cond/Targ	Nullify
	hex	hex	hex	hex	hex	binary
	bits 0:5	bits 23:25	bits 21:22	bits 14:16	bits 27:31	bit 26
FCNV (float/float)	0C	0	1	0	t	0
FCNV (int/float)	0C	0	1	1	t	0
FCNV (float/int)	0C	0	1	2	t	0
FCNV,T (float/int)	0C	0	1	3	t	0
FCNV (uint/float)	0C	0	1	5	t	0
FCNV (float/uint)	0C	0	1	6	t	0
FCNV,T (float/uint)	0C	0	1	7	t	0

Table C-18. Floating-Point Class Two - Major Opcode 0C Instructions

Instruction	Opcode	Uid	Class	Sub-Op	Cond/Targ	Nullify
	hex	hex	hex	hex	hex	binary
	bits 0:5	bits 23:25	bits 21:22	bits 16:18	bits 27:31	bit 26
FCMP	0C	0	2	y	c	0
FTEST	0C	0	2	y	c	1

Table C-19. Floating-Point Class Three - Major Opcode 0C Instructions

Instruction	Opcode	Uid	Class	Sub-Op	Cond/Targ	Nullify
	hex	hex	hex	hex	hex	binary
	bits 0:5	bits 23:25	bits 21:22	bits 16:18	bits 27:31	bit 26
FADD	0C	0	3	0	t	0
FSUB	0C	0	3	1	t	0
FMPY	0C	0	3	2	t	0
FDIV	0C	0	3	3	t	0
Reserved	0C	0	3	4-6	–	0
Undefined	0C	0	3	7	–	0

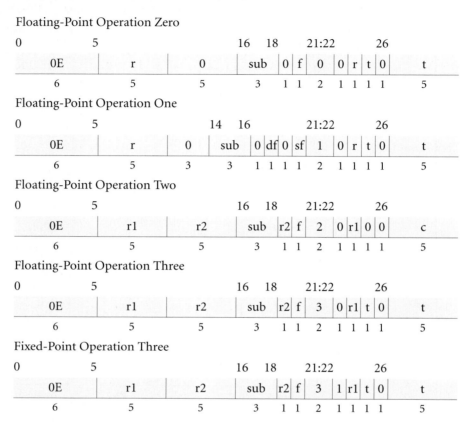

Figure C-14. Formats for Floating-Point Operations - Major Opcode 0E

Table C-20. Floating-Point Class Zero - Major Opcode 0E Instructions

Instruction	Opcode	Class	Sub-Op	Fixed	Nullify	Format	Cond/Targ
	hex	hex	hex	binary	binary	hex	hex
	bits 0:5	bits 21:22	bits 16:18	bit 23	bit 26	bits 19:20	bits 25,27:31
FCPY	0E	0	2	0	0	fmt	t
FABS	0E	0	3	0	0	fmt	t
FSQRT	0E	0	4	0	0	fmt	t
FRND	0E	0	5	0	0	fmt	t
FNEG	0E	0	6	0	0	fmt	t
FNEGABS	0E	0	7	0	0	fmt	t

Table C-21. Floating-Point Class One - Major Opcode 0E Instructions

Instruction	Opcode hex bits 0:5	Class hex bits 21:22	Sub-Op hex bits 14:16	Fixed binary bit 23	Nullify binary bit 26	Format hex bits 17:20	Cond/Targ hex bits 25,27:31
FCNV (float/float)	0E	1	0	0	0	df,sf	t
FCNV (int/float)	0E	1	1	0	0	df,sf	t
FCNV (float/int)	0E	1	2	0	0	df,sf	t
FCNV,T (float/int)	0E	1	3	0	0	df,sf	t
FCNV (uint/float)	0E	1	5	0	0	df,sf	t
FCNV (float/uint)	0E	1	6	0	0	df,sf	t
FCNV,T (float/uint)	0E	1	7	0	0	df,sf	t

Table C-22. Floating-Point Class Two - Major Opcode 0E Instructions

Instruction	Opcode hex bits 0:5	Class hex bits 21:22	Sub-Op hex bits 16:18	Fixed binary bit 23	Nullify binary bit 26	Format binary bit 20	Cond/Targ hex bits 25,27:31
FCMP	0E	2	y	0	0	f	0,c

Table C-23. Floating-Point Class Three - Major Opcode 0E Instructions

Instruction	Opcode hex bits 0:5	Class hex bits 21:22	Sub-Op hex bits 16:18	Fixed binary bit 23	Nullify binary bit 26	Format binary bit 20	Cond/Targ hex bits 25,27:31
FADD	0E	3	0	0	0	f	t
FSUB	0E	3	1	0	0	f	t
FMPY	0E	3	2	0	0	f	t
FDIV	0E	3	3	0	0	f	t
Undefined	0E	3	4	0	0	–	–
Reserved	0E	3	5-6	0	0	–	–
Undefined	0E	3	7	0	0	–	–

Table C-24. Fixed-Point Class Three - Major Opcode 0E Instructions

Instruction	Opcode hex bits 0:5	Class hex bits 21:22	Sub-Op hex bits 16:18	Fixed binary bit 23	Nullify binary bit 26	Format binary bit 20	Cond/Targ hex bits 25,27:31
XMPYU	0E	3	2	1	0	0	t

0	5			20		26	
2E	r1	r2	r3	r2	f	r3	r1	t	s	t
6	5	5	3	1	1	3	1	1	1	5

Figure C-15. Format for Floating-Point Fused-Operation Instructions

Table C-25. Floating-Point Fused-Operation Instructions

Instruction	Opcode hex bits 0:5	Sub-Op binary bit 26	Format binary bit 20
FMPYFADD	2E	0	f
FMPYNFADD	2E	1	f

Performance Monitor Coprocessor Instructions

Figure C-16 shows the format of the performance monitor coprocessor operation instructions. The opcode extensions for the performance monitor coprocessor instructions (major opcode 0C, uid 2) are listed in Table C-26.

Figure C-16. Format for Performance Monitor Coprocessor Instructions

Table C-26. Performance Monitor Coprocessor Instructions

Instruction	Opcode hex bits 0:5	Uid hex bits 23:25	Sub-Op hex bits 18:22	Nullify binary bit 26
PMDIS	0C	2	1	n
PMENB	0C	2	3	0
Undefined	0C	2	0,2,4..F	–
Reserved	0C	2	10..1F	–

D
Conditions

The condition completer field, *cond*, in the assembly language form of an instruction specifies a condition or the negation of a condition. This field expands in the machine language form to fill the condition field, *c*, (normally 3 bits wide), the 1-bit negation field, *f*, and the 1-bit doubleword field, *d*, as required. For some instructions, the negation or doubleword attributes of the condition are controlled by the opcode.

This appendix defines all conditions for the instruction set.

Arithmetic/Logical Conditions

The arithmetic/logical operations generate the set of conditions as shown in Table D-1. No overflow conditions result from logical operations. In the table, *c* is the machine language encoding indicating the condition. While most instructions perform only doubleword arithmetic/logical operations, both word and doubleword conditions are available. Doubleword conditions are computed based on the 64-bit result of the arithmetic operation, the (leftmost) carry bit of the result, and the overflow indication. Word conditions are computed based on the least significant 32 bits of the 64-bit result of the arithmetic operation, and the carry bit and overflow indication out of bit 32 of the doubleword result.

The terms **signed overflow** and **unsigned overflow** are defined for the arithmetic instructions in Table D-2.

Table D-1. Arithmetic/Logical Operation Conditions

c	Description	
0	never; nothing	
1	all bits are 0	
2	(leftmost bit is 1) xor signed overflow	
3	all bits are 0 or (leftmost bit is 1 xor signed overflow)	
	adds	subtracts/compares
4	no unsigned overflow	unsigned overflow
5	all bits are 0 or no unsigned overflow	all bits are 0 or unsigned overflow
6	signed overflow	
7	rightmost bit is 1	

Table D-2. Overflow Results

Instructions	Unsigned Overflow	Signed Overflow
Adds	The result of an unsigned addition is greater than $2^{size} - 1$ (carry == 1). where *size* is the operand size (either 32 or 64).	The result of signed addition is not representable in two's complement notation (both source operands have the same sign and the sign of the result is different)
Subtracts and Compares	The result of an unsigned subtraction is less than 0 (i.e., *b* is greater than *a* in the operation *c* = *a* - *b*; borrow == 0).	The result of signed subtraction is not representable in two's complement notation (both the source operands have different signs and the sign of the result differs from the sign of the first operand; i.e., *a* has a different sign than *b* and *c* in the operation *c* = *a* - *b*).
Divide Step and Shift and Adds	One or more of the bits shifted out is 1, or the result of the operation is not in the range 0 through $2^{size} - 1$ where *size* is the operand size (either 32 or 64).	One or more of the bits shifted out differs from the leftmost bit following the shift, or the result of the operation is not representable in two's complement notation.

When implementing the DIVIDE STEP and SHIFT AND ADD instructions, the overflow condition XORed into conditions 2 and 3 may optionally include the overflow that is generated during the pre-shift operation. The only overflow that must be included is the one actually generated by the arithmetic operation.

If a signed overflow occurs during the shift operation of a DIVIDE STEP or SHIFT AND ADD instruction, conditions 2 and 3 are not meaningful; therefore, the result of a condition 2 or condition 3 test is not predictable.

Programming Note

The figure below shows signed number addition and indicates the signed overflow condition when both operands are small positive numbers, large positive numbers, large negative numbers, or small negative numbers.

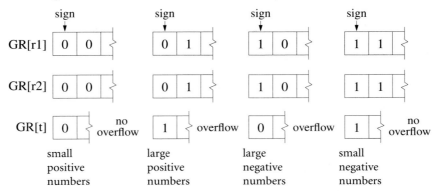

Signed overflow can occur only when adding numbers with the same sign. Addition of numbers with unlike signs will always result with a "no overflow" condition.

The interpretation of the arithmetic/logical conditions varies according to the operation performed. The interpretation for all the subtracts and the register forms of comparisons are shown in Tables D-3 and D-4. The interpretation for the immediate form of comparisons are shown in Table D-5.

In these tables, *cond* is in assembly language format and *c, f,* and *d* are in machine language format. *opd1* denotes operand 1 (an immediate value or a register's contents) in the assembly language instruction format and *opd2* denotes operand 2 (a register's contents). The condition, <<, "opd1 is less than opd2 (unsigned)" is equivalent to unsigned overflow in Table D-1.

Table D-3. Compare/Subtract Instruction Word Conditions

cond	Description	c	f	d
	never	0	0	0
=	opd1 is equal to opd2 (word)	1	0	0
<	opd1 is less than opd2 (signed word)	2	0	0
<=	opd1 is less than or equal to opd2 (signed word)	3	0	0
<<	opd1 is less than opd2 (unsigned word)	4	0	0
<<=	opd1 is less than or equal to opd2 (unsigned word)	5	0	0
SV	opd1 minus opd2 overflows (signed word)	6	0	0
OD	opd1 minus opd2 is odd	7	0	0
TR	always	0	1	0
<>	opd1 is not equal to opd2 (word)	1	1	0
>=	opd1 is greater than or equal to opd2 (signed word)	2	1	0
>	opd1 is greater than opd2 (signed word)	3	1	0
>>=	opd1 is greater than or equal to opd2 (unsigned word)	4	1	0
>>	opd1 is greater than opd2 (unsigned word)	5	1	0
NSV	opd1 minus opd2 does not overflow (signed word)	6	1	0
EV	opd1 minus opd2 is even	7	1	0

Table D-4. Compare/Subtract Instruction Doubleword Conditions

cond	Description	c	f	d
*	never	0	0	1
*=	opd1 is equal to opd2 (doubleword)	1	0	1
*<	opd1 is less than opd2 (signed doubleword)	2	0	1
*<=	opd1 is less than or equal to opd2 (signed doubleword)	3	0	1
*<<	opd1 is less than opd2 (unsigned doubleword)	4	0	1
*<<=	opd1 is less than or equal to opd2 (unsigned doubleword)	5	0	1
*SV	opd1 minus opd2 overflows (signed doubleword)	6	0	1
*OD	opd1 minus opd2 is odd	7	0	1
*TR	always	0	1	1
*<>	opd1 is not equal to opd2 (doubleword)	1	1	1
*>=	opd1 is greater than or equal to opd2 (signed doubleword)	2	1	1
*>	opd1 is greater than opd2 (signed doubleword)	3	1	1
*>>=	opd1 is greater than or equal to opd2 (unsigned doubleword)	4	1	1
*>>	opd1 is greater than opd2 (unsigned doubleword)	5	1	1
*NSV	opd1 minus opd2 does not overflow (signed doubleword)	6	1	1
*EV	opd1 minus opd2 is even	7	1	1

Table D-5. Compare Immediate and Branch Instruction Doubleword Conditions

cond	Description	c
*<<	opd1 is less than opd2 (unsigned doubleword)	0
*=	opd1 is equal to opd2 (doubleword)	1
*<	opd1 is less than opd2 (signed doubleword)	2
*<=	opd1 is less than or equal to opd2 (signed doubleword)	3
*>>=	opd1 is greater than or equal to opd2 (unsigned doubleword)	4
*<>	opd1 is not equal to opd2 (doubleword)	5
*>=	opd1 is greater than or equal to opd2 (signed doubleword)	6
*>	opd1 is greater than opd2 (signed doubleword)	7

The interpretation for the register form of adds are shown in Tables D-6 and D-7. The interpretation for the immediate form of adds are shown in Table D-6.

Cond is in assembly language format and c, f, and d are in machine language format.

Table D-6. Add Instruction Word Conditions

cond	Description	c	f	d
	never	0	0	0
=	opd1 is equal to negative of opd2 (word)	1	0	0
<	opd1 is less than negative of opd2 (signed word)	2	0	0
<=	opd1 is less than or equal to negative of opd2 (signed word)	3	0	0
NUV	opd1 plus opd2 does not overflow (unsigned word)	4	0	0
ZNV	opd1 plus opd2 is zero or no overflow (unsigned word)	5	0	0
SV	opd1 plus opd2 overflows (signed word)	6	0	0
OD	opd1 plus opd2 is odd	7	0	0
TR	always	0	1	0
<>	opd1 is not equal to negative of opd2 (word)	1	1	0
>=	opd1 is greater than or equal to negative of opd2 (signed word)	2	1	0
>	opd1 is greater than negative of opd2 (signed word)	3	1	0
UV	opd1 plus opd2 overflows (unsigned word)	4	1	0
VNZ	opd1 plus opd2 is nonzero and overflows (unsigned word)	5	1	0
NSV	opd1 plus opd2 does not overflow (signed word)	6	1	0
EV	opd1 plus opd2 is even	7	1	0

Table D-7. Add Instruction Doubleword Conditions

cond	Description	c	f	d
*	never	0	0	1
*=	opd1 is equal to negative of opd2 (doubleword)	1	0	1
*<	opd1 is less than negative of opd2 (signed doubleword)	2	0	1
*<=	opd1 is less than or equal to negative of opd2 (signed doubleword)	3	0	1
*NUV	opd1 plus opd2 does not overflow (unsigned doubleword)	4	0	1
*ZNV	opd1 plus opd2 is zero or no overflow (unsigned doubleword)	5	0	1
*SV	opd1 plus opd2 overflows (signed doubleword)	6	0	1
*OD	opd1 plus opd2 is odd (doubleword)	7	0	1
*TR	always	0	1	1
*<>	opd1 is not equal to negative of opd2 (doubleword)	1	1	1
*>=	opd1 is greater than or equal to negative of opd2 (signed doubleword)	2	1	1
*>	opd1 is greater than negative of opd2 (signed doubleword)	3	1	1
*UV	opd1 plus opd2 overflows (unsigned doubleword)	4	1	1
*VNZ	opd1 plus opd2 is nonzero and overflows (unsigned doubleword)	5	1	1
*NSV	opd1 plus opd2 does not overflow (signed doubleword)	6	1	1
*EV	opd1 plus opd2 is even	7	1	1

Table D-8. Add and Branch Instruction Conditions when PSW W-bit is 1

cond	Description	c	f
	never	0	0
=	opd1 is equal to negative of opd2 (word)	1	0
<	opd1 is less than negative of opd2 (signed word)	2	0
<=	opd1 is less than or equal to negative of opd2 (signed word)	3	0
NUV	opd1 plus opd2 does not overflow (unsigned word)	4	0
*=	opd1 is equal to negative of opd2 (doubleword)	5	0
*<	opd1 is less than negative of opd2 (signed doubleword)	6	0
*<=	opd1 is less than or equal to negative of opd2 (signed doubleword)	7	0
TR	always	0	1
<>	opd1 is not equal to negative of opd2 (word)	1	1
>=	opd1 is greater than or equal to negative of opd2 (signed word)	2	1
>	opd1 is greater than negative of opd2 (signed word)	3	1
UV	opd1 plus opd2 overflows (unsigned word)	4	1
*<>	opd1 is not equal to negative of opd2 (doubleword)	5	1
*>=	opd1 is greater than or equal to negative of opd2 (signed doubleword)	6	1
*>	opd1 is greater than negative of opd2 (signed doubleword)	7	1

The interpretation of the condition completers for the SHIFT AND ADD instructions is similar to the ADD instructions (Tables D-6 and D-7). If no overflow occurs, *opd1* is the shifted value. For example, the completer "=" implies that the shifted *opd1* equals the negative of *opd2*. If overflow occurs, the interpretations in Tables D-6 and D-7 do not apply. Table D-1 and the definition of overflow in Table D-2 can be used to determine if the condition is satisfied.

The interpretation of the condition completers for the DIVIDE STEP instruction are similar to the subtract or add conditions, depending on the state of the PSW V-bit. If no overflow occurs, then *opd1* is the shifted value. If overflow occurs, the interpretations in Tables D-3 and D-6 do not apply. Again, Tables D-1 and D-2 can be used to determine if the condition is satisfied.

For logical operations, the conditions are computed based only on the result. The interpretation of the arithmetic/logical conditions for logical instructions is shown in Tables D-9 and D-10. In these tables, *cond* is in assembly language format and *c*, *f*, and *d* are in machine language format. Other values of the condition field are undefined for the logical operations.

Table D-9. Logical Instruction Word Conditions

cond	Description	c	f	d
	never	0	0	0
=	all bits in word are 0	1	0	0
<	leftmost bit in word is 1	2	0	0
<=	leftmost bit in word is 1 or all bits in word are 0	3	0	0
OD	rightmost bit is 1	7	0	0
TR	always	0	1	0
<>	some bits in word are 1	1	1	0
>=	leftmost bit in word is 0	2	1	0
>	leftmost bit in word is 0, some bits in word are 1	3	1	0
EV	rightmost bit is 0	7	1	0

Table D-10. Logical Instruction Doubleword Conditions

cond	Description	c	f	d
*	never	0	0	1
*=	all bits in doubleword are 0	1	0	1
*<	leftmost bit in doubleword is 1	2	0	1
*<=	leftmost bit in doubleword is 1 or all bits in doubleword are 0	3	0	1
*OD	rightmost bit is 1	7	0	1
*TR	always	0	1	1
*<>	some bits in doubleword are 1	1	1	1
*>=	leftmost bit in doubleword is 0	2	1	1
*>	leftmost bit in doubleword is 0, some bits in doubleword are 1	3	1	1
*EV	rightmost bit is 0	7	1	1

Unit Conditions

The operations concerned with sub-units of a doubleword generate the conditions shown in Tables D-11 and D-12. The conditions are computed based on the 64-bit result of the unit operation and the sixteen 4-bit carries. In these tables, *cond* is in assembly language format and *c*, *f*, and *d* are in machine language format.

Table D-11. Unit Instruction Word Conditions

cond	Description	c	f	d
	never	0	0	0
	undefined	1	0	0
SBZ	Some Byte in word Zero	2	0	0
SHZ	Some Halfword Zero	3	0	0
SDC	Some Digit in word Carry	4	0	0
	undefined	5	0	0
SBC	Some Byte in word Carry	6	0	0
SHC	Some Halfword Carry	7	0	0
TR	always	0	1	0
	undefined	1	1	0
NBZ	No Bytes in word Zero	2	1	0
NHZ	No Halfwords Zero	3	1	0
NDC	No Digit in word Carries	4	1	0
	undefined	5	1	0
NBC	No Byte in word Carries	6	1	0
NHC	No Halfword Carries	7	1	0

Table D-12. Unit Instruction Doubleword Conditions

cond	Description	c	f	d
*	never	0	0	1
*SWZ	Some Word in doubleword Zero	1	0	1
*SBZ	Some Byte in doubleword Zero	2	0	1
*SHZ	Some Halfword in doubleword Zero	3	0	1
*SDC	Some Digit in doubleword Carry	4	0	1
*SWC	Some Word in doubleword Carry	5	0	1
*SBC	Some Byte in doubleword Carry	6	0	1
*SHC	Some Halfword in doubleword Carry	7	0	1
*TR	always	0	1	1
*NWZ	No Words in doubleword Zero	1	1	1
*NBZ	No Bytes in doubleword Zero	2	1	1
*NHZ	No Halfwords in doubleword Zero	3	1	1
*NDC	No Digit in doubleword Carries	4	1	1
*NWC	No Words in doubleword Carry	5	1	1
*NBC	No Byte in doubleword Carries	6	1	1
*NHC	No Halfword in doubleword Carries	7	1	1

Shift/Extract/Deposit Conditions

The shift, extract, and deposit operations generate the conditions shown in Tables D-13 and D-14. The conditions are computed based on the result of the operation. In these tables, *cond* is in assembly language format and *c* and *d* are in machine language format. The MOVE AND BRANCH and MOVE IMMEDIATE AND BRANCH instructions also use the extract/deposit conditions.

Table D-13. Shift/Extract/Deposit Word Instruction Conditions

cond	Description	c	d
	never	0	0
=	all bits in word are 0	1	0
<	leftmost bit in word is 1	2	0
OD	rightmost bit is 1	3	0
TR	always	4	0
<>	some bits in word are 1	5	0
>=	leftmost bit of word is 0	6	0
EV	rightmost bit is 0	7	0

Table D-14. Shift/Extract/Deposit Doubleword Instruction Conditions

cond	Description	c	d
*	never	0	1
*=	all bits in doubleword are 0	1	1
*<	leftmost bit in doubleword is 1	2	1
*OD	rightmost bit is 1	3	1
*TR	always	4	1
*<>	some bits in doubleword are 1	5	1
*>=	leftmost bit in doubleword is 0	6	1
*EV	rightmost bit is 0	7	1

Branch On Bit Conditions

The branch on bit operations generate the conditions shown in Table D-15. In this table, *cond* is in assembly language format and *c* and *d* are in machine language format.

Table D-15. Branch On Bit Instruction Conditions

cond	Description	c	d
<	leftmost bit in word is 1	0	0
>=	leftmost bit in word is 0	1	0
*<	leftmost bit in doubleword is 1	0	1
*>=	leftmost bit in doubleword is 0	1	1

E   Instruction Notation Control Structures

The control structures used in the instruction notation in Chapter 7, "Instruction Descriptions" and Chapter 9, "Floating-Point Instruction Set" are relatively standard. The expression statements describe a computation performed by the ALU or some other hardware for its side effects rather than the value of the computation. The functions listed Table E-1 are used to localize long calculations that are used in several places.

Table E-1. Long Calculation Functions

Function	Description
assemble_3(x)	Assembles a 3-bit space register number: $return(cat(x\{2\},x\{0..1\}))$
assemble_6(x,y)	Assembles a 6-bit extract/deposit length specifier: $return(32 * x + 32 - y)$
assemble_12(x,y)	Assembles a 12-bit immediate: $return(cat(y,x\{10\},x\{0..9\}))$

assemble_16(x,y)	Assembles a 16-bit immediate in one of two ways, depending on the PSW W-bit:
	if (PSW[W])
	$\quad return(cat(y\{13\},xor(y\{13\},x\{0\}),xor(y\{13\},x\{1\}),y\{0..12\}))$
	else
	$\quad return(cat(y\{13\},y\{13\},y\{13\},y\{0..12\}))$

assemble_16a(x,y,z)	Assembles a word-aligned 16-bit immediate in one of two ways, depending on the PSW W-bit:
	if (PSW[W])
	$\quad return(cat(z,xor(z,x\{0\}),xor(z,x\{1\}),y,0\{0..1\}))$
	else
	$\quad return(cat(z,z,z,y,0\{0..1\}))$

assemble_17(x,y,z)	Assembles a 17-bit immediate: $return(cat(z,x,y\{10\},y\{0..9\}))$
assemble_21(x)	Assembles a 21-bit immediate: $return(cat(x\{20\},x\{9..19\},x\{5..6\},x\{0..4\},x\{7..8\}))$
assemble_22(a,b,c,d)	Assembles a 22-bit immediate: $return(cat(d,a,b,c\{10\},c\{0..9\}))$
cat(x1, ..., xn)	Concatenates the passed arguments, *x1* through *xn*.
low_sign_ext(x,len)	Removes the rightmost bit of *x* and extends the field to the left with that bit to form a 64-bit quantity. The field is of size *len*: $return(sign\_ext(cat(x\{len-1\},x\{0..len-2\}),len))$
lshift(arg1,arg2)	*arg1* is logically shifted left by the number of bits specified in *arg2*. The size of the result is determined by the size of *arg1*.
mem_load	See "Memory Reference Instructions" on page 6-6.

Function	Description
mem_store	See "Memory Reference Instructions" on page 6-6.
rshift(arg1,arg2)	*arg1* is logically shifted right by *arg2* bits. The size of the result is determined by the size of *arg1*.
send_to_copr(u,t)	Sends the 5-bit value *t* to coprocessor unit *u*.
sign_ext(x,len)	Extends *x* on the left with sign bits to form a 64-bit quantity, taking the leftmost bit for the field of size *len* as the sign bit.
sign_ext_16(x,len)	Extends *x* on the left with sign bits to form a 16-bit quantity, taking the leftmost bit for the field of size *len* as the sign bit.
store_in_memory(space,offset,low,high,hint,data)	The function store_in_memory is identical to mem_store except that it forces the data to be stored into main memory. The data may optionally remain in the cache.
xor(x1, ..., xn)	Produces the bitwise exclusive or of the passed arguments.
zero_ext(x,len)	Extends *x* on the left, for the field of size *len*, with zeros to form a 64-bit quantity.

Miscellaneous Constructs

Numerous mnemonic constructs are used to represent things that do not fit easily into the rest of the notation described in the previous table or whose details are more implementation-dependent than defined. Table E-2 defines these constructs.

Table E-2. Miscellaneous Constructs

Function	Description
absolute_address(space,offset)	Returns the absolute address corresponding to the passed virtual address.
clear_BTS()	Sets the valid bit in every entry of the Branch Target Stack to 0.
coherence_index(space,offset)	Returns the coherence index corresponding to the passed effective address. See "Cache Coherence with I/O" on page F-11.
coherent_system	Boolean; the value is 1 if the system is fully coherent; the value is 0 if the system is partially or completely non-coherent.
coprocessor_condition(id,opcode,n)	A coprocessor specific condition is returned based on the arguments and the current state of the coprocessor.
coprocessor_op(id,opcode,n,priv)	A coprocessor specific operation is performed based on the arguments and the current state of the coprocessor.

Function	Description
DTLB_alloc(space,offset)	Allocates a slot in the data TLB based on the space and offset arguments, and returns a pointer to the slot.
DTLB_purge_broadcast(space,offset,page_size)	In a multiprocessor system, the other processors are made to search their data TLBs for one or more entries which match the address range specified by space, offset, and page_size. All matching entries are removed.
DTLB_purge_entries(space,offset)	Removes one or more data TLB entries. The entries to be removed are selected based on some implementation-dependent function of the arguments space and offset. No address matching is done. If there are entries which would match space and offset, these need not be among the entries removed.
DTLB_purge_local(space,offset)	Removes the specified TLB entry.
DTLB_search(space,offset)	Searches the data TLB for a valid entry whose virtual address range encompasses the page including the virtual address specified by space and offset, and returns a pointer to the slot containing the entry if one is found. If no matching entry is found, NULL is returned.
Dcache_flush(space,offset)	If the cache line containing the effective address is present, it is invalidated. If the line is dirty it is written back to main memory.
Dcache_flush_entries(space,offset)	Zero or more cache lines specified by an implementation-dependent function of the address are invalidated. If any of these lines are dirty, they are written back to main memory. No address matching is done. If there are entries which would match space and offset, these need not be among the entries invalidated.
Dcache_flush_or_purge(space,offset)	If the cache line specified by the effective address is present, it is invalidated. If the line is dirty, it may optionally be written back to memory.
Icache_flush(space,offset)	If the cache line containing the effective address is present, it is invalidated. If the line is dirty, it is written back to main memory.

Table E-2. Miscellaneous Constructs (Continued)

Function	Description
Icache_flush_entries(space,offset)	Zero or more cache lines specified by an implementation-dependent function of the address are invalidated. If any of these lines are dirty, they are written back to main memory (only possible in a combined cache.) No address matching is done. If there are entries which would match space and offset, these need not be among the entries invalidated.
ITLB_alloc(space,offset)	Same as DTLB_alloc except that a new slot is allocated in the instruction TLB.
ITLB_purge_broadcast(space,offset,page_size)	Same as DTLB_purge_broadcast except that the instruction TLB is purged.
ITLB_purge_entries(space,offset)	Same as DTLB_purge_entries except that the instruction TLB is purged.
ITLB_purge_local(space,offset)	Same as DTLB_purge_local except that the instruction TLB is purged.
ITLB_search(space,offset)	Same as DTLB_search except that the instruction TLB is searched.
measurement_enabled	Boolean; when the value is 1, the performance monitor coprocessor is enabled to make measurements; when the value is 0, the measurements are disabled. This condition is independent of the state of CCR bit 2.
phys_mem_load(addr,low,high,hint)	Returns the data in physical memory (consisting of memory and the cache) starting at the low'th bit beyond the beginning of the byte at address, addr, and ending at the high'th bit beyond the beginning of the byte at address, addr. If the PSW E-bit is 1, the data bytes are swapped before they are returned. The cache control hint, hint, is a recommendation to the processor on how to resolve cache coherence. See "Cache Control" on page 6-9. This function is used for absolute accesses to memory.

Function	Description
phys_mem_store(addr,low,high,hint,data)	Stores the data in physical memory (consisting of memory and the cache) starting at the low'th bit beyond the beginning of the byte at address, addr, and ending at the high'th bit beyond the beginning of the byte at address, addr. If the PSW E-bit is 1, the data bytes are swapped before they are stored. The cache control hint, hint, is a recommendation to the processor on how to resolve cache coherence. See "Cache Control" on page 6-9. This function is used for absolute accesses to memory.
pop_from_BTS()	Removes the top entry from the Branch Target Stack. All other entries are moved up one register, and the entry at the bottom of stack is marked invalid. The entry which was removed from the top of stack is returned. The valid bit is returned as bit {62} of the return value.
push_onto_BTS(offset)	All entries in the Branch Target Stack are moved down one register. The value which was at the bottom of stack is discarded. The argument is placed in the top of stack entry, and the valid bit for the top of stack entry is set to 1.
read_access_allowed(space,offset,x)	In non-Level 0 systems, returns 1 if read access is allowed to the effective address at the privilege level given by the two rightmost bits of x. Returns 0 otherwise. Always returns 1 in Level 0 systems.
select_data_cache_entries(space,offset)	An implementation-dependent function which returns a list of zero or more entries.
select_instruction_cache_entries(space,offset)	An implementation-dependent function which returns a list of zero or more entries.
sfu_condition0(opcode,priv) sfu_condition1(opcode,priv) sfu_condition2(opcode,priv,r) sfu_condition3(opcode,priv,r1,r2)	An SFU specific condition is returned based on the SFU instruction format, the arguments, and the current state of the special function unit.
sfu_operation0(opcode,priv) sfu_operation1(opcode,priv) sfu_operation2(opcode,priv,r) sfu_operation3(opcode,priv,r1,r2)	An SFU specific operation is performed based on SFU instruction format, the arguments, and the current state of the special function unit.

Function	Description

space_select(s_field,base,format)	Returns the space ID selected by the s-field of the instruction and the base register value as follows:
	
	if (PSW[W])
	    if (format == LONG_DISP)
	        return(SR[base{0..1} + 4]);
	    else /* short or indexed */
	      if (s_field == 0)
	        return(SR[base{0..1} + 4]);
	      else if (priv == 0)
	        return(SR[s_field]);
	      else
	        undefined;
	else /* PSW[W] == 0 */
	    if (s_field == 0)
	        return(SR[base{32..33} + 4]);
	    else
	        return(SR[s_field]);

virt_mem_load(space,offset,low,high,hint)	Returns the data in virtual memory (consisting of memory and the cache) starting at the low'th bit beyond the beginning of the byte at address, space,offset and ending at the high'th bit beyond the beginning of the byte at address, space,offset. If the PSW E-bit is 1, the data bytes are swapped before they are returned. The cache control hint, hint, is a recommendation to the processor on how to resolve cache coherence. See "Cache Control" on page 6-9. This function is used for virtual accesses to memory.

Function	Description
virt_mem_store(space,offset,low,high,hint,data)	Stores the data in virtual memory (consisting of memory and the cache) starting at the low'th bit beyond the beginning of the byte at address, space,offset and ending at the high'th bit beyond the beginning of the byte at address, space,offset. If the PSW E-bit is 1, the data bytes are swapped before they are stored. The cache control hint, hint, is a recommendation to the processor on how to resolve cache coherence. See "Cache Control" on page 6-9. This function is used for virtual accesses to memory.
write_access_allowed(space,offset,x)	In non-Level 0 systems, returns 1 if write access is allowed to the effective address at the privilege level given by the two rightmost bits of x. Returns 0 otherwise. Always returns 1 in Level 0 systems.

F   TLB and Cache Control

This appendix provides detailed information relating to operation of the TLB (Translation Lookaside Buffer) and cache in a PA-RISC system. It describes how software can control the contents of the TLB under various conditions such as TLB miss handling and also specifies the operation requirements of the TLB.

The appendix also describes the responsibilities of system software in regards to handling address aliasing as well as cache move-in rules. Finally, a brief summary of the guidelines relating to coherency in multiprocessor systems is provided.

TLB Control

TLBs function as buffers for the most frequently used address translations. Terms used to describe TLBs are given below.

Entry	The term **entry** refers to a translation which is present in the TLB. Entries are visible to software through references (such as load, store, and semaphore instructions, access rights probes, and the LOAD PHYSICAL ADDRESS instruction).
Slot	Hardware resources in the TLB which hold entries are referred to as **slots**.
Remove	An entry is **removed** when some action causes it to be inaccessible to software.
	Insertion of translations into the TLB, for example, causes other entries to be removed. Entries can be explicitly removed by purging them.

NOTE

From a hardware perspective, a translation is removed when it is displaced by the insertion of another translation. If each slot has an associated valid bit which causes that slot not to participate in TLB lookup, then a translation is removed if the slot that contains it is marked invalid. This would be one way of implementing TLB purges.

Several mechanisms can be used by software to remove a specific translation from the ITLB or DTLB. First, when a new translation is inserted into the TLB, any old translations which overlap the virtual address range of the new translation are removed. Second, a specific virtual address and page size may be used to purge (remove) the associated translations from the TLB. The PURGE INSTRUCTION TLB and PURGE DATA TLB instructions perform this function. These instructions also optionally cause the translation to be removed from the TLBs of other processors in a multiprocessor system.

Translations may also be removed from the TLB using the PURGE INSTRUCTION TLB ENTRY and the PURGE DATA TLB ENTRY instructions. These purge some machine-specific number of entries in the TLB without regard for the translation. These instructions are used by system software to clear the entire instruction or data TLB.

Because the TLB is managed by a mixture of hardware and software mechanisms, software may not, in general, rely on the existence of translations in the TLB and hardware may, in general, remove TLB entries at any time, provided that forward progress is assured. There are limited situations, however, in which software may rely on a translation existing in the TLB. This means that software may make virtual accesses using this **relied-upon translation**, and no TLB miss fault will occur. Hardware is required to retain this TLB entry as long as the constraints of the limited situation are met. These situations are described in "TLB Operation Requirements" on page F-3.

NOTE

As a result, the following hardware actions are allowed, except in the defined limited situations.

- A TLB miss fault may be taken even though the translation exists in the TLB.

- In the event of a TLB error, one or more entries may be removed.

Note also that software may not rely on the existence of any translations in the TLB immediately after any group 1, 2, or 4 interruption.

Software TLB Miss Handling

In order to insure forward progress, some restrictions are placed on software which performs TLB miss handling.

For instruction TLB miss handling, the following restrictions apply:

- Software can insert multiple instruction address translations into the ITLB, provided that the translation which caused the trap is inserted last.

- Software must not execute a purge TLB instruction using the virtual address corresponding to the data address translation needed for the execution of the trapping instruction.

- Software must not insert translations into the DTLB.

For non-access instruction TLB miss handling, the following restrictions apply:

- Software can only insert into the ITLB up to all of the eight translations for the page group. The translation which caused the trap must be inserted last.

- Software must not execute a purge TLB instruction using the virtual address corresponding to the data address translation needed for the execution of the trapping instruction.

- Software must not insert translations into the DTLB.

For data TLB miss handling and non-access data TLB miss handling, the following restrictions apply:

- Software can only insert into the DTLB up to all of the eight translations for the page group. The translation which caused the trap must be inserted last.

- Software must not execute a purge TLB instruction using the virtual address corresponding to the instruction address translation needed for the execution of the trapping instruction.

The following restrictions apply to all four TLB miss handlers:

- Software must not make any virtual references.

- Software must not execute any PURGE DATA TLB ENTRY or PURGE INSTRUCTION TLB ENTRY instructions.

Hardware TLB Miss Handling

The default endian bit (see "Byte Ordering (Big Endian/Little Endian)" on page 2-19) determines how data from the hardware-visible page table is interpreted by the hardware TLB miss handler, if implemented. If the default endian bit is 0, the hardware-visible page table entries are loaded as doublewords in big-endian format; if the default endian bit is 1, the entries are loaded as doublewords in little-endian format.

If a data prefetch instruction (described in "Data Prefetch Instructions" on page 6-11) references an address which misses in the data TLB, the hardware TLB miss handler should not be invoked.

TLB Operation Requirements

Software may rely on the existence of particular translations in the TLB only in certain situations. The following describes the situations in which software may rely upon the fact that a specific translation will continue to exist in the TLB. In these situations, software may make virtual accesses using the relied-upon translation, and no TLB miss fault will occur (including non-access TLB miss faults).

1. When an instruction takes one of the following interruptions, the associated data address translation will remain in the DTLB, and is termed the relied-upon translation.

Intr. No.	Interruption
18	data memory protection/unaligned data reference trap
19	data memory break trap
20	TLB dirty bit trap
21	page reference trap
22	assist emulation trap
26	data memory access rights trap
27	data memory protection ID trap
28	unaligned data reference trap

The translation will continue to remain in the DTLB, meaning no data TLB miss fault will occur on virtual data accesses which use this translation, for as long as software meets the following constraints:

- No virtual data references are made to pages other than the page corresponding to the relied-upon translation.

- The execution stream does not contain nullified instructions which, had they not been nullified, would have made virtual data references to pages other than the page corresponding to the relied-upon translation.

- No memory management instructions other than LPA are executed. (See "Memory Management Instructions (Mem_Mgmt)" on page C-5 for a list of memory management instructions.)

- No purge TLB instructions which would purge the relied-upon translation are executed by other processors in a multiprocessor system.

- No virtual instruction references are made.

- No DIAGNOSE instructions are executed.

- No attempt is made to execute undefined instructions.

Programming Note

Software may rely upon this translation in order to improve performance in handling the above-mentioned traps. For example, the absolute address which corresponds to the virtual address used in the trapping instruction can be determined by using this code sequence:

```
LPA     x(s,b),t
```

Because no TLB miss fault can occur, the interruption handler need not incur the overhead of making itself interruptible.

---

2. If the PSW Q-bit is 1, and is set to 0 by a RESET SYSTEM MASK or MOVE TO SYSTEM MASK instruction, the instruction address translation used to fetch the RSM or MTSM instruction will continue to remain in the ITLB, and is termed the relied-upon translation. No instruction TLB miss fault will occur on virtual instruction accesses which use this translation for as long as software meets the following constraints:

   - The RSM or MTSM instruction which sets the PSW Q-bit to 0 (the **clearing** RSM or MTSM) is preceded by another RSM, SSM, or MTSM instruction which does not affect the PSW Q-bit, and which appears at least 8 instructions prior.

   - The instructions between the initial RSM, SSM, or MTSM instruction and the clearing RSM or MTSM do not include any memory management instructions, virtual data references, or instruction references to pages other than the code page containing the clearing RSM or MTSM instruction.

   - The clearing RSM or MTSM instruction is not within 8 instructions of a page boundary.

   - No virtual data references are made.

   - The execution stream does not contain nullified instructions which would have made virtual data references had they not been nullified.

   - No FLUSH INSTRUCTION CACHE instructions are executed with the PSW D-bit equal to 1.

   - No memory management instructions are executed. (See Appendix C, "Operation Codes" for a list of memory management instructions.)

   - No purge TLB instructions which would purge the relied-upon translation are executed by other processors in a multiprocessor system.

   - No instruction references are made to pages other than the code page containing the clearing RSM or MTSM instruction.

- No DIAGNOSE instructions are executed.

- No undefined instructions are attempted to be executed.

- No instructions are executed which are followed, within 8 words, by a branch instruction, a memory management instruction, a DIAGNOSE instruction, an undefined instruction, or a page boundary.

Programming Note

Software may rely upon this instruction translation in order to improve performance in process dispatch. For example, in this code sequence:

```
SSM        0,gr0    ; initial RSM, SSM or MTSM
LDW                 ; set up process state
  .                 ; must be at least 7 instructions
  .                 ; between the system mask instructions
  .
LDW
RSM        8,gr0    ; set PSW Q-bit to 0
MTCTL      reg1,cr20; set up IIASQ
MTCTL      reg2,cr20
MTCTL      reg3,cr21; set up IIAOQ
MTCTL      reg4,cr21
LDW                 ; set up last of process state
  .
  .
  .
LDW
RFI                 ; dispatch process
```

Because no TLB miss fault can occur, the interruption handler need not incur the overhead of disabling code translation just prior to process dispatch. Note that the LDW instructions in this sequence must use absolute addresses. (Use absolute loads, or do these with the PSW D-bit equal to 0.)

Address Aliasing

Normally, a virtual address does not translate to two different absolute addresses. It is the responsibility of memory management software to avoid the ambiguity such occurrences would create.

Caches are required to permit a physical memory location to be accessed by both an absolute and a virtual address when the virtual address is equal to the absolute address. Such a virtual address is said to be **equivalently-mapped**. For equivalently-mapped addresses in the memory address space, note that since the upper 2 bits of the offset are not used in forming the absolute address, these bits need not match the corresponding bits in the virtual address for the two addresses to be equivalently-mapped.

The instruction and data caches are required to detect that the same physical memory location is being accessed by two virtual addresses that satisfy all the following requirements:

1. The two virtual addresses map to the same absolute address.

2. Offset bits 44 through 63 are the same in both virtual addresses.

3. If the use of space bits in generating the cache index is enabled, the two virtual addresses have the same values for the following space identifier bits: 36, 37, 38, 39, 40, 41, 42, 43, 44, 45, 46, and 47.

Processors must provide an implementation-dependent mechanism to enable/disable the use of space bits in generating the cache index.

NOTE

Implementations are encouraged to provide a mechanism to enable/disable the three contiguous groups of 4 space bits (bits 36 through 39, bits 40 through 43, and bits 44 through 47) independently.

When space bits are enabled for use in generating the cache index, for each space bit that participates, the corresponding offset bit which gets ORed with it in the generation of virtual addresses is always forced by hardware to 0 for address generation purposes.

These rules provide offset aliasing on 1 Mbyte boundaries, with optional support for offset aliasing on smaller power of two sized boundaries, and either restricted or unlimited space aliasing.

Two virtual addresses that satisfy all of the above requirements are called **equivalent aliases** of each other. Virtual addresses that satisfy rule 1 but violate rule 2 or 3 are **non-equivalent aliases,** and are more restricted in their use. For non-equivalent aliases, **read-only** aliasing is supported with minimal restrictions, and **many-reader/one-writer** aliasing is supported with more significant restrictions.

Generally, if system software must use multiple addresses for the same data, these addresses are equivalent aliases (or are an absolute address and an equivalently-mapped virtual address). This description of non-equivalent aliasing, and the restrictions on software only apply in rare situations when non-equivalent aliasing is necessary.

For the purposes of supporting non-equivalent aliasing, a **read-only translation** is defined as one where the TLB and page table both meet at least one of the following conditions:

- The page type in the access rights field is 0, 2, 4, 5, 6, or 7. (See "Access Control" on page 3-11.)

- The D-bit (dirty bit) is 0.

A translation not meeting this requirement is termed a **write-capable translation.**

Software is allowed to have any number of read-only non-equivalently aliased translations to a physical page, as long as there are no other translations to the page. This is referred to as **read-only** non-equivalent aliasing.

Before a write-capable translation is enabled, *all* non-equivalently-aliased translations must be removed from the page table and purged from the TLB. (Note that the caches are not required to be flushed at this time.) The write-capable translation may then be used to read and/or modify data on that page. Before any non-equivalent aliased translation is re-enabled, the virtual address range for the writable page (the entire page) must be flushed from the cache, and the write-capable translation removed from the page table and purged from the TLB. If an old read-only translation is re-enabled, or a translation is enabled that is equivalently-aliased to an old translation, the virtual address range for the re-enabled translation must be flushed from the cache before accesses are made to the page. (This flushing is only required if the re-enabled virtual page has not been flushed since it was last accessed.) This is referred to as **many-reader/one-writer** non-equivalent aliasing.

Absolute read accesses can be made to a page which is mapped with a non-equivalently-mapped read-only translation, as long as the absolute address range accessed is flushed before enabling any write-capable translation. Since absolute accesses do not cause prefetching, it is not necessary to flush the entire page - only the accessed range need be flushed.

All other uses of non-equivalent aliasing (including simultaneously enabling multiple non-equivalently aliased translations where one or more allow for write access) are prohibited, and can cause machine checks or silent data corruption, including data corruption of unrelated memory on unrelated pages. It is the responsibility of privileged software to avoid non-equivalent aliasing, except as described above. This requires flushing the affected address range from the caches prior to any of the following:

- Changing the address mapping in the TLBs.

- Making an absolute access to a location which might reside in the caches as a result of an access by a virtual address that was not equivalently mapped.

- Making a virtual access to a location which might reside in the caches as a result of an access by its absolute address that was not equivalently mapped.

- Making a virtual access to a location which may reside in the caches as a result of an access by another virtual address that was not equivalently aliased.

NOTE

The restrictions on non-equivalent aliases are necessary to allow the design of high-performance caches and memory interconnect, including multi-level caches (including victim or miss caches) and directory-based coherency structures. Coherency schemes are greatly simplified by allowing the assumption that there is at most a single private copy of a physical line at any time. The read-only translation informs hardware to request a shared or public copy of the line.

Cache Move-in Restrictions

Data and instructions from memory can be brought into cache only under certain circumstances. Two different schemes are used for controlling cacheability – one for virtual accesses and one for absolute accesses.

Virtual Accesses

For virtual accesses, cache move-in is controlled by a **mapping-based** approach. Generally, if a translation exists in the TLB that permits access, the memory on that page may be brought into the cache. The access information in the TLB entry must meet a simple check, however, to permit move-in. This is required in order to allow for translations which can be used for cache flushing purposes, but which do not enable move-in. This is described in detail in following sections.

Since TLB miss handling may insert into the TLB any entry in the page table for which the R-bit (Reference bit) is 1, system software should consider the page table as the main tool for controlling cacheability of memory.

Absolute Accesses

For absolute accesses, cache move-in is controlled by a **reference-based** approach. Generally, only instructions and data referenced by executed instructions may be brought into the cache. The definition of "reference" is somewhat loose to permit instruction prefetching and instruction pipelining.

No data reference may cause a move-in to the instruction cache and no instruction reference may cause a move-in to the data cache. This means that the execution of a FLUSH DATA CACHE or PURGE DATA CACHE instruction guarantees that the addressed line, if it has been referenced as data but not as instructions, is no longer present in the cache system. Similarly, only a FLUSH INSTRUCTION CACHE instruction is required to guarantee that a line which has been referenced as instructions but not as data, is no longer present in the cache system. The actions which constitute a reference are described in "Data Cache Move-In" on page F-8 and "Instruction Cache Move-In" on page F-9.

If implemented, the U (Uncacheable) bit is found in the data TLB entry associated with a page. Whether or not the U-bit is implemented, the state of this bit if implemented, whether the memory reference is virtual or absolute, and whether the reference is made from a page in the memory or I/O address spaces, determine if the reference may be moved into the data cache. The detailed rules for moving references into the data cache are specified in "Data Cache Move-In" on page F-8.

Data Cache Move-In

For virtual accesses, cache move-in is permitted only if there is a translation for the virtual address which meets both of these conditions:

- The page type field in the access rights for the entry contains a value in the range 0 to 3 (access rights allow read access).

- The T-bit in the entry is 0.

For absolute accesses, data lines are brought into the cache only as a result of references. Except where noted, a data reference may move in all of the lines on the page containing the reference. The following actions constitute a data reference, and may cause move-in to the data cache:

- Execution of a load, store, or semaphore instruction

- Interruption of a load, store, or semaphore instruction by any interruption except the ones listed below:

Intr. No.	Interruption
6	instruction TLB miss fault
7	instruction memory protection trap
8	illegal instruction trap
10	privileged operation trap

NOTE

Because protection is checked (interruption 10), the reference cannot bring in any data which could not have been accessed.

- A load or store instruction which is left at the front of the interruption queues because of a prior instruction which took a group 4 interruption, provided that the load or store would not have taken any of the above interruptions (6, 7, 8, 10).

Data items which would have been referenced by a nullified load, store, or semaphore instruction are not moved in.

The instructions LDWA, LDDA, STWA, and STDA are exceptions to the general rule that a data reference may cause all of the lines in the page containing the reference to be moved in. These instructions can cause only the referenced line to be moved into the data cache.

Instruction Cache Move-In

For virtual accesses, cache move-in is permitted only if there is a translation for the virtual address which meets both of these conditions:

- The page type field in the access rights for the entry contains a value in the range 2 to 7 (access rights allow execute access).

- The access rights for the entry does not match this binary pattern: "111 0X 1X", where each X stands for either a 1 or a 0 (execute-only page where PL2 ≤ PL ≤ PL1 but PL2 > PL1).

For absolute accesses, instructions are brought into the instruction cache, or combined data and instruction cache, only as a result of references. Except where noted, an instruction reference may move in all of the lines on the page containing the reference, as well as all of the lines on the next sequential page. The following actions constitute an instruction reference, and may cause move-in to the instruction cache:

- Execution of an instruction

- Execution of a nullified instruction. This action can cause only those lines on the page containing the instruction to be moved in

- Execution of a branch can cause all of the lines on the page containing the target of the branch to be moved in.

- Execution of a branch to a target instruction which is the last instruction on a page, followed by an instruction which traps (in the branch delay slot), can cause all of the lines on the page containing the target instruction, as well as all of the lines on the next sequential page to be moved in.

- Interruption of an instruction by any interruption
- A branch instruction which takes a group 4 interruption can cause all of the lines on the page containing the instruction which would have been branched to, to be moved in.

Instructions which would have been branched to by nullified or untaken branches are not moved in.

Programming Note

If a data page immediately follows an instruction page, it is possible that the entire data page may have been moved into the instruction cache because of these move-in rules. Software must be aware of this fact and flush **both the instruction and the data** caches in order to remove the data page from the cache.

I/O Addresses and Uncacheable Memory

Accesses to the I/O address space, whether through absolute accesses or through virtual accesses that map to the I/O address space, are never cached.

Virtual accesses for which the U-bit in the TLB entry is 1 are not cached.

Cache Flushing

Cache control instructions have two effects on caching. One is that they force particular lines to be removed from the cache. The other is that, for absolute accesses, they disable further cache move-in from the affected memory range until further references to that range are made.

For virtual accesses, a purge TLB instruction stops (disables) any subsequent move-in operations to that page. Subsequent accesses must trigger a TLB miss, and then may move into the cache only if the new translation from the page table allows it.

For absolute accesses, a flush cache or purge cache instruction to a page stops (disables) any subsequent move-in operations to that page until another reference to that page is made. In a multiprocessor system, these instructions stop any subsequent move-in operations to that page on all processors until another reference to that page is made.

Once a line could have been brought into a cache, the only way software can insure that the line has been removed from the cache is to

- Purge the translation from the TLB and insure that the corresponding page table entry does not allow cache move-in (if the cached memory was brought in due to a virtual access), and
- Flush or purge the line and execute a SYNC instruction, or flush the entire cache with flush-entry instructions and execute a SYNC instruction.

Once a line has been made cacheable, even if it is subsequently forced out of the cache by other accesses, the cache system can move it in again at will, until the enabling translation is removed (for virtual accesses) or until the line is flushed (for absolute accesses).

System software can create translations which allow a virtual address range to be flushed from the caches, but which do not enable cache move-in. There are two ways of creating such a translation:

- Create a translation in which the page type field in the access rights has the value 0 or 1 (this prevents I-cache move-in), and has the T-bit 1 (this prevents D-cache move-in), or

- Create a translation in which the page type field in the access rights has the value 7 (this prevents D-cache move-in), and has the special access rights pattern "111 0X 1X" (this prevents I-cache move-in).

Cache Coherence with I/O

Accesses to memory by I/O modules may be either coherent or non-coherent with processor data caches.

Coherent I/O

Processors in systems with coherent I/O modules must implement the LOAD COHERENCE INDEX instruction, which loads the coherence index corresponding to a given virtual address into a general Register. Coherent I/O modules provide the coherence index along with the absolute address of data it is reading from or writing to memory. The coherence index must provide enough information such that, together with the absolute address, the processor can find data that was brought into its data cache by the original virtual address.

Software need not flush or purge data from the data cache when sharing the data with a coherent I/O module. For I/O output (e.g., memory to secondary storage), the coherent I/O module performs coherent read operations which will read the data from memory or a processor's data cache depending on where the most up-to-date copy is located. For I/O input, the coherent I/O module performs coherent write operations which will write the data to memory and also update or invalidate matching lines in processor data caches.

Coherent I/O operations are not coherent with instruction caches. Software is responsible for flushing the appropriate instruction cache lines before or after the I/O operation.

Non-coherent I/O

Non-coherent I/O modules process data in memory; this data can be non-coherent with processor caches. Software is required to insure that:

1. The contents of the appropriate caches are flushed to main memory prior to an I/O output (e.g., memory to secondary storage) operation.

2. The contents of the appropriate caches are purged or flushed prior to an I/O input (e.g., secondary storage to memory) operation.

3. The contents of the appropriate caches are purged following an I/O input operation, if the cache move-in rules would have allowed the processor to move the data into the cache during the I/O operation.

Operations Defined for I/O Address Space

Semaphore instructions are undefined if the address maps to the I/O address space. Additionally, semaphore instructions are undefined if the address maps to a page in the memory address space for which the TLB U-bit is 1.

Cache flush and purge instructions execute as NOPs if the address maps to the I/O address space.

Data prefetch instructions directed to the I/O address space or to a page in the memory address space for which the TLB U-bit is 1 behave as described in "Data Prefetch Instructions" on page 6-11 except that they must not affect the cache state and may optionally generate a transaction to the addressed device.

All accesses other than those listed above are defined to the I/O address space.

Cache and TLB Coherence in Multiprocessor Systems

Multiprocessor systems may include PA-RISC processors as well as other processors.

The cache-coherent part of a multiprocessor system is required to behave as if there were logically a single D-cache and a single I-cache. If there are multiple physical D-caches, they must cross-interrogate for current data and must broadcast purge and flush operations except for FDCE and FICE. Purge and flush operations do not cause TLB faults on other processors. Multiple I-caches require only that flushes be broadcast. The I-cache is read-only, and software is responsible for coherence when modifications are made to the instruction stream.

The non-cache-coherent part of a multiprocessor system (if any) may either cross-interrogate with the caches in the cache-coherent part of the system, or may have an independent cache system. This design decision is generally based on the frequency of data sharing.

In the cache-coherent part of a multiprocessor system, all data references to cacheable pages must be satisfied by data that was obtained using cache coherence checks, and has remained coherent since the data was moved in. Data references to uncacheable pages do not need to be satisfied by data that was obtained using cache coherence checks. Data from an uncacheable page could be in a cache if it was moved in when that page was marked cacheable, but the page is now marked uncacheable.

Implementations with write buffers must also check buffer contents on cache coherence checks, in order to insure proper ordering of storage accesses.

Instruction references need not be satisfied by data that was obtained using cache coherence checks.

Instruction caches are read-only. In the case of a separate instruction cache implementation, instruction cache lines must never be written back to main memory.

Each processor in a multiprocessor system must have its own TLB system. All TLBs in a multiprocessor system are required to broadcast global purges to all other TLBs. The originating processor's purge instruction suspends until all target processors complete the purge. TLB inserts, local purges and the PDTLBE and PITLBE instructions are not broadcast and do not affect translation on other processors.

G   Memory Ordering Model

This appendix begins with a description of the memory ordering model that must be implemented by PA-RISC systems to ensure proper operation in multiprocessor systems. The informal description is followed by a formal model which describes the behavior of any correct implementation.

Atomicity of Storage Accesses

All load, store, and semaphore instructions (with one exception below) access storage atomically. For example, a double-word load instruction executing on one processor concurrently with a double-word store instruction to the same address executing on another processor will receive either the entire old value or the entire new value.

The STORE BYTES and STORE DOUBLEWORD BYTES instructions, when referencing the memory address space are atomic, but when referencing the I/O address space, are not guaranteed to execute atomically. Doubleword load and store instructions which reference the I/O address space may or may not be atomic, depending on the capabilities of the bus.

Ordering of References

References to the address space (both to memory and I/O) through load, store, and semaphore instructions always appear to the executing processor to be done in program order. However, from the viewpoint of a second processor in a multiprocessor system or from an I/O module, the apparent order of memory references may be different in certain situations.

Ordering Definitions

A processor (or I/O module) A is said to have **observed** a store by another processor B if processor A executes a load instruction and receives the value stored by processor B.

A store is said to be **performed** by a processor when another processor or I/O module observes that store.

A load is said to be **performed** by a processor A if there are no unobserved stores from any processor that could affect the value of that load.

References to the address space through load, store, semaphore, and TLB purge instructions are referred to as **accesses**. Cache flush and purge operations are discussed separately and are not considered accesses. All accesses can be classified as either **strongly ordered**, **ordered**, or **weakly ordered**.

The following accesses are termed **strongly ordered**:

- Accesses to the I/O address space.
- Accesses to any page for which the TLB U-bit is 1.
- The semaphore instructions (LDCW, LDCD).

- The SYNC instruction forces ordering as though it were a strongly ordered access.

- The TLB purge instructions (PITLB, PDTLB).

The following accesses are termed *ordered*:

- Certain loads and stores, when used with a special ordered completer, O.

- Virtual accesses made when the PSW[O] bit is 1, to an address in a page for which the TLB O-bit is 1.

- Absolute accesses made when the PSW[O] bit is 1.

Accesses which are neither strongly ordered nor ordered are termed *weakly ordered*.

Ordering Requirements

An access which is strongly ordered is guaranteed to be performed before any subsequent accesses are performed and is guaranteed not to be performed until after all prior accesses have been performed.

An ordered load is guaranteed to be performed before any subsequent accesses are performed.

All prior accesses are guaranteed to be performed before an ordered store is performed.

An ordered store is guaranteed to be performed before any subsequent ordered load.

Weakly ordered accesses may appear to another processor or I/O module to be performed in any order, provided that they meet the constraints of other strongly ordered accesses and of other ordered loads and ordered stores.

The effect of these ordering constraints is transitive. That is,

if	a sequence of memory accesses initiated by a first processor must, according to these rules, be observed by a second processor to have been performed prior to a sequence of memory accesses initiated by this second processor,
and if	the same sequence of memory accesses initiated by the second processor must, according to these rules, be observed by a third processor to have been performed prior to a sequence of memory accesses initiated by this third processor,
then	the sequence of memory accesses initiated by the first processor must be observed by the third processor to have been performed prior to the sequence of transactions initiated by the third processor.

NOTE

An example of the observability of the ordering of accesses can be seen by considering two processes, A and B, running concurrently on a multiprocessor system.

process A	process B
load x	load y
store y	store x

If process B observes A's store to y, and the references to y are ordered accesses, then process B may rely on the fact that its store to x will not affect the value seen by process A.

Cache flush operations are weakly ordered. Flush operations may be delayed or held pending, and a sequence of flush operations may be executed in any order. There are some constraints, however, on their ordering:

- A flush data cache operation is guaranteed not to be performed until after all prior accesses to addresses within the same cache line have been performed.

- A flush data cache operation is guaranteed to be performed before any subsequent purge operation to the same cache line, to prevent loss of data.

If a combined cache is implemented, these same constraints apply to flush instruction cache operations.

Cache purge operations are weakly ordered. Cache purge operations may be delayed or held pending, and a sequence of cache purge operations may be executed in any order. There are some constraints, however, on their ordering:

- A purge data cache operation is guaranteed not to be performed until after all prior accesses to addresses within the same cache line have been performed.

- A purge data cache operation is guaranteed to be performed before any subsequent access of any address within the same cache line, to prevent loss of data.

The SYNC instruction is used to ensure ordering of cache flush and purge operations, when necessary. After executing a SYNC instruction, any pending flush and purge operations are completed before performing any subsequent load, store, semaphore, flush, or purge instructions.

The SYNC instruction enforces the ordering of only those flush and purge operations caused by the instructions executed on the same processor which executes the SYNC instruction.

In multiprocessor systems, to allow non-privileged code to do cache management, system software must execute a SYNC instruction when switching processes.

Programming Note

It is important to be aware of the delayed nature of cache flush and purge operations, and to use SYNC instructions to force completion where necessary. The following example illustrates this.

Consider two processes sharing a memory location x which is protected by a semaphore s.

process A on Processor 1	process B on Processor 2	note
LDCW s		A acquires semaphore
PDC x		A executes purge
SYNC		Force completion of purge
STW s		A releases semaphore
	LDCW s	B acquires semaphore
	STW x	

In the absence of the SYNC instruction, it would be possible for process B's store to x to complete before the purge of x is completed (since the purge may have been delayed). The purge of x could then destroy the new value.

MTCTL and MFCTL instructions involving the EIR and the EIEM must appear to preserve program order.

Interrupts must be masked immediately following a MTCTL to the EIEM register that masks interrupts or an RSM or MTSM that sets the PSW I-bit to 0.

Modification of resources which affect data access take effect immediately. Acknowledgment of a data TLB purge request from another processor must not be made until after the purge has logically been performed. Data access resources include Protection Identifier Registers, PSW, and TLB entries.

The following table summarizes these ordering requirements.

First Reference	Second Reference					
	Strongly Ordered Access	Ordered Load	Ordered Store	Weakly Ordered Load	Weakly Ordered Store	Cache Flush/ Purge
Strongly Ordered Access	O	O	O	O	O	-[1,3]
Ordered Load	O	O	O	O	O	-[3]
Ordered Store	O	O	O	-	-	-[3]
Weakly Ordered Load	O	-	O	-	-	-[3]
Weakly Ordered Store	O	-	O	-	-	-[3]
Cache Flush/ Purge	-[1,2]	-[2]	-[2]	-[2]	-[2]	-[4]

Sequences marked with O must appear to other processors and I/O modules to be performed in program order.

Notes:

1. The SYNC instruction is different from other strongly ordered accesses in that it also forces ordering with respect to cache flush and purge operations.

2. A purge operation is guaranteed to be performed before any subsequent access is performed to an address within the same cache line.

3. Any access is guaranteed to be performed before a subsequent flush data cache or purge operation is performed to an address within the same cache line. If a combined cache is implemented, then additionally any access is guaranteed to be performed before a subsequent flush instruction cache operation is performed to an address within the same cache line.

4. Any flush data cache operation is guaranteed to be performed before a subsequent purge operation is performed to the same cache line. If a combined cache is implemented, then additionally any flush instruction cache operation is guaranteed to be performed before a subsequent purge operation is performed to the same cache line.

Completion of Accesses

PA-RISC processors are inherently asynchronous and software may not rely on instruction timing for correct operation. Implementations are permitted to execute instructions out of order and need only preserve the appearance of sequential execution. For example, in the absence of other constraints which would force execution, flush and purge operations may be indefinitely delayed. To insure that progress is made, however, the following requirements must be met.

- Instruction streams must make forward progress. This means that any operation, on which an instruction stream is dependent, must be performed in some finite period.

- All load and store operations to the I/O space must be performed in some finite period.

- Execution of a SYNC instruction forces all prior flush operations from the same instruction stream to be performed in some finite period.

For performance and testability reasons, it is occasionally necessary to know when an access to I/O space has completed. This would not normally be possible due to the asynchronous nature of execution. In order to provide this capability, the following two special sequences are defined. These sequences place additional requirements on implementations for the completion of accesses. When these code sequences are used, the additional completion requirements hold.

When this code sequence is executed, the instruction labeled 'access A completed on bus' is not executed, and the source registers not read until after the LDW (or STW) labeled 'access A' has completed on the bus.

```
LDW (or STW)        from (to) I/O space                        ; access A
SYNC
LDW              from I/O space, but not to GR 0
(at least seven instructions)
Instruction                                                    ; access A completed on bus
```

When this code sequence is executed, the instruction labeled 'access B completed on module' is not executed, and the source registers not read until after the STW instruction labeled 'access B' has completed on the I/O module.

```
STW              to I/O space                                  ; access B
LDW              from the same I/O space module
SYNC
LDW              from I/O space, but not to GR 0
(at least seven instructions)
Instruction                                                    ; access B completed on module
```

Formal Memory Model

The purpose of this Memory Model is to define the values which may be returned by the Load instructions within any program. Any correct system implementation must, for every possible program, return only the Load values permitted by this Memory Model. Likewise, any correct program must behave according to its specification for all combinations of Load return values permitted by this Memory Model. The Model therefore represents the full range of behaviors allowed in the memory system, including all caches and interconnect.

The Model accepts as input an "Execution Trace" (a description of the behavior of a hypothetical program running on a hypothetical machine) and determines whether the behavior is consistent with the rules governing the memory system. The strategy used by the Model is to include the Execution Trace with hardware-generated cache control operations in a "Memory Trace" which must obey certain rules. Each cache line in memory is modelled as a Finite State Machine which takes values from Store operations in the Execution Trace and determines what values can be returned to Load operations. Although the Model may mimic the mechanisms used by some implementations, this does not imply that these are the only acceptable mechanisms for enforcing memory ordering; any implementation is acceptable if it always produces only Load values that are permitted by this Model.

This Model makes some simplifications in order to remain small enough to be useful. First, the Model assumes a static page table. That is, mappings for virtual pages must not change physical address, permissions, or cacheability during the interval studied by the Model. Second, there must be no non-equivalent aliasing of virtual addresses. Third, the move-in restrictions which are specific to STWA and LDWA instructions are not modelled.

This Memory Model is expressed both in natural language and in Formal syntax to facilitate reasoning about memory properties and the verification of new designs.

The Execution Trace

The Execution Trace is defined to represent all software-controlled memory operations executing in a system during some interval. The interval may begin with power-up or some appropriate initial state. This Memory Model is concerned with the behavior of Memory rather than with the internal state of processors or other modules, so the Execution Trace includes only operations which affect memory. The system may include any number of processors and I/O devices, and the Execution Trace is defined to include the memory operations executed by all these modules. These operations include all PA instructions executing on processors, as well as all memory references sourced by I/O devices and non-PA processors. The Execution Trace therefore includes the memory-related instruction stream of every module in the system.

The Execution Trace is analogous to a hardware logic analyzer trace which monitors the memory activity of every module in the system, with two differences. First, the Execution Trace records every memory operation as if it were instantaneous and atomic, as described at the beginning of this appendix. A real hardware logic analyzer might observe that each operation progresses through several phases which might be pipelined or overlapped with other operations. Second, the Execution Trace records no ordering information between different modules. A real hardware logic analyzer would at least have an approximate notion of whether an operation on one module occurred before or after an operation on another module. The Execution Trace is therefore consistent with software's limited view of the system, where a program executing on one processor cannot directly observe the activity of another processor.

We represent an Execution Trace as a partially-ordered set of memory references. These memory references are a collection of the following:

Reference	Description
Load	Data or Instruction fetch
Store	Data store
Flush	Request to remove a line from cache
Sync	Synchronize caches
TLB_Purge	Remove TLB entry

A Semaphore (e.g. a LDCW instruction) is represented as an atomic combination of a Load and a Store. There is no cache Purge operation in this list, because this model takes advantage of the fact that any cache Purge is allowed to be treated as a Flush. All known HP implementations use this simplification, so this Model does, too.

Each memory reference in the Execution Trace may have the following attributes:

Attribute	Description
Type	Load, Store, TLB_Purge, Flush, or Sync.
Strength	Strong, Ordered, or Weak.
Coherent	T or F. Distinguishes between Coherent and Non-coherent access.
Virtual	T or F. Distinguishes between Virtual and Absolute addressing.
Icache	T or F. Determines whether a reference will use the I-cache or D-cache (if one exists).
SemaLd	T or F. Indicates this Load is part of a Semaphore. The Store follows immediately.
Value	The sequence of bytes stored or loaded by the reference.
Size	The number of bytes stored or loaded (the length of the Value sequence).
Page	The physical memory page addressed by the reference.
Line	The line offset addressed within the page.
Byte	The byte offset addressed within the line.
Source	The module which originated the reference.
RefNum	A consecutive numbering of memory references from each Source.

The last six attributes are all modeled as non-negative integers. The attributes of a memory reference are accessed in this model using extractor functions. For example, "Page(x)" is the physical page number addressed by reference "x", and "Type(x)" is "Load" when "x" is any Load reference.

There are many restrictions on the values of these attributes. For example, the Line offset must be less than the page size, the Byte offset plus the Size of a reference must not exceed the line size, semaphore operations must be properly aligned, the Byte of a TLB_Purge operation is undefined, and the Strength of a TLB_Purge is always Strong. For the sake of brevity, these restrictions are not described here, but they should be obvious from other chapters.

In this Model, each Load reference in the Execution Trace has a Value. This represents the data value returned to that Load in the single run represented by the Execution Trace. The goal of this Memory Model is to determine whether the Load Values included in any given Execution Trace are consistent with the allowed behavior of a memory system.

Instruction Order

The ordering of memory references within an Execution Trace is described by the Instruction Order relationship. Instruction Order is determined by the code or internal behavior of each module. Instruction Order is a partial order over the complete set of memory references in an Execution Trace, but it is a total order over the set of references sourced by any single module. That is, any two references from a single processor have an explicit order (as given in the code executing on that processor), while two references from different modules are not related by Instruction Order.

Every memory reference in an Execution Trace is assigned a numeric reference index which indicates its position in its source module's instruction stream. For any given module, the index numbers of the references in its instruction stream increase monotonically with time. Two operations which form an atomic semaphore must be consecutively numbered.

The Instruction Order relationship is represented by the overloaded binary infix operator "<". The expression "ref1 < ref2" should be read "ref1 precedes ref2 in some module's instruction stream." This also implies that ref1 and ref2 are both references in the Execution Trace.

Relation	Abbreviation for
$(x < y)$	$(\text{Source}(x)=\text{Source}(y)$ and $\text{RefNum}(x)<\text{RefNum}(y))$

Many properties follow directly from the fact that Instruction Order is represented by a sequence of integers. The following are only examples:

Theorem	Note
$(x < y)$ and $(y < z) \Rightarrow (x < z)$	Order is transitive
$(x < y) \Rightarrow \sim(y < x)$	Order is antisymmetric
$(\text{Source}(x)=\text{Source}(y)) \Rightarrow (x < y)$ or $(y < x)$ or $(x = y)$	Trichotomy

The Execution Trace, then, is specified as a set of memory references with its Instruction Order relationship. The Execution Trace is the only input to the Memory Model, and the only output of the Model will be a binary value to indicate whether the given Execution Trace (with its included Load values) is possible in a correct memory system.

Line States

This Memory Model is concerned with the possible values that each cache line may have in main memory and in the cache system. Each line is modelled as a Finite State Machine which includes state representing the line's value and its status in the cache system.

Assume that all cache lines contain n bytes. A line value w is then a sequence of n bytes $w_0, \ldots, w_{n-1}$. We define two functions Get and Put to extract and modify bytes within a line. If *offset* is a byte offset within a cache line, *size* is a positive integer such that *offset* + *size* $\leq n$, and *val* is a sequence of *size* bytes, then:

Function	Definition
Get(*w*,*offset*,*size*)	Returns the sequence $w_{offset}, \ldots, w_{offset+size-1}$
Put(*w*,*offset*,*val*)	Returns w', the sequence of n bytes identical to w, except that $w'_{offset}=val_0, \ldots, w'_{offset+size-1}=val_{size-1}$

A cache-coherent system must behave as if it contains a single D-cache and a single I-cache, shared by all modules. A data cache may consist of data-only and combined caches, and an instruction cache may consist of instruction-only and combined caches. Software must be aware of the possible existence of these different kinds of caches, because of possible interference between coherent data accesses, non-coherent instruction accesses, and DMA. Likewise, this Model must be aware of the possible states of these caches.

A physical system might include multiple processor modules, each of which has an I-cache and a D-cache consisting of several levels. The system is free to transfer data lines between these caches and levels in order to satisfy coherent Load requests. At any given time, several copies of a line may exist in various parts of the cache structure.

The Model allows multiple copies of any line to be moved into the cache system. A Load from any module may then access any of these multiple copies. All of these multiple copies may remain valid simultaneously in cache until a Flush is executed, a coherent Store requires a private copy of a line, or hardware spontaneously chooses to invalidate one or more copies of the line to make room for other data in the cache.

The state *s* of a given line in the memory system consists of the following five components:

Component	Meaning	Description
MemVal(*s*)	Memory Value	Value of the line in memory.
Status(*s*)	Data Cache Status	One of: PrivClean (private clean), PrivDirty (private dirty), or Public (shared or not present in any data cache).
DonlyCVs(*s*)	Data-only Cache Values	Set of distinct values of copies of the line present in data-only caches.
IonlyCVs(*s*)	Instruction-only Cache Values	Set of distinct values of copies of the line present in instruction-only caches.
CombCVs(*s*)	Combined Cache Values	Set of distinct values of copies of the line present in combined caches.

In addition to these components we define the following shorthand:

Notation	Abbreviation for	Description
DataCVs(s)	CombCVs(s) $\cup$ DonlyCVs(s)	Set of distinct values of copies of the line present in data caches, including both data-only and combined caches.
InstCVs(s)	CombCVs(s) $\cup$ IonlyCVs(s)	Set of distinct values of copies of the line present in instruction caches, including both instruction-only and combined caches.
AllCVs(s)	CombCVs(s) $\cup$ DonlyCVs(s) $\cup$ IonlyCVs(s)	Set of distinct values of copies of the line present in caches of any kind.

The Memory Trace

The Memory Trace, like the Execution Trace, is a set of memory operations which includes some ordering information. The Memory Trace is a super-set of the Execution Trace, so every memory reference in the Execution Trace also appears in the Memory Trace. In addition, the Memory Trace includes cache management operations and a Memory Order which are not under program control, but rather are controlled by the hardware.

The cache management operations may transfer data lines between cache and memory, and may also modify the data cache status. Like the memory references in the Execution Trace, these operations have a Type attribute and some additional attributes. A cache management operation must have one of the following five types, with the listed attributes in addition to its Type attribute:

Type	Description	Attributes
MoveIn	Move a line into cache. This operation takes a "snap-shot" of a line in memory and copies it into I-cache or D-cache.	Icache, Page, Line
MakePrivate	Change the data cache status from Public to PrivClean.	Page, Line
CopyOut	Copy a dirty line to memory, leaving a clean copy in cache.	Page, Line
MakePublic	Change the data cache status from PrivClean to Public.	Page, Line
Invalidate	Remove a copy of a line from I-cache or D-cache.	Icache, Page, Line

Implementations often combine several of these conceptual operations into a single hardware operation.

The Memory Trace is then a uniform set of operations, the Type of each operation being Load, Store, Flush, Sync, TLB_Purge, MoveIn, MakePrivate, CopyOut, MakePublic, or Invalidate. In all the formal notation in this Model, the variables x, y, and z are assumed to be members of the set of operations defined by the Memory Trace.

Memory Order

The Memory Trace includes a Memory Order relation that determines the order in which all operations "appear" to be executed by the memory system. This ordering interleaves the instruction orderings of the modules while allowing some specific reordering of the memory references issued by each module; in addition, it incorporates the cache management operations listed above.

The Memory Order relationship is a total ordering over the complete set of operations in the Memory Trace. Two operations in a given Memory Trace may be completely independent of each other, but they are still given an explicit (though arbitrary) ordering in the Memory Order relationship. We write O_i for the i-th operation in this total ordering. The index i is in the range $0 \leq i < \text{NumOpns}$, where NumOpns is the number of operations in the Memory Trace. The operations in the Memory Trace affect the state of the memory system. Thus the sequence of operations O_i results in a sequence of states $\text{State}(p,l,i)$, $0 \leq i < \text{NumOpns}$, for every line with page address p and line offset l within p, the initial state of the line being $\text{State}(p,l,0)$. For a given Execution Trace, the Memory Order and the cache management operations are constrained by a set of ordering rules, coherence rules and move-in rules that are stated later.

Function	Definition
O_i	The i-th operation in the Memory Trace.
$\text{State}(p,l,i)$	The state s of the line l on page p immediately prior to the execution of operation O_i.

Final Goal

The behavior of the memory system is observed through the values returned by the Load operations. Hence the ultimate goal of this Memory Model is to determine whether the values returned by the Load operations in a given Execution Trace are permissible in a correct memory system. An Execution Trace is said to be "OK in PA" if and only if there exists a Memory Trace that extends the Execution Trace as described above (and therefore includes its load values), and also satisfies the ordering rules, coherence rules, and move-in rules given in the following sections.

Definition
OK_in_PA(ExecutionTrace) =
there exists MemTrace such that
((MemTrace extends ExecutionTrace) and
ObeysRule1(ExecutionTrace,MemTrace) and
ObeysRule2(ExecutionTrace,MemTrace) and ...
)

We now define the order, coherence, and move-in rules. For clarity, the formal notation given here will avoid passing ExecutionTrace and MemTrace as parameters into every function, and will instead assume that the relationship "<" and the function O_i are globally defined to match the current ExecutionTrace and MemTrace. O_i, O_j, and O_k are arbitrary operations within the current MemTrace, unless otherwise specified. (Formally, free occurrences of the variables i, j, k are to be considered universally quantified over the range $0 \leq i,j,k < \text{NumOpns}$.) To simplify the notations, we define some more shorthand:

Notation	Abbreviation for	Description
Before(i)	State(Page(O_i),Line(O_i),i)	The state of a line *before* it is operated on by O_i
After(i)	State(Page(O_i),Line(O_i),i+1)	The state of a line *after* it is operated on by O_i

Note that Before(i) and After(i) refer implicitly to a specific line, the one that O_i is concerned with, and that this line changes from one operation O_i to the next. These notations are well-defined whenever Type(O_i) $\notin$ {Sync, TLB_Purge}, since Sync and TLB_Purge operations are the only ones that do not have both Page and Line attributes.

Order Rules

We define a relationship called OrderSensitive which represents the ordering requirements from the informal description at the beginning of this appendix. Pairs of operations for which this relationship holds are required to retain their relative ordering as they are processed by the memory system. In addition to the explicit rules stated in the informal description, there is the implicit requirement that all accesses from a single source to a single line are OrderSensitive. Note that the OrderSensitive function is neither symmetric nor transitive. Thus, OrderSensitive(x,y) does not necessarily imply OrderSensitive(y,x).

Definition

IsAccess(x) = (Type(x)=Load or Type(x)=Store or Type(x)=TLB_Purge)
IsLdOrSt(x) = (Type(x)=Load or Type(x)=Store)

StronglyOrdered(x,y) =
 (IsAccess(x) and IsAccess(y)) and
 (Strength(x)=Strong or Strength(y)=Strong)
Ordered(x,y) =
 (Type(x)=Load and Strength(x)=Ordered and IsAccess(y)) or
 (IsAccess(x) and Type(y)=Store and Strength(y)=Ordered) or
 (Type(x)=Store and Strength(x)=Ordered and Type(y)=Load and Strength(y)=Ordered)
FlushOrdered(x,y) =
 (IsLdOrSt(x) and Type(y)=Flush and Page(x)=Page(y) and Line(x)=Line(y)) or
 (Type(x)=TLB_Purge and Type(y)=Flush and Page(x)=Page(y))
SyncOrdered(x,y) =
 (Type(x)=Sync) or
 (Type(y)=Sync)
AccessOrdered(x,y) =
 (IsLdOrSt(x) and IsLdOrSt(y) and Source(x)=Source(y) and
  Page(x)=Page(y) and Line(x)=Line(y))

OrderSensitive(x,y) =
 (StronglyOrdered(x,y) or
  Ordered(x,y) or
  FlushOrdered(x,y) or
  SyncOrdered(x,y) or
  AccessOrdered(x,y)
)

Rule 1 is obeyed when the Memory Order relationship of MemTrace preserves the Instruction Order relationship of ExecutionTrace for all memory references which are considered OrderSensitive:

Rule 1 (Required ordering)

If OrderSensitive(O_i,O_j) and ($O_i < O_j$)
then ($i < j$).

If two operations are atomically linked as a semaphore in the Instruction Order, then Rule 2 states that they must be consecutive in the Memory Order:

Rule 2 (Semaphore atomicity)

If

$\quad\quad$ Source(O_i) = Source(O_j) and
$\quad\quad$ SemaLd(O_i) and
$\quad\quad$ RefNum(O_i)+1 = RefNum(O_j)

then (i+1 = j).

Coherence and Move-in Rules

The first rule in this section specifies that loads, flushes, syncs and TLB purges do not directly change the state of the memory system. (Flushes, however, change the state indirectly, by instructing the hardware to initiate cache line invalidations, as we shall see later.) The rule also specifies that an operation that concerns a specific line does not change the state of any other line. Note that syncs and TLB purges are the only operations that do not have a Line attribute.

Rule 3 (Stability)

For every p, l, if

$\quad\quad$ Type(O_i) $\in$ {Load, Flush, Sync, TLB_Purge} or
$\quad\quad$ (Type(O_i) $\notin$ {Sync, TLB_Purge} and Page(O_i) $\neq p$) or
$\quad\quad$ (Type(O_i) $\notin$ {Sync, TLB_Purge} and Line(O_i) $\neq l$)

then

$\quad\quad$ State(p,l,i+1) = State(p,l,i).

The following few rules concern move-ins. The Icache attribute of a move-in operation O_i specifies whether the operation is an instruction cache move-in (Icache(O_i)=T) or a data cache move-in (Icache(O_i)=F). The Value attribute gives the value of the cache line that is moved in. An instruction move-in may bring a copy of a line into an instruction-only or a combined cache, but not into a data-only cache. The copy of the line may be obtained from memory or from another cache of any kind, including a data-only cache. If the data cache status is private clean or private dirty, then an instruction move-in cannot result in an additional line value being added to the set of line values already present in the combined caches.

(Note that, although we mention line copies in the informal descriptions of the rules, the formal rules are concerned with *values of line copies*, rather than with the copies themselves.)

Rule 4 (Move-in to instruction caches)

If Type(O_i)=MoveIn and Icache(O_i)=T
then
    MemVal(After(i)) = MemVal(Before(i)) and
    Status(After(i)) = Status(Before(i)) and
    Value(O_i) ∈ AllCVs(Before(i)) ∪ {MemVal(Before(i))} and
    InstCVs(After(i)) = InstCVs(Before(i)) ∪ {Value(O_i)} and
    DonlyCVs(After(i)) = DonlyCVs(Before(i)) and
    if Status(Before(i)) ∈ {PrivClean, PrivDirty}
    then CombCVs(After(i)) = CombCVs(Before(i)).

A move-in operation to the data caches for a given line is only allowed when the data cache status for that line is Public. A data move-in may bring a copy of a line into a data-only or a combined cache, but not into an instruction-only cache. The copy of the line may be obtained from memory or from a cache other than an instruction-only cache.

Rule 5 (Move-in to data caches)

If
    Type(O_i) = MoveIn and
    Icache(O_i) = F
then
    Status(Before(i)) = Public and
    Status(After(i)) = Public and
    MemVal(After(i)) = MemVal(Before(i)) and
    IonlyCVs(After(i)) = IonlyCVs(Before(i)) and
    Value(O_i) ∈ DataCVs(Before(i)) ∪ {MemVal(Before(i))} and
    DataCVs(After(i)) = DataCVs(Before(i)) ∪ {Value(O_i)}.

The following move-in rules are a simplified version of what appears in Appendix F. Full details can be found there.

Move-ins are allowed or disallowed on a per-page basis. If a physical page belongs to I/O space, its lines cannot be moved in. Otherwise they can be moved in under two circumstances: (i) the physical page is the translation of a virtual page that is mapped cacheable, or (ii) the move-in is justified by an absolute reference. In the latter case, the absolute reference must be a store or data load to the same page (in the case of a data move-in), or an instruction load to the same or to the preceding page (in the case of an instruction move-in). Furthermore, the reference must precede the move-in with no intervening flush, or else the move-in must immediately precede the memory reference (with perhaps an intervening MakePrivate operation, since MakePrivate is separate from MoveIn in the Memory Model).

Rule 6 (Allowable instruction move-ins)

If

    $Type(O_i) = MoveIn$ and
    $Icache(O_i) = T$

then

    $Page(O_i) \notin IO\_Space$ and
    $(MappedCacheable(Page(O_i))$ or
    there exists $j < NumOpns$ such that
    $Virtual(O_j) = F$ and
    $Type(O_j) = Load$ and
    $Icache(O_j) = T$ and
    $Page(O_j) \in \{Page(O_i), Page(O_i)-1\}$ and
    $(j = i+1$ or

                $(\quad j < i$ and there is no k such that

    $j < k < i$ and
    $Type(O_k) = Flush$ and
    $Icache(O_k) = T$ and
    $Page(O_k) = Page(O_i)$
    $)))$.

Rule 7 (Allowable data move-ins)

If

    $Type(O_i) = MoveIn$ and
    $Icache(O_i) = F$

then

    $Page(O_i) \notin IO\_Space$ and
    $(MappedCacheable(Page(O_i))$ or
    there exists $j < NumOpns$ such that
    $Virtual(O_j) = F$ and
    $Type(O_j) \in \{Load, Store\}$ and
    $Icache(O_j) = F$ and
    $Page(O_j) = Page(O_i)$ and
    $(j = i+1$ or
    $(j = i+2$ and $Type(O_{i+1}) = MakePrivate)$ or
    $(j < i$ and there is no k such that
    $j < k < i$ and
    $Type(O_k) = Flush$ and
    $Icache(O_k) = F$ and
    $Page(O_k) = Page(O_i)$
    $)))$.

A MakePrivate operation on a given line may take place when the data cache status for the line is Public and there is only one distinct line value in the data-only and combined caches. (If there are more than one, hardware may use invalidations to reduce the number to one prior to executing the MakePrivate operation; MakePrivate and those preceding invalidations are usually combined into a single hardware operation.)

Rule 8 (MakePrivate)

If

$\quad\quad$ Type(O_i) = MakePrivate

then

$\quad\quad$ Status(Before(i)) = Public and
$\quad\quad$ (there exists w such that DataCVs(Before(i)) = $\{w\}$) and
$\quad\quad$ Status(After(i)) = PrivClean and
$\quad\quad$ MemVal(After(i)) = MemVal(Before(i)) and
$\quad\quad$ IonlyCVs(After(i)) = IonlyCVs(Before(i)) and
$\quad\quad$ CombCVs(After(i)) = CombCVs(Before(i)) and
$\quad\quad$ DonlyCVs(After(i)) = DonlyCVs(Before(i)).

A CopyOut operation on a given line may take place when the data cache status for the line is PrivDirty, the resulting status being PrivClean. The rule asserts that the value of the line in memory after the operation is one of the values of the line in the data-only or combined caches before the operation. In fact, when the data cache status is private (clean or dirty), there is only one such value; this is not asserted by any one rule, but it follows globally from the set of rules, as we shall see at the end of the section (cf. Theorem 1).

Rule 9 (CopyOut)

If

$\quad\quad$ Type(O_i) = CopyOut

then

$\quad\quad$ Status(Before(i)) = PrivDirty and
$\quad\quad$ Status(After(i)) = PrivClean and
$\quad\quad$ MemVal(After(i)) $\in$ DataCVs(Before(i)) and
$\quad\quad$ IonlyCVs(After(i)) = IonlyCVs(Before(i)) and
$\quad\quad$ CombCVs(After(i)) = CombCVs(Before(i)) and
$\quad\quad$ DonlyCVs(After(i)) = DonlyCVs(Before(i)).

A MakePublic operation for a given line may take place when the data cache status is PrivClean for that line.

Rule 10 (MakePublic)

If

$\quad\quad$ Type(O_i) = MakePublic

then

$\quad\quad$ Status(Before(i)) = PrivClean and
$\quad\quad$ Status(After(i)) = Public and
$\quad\quad$ MemVal(After(i)) = MemVal(Before(i)) and
$\quad\quad$ IonlyCVs(After(i)) = IonlyCVs(Before(i)) and
$\quad\quad$ CombCVs(After(i)) = CombCVs(Before(i)) and
$\quad\quad$ DonlyCVs(After(i)) = DonlyCVs(Before(i)).

Hardware is allowed to perform invalidations at any time. The intended meaning of an Invalidate operation is the removal of *one* copy rather than *all* copies. Removing all copies from the cache structure, or from the instruction-only caches, combined caches, or data-only caches, can be accomplished by multiple invalidations, but it is not an atomic hardware operation.

If O_i is an Invalidate operation, then $Icache(O_i) = T$ is used to indicate that the invalidation occurs in an instruction-only cache, while $Icache(O_i) = F$ is used to indicate that it occurs in a combined or data-only cache.

Rule 11 (Invalidate copy in an instruction-only cache)

If

      $Type(O_i) = $ Invalidate and
      $Icache(O_i) = T$

then

      $Status(After(i)) = Status(Before(i))$ and
      $MemVal(After(i)) = MemVal(Before(i))$ and
      $IonlyCVs(After(i)) \subseteq IonlyCVs(Before(i))$ and
      $CombCVs(After(i)) = CombCVs(Before(i))$ and
      $DonlyCVs(After(i)) = DonlyCVs(Before(i))$.

In the case of a data or combined cache, an invalidation is allowed only if the data cache status is public. If the status is private clean, a MakePublic must be done first, and if the status is private dirty, an invalidation must be preceded by a CopyOut and a MakePublic. Hardware often combines these conceptual operations into a single hardware transaction.

Rule 12 (Invalidate copy in a data or combined cache)

If

      $Type(O_i) = $ Invalidate and
      $Icache(O_i) = F$

then

      $Status(Before(i)) = $ Public and
      $Status(After(i)) = $ Public and
      $MemVal(After(i)) = MemVal(Before(i))$ and
      $IonlyCVs(After(i)) = IonlyCVs(Before(i))$ and
      $CombCVs(After(i)) \subseteq CombCVs(Before(i))$ and
      $DonlyCVs(After(i)) \subseteq DonlyCVs(Before(i))$.

A flush operation O_i for a given line causes no immediate change in the state of the line, but it instructs the hardware to perform a series of invalidations of copies of the line. An instruction flush operation, indicated by $Icache(O_i) = T$, is a request to invalidate all copies in the instruction-only and combined caches. A subsequent Sync operation must wait for these invalidations to be completed. Thus, in the state before the Sync, any copies of the line in those caches must be new copies, brought into the caches by move-ins following the Flush.

Rule 13 (Flush instruction cache)

If

$\quad$ $\text{Type}(O_i) = \text{Flush and}$
$\quad$ $\text{Icache}(O_i) = \text{T and}$
$\quad$ $\text{Type}(O_k) = \text{Sync and}$
$\quad$ $O_i < O_k$

then

$\quad$ for every $w \in \text{InstCVs}(\text{State}(\text{Page}(O_i),\text{Line}(O_i),k))$
$\quad$ there exists j in the range $i < j < k$ such that
$\quad$ $\text{Type}(O_j) = \text{MoveIn and}$
$\quad$ $\text{Page}(O_j) = \text{Page}(O_i)$ and
$\quad$ $\text{Line}(O_j) = \text{Line}(O_i)$ and
$\quad$ $\text{Value}(O_j) = w.$

A data flush operation, indicated by $\text{Icache}(O_i) = \text{F}$, is a request to invalidate all copies in the data-only and combined caches. A subsequent Sync operation must wait for these invalidations to be completed. Thus, in the state before the Sync, any copies of the line in those caches must be new copies, brought into the caches by move-ins following the Flush.

Rule 14 (Flush data cache)

If

$\quad$ $\text{Type}(O_i) = \text{Flush and}$
$\quad$ $\text{Icache}(O_i) = \text{F and}$
$\quad$ $\text{Type}(O_k) = \text{Sync and}$
$\quad$ $O_i < O_k$

then

$\quad$ for every $w \in \text{DataCVs}(\text{State}(\text{Page}(O_i),\text{Line}(O_i),k))$
$\quad$ there exists j in the range $i < j < k$ such that
$\quad$ $\text{Type}(O_j) = \text{MoveIn and}$
$\quad$ $\text{Page}(O_j) = \text{Page}(O_i)$ and
$\quad$ $\text{Line}(O_j) = \text{Line}(O_i)$ and
$\quad$ $\text{Value}(O_j) = w.$

A non-coherent store to a given line modifies the memory copy of the line.

Rule 15 (Non-coherent store)

If

$\quad$ $\text{Type}(O_i) = \text{Store and}$
$\quad$ $\text{Coherent}(O_i) = \text{F}$

then

$\quad$ $\text{Status}(\text{After}(i)) = \text{Status}(\text{Before}(i))$ and
$\quad$ $\text{MemVal}(\text{After}(i)) = \text{Put}(\text{MemVal}(\text{Before}(i)),\text{Byte}(O_i),\text{Value}(O_i))$ and
$\quad$ $\text{IonlyCVs}(\text{After}(i)) = \text{IonlyCVs}(\text{Before}(i))$ and
$\quad$ $\text{CombCVs}(\text{After}(i)) = \text{CombCVs}(\text{Before}(i))$ and
$\quad$ $\text{DonlyCVs}(\text{After}(i)) = \text{DonlyCVs}(\text{Before}(i)).$

If the data cache status of a given line is private (clean or dirty), then a coherent store modifies the copy or copies of the line present in the data or combined caches, the resulting status being private dirty.

Even though the status is private, there may be multiple copies: for example, there could be a valid copy in a level-1 cache and a valid copy in the corresponding level-2 cache. However, as we shall see later, it follows globally from the set of rules that there must be only one distinct value for the line in the data or combined caches. Thus, if there are multiple valid copies, they must have the same value. A coherent store modifies this unique value in each of those copies.

Rule 16 (Coherent store to cache)

If

$\text{Type}(O_i)=\text{Store}$ and
$\text{Coherent}(O_i) = \text{T}$ and
$\text{Status}(\text{Before}(i)) \in \{\text{PrivClean, PrivDirty}\}$

then

$\text{Status}(\text{After}(i)) = \text{PrivDirty}$ and
$\text{MemVal}(\text{After}(i)) = \text{MemVal}(\text{Before}(i))$ and
$\text{IonlyCVs}(\text{After}(i)) = \text{IonlyCVs}(\text{Before}(i))$ and
for every w
(if $\text{CombCVs}(\text{Before}(i)) = \{w\}$ then $\text{CombCVs}(\text{After}(i)) = \{\text{Put}(w,\text{Byte}(O_i),\text{Value}(O_i))\}$) and
(if $\text{CombCVs}(\text{Before}(i)) = \varnothing$ then $\text{CombCVs}(\text{After}(i)) = \varnothing$) and
(if $\text{DonlyCVs}(\text{Before}(i)) = \{w\}$ then $\text{DonlyCVs}(\text{After}(i)) = \{\text{Put}(w,\text{Byte}(O_i),\text{Value}(O_i))\}$) and
(if $\text{DonlyCVs}(\text{Before}(i)) = \varnothing$ then $\text{DonlyCVs}(\text{After}(i)) = \varnothing$).

If the data cache status is public, a coherent store is allowed to write directly to memory, but only if there are no copies of the line in the data-only or combined caches. It then has the same effect as a non-coherent store. (The concept of a coherent store to memory is included for the sake of completeness. It may be useful in implementations where some of the processors have no data cache, while others do.)

Rule 17 (Coherent store to memory)

If

$\text{Type}(O_i) = \text{Store}$ and
$\text{Coherent}(O_i) = \text{T}$ and
$\text{Status}(\text{Before}(i)) = \text{Public}$

then

$\text{DataCVs}(\text{Before}(i)) = \varnothing$ and
$\text{Status}(\text{After}(i)) = \text{Public}$ and
$\text{MemVal}(\text{After}(i)) = \text{Put}(\text{MemVal}(\text{Before}(i)),\text{Byte}(O_i),\text{Value}(O_i))$ and
$\text{IonlyCVs}(\text{After}(i)) = \text{IonlyCVs}(\text{Before}(i))$ and
$\text{DataCVs}(\text{After}(i)) = \varnothing$.

An instruction load from a given line may get its value from memory or from any copy of the line in an instruction or combined cache.

Rule 18 (Value returned by instruction load)

If

$\text{Type}(O_i) = \text{Load}$ and
$\text{Icache}(O_i) = \text{T}$

then

there exists $w \in \{\text{MemVal}(\text{Before}(i))\} \cup \text{InstCVs}(\text{Before}(i))$ such that
$\text{Value}(O_i) = \text{Get}(w,\text{Byte}(O_i),\text{Size}(O_i))$.

A non-coherent data-load is allowed to obtain its value from memory or a data-only or combined cache.

Rule 19 (Value returned by non-coherent data load)

If

$\quad$ Type(O_i) = Load and

$\quad$ Icache(O_i) = F and

$\quad$ Coherent(O_i) = F

then

$\quad$ there exists $w \in$ {MemVal(Before(i))} $\cup$ DataCVs(Before(i)) such that

$\quad$ Value(O_i) = Get(w,Byte(O_i),Size(O_i)).

A coherent data load from a given line may get its value from memory or from any copy of the line in a data-only or combined cache. However, if the data cache status is PrivDirty, then a copy of the line in a data or combined cache must be used. As mentioned earlier, it follows from the global set of rules that there is only one distinct value of the line in the data-only and combined caches.

Rule 20 (Value returned by coherent data load)

If

$\quad$ Type(O_i) = Load and

$\quad$ Icache(O_i) = F and

$\quad$ Coherent(O_i) = T

then

$\quad$ there exists w such that

$\quad$ Value(O_i) = Get(w,Byte(O_i),Size(O_i)).

and

$\quad$ if Status(Before(i)) = PrivDirty

$\quad$ then $w \in$ DataCVs(Before(i))

$\quad$ else $w \in$ DataCVs(Before(i)) $\cup$ {MemVal(Before(i))}.

In the initial state, all caches must be empty, and the data cache status must be public.

Rule 21 (Initial State)

For every $p, l,$

$\quad$ Status(State($p,l,0$)) = Public and

$\quad$ IonlyCVs(State($p,l,0$)) = $\varnothing$ and

$\quad$ CombCVs(State($p,l,0$)) = $\varnothing$ and

$\quad$ DonlyCVs(State($p,l,0$)) = $\varnothing$.

This ends the rules of the Memory Model. Additional architectural rules are derivable as logical consequences of these rules. As an example, the next section proves a sample theorem.

Proof of Coherence for Private Lines

> Theorem 1 (Coherence of private lines)
>
> If a memory trace obeys the coherence and move-in rules, then for every $i <$ NumOpns, for every physical page address p, and for every line offset l, if $s =$ State(p,l,i) and Status(s) $\in$ {PrivClean, PrivDirty}, then the set DataCVs(s) has exactly one element.

PROOF. For arbitrary p and l, we prove by induction on i the invariant: if $s =$ Status(p,l,i), then either Status(s) = Public or DataCVs(s) has one element.

The invariant holds for the initial state, since

$$\text{Status(State}(p,l,0)) = \text{Public}.$$

Assume that it holds for $i <$ NumOpns and let $s' =$ State($p,l,i+1$). We reason by cases on the operation O_i. If $s' = s$, then the invariant holds for $i+1$; hence we need only consider operations that change the state of the line addressed by p and l. By Rule 3 such an operation must be a store or a cache management operation concerning the line. We check now that in every case the invariant holds for $i+1$.

By Rule 15, if O_i is a non-coherent store, then Status(s') = Status(s) and DataCVs(s') = DataCVs(s), Hence, since the invariant holds for i by induction hypothesis, it holds for $i+1$.

By Rule 16, if O_i is a coherent store to cache, then Status(s) $\in$ {PrivClean, PrivDirty}. In that case, by the induction hypothesis, DataCVs(s) has one element. This means that either

$$\text{DonlyCVs}(s) = \text{CombCVs}(s) = \{w\} \text{ or}$$

$$(\text{DonlyCVs}(s) = \{w\} \text{ and CombCVs}(s) = \varnothing) \text{ or}$$

$$(\text{DonlyCVs}(s) = \varnothing \text{ and CombCVs}(s) = \{w\})$$

for some line value w. Then, again by Rule 16, we have

$$\text{DonlyCVs}(s) = \text{CombCVs}(s) = \{w'\} \text{ or}$$

$$(\text{DonlyCVs}(s) = \{w'\} \text{ and CombCVs}(s) = \varnothing) \text{ or}$$

$$(\text{DonlyCVs}(s) = \varnothing \text{ and CombCVs}(s) = \{w'\})$$

respectively, with

$$w' = \text{Put}(w, \text{Byte}(O_i), \text{Value}(O_i)).$$

Hence DataCVs(s') has one element, and the invariant holds for $i+1$.

By Rule 17, if O_i is a coherent store to memory, then Status(s') = Public, and hence the invariant holds for $i+1$.

By Rule 4, if O_i is a move-in to the instruction caches, Status(s) = Status(s'). Hence if Status(s) = Public, then Status(s') = Public, and the invariant holds for $i+1$. If, on the other hand, Status(s) $\in$ {PrivClean, PrivDirty}, then DataCVs(s) must have one element by induction hypothesis, and Rule 4 specifies in this case that CombCVs(s') = CombCVs(s), in addition to the requirement that DonlyCVs(s) = DonlyCVs(s') which applies to any status. Thus DataCVs(s') coincides with DataCVs(s) and therefore has one element.

By Rule 5, if O_i is a move-in to the data caches, then Status(s') = Public, and hence the invariant holds for i+1.

By Rule 8, if O_i is a MakePrivate operation, then DataCVs(s) has one element, and DataCVs(s') = DataCVs(s). Hence DataCVs(s') has one element and the invariant is satisfied for i+1.

By Rule 9, if O_i is a CopyOut operation, then Status(s) = PrivDirty. Hence, by induction hypothesis, DataCVs(s) must have one element. But, by Rule 9 again, DataCVs(s') coincides with DataCVs(s). Thus DataCVs(s') has one element, and the invariant holds for i+1.

By Rule 10, if O_i is a MakePublic operation, then Status(s') = Public and the invariant holds for i+1.

By Rule 11, if O_i is an invalidation in an instruction-only cache, then

> Status(s') = Status(s) and
>
> DataCVs(s') = DataCVs(s).

Hence, since the invariant holds for i by induction hypothesis, it holds for i+1.

Finally, by Rule 12, if O_i is an invalidation in a data or combined cache, then Status(s') = Public and the invariant holds for i+1.

We have now examined all cases, and thus completed the induction step and the proof.

H   Address Formation Details

This appendix provides detailed descriptions and illustrations of how various types of addresses are formed in a PA-RISC processor.

Memory Reference Instruction Address Formation

Addresses are formed by the combination of a Space ID and an address Offset. Address Offsets may be formed as the sum of a base register and any one of the following: a long displacement, a short displacement (which leaves more instruction bits for other functions), or an index register.

Long Displacement Addressing

Memory reference instruction formats that have long displacements form the effective memory reference address by adding a displacement to a base value specified through the instruction. The entity being transferred can be a doubleword, word, halfword, or a byte.

The displacement can be any of the following:

- a 16-bit byte displacement (restricted to 14 bits when PSW W-bit =0)
- a 12-bit word displacement for word loads and stores
- an 11-bit doubleword displacement for doubleword loads and stores.

The opcode specifies the particular data transfer to be performed and the form of the displacement. The displacements are encoded in two's complement notation with the sign bit always placed in instruction bit 31. The formats for long displacement instructions are:

op	b	t/r	s	im14		
6	5	5	2	14		

op	b	t/r	s	im11a	op	i
6	5	5	2	11	2	1

op	b	t/r	s	im10a	m	op	i
6	5	5	2	10	1	2	1

Space selection is done differently for 64-bit programs (when the PSW W-bit is 1) than it is for 32-bit programs (when the PSW W-bit is 0). For 64-bit programs, there is little need for providing direct user program access to an address space larger than 64 bits. Therefore, it is anticipated that most programs (other than system software) will use only implicit pointers. For this reason, for 64-bit programs, all long displacement loads and stores inherently compute their addresses as implicit pointers, and the s-field is used to extend the displacement by 2 bits, providing an effective 16-bit displacement. When the s-field is used to encode more displacement bits, they are encoded in a special fashion in order to. allow the encoding for displacements which do not require the additional 2 bits of range to be the same for 32-bit and for 64-bit programs. (See the function "assemble_16" in "Instruction Notation Control Structures" on page E-1 for more details on encoding.) For 32-bit programs, the s-field simply specifies the space register.

When data translation is enabled, the effective space ID is the contents of a selected space register. If the PSW W-bit is 0 (a 32-bit program), and the s-field is non-zero, the space register is selected directly by the s-field (explicit pointer). If the PSW W-bit is 0 and the s-field is 0, the effective space ID is the contents of the space register whose number is the sum of 4 plus bits 32..33 of GR b (implicit 32-bit pointer). If the PSW W-bit is 1 (a 64-bit program), the effective space ID is the contents of the space register whose number is the sum of 4 plus bits 0..1 of GR b (implicit 64-bit pointer). When data translation is disabled, no space register selection is done and the offset is used directly as the address.

The effective offset is the sum of the contents of GR b and the sign-extended displacement d. For 32-bit programs, the offset is truncated to 32 bits (the upper 32 bits are forced to 0).

The address calculation is shown in Figure H-1 and Figure H-2 in three parts: Figure H-1 shows space identifier selection, and Figure H-2 shows offset computation. Space and offset are then bit-wise ORed, as shown in Figure H-3 to form the full virtual address.

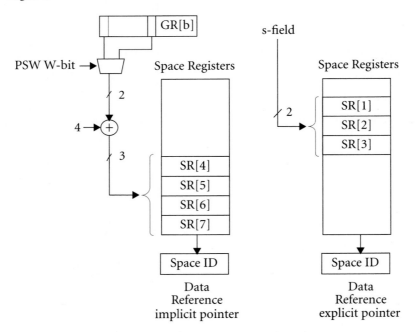

Figure H-1. Space Identifier Selection

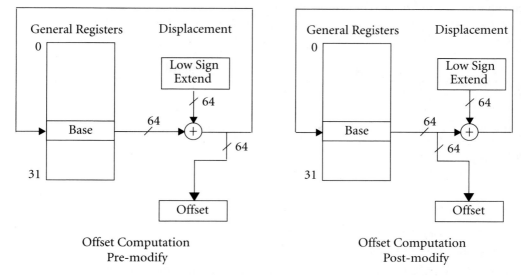

Figure H-2. Offset computation with long displacement

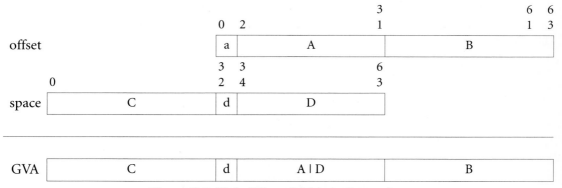

Figure H-3. Global Virtual Address Formation

Base register modification can be optionally performed, and can either be done before or after the offset calculation, as shown in Figure H-2. Base register modification is specified by the opcode, or in the case of doubleword loads and stores, by the m-field.

Short Displacement Addressing

This section describes memory reference instruction formats, where the effective memory reference address is formed by the addition of a short 5-bit displacement to a base value specified in the instruction. The sign bit of the short displacement is the rightmost bit of the 5-bit field, which is in two's complement notation. The entity being transferred can be a doubleword, word, halfword, or a byte.

The format of the short displacement load instructions is:

03	b	im5	s	a	1	cc	ext4	m	t
6	5	5	2	1	1	2	4	1	5

and that of the short displacement stores is:

03	b	r	s	a	1	cc	ext4	m	im5
6	5	5	2	1	1	2	4	1	5

The *ext4* field in the instruction format above specifies a load or a store and the data size. The *a* and *m* fields specify the following functions:

$a = 0$ modify after if m = 1.
    $= 1$ modify before if m = 1.

$m = 0$ no address modification.
    $= 1$ address modification.

In addition the combination $a = 0$, $m = 1$, and $im5 = 0$ specifies an ordered load or store.

The *cc* field specifies the cache control hint (see Table 6-7 on page 6-10, Table 6-8 on page 6-10, and Table 6-9 on page 6-11).

In the instruction descriptions that follow, some information is coded into the instruction names and the remainder is coded in the completer field (denoted by *cmplt* in the descriptions). Table H-1 lists the assembly language syntax of the completer, the functions performed, and the values coded into the *a*, *m*, and *im5* bit fields of the instruction.

Table H-1. Short Displacement Load and Store Instruction Completers

cmplt	Description	a	m	im5
<none>	don't modify base register	x	0	x
MA	Modify base register After	0	1	$\neq 0$
MB	Modify base register Before	1	1	x
O	Ordered access	0	1	0

Notes: x indicates don't care.

In the above table, *cmplt* is in assembly language format and *a*, *m*, and *im5* are in machine language format.

The space identifier is computed like any other data memory reference (see Figure H-1 on page H-2). The calculation of the offset portion of the effective address for different completers is shown in Figure H-4. Space and offset are combined like any other data memory reference (see Figure H-3 on page H-3).

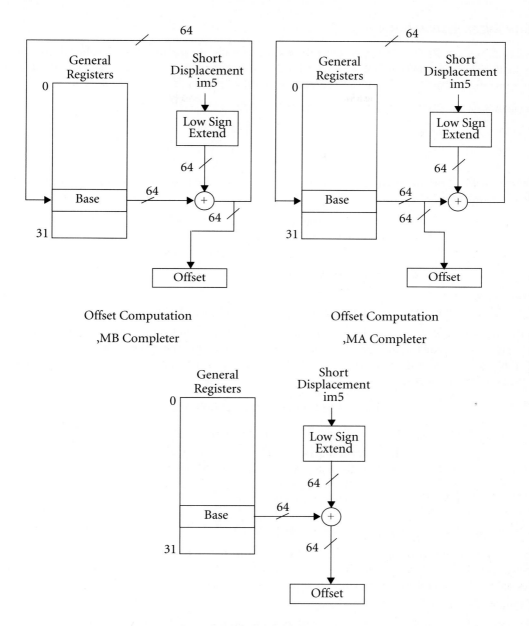

Offset Computation

,MB Completer

Offset Computation

,MA Completer

Offset Computation

No Completer Specified

Figure H-4. Offset computation with short displacement

Store Bytes Instructions

STORE BYTES and STORE DOUBLEWORD BYTES provide the means for doing unaligned byte moves efficiently. These instructions use a short 5-bit displacement to store bytes to unaligned destinations. The short displacement field is in two's complement notation with the sign bit as its rightmost bit.

The format of the STORE BYTES and STORE DOUBLEWORD BYTES instructions is:

03	b	r	s	a	1	cc	ext4	m	im5
6	5	5	2	1	1	2	4	1	5

The *ext4* field in the instruction format above specifies the data size. The a and m fields specify the following functions:

a	= 0	store bytes beginning at the effective byte address in the word or doubleword.
	= 1	store bytes ending at the effective byte address in the word or doubleword.
m	= 0	no address modification.
	= 1	address modification.

The *cc* field specifies the cache control hint (see Table H-2 on page H-6).

In the instruction descriptions that follow, some information is coded into the instruction names and the remainder is coded in the completer field (denoted by *cmplt* in the descriptions). Table H-2 lists the assembly language syntax of the completer, the functions performed, and the values coded into the a and m fields of the instruction.

Table H-2. Store Bytes Instruction Completers

cmplt	Description	a	m
<none> or B	Beginning case, don't modify base register	0	0
B,M	Beginning case, Modify base register	0	1
E	Ending case, don't modify base register	1	0
E,M	Ending case, Modify base register	1	1

In the above table, *cmplt* is in assembly language format and a and m are in machine language format.

The space identifier is computed like any other data memory reference (see Figure H-1 on page H-2). The calculation of the offset portion of the effective address for different completers is shown in Figure H-5. Space and offset are combined like any other data memory reference (see Figure H-3 on page H-3).

The actual offset and modified address involves some alignment and other considerations. Refer to the instruction description pages for an exact definition.

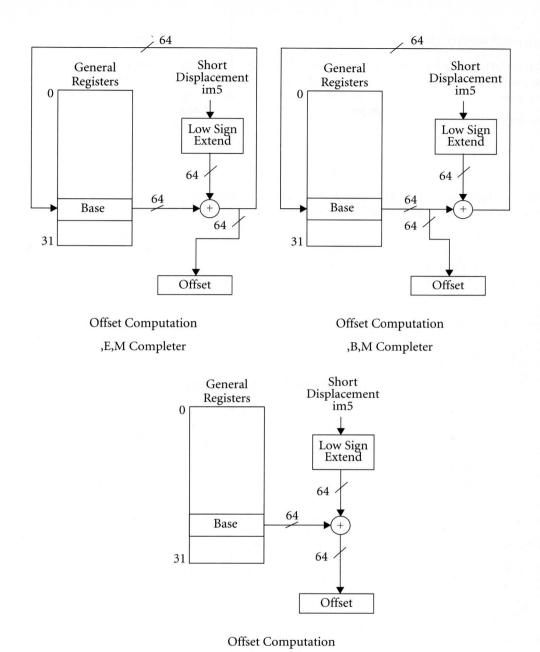

Figure H-5. Offset computation for Store Bytes and Store Doubleword Bytes

Indexed Addressing

This section describes memory reference instruction formats, where the effective memory reference address is formed by the addition of an index value to a base value specified in the instruction. The entity being transferred can be a doubleword, word, halfword, or a byte.

The format for indexed instructions is:

03	b	x	s	u	0	cc	ext4	m	t
6	5	5	2	1	1	2	4	1	5

The u field specifies is the index register is shifted by the data size specified in the $ext4$ field and the m field specifies if base register modification is performed.

Index shift by data size means that the index value (contents of GR x) is multiplied by the size of the data item being referenced - 1 if it is a byte, 2 for a halfword, 4 for a word, and 8 for a doubleword (these correspond to shifts by 0, 1, 2, and 3 bits, respectively). Base register modification also results in the contents of GR b being replaced by the sum of the index value and the previous contents of GR b.

The cc field specifies the cache control hint (see Table 6-7 on page 6-10 and Table 6-9 on page 6-11).

In the instruction descriptions, the term $cmplt$ is used to denote the completer which is encoded in the u and m fields. The list of completers and the address formation functions they specify appear in Table H-3.

Table H-3. Indexed Instruction Completers

cmplt	Description	u	m
\<none>	no index shift, don't modify base register	0	0
M	no index shift, Modify base register	0	1
S	Shift index by data size, don't modify base register	1	0
SM or S,M	Shift index by data size, Modify base register	1	1

In the above table, $cmplt$ is in assembly language format and u and m are in machine language format.

The space identifier is computed like any other data memory reference (see Figure H-1 on page H-2). The calculation of the offset portion of the effective address for different completers is shown in Figure H-6. Space and offset are combined like any other data memory reference (see Figure H-3 on page H-3).

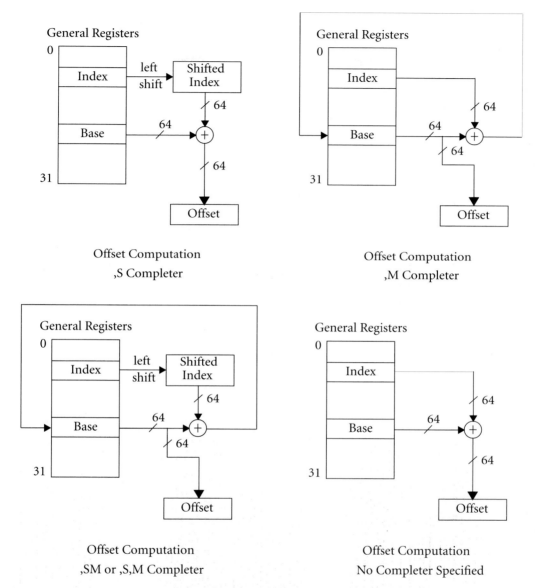

Figure H-6. Offset computation with indexed addressing

Absolute Address Formation

The formation of absolute addresses varies depending on the setting of the PSW W-bit which specifies whether the system is to support full 64-bit offsets or the 32-bit offsets compatible with PA-RISC 1.0 and 1.1 systems.

Absolute Accesses when PSW W-bit is 1

When the PSW W-bit is 1 (see "Processor Status Word (PSW)" on page 2-7 for the definition of the PSW W-bit), an absolute address is a 62-bit unsigned integer whose value is the address of the lowest-addressed byte of the operand it designates (see Figure H-7).

ne	Absolute Byte Address
2	62

Figure H-7. 62-bit Absolute Pointer

The 2-bit *ne* field is a non-existent field (i.e., software may write any value, but hardware implementations must ignore them).

A 64-bit physical address is formed by extending a 62-bit absolute address as shown in Figure H-8 and described by the following pseudo-code:

```
if (abs_addr{2..9} != 0xF0) {              /* if not in PDC Address Space */
    phys_addr{2..63} ← abs_addr{2..63};
    if (abs_addr{2..5} == 0xF)             /* if I/O Address Space */
        phys_addr{0..1} ← 0x3;
    else                                   /* if Memory Address Space */
        phys_addr{0..1} ← 0x0;
} else {                                   /* if PDC Address Space */
    phys_addr{0..7} ← 0xF0;
    phys_addr{8..9} ← processor-specific;
    phys_addr{10..63} ← abs_addr{10..63};
}
```

NOTE

Restricting absolute addresses when the PSW W-bit is 1 to 62 bits in size enables software to access any objects in a quarter of the 64-bit Physical Address Space by two means:

- Using a 62-bit absolute address

- Using a virtual address which implicitly uses any of Space Registers 4 through 7.

Maintaining a 64-bit virtual address space enables software to virtually access hardware subsystems such as I/O busses which define 64 bit physical addresses.

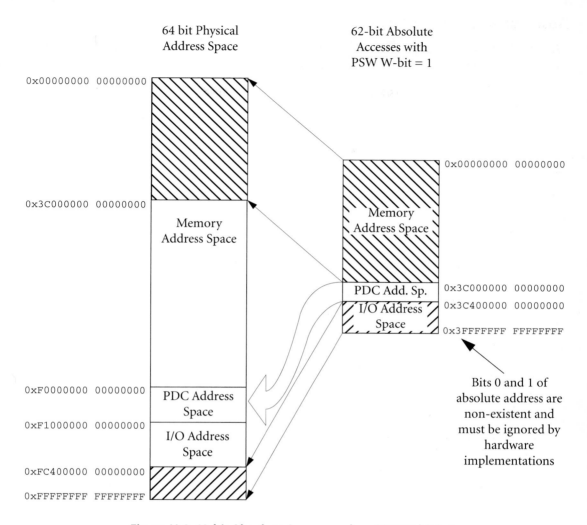

Figure H-8. 62-bit Absolute Accesses when PSW W-bit is 1

Absolute Accesses when PSW W-bit is 0

When the PSW W-bit is 0, an absolute address is a 32-bit unsigned integer whose value is the address of the lowest-addressed byte of the operand it designates (see Figure H-9)

non-existent	Absolute Byte Address
32	32

Figure H-9. 32-bit Absolute Pointer

A 64-bit physical address is formed by extending the 32-bit Absolute Address as shown in Figure H-10 and described by the following pseudo-code:

```
if (abs_addr{32..39} != 0xF0) {                    /* if not in PDC Address Space */
    phys_addr{32..63} ← abs_addr{32..63};
    if (abs_addr{32..35} == 0xF)                        /* if I/O Address Space */
        phys_addr{0..31} ← 0xFFFFFFFF;
    else                                             /* if Memory Address Space */
        phys_addr{0..31} ← 0x00000000;
} else {                                              /* if PDC Address Space */
    phys_addr{0..7} ← 0xF0;
    phys_addr{8..39} ← processor-specific;
    phys_addr{40..63} ← abs_addr{40..63};
}
```

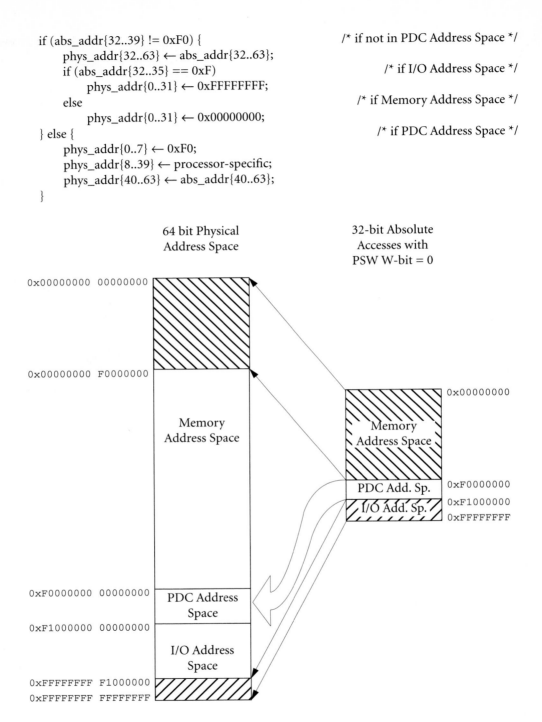

Figure H-10. 32-bit Absolute Accesses when PSW W-bit is 0

Figure H-11 illustrates the relationship between the 64-bit Physical Address Space, absolute accesses when the PSW W-bit is 0, and an example, 40-bit, implemented physical address space.

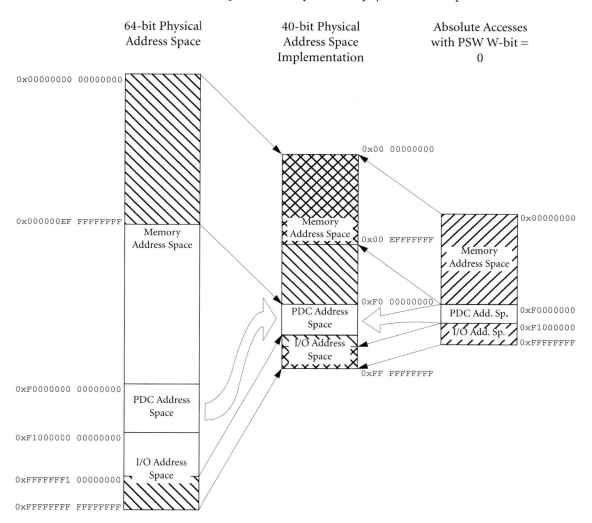

Figure H-11. Physical Address Space Mapping - An Example

I

Programming Notes

This appendix is a collection of programming tips and notes that provide brief examples of how to effectively use the PA-RISC instruction set to accomplish commonly needed operations.

The following topics are covered:

- privilege level changes
- testing the current state of the PSW[W] bit
- branching
- static branch prediction
- returning from interruption
- trap handlers
- reserved op exception
- endian byte swapping
  - halfword byte swap
  - word byte swap
  - doubleword byte swap

Privilege Level Changes

Branch instructions may change the privilege level depending on the type of branch performed. Since privilege levels are determined by the two rightmost bits in the offset part of the instruction address, privilege level changes are a function of the offset computation.

Since a branch instruction may be executed in the delay slot of another branch instruction, an interesting case arises because of the way the privilege level changes are defined to take effect.

Consider the case where a taken IA relative branch is placed in the delay slot of a base relative branch that lowers the privilege level of its target instruction. First, the base relative branch will execute and schedule change of privilege level for its target. Then, in the delay slot, the IA relative branch will execute and it will schedule its target to execute at the same privilege level as its own. Then, the target of the base relative branch will execute at the new (demoted) privileged level. The next instruction, however, which is the target of the IA relative branch, will have the same privilege level as that of the IA relative branch, and thus will cause the privilege level to be restored to the original (higher) value as shown in the following:

PROGRAM SEGMENT		
Location	Instruction	Comment
100	STW r7, 0(r8)	; non-branch instruction
104	BV r0(r7)	; branch vectored to 200 and change priv -> 2
108	BLR r4, r0	; IA relative branch to location 400
10C	ADD r2,r6, r9	; next instruction in linear code sequence
.	.	
.	.	
.	.	
200	LDW 0(r3), r11	; target of branch vectored instruction
.	.	
.	.	
.	.	
400	LDW 0(r15), r4	; target of IA relative branch instruction
404	STW r4, 0(r18)	

EXECUTION SEQUENCE		
Location	Instruction	Comment
100	STW r7, 0(r8)	; priv = 0
104	BV r0(r7)	; priv = 0
108	BLR r4, r0	; priv = 0
200	LDW 0(r3), r11	; priv = 2 decreased by branch vectored instr
400	LDW 0(r15), r4	; priv = 0 changed back by IA relative branch
404	STW r4, 0(r18)	; priv = 0

Testing the Current State of the PSW W-Bit

Some code may wish to be callable from code which may be running with either narrow or wide addressing.

The following instruction sequence can be used to determine whether wide 64-bit address generation is enabled. The value of PSW[W] is returned in register r28 (0=narrow, 1=wide).

PROGRAM SEGMENT		
Location	Instruction	Comment
100	ADDB,*=,N %r0,%r0,%label	; branch if narrow addressing
104	BV 0(2)	; return

PROGRAM SEGMENT			
108	LDI	1,%r28	; return a 1
label:			
10C	BV	0(2)	; return
110	LDI	0,%r28	; return a 0

Procedure Call and Return

Example instruction sequences which perform the different types of procedure calls are shown below. The following examples illustrate ways to use offsets of different lengths. The simplest case is that of intraspace calls which can be done by any of the following code sequences, assuming that the convention that SR 4 tracks IASQ is observed:

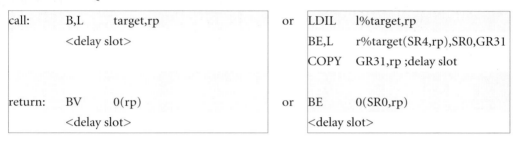

```
call:    B,L      target,rp            or   LDIL    l%target,rp
         <delay slot>                       BE,L    r%target(SR4,rp),SR0,GR31
                                            COPY    GR31,rp ;delay slot


return:  BV       0(rp)               or   BE      0(SR0,rp)
         <delay slot>                       <delay slot>
```

Making interspace calls which might decrease privilege level is shown below:

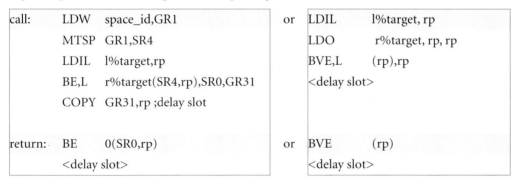

```
call:    LDW    space_id,GR1           or   LDIL      l%target, rp
         MTSP   GR1,SR4                      LDO       r%target, rp, rp
         LDIL   l%target,rp                  BVE,L     (rp),rp
         BE,L   r%target(SR4,rp),SR0,GR31    <delay slot>
         COPY   GR31,rp ;delay slot


return:  BE     0(SR0,rp)             or   BVE       (rp)
         <delay slot>                       <delay slot>
```

Static Branch Prediction

Branch prediction is quite important to overall performance. PA-RISC includes a set of conventions which allow the programmer to indicate whether a particular branch is more likely to be taken or not taken (based on static information, or on information obtained from feedback-directed compilation). The way this information is encoded in the branch instructions does not change the semantics of the instructions, but only provides hints to improve the success in predicting branch outcomes.

The static prediction hints are encoded by utilizing the fact that there are, in many of the important cases, two ways of specifying the same branching operation. For such cases, one of these ways has been defined to carry the static hint of 'likely taken', and the other, the static hint of 'likely not taken'. These hints also take into account whether the branch is backward or forward.

All of the unconditional branches (B, BLR, BV, BE, BVE) are defined to carry the hint of 'likely taken'.

For the conditional branches, the hint is defined as follows. If the ,TR completer is specified (always taken), then the hint is defined to be 'likely taken'. For other branch conditions, the hint depends on whether the branch is forward (positive displacement) or backward (negative displacement). For most of the conditional branches (ADDB, ADDIB, BB, CMPIB, MOVB, MOVIB), backward branches have the hint 'likely taken' and forward branches have the hint 'likely not taken'.

For CMPB, there is additional flexibility. Since the same comparison can be made by swapping the two operands and choosing the opposite condition, this can be used to encode the branch hint. If the r1 register specifier is a lower-numbered register than the r2 register specifier, then backward branches have the hint 'likely taken' and forward branches have the hint 'likely not taken', otherwise the hint is the opposite.

These branch hints are summarized in the following table.

STATIC BRANCH PREDICTION HINTS			
Uncondi-tional	Conditional		
B, BLR, BV, BE, BVE	,TR condition	other conditions	
	ADDB, ADDIB, BB, CMPIB, MOVB, MOVIB, CMPB	ADDB, ADDIB, BB, CMPIB, MOVB, MOVIB, CMPB with r1<r2	CMPB with r1>=r2
taken	taken	backward: taken forward: not taken	backward: not taken forward: taken

Additionally, if a branch is executed in the shadow of a 'likely taken' branch, then the prediction for the second branch is 'likely not taken', regardless of the above table.

There are situations where it is desirable to code a branching sequence as a nullifying instruction followed by an unconditional branch. An example would be if one wanted to branch based on an extract/deposit condition. In such cases, if the branch is likely taken, then a normal unconditional branch can be used.

EXECUTION SEQUENCE		
Location	Instruction	Comment
100	EXTR,= r4,15,16,r0	; if bit field is not zero
104	B target	; then branch (predicted taken)

If the branch is likely not taken, this can be achieved by using a conditional branch which will always be taken, and which has the desired hint. The branch to use depends on whether the target is forward or back. The two cases are shown below.

If the target of the branch is forward, then we can use the following sequence. The COMIB is effectively an unconditional branch. Since the branch is forward, the above table shows the COMIB to be likely not taken.

EXECUTION SEQUENCE		
Location	Instruction	Comment
100	EXTR,= r4,15,16,r0	; if bit field is not zero
104	COMIB,<> 1,r0,forward_target	; then branch (predicted not taken)

If the target of the branch is backward, then we can use this sequence. Here again, the COMB is effectively an unconditional branch. Since the branch is backward, and since r1 = r2, the above table shows the COMB to be likely not taken.

EXECUTION SEQUENCE		
Location	Instruction	Comment
100	EXTR,= r4,15,16,r0	; if bit field is not zero
104	COMB,= r0,r0,backward_target	; then branch (predicted not taken)

Return from Interruption

Only those interruptions which are themselves uninterruptible (they leave the PSW Q-bit 0) may return from the interruption using the RFI,R instruction. Interruption handling code which is interruptible (they set the PSW Q-bit to 1) must return from the interruption using the RFI instruction.

Fast interruption handling is achieved using shadow registers, since GRs 1, 8, 9, 16, 17, 24, and 25 are copied to the shadow registers on interruptions. In this example, it is assumed that at most seven general registers need to be used in the interruption handling routine.

```
using RFI              using RFI,R
interrupt              interrupt
save GRs               <no save>
[process interrupt]    [process interrupt]
restore GRs            <no restore>
RFI                    RFI,R
```

Trap Handlers

The IEEE standard strongly recommends that users be allowed to specify a trap handler for any of the five standard exceptions. The mechanisms to accomplish this are programming language and operating system dependent.

Since the coprocessor continues to trap if the Status Register T-bit is 1, the trap handler must first set the bit to 0 by executing a double-word store of register 0. The trap handler may then emulate the instructions in the exception queue beginning with the instruction in Exception Register 1 and proceeding sequentially to the end.

The trap handler must clear all the exception registers before returning with the T-bit cleared to 0. If the trap handler chooses not to emulate all the instructions, it must set the T-bit to 1 before returning to the trapped process to trap immediately again.

To emulate an instruction, the trap handler computes or specifies a substitute result to be placed in the destination register of the operation. The trap handler may determine what operation was being performed and what exceptions occurred during the operation by examining the corresponding exception register. On overflow, underflow, and inexact exceptions, the trap handler has access to the correctly rounded result by examining the destination register of the operation. On unimplemented, invalid operation, and divide-by-zero exceptions, the trap handler has access to the operand values by examining the source registers of the instruction.

Reserved-op Exception

When a non-load/store instruction has a reserved sub-opcode, an implementation signals either a reserved-op exception or an unimplemented exception.

A reserved-op exception always forces the processor to take an immediate assist exception trap. It does not set the exception registers or the T-bit, and does not change any of the flag bits in the Status Register. The reserved-op exception cannot be disabled.

Trapping is immediate for reserved-op exceptions. The trap handler must check for a Status Register T-bit equal to 0 to determine that the trap was caused by a reserved-op exception. When a reserved-op exception occurs, software interprets the contents of the IIR, nullifies the instruction pointed to by the front of the IIA queues, and returns control to the trapping process.

Endian Byte Swapping

Rearranging bytes within halfwords, words or doublewords from little endian to big endian or vice versa can be accomplished with just a few instructions. The three examples that follow illustrate byte swapping for the common cases.

Halfword Byte Swap

The following instruction sequence returns in register r28 the byte-reversed halfword value held in r26.

PROGRAM SEGMENT			
Location	Instruction		Comment
100	EXTRW,U	%r26,23,8,%r28	; extract instruction
104	BV	0(2)	; return
108	DEPW	%r26,23,8,%r28	; deposit instruction

The following figure illustrates how the bytes are manipulated during this instruction sequence

Word Byte Swap

The following instruction sequence returns in register r28 the byte-reversed word value held in r26.

PROGRAM SEGMENT			
Location	Instruction		Comment
100	SHRPW	%r26,%r26,16,%r28	; shift right instruction
104	DEPW	%r28,15,8,%r28	; deposit instruction
108	BV	0(2)	; return
10C	SHRPW	%r26,%r28,8,%r28	;shift right

The following figure illustrates how the bytes are manipulated during this instruction sequence

Inputs		Instruction	Output
r26: a b c d	r26: a b c d	SHRPW r26, r26, 16, r28	r28: c d a b
r28: c d a b		DEPW r28, 15, 8, r28	r28: c b a b
r26: a b c d	r28: c b a b	SHRPW r26, r28, 8, r28	r28: d c b a

Doubleword Byte Swap

The following instruction sequence returns in register r28 the byte-reversed doubleword value held in r26. The original value in r26 is destroyed.

PROGRAM SEGMENT		
Location	Instruction	Comment
100	PERMH,3210 %r26,%r26	;permute instruction
104	HSHL %r26,8,%r28	; shift
108	HSHR,U %r26,8,%r26	; shift
10C	BV 0(%r2)	;return
202	OR %r28,%r26,%r28	;OR the shifted registers

The following figure illustrates how the bytes are manipulated during this instruction sequence:

Inputs		Instruction	Output
r26: a b c d e f g h		PERMH,3210 r26, r26	r26: g h e f c d a b
r26: g h e f c d a b		HSHL r26, 8, r28	r28: h 0 f 0 d 0 b 0
r26: g h e f c d a b		HSHR,U r26, 8, r26	r26: 0 g 0 e 0 c 0 a
r26: h 0 f 0 d 0 b 0	r26: 0 g 0 e 0 c 0 a	OR r28, r26, r28	r28: h g f e d c b a

J   PA-RISC 2 Instruction Completers & Pseudo-Ops

The instruction set descriptions provided in this book use instruction mnemonics that differ in some subtle (and not so subtle) ways from the earlier PA-RISC instruction set descriptions. This appendix is intended as an aid to those who were familiar with the 1.0 and 1.1 instruction mnemonics and may wonder where their favorite instructions that they remember from the old days have gone. Generally, the answer is that those instructions have simply been given a new, sleeker identity.

The motivation behind this renaming/reorganizing effort was to present a simpler, more easily understood view of the PA-RISC instruction set. The major changes involve the use of more completers and the introduction of a number of new pseudo-op mnemonics .

PA-RISC 2 Instruction Completers

The 2.0 instruction mnemonics use more completers instead of separate instructions for closely related functions. For example, the 1.x read and write versions of the PROBE instruction were replaced in 2.0 by a single PROBE instruction with two completers, R and W. All 64-bit conditions on the arithmetic and logical instructions provide new condition completers using the existing 32-bit symbols but with a "*" prepended.

One problem which occurs when multiple encodings are compressed into a single mnemonic is how to force a particular encoding if you really care (for example, when writing test code). New completers have been added in 2.0 to allow the programmer to force the desired encoding. Table J-1 shows all of the completers that can be used with PA-RISC 2.0.

Table J-1. Summary of PA 2.0 Instruction Completers

Completer	Meaning
B	borrow
C	carry
CA0 – CA6	floating-point condition array bits 0 – 6
DB	doubleword borrow
DC	doubleword carry
DW	doubleword
GATE	gateway
I	intermediate
L	logical local link left
NWC	no word carries
NWZ	no words zero
POP	pop branch target stack

Completer	Meaning
PUSH	push branch target stack
QW	quadword
R	read
	restore
	right
S	signed
SWC	some word carry
SWZ	some word zero
T	truncate
TC	trap on condition
TSV	trap on signed overflow
U	unsigned
UDW	unsigned doubleword
UQW	unsigned quadword
UW	unsigned word
W	wide
	word
	write
Z	zero
*	64-bit never condition
*=	64-bit equal condition
*<	64-bit less than condition
*<=	64-bit less than or equal to condition
*<<	64-bit unsigned less than condition
*<<=	64-bit unsigned less than or equal-to condition
*SV	64-bit signed overflow condition
*OD	64-bit odd condition
*TR	64-bit always condition
*<>	64-bit not equal condition
*>=	64-bit greater than or equal to condition
*>	64-bit greater than condition
*>>=	64-bit unsigned greater than or equal to condition
*>>	64-bit unsigned greater than condition
*NSV	64-bit no signed overflow condition
*EV	64-bit even condition
*NUV	64-bit no unsigned overflow condition
*ZNV	64-bit zero or no unsigned overflow condition
*UV	64-bit unsigned overflow condition
*VNZ	64-bit nonzero and unsigned overflow condition
*NBC	64-bit no byte carries condition
*NBZ	64-bit no bytes zero condition
*NDC	64-bit no digit carries condition
*NHC	64-bit no halfword carries condition

Completer	Meaning
*NHZ	64-bit no halfwords zero condition
*NWC	64-bit no word carries condition
*NWZ	64-bit no words zero condition
*SBC	64-bit some byte carry condition
*SBZ	64-bit some byte zero condition
*SDC	64-bit some digit carry condition
*SHC	64-bit some halfword carry condition
*SHZ	64-bit some halfword zero condition
*SWC	64-bit some word carry condition
*SWZ	64-bit some word zero condition
LDISP	force long-displacement encoding for loads, stores, branches
SDISP	force short-displacement encoding for loads, stores, branches
0C	force 0C encoding for floating-point
0E	force 0E encoding for floating-point
0A	force 0A encoding for FIC
4F	force 4F encoding for FIC

Pseudo-Op Mnemonics

All 1.x instruction mnemonics are supported either directly or via 2.0 pseudo-ops as listed in Table J-2. Note that only 1.x instructions whose mnemonics changed are listed in Table J-2.

Table J-2. 1.x versus 2.0 Mnemonics

1.x Instruction	2.0 Instruction
ADDBF,cond,n r1,r2,target	ADDB,cond,n r1,r2,target
ADDBT,cond,n r1,r2,target	ADDB,cond,n r1,r2,target
ADDC,cond r1,r2,t	ADD,C,cond r1,r2,t
ADDCO,cond r1,r2,t	ADD,C,TSV,cond r1,r2,t
ADDIBF,cond,n i,r,target	ADDIB,cond,n i,r,target
ADDIBT,cond,n i,r,target	ADDIB,cond,n i,r,target
ADDIL i,r	ADDIL i,r,%R1
ADDIO,cond i,r,t	ADDI,TSV,cond i,r,t
ADDIT,cond i,r,t	ADDI,TC,cond i,r,t
ADDITO,cond i,r,t	ADDI,TSV,TC,cond i,r,t
ADDL,cond r1,r2,t	ADD,L,cond r1,r2,t
ADDO,cond r1,r2,t	ADD,TSV,cond r1,r2,t
BL,n target,t	B,L,n target,t
BLE,n wd(sr,b)	BE,L,n wd(sr,b),%SR0,%R31
BVB,cond,n r,target	BB,cond,n r,%SAR,target
CLDDS,uid,cmplt,cc d(s,b),t	CLDD,uid,cmplt,cc d(s,b),t

Table J-2. 1.x versus 2.0 Mnemonics (Continued)

1.x Instruction	2.0 Instruction
CLDDX,uid,cmplt,cc x(s,b),t	CLDD,uid,cmplt,cc x(s,b),t
CLDWS,uid,cmplt,cc d(s,b),t	CLDW,uid,cmplt,cc d(s,b),t
CLDWX,uid,cmplt,cc x(s,b),t	CLDW,uid,cmplt,cc x(s,b),t
COMBF,cond,n r1,r2,target	CMPB,cond,n r1,r2,target
COMBT,cond,n r1,r2,target	CMPB,cond,n r1,r2,target
COMIBF,cond,n i,r,target	CMPIB,cond,n i,r,target
COMIBT,cond,n i,r,target	CMPIB,cond,n i,r,target
COMICLR,cond i,r,t	CMPICLR,cond i,r,t
CSTDS,uid,cmplt,cc r,d(s,b)	CSTD,uid,cmplt,cc r,d(s,b)
CSTDX,uid,cmplt,cc r,x(s,b)	CSTD,uid,cmplt,cc r,x(s,b)
CSTWS,uid,cmplt,cc r,d(s,b)	CSTW,uid,cmplt,cc r,d(s,b)
CSTWX,uid,cmplt,cc r,x(s,b)	CSTW,uid,cmplt,cc r,x(s,b)
DEP,cond r,p,len,t	DEPW,cond r,p,len,t
DEPI,cond i,p,len,t	DEPWI,cond i,p,len,t
EXTRS,cond r,p,len,t	EXTRW,S,cond r,p,len,t
EXTRU,cond r,p,len,t	EXTRW,U,cond r,p,len,t
FCNVFF,sf,df r,t	FCNV,sf,df r,t
FCNVFX,sf,df r,t	FCNV,sf,df r,t
FCNVFXT,sf,df r,t	FCNV,T,sf,df r,t
FCNVXF,sf,df r,t	FCNV,sf,df r,t
FLDDS,cmplt,cc d(s,b),t	FLDD,cmplt,cc d(s,b),t
FLDDX,cmplt,cc x(s,b),t	FLDD,cmplt,cc x(s,b),t
FLDWS,cmplt,cc d(s,b),t	FLDW,cmplt,cc d(s,b),t
FLDWX,cmplt,cc x(s,b),t	FLDW,cmplt,cc x(s,b),t
FSTDS,cmplt,cc r,d(s,b)	FSTD,cmplt,cc r,d(s,b)
FSTDX,cmplt,cc r,x(s,b)	FSTD,cmplt,cc r,x(s,b)
FSTWS,cmplt,cc r,d(s,b)	FSTW,cmplt,cc r,d(s,b)
FSTWX,cmplt,cc r,x(s,b)	FSTW,cmplt,cc r,x(s,b)
GATE,n target,t	B,GATE,n target,t
IDCOR,cond r,t	DCOR,I,cond r,t
LDBS,cmplt,cc d(s,b),t	LDB,cmplt,cc d(s,b),t
LDBX,cmplt,cc x(s,b),t	LDB,cmplt,cc x(s,b),t
LDCWS,cmplt,cc d(s,b),t	LDCW,cmplt,cc d(s,b),t
LDCWX,cmplt,cc x(s,b),t	LDCW,cmplt,cc x(s,b),t
LDHS,cmplt,cc d(s,b),t	LDH,cmplt,cc d(s,b),t
LDHX,cmplt,cc x(s,b),t	LDH,cmplt,cc x(s,b),t
LDWAS,cmplt,cc d(b),t	LDWA,cmplt,cc d(b),t

1.x Instruction	2.0 Instruction
LDWAX,cmplt,cc x(b),t	LDWA,cmplt,cc x(b),t
LDWM d(s,b),t	LDW,cmplt ld(s,b),t
LDWS,cmplt,cc d(s,b),t	LDW,cmplt,cc d(s,b),t
LDWX,cmplt,cc x(s,b),t	LDW,cmplt,cc x(s,b),t
PROBER (s,b),r,t	PROBE,R (s,b),r,t
PROBERI (s,b),i,t	PROBEI,R (s,b),i,t
PROBEW (s,b),r,t	PROBE,W (s,b),r,t
PROBEWI (s,b),i,t	PROBEI,W (s,b),i,t
RFIR	RFI,R
SH1ADD,cond r1,r2,t	SHLADD,cond r1,1,r2,t
SH1ADDL,cond r1,r2,t	SHLADD,L,cond r1,1,r2,t
SH1ADDO,cond r1,r2,t	SHLADD,TSV,cond r1,1,r2,t
SH2ADD,cond r1,r2,t	SHLADD,cond r1,2,r2,t
SH2ADDL,cond r1,r2,t	SHLADD,L,cond r1,2,r2,t
SH2ADDO,cond r1,r2,t	SHLADD,TSV,cond r1,2,r2,t
SH3ADD,cond r1,r2,t	SHLADD,cond r1,3,r2,t
SH3ADDL,cond r1,r2,t	SHLADD,L,cond r1,3,r2,t
SH3ADDO,cond r1,r2,t	SHLADD,TSV,cond r1,3,r2,t
SHD,cond r1,r2,p,t	SHRPW,cond r1,r2,p,t
STBS,,cmplt,cc r,d(s,b)	STB,,cmpltcc r,d(s,b)
STBYS,cmplt,cc r,d(s,b)	STBY,cmplt,cc r,d(s,b)
STHS,cmplt,cc r,d(s,b)	STH,cmplt,cc r,d(s,b)
STWAS,cmplt,cc r,d(b)	STWA,cmplt,cc r,d(b)
STWM r,d(s,b)	STW,cmplt r,ld(s,b)
STWS,cmplt,cc r,d(s,b)	STW,cmplt,cc r,d(s,b)
SUBB,cond r1,r2,t	SUB,B,cond r1,r2,t
SUBBO,cond r1,r2,t	SUB,B,TSV,cond r1,r2,t
SUBIO,cond i,r,t	SUBI,TSV,cond i,r,t
SUBO,cond r1,r2,t	SUB,TSV,cond r1,r2,t
SUBT,cond r1,r2,t	SUB,TC,cond r1,r2,t
SUBTO,cond r1,r2,t	SUB,TSV,TC,cond r1,r2,t
UADDCMT,cond r1,r2,t	UADDCM,TC,cond r1,r2,t
VDEP,cond r,len,t	DEPW,cond r,%SAR,len,t
VDEPI,cond i,len,t	DEPWI,cond i,%SAR,len,t
VEXTRS,cond r,len,t	EXTRW,S,cond r,%SAR,len,t
VEXTRU,cond r,len,t	EXTRW,U,cond r,%SAR,len,t

Table J-2. 1.x versus 2.0 Mnemonics (Continued)

1.x Instruction	2.0 Instruction
VSHD,cond r1,r2,t	SHRPW,cond r1,r2,%SAR,t
ZDEP,cond r,p,len,t	DEPW,Z,cond r,p,len,t
ZDEPI,cond i,p,len,t	DEPWI,Z,cond i,p,len,t
ZVDEP,cond r,len,t	DEPW,Z,cond r,%SAR,len,t
ZVDEPI,cond i,len,t	DEPW,Z,cond i,%SAR,len,t

Index

virt_mem_store()   E-7
virtual accesses   3-1

W

WD bit   2-12
weakly ordered   G-1
write_access_allowed()   E-7
write-capable translation   F-6

X

XMPYU (*see* FIXED-POINT MULTIPLY UNSIGNED)
XOR (*see* EXCLUSIVE OR)
xor()   E-2

Z

zero_ext()   E-2